ADULT ESL: POLITICS, PEDAGOGY, AND PARTICIPATION IN CLASSROOM AND COMMUNITY PROGRAMS

ADULT ESL: POLITICS, PEDAGOGY, AND PARTICIPATION IN CLASSROOM AND COMMUNITY PROGRAMS

Edited by

Trudy Smoke
Hunter College, City University of New York

LEA LAWRENCE ERLBAUM ASSOCIATES, PUBLISHERS
1998 Mahwah, New Jersey London

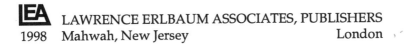

Lawrence Erlbaum Associates, Inc., Publishers
10 Industrial Avenue
Mahwah, New Jersey 07430

Cover design by Kathryn Houghtaling Lacey

Library of Congress Cataloging-in-Publication-Data

Adult ESL: politics, pedagogy, and participation in classroom and community programs / Trudy Smoke, editor.
p. cm.
Includes bibliographical references and index.
ISBN 0-8058-2261-5 (cloth : alk. paper). — ISBN 0-8058-2262-3 (pbk. : alk. paper)
1. English language—Study and teaching—Foreign speakers. 2. English language—Study and teaching—United States. 3. Adult education—Political aspects—United States. 4. Adult education—Social aspects—United States. 5. Community education—United States. I. Smoke, Trudy.
PE1128.A2A326 1997
428'.0071'50973—dc21 97-13493
CIP

Books published by Lawrence Erlbaum Associates are printed on acid-free paper, and their bindings are chosen for strength and durability.

Printed in the United States of America
10 9 8 7 6 5 4 3 2 1

Contents

Part II – Pedagogy

Part III – Participation

Preface

In designing this book, I decided to use the term *adult* ESL in its broadest sense—non-native English-speaking adults who participate in ABE (adult basic education), community college, or senior college programs. I would like *Adult ESL: Politics, Pedagogy and Participation in Classroom and Community Programs* to be a step in creating better communication between the faculty who work in ABE community programs and those who work in college classrooms. Although teachers in both types of programs often have different needs, many of our students cross over from one program to another. As a result, we have a similar political agenda. As we end this millennium, our task seems to be to find some positive common ground to present to a public that seems anxious to locate the problems of our society in the immigrant population. Perhaps by reading each other's experiences in books such as this, we may discover that we have much to gain from working together, Together, we can learn not only about the needs and political realities of our students and programs that have worked for them but also about successful methods of advocating for adequate funding and support to maintain programming and serve our students' needs.

The TESOL Resolution on Adult Education (1996)[1] itself presented some common concerns that apply to both community and college ESL programs:

- The United States needs to develop and maintain an informed citizenry and a high-quality work force prepared to meet the demands of a world economy in the 21st century.
- Adult learners have diverse educational needs, including literacy, basic skills, vocational training, and rigorous preparation for higher education; and these needs are met in a variety of educational programs and settings.
- Educated adults, committed to and participating in a program of lifelong learning, serve as the best role models and take an active role in their children's education.

---

[1]Resolutions passed at the Annual Business Meeting at TESOL '96 (June/July 1996), *TESOL Matters*, 6(3), 4.

- Educational services to adult learners are best provided by trained professionals who are themselves participants in ongoing education addressing new developments in their field.
- Adult learners are most successful in stable, continuously operating programs that have sufficient resources available to create an effective learning environment.

In the past several years, as budgets for public "entitlements" have dwindled: ESL programs, which tend to exist on the margins of larger systems, have been forced to shrink or close; community language programs have been defunded; teachers have lost their jobs; and, worst of all, students who wanted to attend school, wanted to learn English, and wanted to turn their lives around have been denied classes. This situation can result in practitioners in the field and ESL students themselves feeling passive and helpless. The purpose of this book is to present the research, pedagogy, and reflections of ESL practitioners who are making an effort to enable their students to become more active and literate individuals who are aware of social and political issues that face our world today.

A cursory glance at the table of contents reveals that the majority of authors in the book are women. In fact, many teachers in ESL programs are women, and many of the innovators in our field are women. I did not choose the contributors to this book on the bases of gender, but I did find that much of the collaborative and progressive work in adult ESL is being done and written about by women. This trend is reflected in the essays selected for inclusion in the book.

This book is meant to help both practitioners in our field and students in graduate programs who are entering the field of adult ESL understand and confront the problems that today's sociopolitical climate poses for adult ESL programs. I have included a variety of educational models, training programs, and support services from across the United States and Canada that have enabled adult ESL learners to become more knowledgeable and effective participants in our society. The hope is that information about such programs will help keep these programs alive and encourage their replication at other sites.

THE STRUCTURE

When I first conceived of this book I knew that I wanted it to focus on participatory, pedagogically sound responses to the sociopolitical situation that resulted in reduced support for ESL programs. As I reflected on the issues facing our field, it seemed logical to divide the book into the three categories of politics, pedagogy, and participation. But, of course, there is overlap in the content of essays, and although placement of some chapters was obvious from the start, several chapters could fit well under two of the categories, and some chapters into any of the three categories. I hope as you read the book you will think about why a chapter was placed in its category of politics, pedagogy, or participation, and how this chapter relates to the other categories as well as the one in which it has been placed.

Politics

The six chapters in this section of the book deal with power, where it comes from, how it is disseminated, how having or not having it affects teachers and students, and how to advocate for it. Within the section itself, the essays move from macro- to microlevel, from essays that focus on whole communities to one that focuses on one student.

In chapter 1, Pamela Ferguson addresses what happened in a central Washington state community when previously invisible migrant workers became visible and had needs. She describes how student and faculty activism enabled her to gain funding for ESL classes despite the community's initial reluctance to provide these services to limited English speakers. Ferguson writes, "We do not have to be experts before we state to advocate. We only need to reflect and act with awareness."

In "Learning to Be Legal: Unintended Meanings for Adult Schools" (chap. 2), Pia Moriarty explains how, as a result of the 1986 Immigration Reform and Control Act (IRCA), over a million individuals in California applied for amnesty, thereby exposing their illegal status and making themselves vulnerable to deportation. By examining videotapes of the ESL/civics classes that these individuals were forced to attend to attain "legal" status, Moriarty show how people respond to powerlessness. She shows how adult students in such jeopardy responded to what might be thought of as simple literacy activities involving name, address, social security number, and family status.

Judy Manton, in chapter 3, tells about how she reconstructed her ESL classes to meet the needs of her adult students who had children in public school classes. Manton found that these limited English-speaking parents could not understand their communications with the schools: They were signing some papers and throwing out others that often were consequential for their children's education. Manton developed lessons that helped her students learn English through learning about the public schools, thereby helping them to embolden themselves to deal with the oppressive public school system more effectively.

The last three chapters in this section deal with feminist issues. Bonny Norton's chapter (chap. 4) describes her investigation into the language-learning experiences of five women immigrants in Canada. Her supposition was that by focusing on social identity and second language learning, she would be able to better comprehend in what situations individuals have power and privilege. Believing that identity is not fixed but instead subject to change and contradictions, Norton used a journal study to help the participants analyze their encounters with Anglophone Canadians and to reflect on the impact of these encounters.

In chapter 5, Stephanie Vandrick explains how the goals of equity and justice that are familiar to many ESL instructors are also the goals of feminist pedagogy.

In addition to presenting a clear theoretical description of feminist pedagogy, Vandrick points to specific "feminist" classroom practices that all ESL teachers need to keep in mind: women's names and feminine pronouns should be equally represented; tests need to be written in a gender-neutral manner; female students should be called on as often as male students; female students should be asked substantive, not just information-type questions; and issues of language and gender should be explicitly addressed in the classroom.

In my chapter (chap. 6) I introduce the concept of critical multiculturalism and illustrate it by examining the long-term experiences of an ESL student. I look at how the multicultural education to which she was exposed affected the identity issues she faced. At first, she dealt with the paradox of being the best speaker of English in her family and the responsibilities that entailed while, at the same time, being a weak often failing student in her college English classes. Then, after she received her bachelor's and master's degrees, she continued to struggle with issues related to aggression, ambition, responsibility, and tradition. Her exposure to multicultural texts and experiences offered her tools that help her to better understand her identity conflicts.

Pedagogy

The seven chapters in this section of the book describe and reflect on assignments and methods designed and taught by the authors. These chapters are not designed to be models of what an ESL class should be, but are instead examples of a variety of learner-centered approaches to teaching, approaches that encourage participation and self-reflection.

In "Anorexia: A Feminist EAP Curriculum" (chap. 7), Sarah Benesch describes an English for Academic Purposes (EAP) class that focuses on anorexia, commonly acknowledged as a women's issue and rarely discussed in ESL or in other traditional classes. Benesch illustrates how the responses to this topic tended to be gender specific, with men resisting it and women identifying with it, and with students admitting that discussing issues such as anorexia was unfamiliar to them. These responses reinforced the notion that feminist pedagogy creates dialogue across races, classes, and genders, in contrast to the passivity that might be engendered by more traditional pragmatic EAP approaches.

In chapter 8, Kate Mangelsdorf explains why literature is crucial for the adult ESL learner. she believes that, through literature, students learn to deal with cultural conflicts and to be able to create and communicate meaning. Mangelsdorf not only stresses multicultural literature that she believes has a powerful effect on ESL readers, but also explains why some of the traditional canon of novels, poems, and stories should continue to be a part of adult ESL classes.

In advocating the "Fluency First" approach in her classroom (chap. 9), Rebecca Williams Mlynarczyk also stresses the importance of reading for ESL students, but she suggests that it is the act of reading and writing even more than the literary value of each work that makes the experiences worthwhile. She explains in detail how and why Fluency First builds literacy, and how it helps students to improve their understanding of English.

In chapter 10, Loretta Frances Kasper questions the need for literature in adult ESL classes, and instead focuses on academic literacy as a means of enabling students to succeed in the college setting. Kasper presents compelling statistics that illustrate the high pass rate and the high retention rate of students being taught by her method of teaching ESL through content areas. Juxtaposing the Mlynarczyk and Kasper chapters was purposeful and intended to reveal the complexities of designing effective programs and choosing one or another pedagogy as "the" pedagogy. As teachers gain control over their classrooms, they may feel more confident in trying a variety of pedagogical approaches and in ultimately developing a pedagogy that works for them personally, works for their students, and works for their program.

In their chapter "Democracy and the ESL Classroom" (chap. 11), Timotha Doane presents as an example of liberatory pedagogy Doane's showing to her intermediate ESL class a short film called *Hero*. Doane explains how this 30-second video tape problematized the issues of prejudice and was generative in getting adult students to recognize their own participation in discrimination and to deal with the contradictions of the situation.

In "The Politics of Pronunciation and the Adult Learner" (chap. 12), Angela Parrino problematizes the issue of "correct" pronunciation for adult ESL learners. Parrino writes, "We define ourselves by what we say, but more notably by how we say it. . . . Our pronunciation allies or isolates us from a community of speakers. Even when we whisper, it screams out at our audience. It precedes our intentions and completes our utterances."

In chapter 13, Carol Severino questions how the ideology we bring to our role as teachers affects our responses to our student's writing. To what degree do we respond to students based on their needs, and to what degree do we respond based on our own? How much do we need to know about our students before we know how to respond to them? How important is correctness? How do we decide on what elements in their texts to focus our responses? Should we respond to students differently because of their different language backgrounds, a contrastive analysis of writing? How much power should students have over the kinds of responses they get to their work? Severino deals with these and other serious issues in this chapter.

Participation

The seven chapters in this section of the book are about programs or methods that connect ESL students to the broader community. Whether the chapter describes ESL and non-ESL students working together in a setting, former ESL students teaching other ESL students, native speakers working with ESL students, or ESL teachers working together, each chapter presents a connection—a step toward participation—enabling the adult ESL student to join the larger community and society.

In chapter 14, Elsa Auerbach, Joanne Arnaud, Carol Chandler, and Ana Zambrano describe the university–community collaboration they developed in which immigrants and refugees themselves become adult ESL and native literacy instructors in their own communities. The authors explain how students' first language can be used as a resource for attaining literacy and ESL acquisition.

In chapter 15, J. Milton Clark and Carol Peterson Haviland tell about how they enabled ESL students to become the authorities in their classrooms. Using Spanish, Chinese, and French texts in addition to the customary English texts, ESL students got the opportunity to share their knowledge of language and culture. This process offers the other students in the class the opportunity to learn from the ESL learners and gain from the diversity of students in their classes.

The English Language Fellows program that Richard Blakely designed, implemented, and directed is the subject of chapter 16. In addition to a detailed description of this highly successful program in which native speakers worked with ESL peers in traditional college classrooms, Blakely descries what happened to a college system bent on downsizing and reducing budgets.

In chapter 17, Leslie Robbins details the life history of one of the most successful refugee language programs in New York City. Although Robbins describes the ideal Riverside Language program as a combination language center and training center for ESL teachers, her introduction reveals the uncertain future of a program that depends on federal and state government funding. How do we ensure that programs such as this one maintain their existence in times of financial crisis? What can we learn from reading the Riverside story?

That we all need to know more about each other's programs and students is the premise with which Jessie M. Reppy and Elaine Coburn began the Resource Language Center for Minority Students at Kean College in New Jersey, (discussed in chap. 18). With a small grant and an enormous output of time and energy, Reppy and Coburn created their center as a repository of information about state ESL, EFL, and EAP programs—including resources, student demographics, and assessment measures. However, as with other publicly funded enterprises, the Resource Center has fallen prey to budget cuts. Reppy and Coburn present their ideas both with the hope that they will be re-funded and that readers will learn from their experiments and find other ways to create similar centers.

In "Electronic Communication, New Technology, and the ESL Student" (chap. 19), Keming Liu explains how she uses e-mail and the World Wide Web to introduce her ESL students to online communication and research. Liu includes resources available to all educators in setting out her premise that, through digital communication, we may find the future of education.

I end, in chapter 20, with a short introduction to electronic communication to enable readers to participate in what we think will be a very exciting interactive web site for our book found through accessing www.erlbaum.com. It is the hope that with the interaction that can occur through electronic means, we will be able to problematize our issues, discuss solutions, and begin to regain some of our power over the future of our programs and our profession.

ACKNOWLEDGMENTS

This book is the result of a tremendous effort on the part of all the contributors who provided multiple drafts of their work, got them in on time, and produced chapters that are thought provoking and intellectually well grounded.

I would like to thank my husband, Alan Robbins, for the patience and love he showed throughout the long process of creating this book.

But most of all I want to thank Naomi Silverman for her commitment to this project, her advice, her intelligence, and her friendship. This book could not have existed without Naomi.

—Trudy Smoke

I

POLITICS

1

The Politics of Adult ESL Literacy: Becoming Politically Visible[1]

Pamela Ferguson
Yakima Valley Community College

> *The idea of democracy as opposed to any concept of aristocracy is that every individual must be consulted in such a way actively not passively that he himself becomes part of the process of authority, of the process of social control; that his needs and wants have a chance to be registered in a way that they count in determining social policy.*
>
> —John Dewey (1859–1952)

> *I can be somebody. I don't have to sit home and do nothing and be nobody.*
>
> —Adult ESL Literacy Student (1993)
> Yakima Valley Community College

The teaching of English as a Second Language to adults is not a new field. It actually was born with all of adult education in this country in the years around World War I. The large wave of immigration at that time from southern and eastern Europe led some U.S. citizenry, then as now, to decry the newcomers' differences in language and custom, railing that the immigrants would never be "like us." That outcry led to the Americanization movement and the teaching of English to adult immigrants. The goal of the movement was to make the newcomers into "good citizens," often meaning meek and accepting of the status quo (Appel & Appel, 1982; Crawford, 1992a, 1992b; Leibowicz, 1992; Weiss, 1982). The aim of

---

[1]Permission to quote is gratefully acknowledged from the *Yakima Herald-Republic* and Addison-Wesley Publishing Company.

education for the public, not individual, good has been a bane of the adult ESL field ever since. Public policy offers funding, still, with the expressed aim of producing newcomers who will be just "like us."

We, in adult ESL, never needed to try so hard. Immigrants, to a large extent, believe in the American Dream more than those of us raised within it. The United States' public relations lives and flourishes in the world. Many, many newcomers to this country are perfectly willing to blame themselves for the reality of their living far from the ideal of the American Dream. Feelings of failure and worthlessness are not uncommon.

As adult ESL literacy instructors, we truly are both in the middle—acting as buffers between our students and often-hostile communities—and on the front lines. We are political workers, whether we intended to be or not, whether we were trained to be or not. And, whether we want to be or not, we are either part of the solutions to the problems surrounding our students, or we are part of the problems.

As both a coordinator and an instructor in a community-college-based adult ESL literacy program serving primarily Mexican immigrants, I find myself in the middle of this dialogue around immigrants' learning of English. My own questions have been: How do immigrants gain a voice, a political visibility? How do their needs become a rightful consideration of the dominant community? How do immigrants gain access to opportunities for education and jobs?

What we are experiencing here in the Yakima Valley seems, to me, to be an intense microcosm of the impact of current immigration in other parts of the United States. At the local level, there is political advocacy work to be done and visibility to be gained within the classroom, within the adult education department, within the college, and within the community. Many of these relationships overlap and intertwine in a smaller city, as they do where I live and work. I have opportunities to know people in many facets of their lives: at work, at their children's school functions, at social occasions, and in just doing errands around town. It's a balancing act to practice advocacy along with sensitivity to people's receptiveness to listen.

I take my resolve to build the positive visibility of immigrants in this community with me into the adult ESL literacy classroom. ESL programs need both internal and external support. In the classroom, I use problem-posing as the basis for my ESL teaching. The real-life issues that affect us, as students and teacher, are the basis for language learning in the classroom. We look for the problems behind the issues we discuss. We look for ways to have impact on the problems. Students become political advocates for issues that are important to them, including ESL classes. As Wallerstein (1987) noted:

> [Brazilian literacy educator Paulo] Freire's central premise is that education is not neutral; whether it occurs in a classroom or in a community setting, the interaction of teacher and student does not take place in a vacuum. People bring with them their cultural expectations, their experiences of social discrimination and life pressures, and their strengths in surviving. Education starts from the experiences of people, and either reinforces or challenges the existing social forces that keep them passive. . . . Problem-posing is a group process that draws on personal experience to create social connectedness and mutual responsibility. (pp. 33–34)

Questions of who the students are and what they want become the basis for learning. The point of my instruction is to help students give label and voice in a new language to their own life experiences and needs. Immigrants come as students to the program with widely different levels of formal education and first language literacy. Students start their language learning with who they are. My instruction starts with that. The students are the the instructor's manual. The language is the text.

Students at the intermediate level of my classes extend their learning into the action phase of Freire's problem-posing process. At the beginning level, students have learned to describe and define some of their life situations. At the next level of classes, they continue into analyzing problems they share and planning for action. (If bilingual instruction were available [there are usually six or more language groups in the classroom], these steps would not need to be separated by language proficiency.)

From the first days in class, students are encouraged to learn about and use services at the college. Through tours and activities like "Scavenger Hunt," they become familiar with the library, cafeteria, nurse's office, gym, registration and financial aid offices, as well as various academic departments. Students learn about and attend free campus art shows and musical performances. They learn that the campus is theirs as well as any other student's.

Intermediate students begin classes by working in small groups to answer these questions: What skill have you learned as an adult? What did you do to learn it? How did you feel while learning? In whole-group dialogue, students report their answers to what they have learned and have included driving a car, cooking, dancing, replacing a roof, changing a diaper, packing apples, and driving a forklift. They said they learned by having a need for the skill (motivation), thinking about the skill, demonstrating the skill, practicing, watching, and asking questions. While learning they felt nervous, scared, embarrassed, insecure, worried, and uncomfortable; later they felt happy, proud, and relaxed about their accomplishments.

I want students to understand that they know how to learn. They, as adults, already have the knowledge of successful learning practices and how learning feels. Just as they have been successful in other adult learning, they will be successful in learning English. From this, we talk about the learning environment they will need to be successful in the language classroom. Small groups write lists of the students' and teacher's responsibilities in the classroom. The lists are consolidated to make a poster to hang in the classroom. One year students wrote:

Students' Responsibilities	*Teacher's Responsibilities*
Pay attention	Explain to students
Participate	Don't be absent
Sign attendance daily	Teach different topics
Do homework	Be patient with all students
Write in journal quietly	Answer questions
Be on time to class	Respect the students
Listen to the teacher	Give homework, but not every day
Respect each other	Correct the students
Don't be absent	Give students motivation
Speak English	Help with pronunciation
Practice	Be in charge of the classroom
Bring supplies to class	Listen to the students
Help each other	Respect the students
Be motivated	

We reviewed the lists to see if we each were willing to accept the responsibilities the class had determined necessary. The only thing asked of me that I was unsure of was "give the students motivation." We talked about the limits of my abilities to do this. I got out a "magic wand" that I keep in the classroom and told them I would use it if it helped! We agreed to the lists.

One year students wanted one rule only for the classroom: "No one laughs when someone makes a mistake." That was also posted on the wall. I realize that I am more fortunate than many teachers in that I have (after years of advocating for it) dedicated classroom space that I do not share. Dedicated space allows me to hang pictures and posters on the walls. As students have brought in family snapshots to share, I have borrowed especially colorful ones that are representative of an aspect of family or culture. I have large, inexpensive, color photocopies made of them. I mount each photocopy on top of bright poster board and put the whole thing inside an acrylic poster frame. The pictures are frequently a topic of discussion for both visitors and students.

Since realizing that some students come to class without eating first, I have kept a snack table and a small refrigerator in the classroom. Snacks include dry mixes for coffee, tea, cocoa, juice, and soup, and also crackers. There is a cup for donations and a sign that says "25 cents, please."

Somehow, it always works out that there is enough money to replace what is used.

To get at common class themes, intermediate students begin by comparing their living situations in their native countries and in Yakima (see Auerbach, 1993, for extensive information on generating themes). In small groups, they brainstorm what was/is positive and negative in each context. Each small group makes a poster representing their themes and presents it to the class. The class analyzes what the common themes are among the groups. One year, they discovered that most of the class members were concerned with the crime rate, gangs, and graffiti in Yakima, as well as with immigration law, with domestic violence and child abuse, with the transportation system in Yakima, and with recreational opportunities available to them here. They decided they needed more information about each of these areas of concern. They brainstormed about ways to get information. The direction of our next several classes was set.

The class decided to start with the most pressing concern: the crime rate, gangs, and graffiti in the community. As a class, they composed a letter to the city's chief of police, stating their concerns and need for information. They invited him to speak to the class. (This was authentic, meaningful literacy practice of letter writing form and content.) He responded and arranged to come to the class along with a gang specialist from the school district. The two men came to the classroom with confiscated gang clothing, weapons, symbolic paraphernalia, and a slide show of local graffiti. The class members, mostly parents, listened to graphic information on identifying gang-related behaviors. They actively questioned the speakers on preventative measures parents can take with their children, and on ways to organize neighborhoods to counteract gang influence.

My notes on the lectures and questions became class reading material to once again provide meaningful literacy practice, this time in reading. Over the next several classes, students continued to compare and report on plans for organizing neighborhood watch programs. For their next speaker, students invited the founder of an immigrants' rights project in Seattle to come to speak to our class.

The community comes to the classroom. Governmental agencies as well as social service agencies often have employees whose job is to speak to the public about their services. Students get practice in asking clarifying and informational questions while they learn about the community. We routinely have judges, police and state patrol officers, housing authority officers, employment and welfare workers, and health officials speak to the class. Groups like Habitat for Humanity have also given presentations. (Three families of former students now have homes through Habitat!) Former students also return to talk about "life after ESL class."

Students share community resources they hear about with each other, and make use of the resources. One class listened quietly to an Employment Security worker's spiel about computer job searches and job placements. When the state employee asked if there were questions, one student started by asking, "Is this reality or is this fantasy?" and told of his experiences at the employment office. Students spoke, one after another around the room, telling of their dissatisfactions with their treatment at the office. The worker, appearing shaken, apologized for their experiences and said he would "look into it." He left, and the students cheered for themselves.

I open my ESL classroom, and encourage other teachers in the program to do the same, to visitors. Many, many curious community members as well as teachers and administrators have observed my classes. We usually have a couple of visitors a week. Students are used to their presence. We've talked about the hoped-for benefits of having visitors watch us. Sometimes the visitors participate in class discussions; sometimes they don't. Sometimes visitors are excited by the processes they see; sometimes they are not. At the very least, I expect that visitors will be able to put faces to the anonymous issues of "immigration" and "learning English." Media representatives were, at first, invited and now frequently ask to return to the classroom. Students have learned to say, "Must be a slow news day!"

Whenever the ESL classes have a party (which usually means potluck), some administrators, staff, and faculty are invited to join us. Students write and deliver the invitations to offices around campus. They return to class and report on their receptions. After several years, I have found that administrators now anticipate the delivery of their invitations and look forward to that as a herald of the season! People's thinking can begin to change as they eat and talk together. Social revolutions have started through the simple acts of eating, talking, and walking together. We are not near revolution on campus, but the adult ESL literacy program is now seen and spoken of by administrators as an integral part of the college's mission to the community. We are no longer the temporary program housed inconspicuously in a corner of the second floor of the library.

The end-of-the-program-year graduation ceremony is an event that brings together students and their families and friends, faculty and administrators, community members, agency representatives, local politicians, and media. Speeches are given by students and officials. Certificates are handed out. Pictures are taken. Refreshments are served.

Students have learned to make their presence known. In preparation for my speech at one year's graduation ceremony, I asked an intermediate class what they thought I should say. One man said, "We do not need you to speak for us anymore. We have learned to speak for ourselves!" The class agreed.

Students were brought into the concerns for program funding. They learned that the problems were not just mine, but theirs as well. Intermediate ESL students learned to write letters to the editor of the newspaper and to the legislature, and to speak on television. An ESL student was chosen by his classmates to accompany me and other faculty and the college president to visit the state legislature and meet with representatives and senators from the college's service district. ESL students joined a college field trip to tour the state capital and met the governor and the executive director of the State Board for Community and Technical Colleges (SBCTC).

As the end of one program year approached, program coordinators had been assured by state-level adult education administrators that the SBCTC had included continued funding for ESL programs in eastern Washington in its budget request to the legislature. Grant applications for continued funding had been completed as required by the SBCTC. Two weeks before the legislative sessions ended, I learned that the ESL funding request had been dropped. I also learned that this information was kept from ESL program coordinators with deliberate intent at the state level.

I learned this on a Friday afternoon in a casual phone call to the SBCTC, when most of the campus and state offices were closing for the weekend. I spent several hours over the weekend wringing my hands and wondering what to do, and came to the realization that I had little to lose in making an effort to secure continued funding. I called an acquaintance who worked at the SBCTC who said to me, "The only chance you have is to get the college presidents to put pressure on the SBCTC. But [the State Board] considers this their money and they don't like the legislature or the college presidents telling them what to do with it." (That, in itself, was an insight about some appointed government officials!) Another person experienced with working with the SBCTC advised me to, in this case, work directly with the college president on the issue.

I wrote a short memo and hand delivered it to the college president's office early Monday morning. I asked him for further information about the status of ESL funding for eastern Washington, and requested him to appeal to our legislative representatives and senators to renew their mandate to the SBCTC to continue ESL funding in eastern Washington. To allay future criticism, I also informed the college vice president and my dean of the crisis, and told them I had been advised to work directly with the president on this issue because of the short timeline involved.

The college president called and asked to meet with me that same day. I prepared some notes to take with me, broadly outlining the history of

ESL funding at the college, the current situation, and ways he could help. The president asked me to draft a letter from him to the executive director of the SBCTC and a memo from him to the other college presidents in eastern Washington about the crisis, asking them to immediately notify the SBCTC of the need for continued ESL funding. I also supplied drafts of letters from him to state legislators. I wrote the draft of a letter to the chairman of the SBCTC for the chairman of the college's board of trustees to sign. The letters and memos went out the next day. I realized that my words may be effective, but others' more significant signatures would lend the words more impact in this case. I also wrote my own letter to the executive director of the SBCTC, inviting him to "join in our advocacy for the education of *all* our populations in the state, eastside and westside, citizen and immigrant."

The college vice president spoke to the teachers' union president on campus about the funding crisis. The union president met with me (at that time, I was not a union member), and then asked the state union representative to speak about the need for ESL funding to a meeting of the SBCTC later that same week. I also learned that the executive director of the state Commission for Hispanic Affairs was slated to speak at this same meeting of the SBCTC. Through intermediaries in the community, he was informed of and asked to speak about the need for continued ESL funding at the meeting. He did. Multiple sources reported to me that he pointed to the executive director of the state board and said, "If these ESL classes don't continue in eastern Washington, expect a large contingent of Hispanic people *in your office*!"

I began to receive copies, passed on to me by the college president, of letters to the chairman and to the executive director of the SBCTC from other eastern Washington college presidents. At the same time I was working with the president, my colleagues in the adult education department were writing and calling and inviting students to write and call members of the community, the legislature, the media, and the SBCTC. They sent out 250 pieces of mail on one day of the funding crisis. Letters were published in the local newspaper. Television stations included segments about the issue on the local news, and followed the issue until its resolution. My students and I were interviewed four times in our classroom about the crisis.

A member of the local Democratic party caucus, on staff at the college, asked me to speak to an upcoming meeting of the caucus about the funding crisis. I had repeated my story so many times by then that I spoke and answered questions for 45 minutes without preparation or notes. The caucus members, themselves a beleaguered group in a very conservative town, responded enthusiastically with their own letter-writing campaign.

Although I had sleepless nights and "what if" scenarios running through my mind during this crisis, I also had immediate cooperation and support from everyone I approached at the college and in the community. (Of course, I knew whom to approach!) I was not aware of any reluctance to support the fight at the local level. There was nothing for anyone at the college to lose in fighting for supplemental funds from the SBCTC: No other local college program budgets would be affected by the continuation of funding (although, without the funding, the issue of how to meet the demand for ESL classes would have to be faced). The funding crisis allowed us to take an "us against them" stance at the college, always more comfortable than a interdepartmental struggle within the college.

I had no idea what the effect of the campaign would be at the state level. I had no control over reactions at the SBCTC. The best I could do was to keep the flow of letters, faxes, telephone calls, and media attention going. It was a wearing process for me (as it was also, I imagine, for the executive director of the SBCTC—a local television reporter told me of tracking the executive director down in a hotel to get a quote for the evening news). At a meeting with the college president, vice president, and colleagues from my department about 2 weeks into the process, I was asked to give an update on the crisis. I reported what had been done and ended, wearily, with, "I don't know what else to do. I'm feeling tired and emotional about it all right now."

The vice president, a man not known for his nurturing, said, "I think you've done enough for now. You can let it go."

A short while later, an informant at the SBCTC called me and said, "You people in Yakima have really put the pressure on! The controversy over discontinued funding of ESL classes in eastern Washington has become too big to ignore. The funding seems to be back in the SBCTC's budget."

The State Board for Community and Technical Colleges agreed to continue funding for ESL classes in eastern Washington for fiscal years 1993 through 1997 at $560,085 for each year. In a letter to me dated May 5, 1993, the executive director of the SBCTC wrote, "Our board is strongly committed to basic skills programs in general and the ESL programs in particular. We're glad that this funding will provide the continuity needed for their continued operation."

The executive director of the SBCTC was asked by the college president, in an effort to mend the adversarial stance, to speak at the college academic graduation ceremony a few weeks later. In his address, the executive director said, "You people in this community really know how to get behind a cause." As reported in the *Yakima Herald-Republic*, "[He] noted the furious lobbying effort made to his office by college and community leaders [to continue funding for ESL classes]. 'Actually, they hammered the heck out of us,' he said" (Christie, 1993).

Coincidentally, the State Advisory Council on Adult Education met at Yakima Valley Community College in early June. The president of the college asked my two department program coordinator peers and me to prepare a presentation. We showed the council a video of students telling why they attend adult education classes and changes they have experienced in their lives as a result, interspersed with our own oral presentation on program designs. After the presentation, many of the people attending (from the legislature and governor's office, as well as from community organizations) came to us, some in tears, to thank us.

The executive director of the SBCTC came up to me, extended his hand for me to shake, and said, "Well, you got your funding."

I answered, "Yes, thank you very much."

He replied, "You're doing God's work here," turned and left.

I have thought about that: God's work. From a state administrator's point of view, that may be exactly the point. Adult education is not the work of the government, national or state; it's God's work. God is to provide, apparently, because the government willingly does not. As a SBCTC employee said to me, "You think your problem is funding? It's not. It's politics."

Thus, the responsibility for political advocacy really comes down to the program level. There is no one at the state or federal levels whose primary responsibility is advocacy for adult ESL programs. Once I realized that fact, I stopped waiting for someone else to come forward to take the lead. It was a critical acknowledgment: There is no one else. I started making plans for action.

The cultivation of relationships and a positive stance for political advocacy doesn't guarantee success for ESL programs at the local level. However, it becomes more likely that there are informed, friendly, and willing people to call on in times of crisis. It would be even better to move beyond reacting to crisis toward leadership for proactive change in support of ESL programs.

As individuals working in the field, we probably have our biggest influence at the local level. This is where we have the most opportunity to bring people, both friends and opponents, together with students. This is where our students begin to speak for themselves. Our students will learn from our modeling of advocacy. Many of our students come from countries where they had no experience with democracy because of politics or poverty. This is true citizenship preparation. This country gains strength when all of its inhabitants and their needs are regarded.

We who work in ESL classrooms need to broaden our vision beyond the walls of our classrooms. The politics outside of our classrooms set, to a large extent, the structure of our classrooms: who will instruct, how they will instruct, who will be served, how long they will be served, and to what degree they will be served. It is time to focus our attention and work for impact on those political policies that shape both our own and our students' lives inside the classroom. We often assume we are independent in our classrooms: We think we define our classroom worlds. We don't. Many parameters are set for us without our input. But we have voice, and as our students gain voice, we must give voice to their needs. We need to become politically visible.

Few, if any, ESL teachers receive training in how to become politically aware and politically effective. We learn when we have to, usually when facing a crisis, on the job and with hit-and-miss success. However, we can educate ourselves. We can ask that the political realities of adult ESL be addressed at training seminars and conferences we attend. We can give presentations on political advocacy at these conferences. We can insist that this is part of what we need to know to be effective language teachers, and demand that it be part of our formal schooling.

We, as ESL practitioners, can look at our field of work and easily say, "It's hopeless!" The inadequacies in the field are great: in recognition of the need for ESL services for adults, in funding for service delivery, in amount of service available, in employment opportunities for teachers, and on and on. However, we can just as easily say, "It's wide open!" There is so much room for improvement that small actions toward building political visibility can be significant. Any expertise we gain is valuable. Any progress we make is laudable.

Nancy Amidei, Associate Director and Senior Lecturer at the Center for Policy and Practice Research at the University of Washington, told a story about political activism: The two "good guys" were on a hill, looking down at the horde of "bad guys" galloping on horses through the ravine below, gaining on the good guys. One good guy said to the other, "I'll pound these rocks together to make it sound like there are lots of horses up here! You take this stick and whip up the dust to make it look like a lot of horses!" The bad guys looked up, heard all the noise, and saw all the dust. They said, "There sure are a lot of them!" and turned back. Amidei concluded, "[In advocating for political change,] it only takes two of you: one to make noise and one to whip up the dust!" (Amidei, 1993). We do not need large numbers to begin to take action. We just need *someone* to take action.

The task of advocacy for adult ESL comes to us, as ESL practitioners, by default. The task is not ours because of our expertise or our preference. Advocacy is ours simply because there is no one else to do it. However, we are equipped for the task: We, of all possible advocates for our students in this country, know them well. We, more than a neighbor and more than a friend, hear multiple stories of lives filled with change and need. We are positioned, in our classrooms, to work not only inside those walls, but beyond them as well.

We must gain expertise in the politics of adult ESL literacy. We, as practitioners, have gained expertise in approaches and methods for teaching the language. We have become reflective in our teaching practice, and we have honed our skills. The same practice that we give to our pedagogy needs to be given to our advocacy. The best pedagogy in the world is useless without students and without a classroom.

We must determine how our classrooms are placed. There are questions to ask: How is this class funded? How long does the funding last? How is the funding renewed? How does this institution view this class? Who knows about this class? Who needs to know? How can we let people know what happens in this classroom? Who can join us in advocacy for this class of students? We need to work for advocacy in all directions emanating from our classrooms: with our students, with our colleagues, with our administrators, with our legislators, and with the members of the communities in which we are placed.

We do not need to be experts before we start to advocate—we only need to reflect and act with awareness: What can be gained (or lost) by this action? Do we gain (or lose) allies by this action? Changes in adult ESL literacy will not come by one person's actions at one time; changes will come when we address the needs for advocacy outside our classrooms as often as we address the needs inside, over and over again. Changes will come when we all do this in each of our classrooms, wherever we are placed, and when we share our experiences and build on our alliances. We will be heard and we will make a difference.

REFERENCES

Amidei, N. (1993, November). *Poverty and advocacy.* Keynote speech presented as part of the symposium "Building Bridges" at the annual conference of Adult Basic and Literacy Educators of Washington State, Bellevue, Washington.

Appel, J., & Appel, S. (1982). The huddled masses and the little red schoolhouse. In B. Weiss (Ed.), *American education and the European immigrant* (pp. 17–30). Chicago: University of Chicago Press.

Auerbach, E. (1993). Putting the P back in participatory. *TESOL Quarterly, 27*(3), 543–545.

Christie, T. (1993, June). YVCC grads see dreams come true. *Yakima Herald-Republic.* Yakima, WA.

Crawford, J. (1992a). *Hold your tongue: Bilingualism and the politics of "English only."* Reading, MA: Addison-Wesley.

Crawford, J. (Ed.). (1992b). *Language loyalties: A source book on the Official English controversy.* Chicago: University of Chicago Press.

Dewey, J. (1966). *Democracy and education.* New York: The Free Press. (Original work published 1916)

Leibowicz, J. (1992). Official English: Another Americanization campaign? In J. Crawford (Ed.), *Language loyalties: A sourcebook on the Official English controversy* (pp. 101–111). Chicago: University of Chicago Press.

Wallerstein, N. (1987). Problem-posing education: Freire's method for transformation. In I. Shor (Ed.), *Freire for the classroom: A sourcebook for liberatory teaching* (pp. 33–44). Portsmouth, NH: Boynton/Cook.

Weiss, B. (Ed.). (1982). *American education and the European immigrant: 1840–1940.* Chicago: University of Chicago Press.

Yakima Valley Community College Video. (1993). *Student's voices: Who we are.* Yakima, WA.

2

Learning to Be Legal: Unintended Meanings for Adult Schools

Pia Moriarty
Santa Clara University

As teachers of adult basic education with immigrants and refugees, we like to think we know what we are talking about. What's the mystery, after all, of the ABCs or the foundational phrases of identification and welcome that start off virtually every beginning textbook in English as a Second Language (ESL)? We know what they mean, and we teach those received meanings to our students. What follows here is a story of the remaking of classroom meanings that most teachers neither recognized nor intended, in spite of our key role in implementation. This is a close-in analysis of one contemporary transformation of adult school culture that is redefining the context and consequence of such fundamental curriculum content as "What's your name?" and "What is an adult school?"

I should have seen it coming. I had helped to establish the new field of ESL/literacy with Southeast Asian refugees in the late 1970s. I remember the first classes: I would say, "Good morning," and they would respond in chorus, "Good morning!" Then I would say, "How are you?" and without understanding, they would repeat, "How are you?" It became clear that the teaching task was to establish a foothold of meaning in what was startlingly new learning territory. But wasn't reading always supposed to be a process of getting meaning from print? As a literacy teacher, I became a specialist in making understandable connections in the English language, in the New World of formal schooling and its conventions, and on the often mean streets of San Francisco's Tenderloin neighborhood. I knew then that commonsense meanings could no longer be taken for granted.

I also realized that the correct grammatical responses that began to emerge in class were often polite masks for the deeper stories that students knew. In our efforts to introduce applications of Paulo Freire's pedagogy, Nina Wallerstein and I had offered "Hidden Voices" conference presentations that revealed some of the reasons why Hmong students had such a hard time learning to answer "I am from Laos," and why questions like "How many children do you have?" could silence half a classroom. We were well aware that conflicting cultural systems of self-identification and recent histories of personal trauma created formidable barriers to learning the ESL curriculum that we had initially assumed to be emotionally neutral (or even encouraging) to students (Moriarty & Wallerstein, 1980; Wallerstein, 1983). What we did not notice was that the promise of a safer future that we implied and reinforced daily in immigrant/refugee classrooms might have been foundational curriculum content in itself.

UNDOCUMENTED DOCUMENTATION AND OTHER IRCA IRONIES

Some years later, in a different community and a different classroom, the 1986 "amnesty" immigration law[1] promised legalized status to half the adult students in my ESL class and denied it to the rest. Because my class had been funded by that same law, this discrepancy created a nagging tension within the classroom. As we practiced literacy skills, we unavoidably tripped and wrestled over the meaning of that legal/illegal distinction.

Dice que ningún ser humano es ilegal
Pero todos somos ilegales Porque somos
mejicanos. Pero estamos arreglando para
ser ciudadanos, tener la tarjeta de
los Estados Unidos, Para que si la migra
nos agarre no ser deportados.
Poramdar on di quiera
no te ner mi edo

It says that no human being is illegal but we are all illegals because we're Mexicans. But we are arranging to be citizens, to have the green card of

[1]This was the Immigration Reform and Control Act (IRCA; 1986). Spanish-speaking students regularly referred to this law as "the amnesty," and educational planners called it *IRCA* (/ear-kah/). I use the terms interchangeably here.

> the United States. So that if the *migra* catches us we won't be deported. So we can go anywhere and not be afraid. (written by Ramona, age 23, amnesty participant)[2]

Many of the students in that lit- eracy classroom had arrived *sin papeles*—without papers in an ambiguous and multiple sense. They had crossed the U.S./Mexico border without the blessings of visas or proper work authorizations. Most lacked any experience of formal schooling in their first language, Spanish. The everyday English—written or spoken—that surrounded them in the United States was largely unintelligible, and had been so for years. By entering my amnesty classroom, they hoped to earn papers—both legal documentation and literacy.

As illiterate adults living in a highly literate country, they had worked around the meanings available in written symbols in the same way they had worked around the need to learn English. When faced with classroom worksheets, they were unsure which differences mattered. With this pitfall in mind, I designed beginning writing assignments that were carefully controlled and focused. An example is shown in Table 2.1.

TABLE 2.1
Student Worksheet Excerpt, First Week of Class

Name: ______________________	
First Last	
Where are you from?	
	Mexico
I am from ______________________.	
	El Salvador
Where do you come from?	
	Vietnam
I come from ______________________.	
	Guatemala
Where were you born?	
	Laos
I was born in ______________________.	
	USA
Country of origin: ______________________	

But at the same time I was teaching such a carefully simplified and sequenced curriculum, the adult literacy students in my class were successfully negotiating the intricate legal paperwork of the amnesty immigration program. It looked more like the form shown in Fig. 2.1.

---

[2]All student names in this chapter are aliases. Class participants gave permission for videotaping, audiotaping, and selecting quotations from their course work as part of this research.

OMB No. 1115-0155

U.S. Department of Justice
Immigration and Naturalization Service

Application to Adjust Status from Temporary to Permanent Resident (Under Section 245 A of Public Law 99-603)

Please read instructions: fee will not be refunded.	Fee Stamp
INS Use: Bar Code	
Address Label	
(Place adhesive address label here from booklet or fill in name and address, and A 90 million file number in appropriate blocks.)	Applicant's File No. A - 9 _ _ _ _ _ _ _

1. Family Name *(Last Name in CAPITAL Letters) (See instructions) (First Name) (Middle Name)*	2. Sex ☐ Male ☐ Female
3. Name as it appears on Temporary Resident Card *(I-688)* if different from above.	4. Phone No.'s *(Include Area Codes)* Home: Work:
5. Reason for difference in name *(See instructions)*	
6. Home Address *(No. and Street) (Apt. No.) (City) (State) (Zip Code)*	
7. Mailing Address *(if different) (Apt. No.) (City) (State) (Zip Code)*	
8. Place of Birth *(City or Town) (County, Province or State) (Country)*	9. Date of Birth *(Month/Day/Year)*
10. Your Mother's First Name / 11. Your Father's First Name	12. Enter your Social Security Number _ _ _-_ _-_ _ _ _

13. Absences from the United States since becoming a Temporary Resident Alien. *(List most recent first.) (If you have a single absence in excess of 30 days or the total of all your absences exceeds 90 days, explain and attach any relevant information).*

Country	Purpose of Trip	From (Month/Day/Year)	To (Month/Day/Year)	Total Days Absent

FIG. 2.1. U.S. Department of Justice, Immigration and Naturalization Service, "Application to Adjust Status From Temporary to Permanent Resident (Under Section 245 A of Public Law 99-603)." Page 1 of Form I-698.

Obviously, something was happening with these students that went well beyond my ESL/literacy teacher assumptions. I soon learned that illiterate participants in the amnesty program had all succeeded in gathering a bewildering complexity of official papers and proofs of residence required by the Immigration and Naturalization Service (INS). By presenting forms that they themselves probably had difficulty reading—among them rent receipts, paycheck stubs, medical records, bank statements, written affidavits in English—they had performed the contradictory transformation required by the new law. They had documented that they had been undocumented for at least 5 years in the United States. By displaying multiple papers in exhaustive detail, they had proven that they had "no papers." They were attending my literacy class as part of a sequence of bureaucratic processing that would transform them from "illegal aliens" into legal permanent residents.

Once they had passed the initial screening for the legalization program, my "unpapered" students continued to deal effectively with an impressive array of documentation, such as Immigration and Naturalization Service applications, requests for additional verifications and subsequent notices of appointments, various stages of work permits and identification cards, school registration forms, and lawyers' bills. Within my amnesty/ESL classroom, they acquired even more papers—the ubiquitous dittoed worksheets for reading and writing practice, a certificate that they had completed the law's school attendance requirement, and ultimately a green card (legal documentation to work and remain in the United States). From the students' point of view, the classes were a means of *arreglando papeles*; literally, straightening out or fixing up papers, especially the all-important green card. From the viewpoint of INS and adult schools, the students were learning to be "legal" by studying the English language and U.S. history and government.

ADULT BASIC EDUCATION MEETS IMMIGRATION CONTROL

The adult schools were learning to be legal as well. With the amnesty program, adult schools began learning to differentiate between students who "had papers" and those who lacked official INS authorizations. Initially, this sorting merely identified which students had qualified for federal reimbursements within amnesty's categorical funding.

The Immigration Reform and Control Act of 1986 promised legalization through a process of properly timed and documented applications and screenings by the INS. Applicants had to prove continuous residency in the United States for the 5 years since January 1, 1982, or they could alternatively qualify as "special agricultural workers." In order to demonstrate the sincerity of their requests for amnesty, legalization seekers were further required to attend classes that combined ESL with United States history and government. This implication of adult schools as part of an immigration control law was unprecedented in U.S. educational history.

Nevertheless, adult educators were initially optimistic about the amnesty law's opportunities for funding underserved student populations. In May 1989, the California Postsecondary Education Commission released "Out of the Shadows: The IRCA/SLIAG Opportunity."[3] The dis-

---

[3]SLIAG refers to the State Legalization Impact Assistance Grants, or federal monies designated to reimburse states for health, education, and public assistance expenditures under IRCA.

crimination that overshadowed the lives of persons who had entered the United States illegally was to be lifted by declaring some of them to be legal permanent residents:

> The legalization program provides an opportunity to bring many undocumented aliens out of the shadows into full participation in America's society and economy. It provides the vehicle by which the alien population will be able to contribute more fully to our society as well as an opportunity to address some of the problems evidenced in the undocumented population—particularly those related to poor health, restricted employment, limited English fluency, victimization, inadequate housing, and educational attrition. (Olson, 1989, p. 8)

The "Shadows" report argued persuasively for additional funding to meet the need for IRCA's mandated ESL/civics classes. It made statistical predictions that accurately anticipated an overload on California's adult schools as they tried to meet student needs. By adult education standards, the numbers of people seeking classes within the limited time period specified by IRCA were massive:

- Over 3 million people nationwide passed the initial INS screening for legalization.
- Approximately 1.8 million people nationwide needed to take ESL/civics classes. (Agricultural workers were exempted from this requirement.)
- Fully half of of IRCA's legalization participants lived in California. The California Department of Education projected an IRCA enrollment of 900,000 over a 3-year period. During the 4 school years spanning 1987 to 1991, actual enrollment in amnesty classes totaled 1,348,477.
- Almost all the amnesty participants in California (99%) were Latinos who spoke Spanish as their first language; 85% were of Mexican origin (CASAS, 1992; note that CASAS' enrollment figures are based on data from the 1991 California Department of Education Transition Plan).

Technically, the new law gave amnesty applicants two options: They could attend classes in ESL and civics, demonstrating "satisfactory progress" by clocking in at least 40 hours of seat time; or they could pass an Immigration and Naturalization Service test in English. As it turned out, most amnesty applicants in California lacked the formal educational background to make the INS test any real option. More than one third were not literate in their first language, Spanish. Over 85% scored below the recognized state levels for functional literacy in English (CASAS, 1992). In order to avoid the INS test, they came to school.

They came in overwhelming numbers and, because they had exposed their illegal status by deciding to participate in legalization, they had a sense of urgency unusual even for adult education students. They had formally admitted to having crossed the border illegally, and INS had already checked and recorded their names, addresses, and family connections. This made them eligible for the IRCA classes. Now they found themselves in the middle of a bureaucratic nightmare. In its attempts at fairness, IRCA had adopted calendar- and paper-based standards of eligibility that were complicated and confusing. To make it worse, those standards kept changing. At the same time as it was difficult to follow the new law's requirements, the consequences of misunderstanding them were serious (i.e., possible deportations). Requirements were disseminated in English "legalese," a language that virtually none of the amnesty participants—teachers or students—understood.

The "Shadows" report focused on maximizing direct educational services; it never questioned the adult schools' role in implementing IRCA. It portrayed adult schools as the overwhelmed but willing servants of the hundreds of thousands of needy students who would seek out amnesty classes. The report's apolitical orientation was typical of educational discussions while the amnesty classes were in operation. Adequate funding, curriculum, teachers, and space for IRCA classes dominated exchanges among practicing educators. The few articles that appeared in professional journals concentrated on IRCA's potential fiscal impacts.[4]

As compelling as these practical issues were, they were overshadowed by structural changes that allowed INS authority, scrutiny, and procedures into the adult schools on a regular basis. However, educators did not publicly discuss the fact that IRCA had opened up a whole new field of overlap and interaction between INS and adult schools. As they turned their energies toward service relationships between schools and students, educational leaders turned away from recognition and analysis of IRCA's implications for their own ongoing institutions. But even as their undocumented students moved "out of the shadows" through the amnesty legalization program, the adult schools themselves came under the lingering shadow of INS influence and control.

---

[4]An ERIC search for articles on immigrants from 1986–1990 found only two IRCA references within mainstream educational circles. One special issue of *CUPA Journal* (1988), *39*(1), devoted itself entirely to a discussion of the impact of employer sanctions on college and university personnel practices. *Chronicle of Higher Education* (1988), *34*(38), p. A1, 31, June 1 ran a discussion of whether immigrants' college aid might jeopardize their eligibility for legalization under IRCA. A review of the *Education Index* yielded similar results.

"FISH EPISTEMOLOGY" AS TEACHER/RESEARCHER METHOD

What can a fish know about the water? Submerged, accustomed, desensitized—fish are reputedly unconscious of the very medium of their survival. Similar claims get made about the limitations of teachers' awareness of patterns within their schools. Daily social intercourse within the classroom becomes transparent to practitioners, or so the logic goes. A fish may need help in seeing its water, but the fish knows better than anyone when the water changes. The fish's very familiarity and immersion heighten its sensitivity to any shift in content or currents that may prove life threatening. This is the basis of my authority as a teacher/researcher conducting this study. As a long-time teacher of adult basic education among immigrant families in California, I sensed a potential sea change happening within the amnesty classes. It was with this suspicion that I accepted a summer job teaching a literacy-level amnesty class in the San Francisco Bay Area in 1989.

My objective was to introduce students to literacy and citizenship skills, and I did that using both English and Spanish, teaching basic literacy skills by helping students to articulate their experiences in IRCA's legalization program. With students' permission, I videotaped 5 weeks of class sessions, screening the day's class each evening, providing feedback and building on amnesty-relevant themes, and saving 24 hours of video segments for future analysis. I elicited and collected student compositions and kept daily field notes in three categories: amnesty-related content, overall classroom process and curriculum, and a journal of my own feelings and insights. I also conducted audiotaped interviews with my students, both at school and in some of their homes, and with other teachers and administrators at the school site.

My method was to expand my analysis progressively, first paying attention to the small inner circle of classroom experience and then widening the research focus to take in the larger historical and political circles that gave that particular experience meaning. In an effort to pursue questions raised by my local field observations, I subsequently conducted archival research into the development of IRCA's educational requirement, as evidenced in the *Congressional Record* over the 15-year history of the law. I supplemented and corrected my findings with interviews with key congressional figures and community lobbyists. Parallel information regarding California's implementation of IRCA classes and comparative demographic descriptors were made available to me through the Comprehensive Adult Student Assessment System (CASAS), the prime IRCA evaluation contractor in California, and the Amnesty Education Office in Sacramento. Over a 2-year period beginning in 1989, I conducted telephone and face-to-face interviews and collected written reports about the IRCA implementation from an array of amnesty class teachers, local district administrators, state planners, and evaluators.

LISTENING FOR THE HIDDEN VOICES IN IRCA ENGLISH

My ESL/literacy class met afternoons from 1:00 to 4:00 in classrooms rented from a public elementary school in a first-generation Mexican immigrant neighborhood. The personal identification questions with which we began were standard textbook fare, but the amnesty context gave them a particular consequence and significance for the students. The field of "cultural electricity" around INS and amnesty charged even the most innocent beginning English lessons, literally changing the meaning of the words that had come out of my mouth in so many literacy classes before.

The following descriptive examples use standard ESL questions to highlight the difference that it made that these questions were being posed and learned in the context of an amnesty class. Taken one by one, they are merely anecdotal evidence of the students' heightened sense of vulnerability from being part of the amnesty program. Taken as a pattern, they reflect a significant deviation from the usual safety and confidence within an adult ESL/literacy classroom. Examination of these normal beginning questions and answers in ESL opens a window onto the content of my literacy class that summer. Realization of the cultural force behind these simple questions moves my analysis from traditional teacher assumptions that the ESL curriculum is existentially neutral into the loaded political reality that the students were negotiating on a daily basis.

Classroom interactions are characterized by a prevailing sequence of linked utterances: question/answer/evaluation (Mehan, 1975). In a language class, the *form* of the questions and answers becomes the major focus. People concentrate on learning how to say things. But the evaluation component (Is the answer correct? Is it true?) applies to both form and content. There is the tacit expectation that students will tell the truth within the classroom. Usually they do, even at some personal cost. For example, flirtations that had kept my classroom lively all summer died a silent death once we started practicing the English words to describe marital status, because the two men involved admitted in grammar exercises that they were already married.

Identification questions and what is called "survival English" are generally considered socially appropriate within the classroom. They are supposed to be mere practice at expressing existing realities in a new language. They are supposed to be publicly neutral and, at the very least, not harmful to students. But when the classroom is part of a program in which many people have qualified for legalization by begging, borrowing, or buying various forms of documentation, telling the truth becomes a survival problem in itself. Personal identification questions aren't so simple any more. They reveal an underlying cultural reality that is not acknowledged in the textbooks, as the following instances illustrate.

1. What's Your Name?

Miguel knew his own name, but three weeks into the course he was arrested for answering this question incorrectly. His hesitation with the police officer and his attempt to hide behind aliases revealed his vulnerability both as an amnesty program participant and as an undocumented person working in the United States. As far as he was concerned, the key to survival was anonymity, lest the police use his name to add up the charges against him and disqualify his legalization. "What is your name?" was a dangerous question. Miguel gave three different answers and landed in jail.

2. Sign Your Name.

Making a signature for the first time is one of the magical moments of a literacy class. For students, it is a breakthrough from what feels like humiliating and childish printing to producing something worthy of an adult. I teach people how to sign their names as soon as possible after they have learned to recognize print letters, so the signature transformation becomes an easy tracing process.

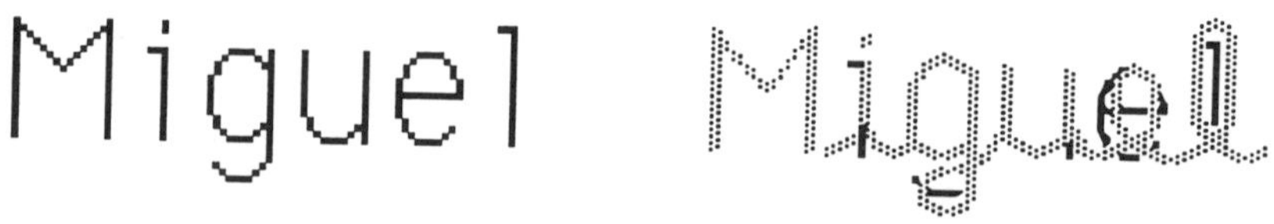

The first blackboard demonstration of this magic trick never fails to earn *oohs* and *ahs* from the students. They practice refining and giving these simple signatures a more complicated and individual style, filling endless worksheets with lines labeled "signature" or "sign your name."

Fernando knew how to sign his name by the time he received the letter from INS that asked him whether or not he wanted to take a written citizenship test. That letter (all in English) politely explained that he had the option of taking the official English/civics test at this point. If he passed it, he would fulfill both his amnesty requirement and the English proficiency requirement for citizenship when he became eligible in 5 years. The letter, a full page of triple-spaced lines of capital letters, may have looked to Fernando something like this:

XXX XXXXX X XXXXX X XXX XXX XXXXXXXXXXXXX XX XXXXXX X XX
XXXX XX X XXXXXXXXXXX XXX XXXXXXX XXXXXXXXXX XXXXX
XXXX

__ YES   __ NO

____________________   ____________________
SIGNATURE   DATE

So he did exactly what he had practiced mechanically in class. He checked the "yes" box and signed and dated the document. Fortunately, when he presented this form to an alert INS clerk, she noticed the roughness of his lettering. She asked him in Spanish if he really wanted to take the written test that day and found out that he had no such intention. Had she not been there to double check, Fernando would have had one more IRCA knot to unravel before he got his green card.

3. What Is Your Address?

Addresses are difficult for literacy students. At the same time, they are among the most important aspects of beginning literacy because they enable a person to write letters and send money home to family members in Mexico, something that most of my students did regularly. Addresses have strange sequencing (house number first), they mix letters and numbers together, and they involve abbreviations with several variants. Spacing is crucial to an address, with the street address below the name and above the city, state, and zip code, and all of this in a certain rectangle on the envelope. There is a lot to remember. Every day I would ask students to write their addresses, first copying and then writing them from memory. This was a challenge, because it meant that they could not use their everyday strategy of helping each other to figure things out; each person had a different address to be memorized.

Pedro had a particularly hard time, and it frustrated him. At 61 years of age, he was a knowledgeable man and impatient with the slowness of others in the Spanish literacy group. He was often the first to answer my questions, eager to show what he knew. He read Spanish with relative ease once he caught on to the system. He knew his way around and had been in the United States for about 2 years this time, just one of his many trips north to visit his children and their families. He had worked with fiberglass in Mexico, and had found a job here as a janitor. Pedro finally explained to me that he couldn't remember his address because he had too many of them. Sometimes he lived with one son, sometimes with another, depending on the work possibilities. The forms to be filled out always required that he give only one address, and he wasn't sure which one would be best to put down.

Pedro claimed to be in the amnesty program, and because I believed him I felt free to ask him questions about it. I was puzzled but not dissuaded when his school record card didn't have the usual IRCA identification number penciled in at the top. When I wanted to learn what the school certificates for completion of 40 hours of schooling looked like, I went ahead and asked Pedro if I could see his. He quickly showed me a half-page cardboard form that said he had completed an English course at another site. At the time, I didn't know that this was an in-house graduation certificate, not the official amnesty documentation. In my ignorance, I kept asking him questions about his experiences in the amnesty program, and he kept finding inventive ways to give me answers.

It was the day after I had pressed him about this that Pedro came to class early, found a broom, and swept the entire room of its usual paper bits and debris. After class he left and never returned. In retrospect, I am afraid that my persistent questions were an unwelcome interrogation. Perhaps he felt he had revealed too much to me. I had no way to check that, because the address that he had given the school turned out to be inaccurate. These clues make me believe that Pedro in fact had not qualified for legalization under amnesty.

Following that assumption, Pedro's comments during earlier discussions with the Spanish literacy group begin to sound much more poignant, cogent, and authoritative than I had noticed at first. The previous week I had introduced an overhead picture that showed three Latinos standing outside an unemployment office, explaining that two of them had legal papers to work in the United States and the other one didn't. I asked how their lives were different because of that. (This is an example of Freire's problem-posing using concrete discussion objects, or codifications; see Moriarty, 1985.) The following rough transcript conveys the explicit content of that discussion but not the excitement, the echoing and overlapping voices, the conflict between my slow transcription and their quick responses. Pedro took the lead in the Spanish discussion.

Pedro: When he goes to work they'll pay less because you don't have papers. They'll pay him two or three dollars an hour.

Anita: He'll resign himself to that. Since he doesn't have papers, he has to put up with it.

(I begin to write these ideas on the board, and they go on as I write.)

Anita: I think he's going to feel bad, he's going to be sad.

Graciela: He's going to feel bad about it.

(somebody): They take advantage of you.
Me: (I turn and ask again) So how will his life be different?
Rosa: I just don't know how to tell you.
Graciela: They'll kick him out.
Pedro: He'll probably just leave on his own accord because he won't find work.
Rosa: If he doesn't find work, maybe he'll have to go back. He'll return to his own country.

(José arrives and this breaks the rhythm.)

Me: How is his life different?
Pedro: He's illegal.
Rosa: Sometimes people abuse you.
Graciela: They take advantage of you. That's the way it is.

(I ask for an example.)

Rosa: If you want to get permanent work, they ask if you have papers and if you can speak English.
Pedro: One is a wetback *(es mojado)* and the others are dry *(son secos).*
Graciela: One is a wetback and the others are dry.

(We read together off the chalkboard, where I have been madly transcribing their words. It is amazing the degree to which reading and writing slows down oral communication.)

Pedro: (to José) And you, what do you think? (José doesn't answer.) He has to go with somebody who will give him directions about how to get his papers, to get the legal procedures started, right? That guy is a wetback *(está mojado),* but he's going to dry himself off *(se va a secar).* (laughing) He's going to dry himself off. Just like everybody does *(como todos).*

4. What Is Your Social Security Number?

Pedro's guardedness was not the whole story. Adult schools have traditionally provided a safe haven for students looking to better their lives. When an adult cannot read in U.S. society, it takes a tremendous leap of faith to admit that in public. The teacher must be seen as *una persona de confianza*—someone who can be trusted with the student's vulnerability. Under amnesty, this vulnerability was multiplied by the fact that virtually all the students had arrived in the United States illegally. Whether or not they had managed to qualify for legalization, the experience of living here without legal protections had taken its toll when it came to trusting unfamiliar people. This applied even to teachers, especially in a school situation in which immigration status had become the object of public discussion. Sometimes, however, the trust that I have come to expect between teacher and student would shine through.

Carlos exhibited that trust. At age 23, he had a quality of innocence, a naiveté that stood out in sharp contrast to the worldly watchfulness of many of the amnesty students. He was a weekend soccer player, married to a young woman who sometimes worked as an aide at the school (so she must have had legal papers). Carlos had none, and I am not sure what he did for work. When it came time to learn about social security numbers, he gave me a wide-eyed look and said, "Teacher, I don't have one." I told him to just leave it blank on his paper. I also immediately told him that he wouldn't be able to admit that so openly with other people, especially potential employers.

I cannot remember having reacted that way before. In my teaching experience, social security numbers had always been strictly in-house identifiers for school computer systems. In a post-amnesty school, it was somehow different. Here the school numbers were required to match society's social control numbers, and so Carlos' lack of documentation became a problem that I, as a teacher, could not automatically ignore within my classroom, so I felt obliged to warn him about the consequences of his admission.

5. What Is Your Telephone Number?

Most of the students had telephones and gave out their numbers readily. However, when I used those numbers one weekend to remind people of an upcoming class exercise, I met with a kind of resistance I had not encountered in ESL students before. People who answered the phone hesitated to talk with me. A surprising number of them reported that the person with whom I wished to speak didn't live there at all. Only on those occasions when I managed to extend the conversation long enough to reassure the person that I was a teacher from the adult school did I make it through to my student.

It is hard to tell just what was going on with this exaggerated guardedness. One student explained that it is unusual for unfamiliar people to call their homes. Although the individuals whom I was calling had themselves qualified for legalization under amnesty, chances were that their households also contained family members who were still illegal. As a nonnative speaker, my colloquial Spanish is quite good but I am often aware that I can get "off the beat" in the stylized rhythmic exchange of telephone conversations. Perhaps, in the climate of amnesty's fact checking, I sounded like a potentially dangerous outsider, from the INS or otherwise. I have some confidence in these suspicions because by the third and final round of phone calls I made that summer, people answering the phone responded in a more comfortable and open manner.

6. How Many Children Do You Have?

Teresa had 10 children, but there were 24 people living in her three-bedroom house. As I came up her walkway one afternoon, five or six teenagers were gathered near the front door. As I approached, one mumbled in Spanish, "I'm not going back to school, no matter what they say," before we could even say "Hello." Their overt defensiveness was intense, compared with the quiet avoidance I had received from some of my adult students when I first asked if I could accompany them home after school for a visit. Consistently, this plan would not work out. Teresa had agreed to a longer conversation about her experiences in the amnesty program, but when I finished closing the classroom I found that she had gone home without me. Sometimes, I accepted such behavior as a tacit denial of my request for more information. In this case, I pursued her.

She greeted me as if nothing had happened, introducing me to another circle of teens in the living room before we went to talk in a bedroom where it was more quiet. The room was crowded with its double bed and dresser covered with family pictures, plastic flowers, and small decorative figures. Calendars and posters with prayerful Christian sayings adorned the walls. Several of the younger children came in and out of the room as Teresa told me her story.

She had been in the literacy class for almost a year. When she had first been forced to enroll by the amnesty requirement, she had been angry and withdrawn. She felt it was a waste of her time, and embarrassing besides. Then she had begun to like the mobility, having a social group to join each day, learning to write her name and understand a little English. It helped her to hold her own with her teenagers. She explained that not all the children I had met on the way in were her own. In addition to her 10 children, another dozen young men in their late teens and early 20s slept on her floors at night. They were in the United States to work, didn't have family here, and needed a place to stay. She hated to see them out on the streets. Sometimes they gave her money toward the mortgage payment, which was a help.

Here was a woman who just that summer had managed to write her address from memory, and she and her husband had successfully negotiated the bureaucracies of a mortgage banker and the amnesty program. She explained how the bank representative had come to the house to explain how important it was that they make the payments each month. She detailed the process she had gone through to qualify the family for amnesty, hauling out a fat manila folder of all the different papers—applications, letters, appointments—that she had amassed along the way.

The family had heard about the amnesty program on the radio and seen flyers at the local church. They suspected that it was an INS plot to locate and deport people. There was a sense of risk involved; Teresa explained, *"No tenía uno confianza.*/You didn't trust it." They had gone initially to the community center for information and for help with the forms. It turned out that they needed a lawyer to handle all the intricacies for each person, and some of the children still weren't qualified. They paid the lawyer $75 per case, and were still saving up to send in applications for the last two children. Teresa had qualified for amnesty because she had been in the United States since 1980; her husband had qualified because he'd been an agricultural worker since 1978.

Once they got the forms, they had to go to the INS office in San Francisco to turn them in. Teresa couldn't drive, didn't have a car, and didn't trust the mails with something so important, so she pressured a friend to drive her to San Francisco's downtown financial district and waited in the car while the friend went inside to submit her amnesty application. She was frightened to be so close to the INS headquarters, but she steeled herself with the knowledge that it had to be done for the sake of her children. She feared that she might be taken and deported at that point, but in fact the errand was completed without incident.

What followed was a series of trips to San Francisco, only to find out that some small piece of information was missing or needed to be notarized. Then there were further investigations at home to come up with the required verifying papers; time spent saving for the lawyer's fee and the INS fee ($185 per application) and the clinic's fee for AIDS tests, TB tests, and children's vaccinations; and then return trips to the INS office. As she showed me the file of her still-outstanding forms and data, it became apparent that she hoped I could help to complete an application. Even though I had been working on this research for some time by then, I found the applications so complicated and intimidating that I didn't venture to fill them out.

Teresa's situation illustrates an uncontradicted pattern in the interviews I did with students. In every case, the decision to participate in the amnesty program was a family decision, not an individual one. One or more family members were designated to run the risks and do the work of submitting an application for legalization, in the hope that they could anchor future legalization proceedings for the whole family. This was equally true for mothers like Teresa and single persons like Rosa and Anita. Teresa had been deported three times by INS—dropped off in Mexicali alone at midnight, held in a paddy wagon for 3 hours, and warned by Mexican border guards that if she was caught again they would take away her children for 2 months and not let her see them. Why did Teresa's family go through the amnesty process? They did so because of hopes, courage, and poverty. Why does she go to school so faithfully? "*Para olvidarme que vine con tanto sacrificio.*/To forget that I got here by so many sacrifices."

> *Es el sueño de todos vivir tranquilos. Todavía tiene uno miedo. Uno no crea que sea cierto. . . . Uno busca una vida mejor. Solo los ricos vienen con papeles.*
> It's everybody's dream to live in peace. You're still scared, though. You don't believe that it's for certain. . . . You're looking for a better life. Only the rich people come here with papers.

These "hidden voices" give an indication of the complexities that the students were negotiating in the amnesty program, and the ways in which they responded to my questions. The key to understanding their reactions is to realize that the beginning ESL I was teaching overlapped almost completely with the INS interview questions that students had had to answer to qualify for the amnesty program. My students had already repeatedly provided answers to the personal identification questions we practiced in English. They had answered in precarious detail on behalf of themselves and their families, and had provided documentation to back up their claims. This experience left the most straightforward questions and answers with a resonance and a politically charged electricity that skewed my simple requests for grammar practice and human connection. Review of classroom videotapes revealed uncharacteristic hesitations and avoidances around standard ESL fare. I believe that the students realized before I did that we were not merely practicing public introductions; we were participating in a high-stakes game of "truth or consequences" for themselves and their families.

The theoretical concept that sheds the best light on these teacher/student interactions is the notion of cultural force, or the power of emotional affect to define and intensify cultural meanings. This theory stresses that what matters the most to people is what will structure their perceptions and responses within a given social situation. Geertz offers a beginning understanding of cultural force as a factor in the analysis of ethnographic patterns: "By 'force' I mean the thoroughness with which such a pattern is internalized in the personalities of the individuals who adopt it, its centrality or marginality in their lives" (Geertz, 1968, p. 111).

In attempting to understand the meaning of students' experiences under IRCA, it became important not only to pay attention to the concepts and categories they used to describe their experiences, but also to note the affect, the charge, what I would call the "cultural electricity" of their meanings. The presence or absence of a given concept says little without an accompanying description of the loadedness of that concept for the people involved. It is not just what happens, but people's understandings of their personal connections to what is happening, that defines the meaning of an experience from the insiders' perspectives. Rosaldo (1989) describes cultural force as constituting *the meaning that matters* by emphasizing attention to the human consequences of a person's positioning and attachments within intersecting social relationships: "[Cultural force] refers to the kinds of feelings one experiences on learning, for example, that the child just run over by a car is one's own and not a stranger's. Rather than speaking of death in general, one must consider the subject's position within a field of social relations in order to grasp one's emotional experience" (Rosaldo, 1989, p. 2).

The cultural force of the new INS presence in my amnesty classroom altered the meaning of even the most basic ESL curriculum components. Teachers, too, were reoriented by IRCA. Everyday teaching practice took on aspects more congruent with INS priorities than with long-standing adult school affirmations of equal educational opportunity. Curriculum had to be developed toward an INS-defined test of dubious educational merit, and admissions practices had to be significantly altered by amnesty's requirements for federal funding reimbursements. In California adult school history, even such a limited systematic inquiry into students' immigration status for categorical funding purposes was unprecedented.

CONFLICTING INSTITUTIONAL VALUES: ADULT SCHOOLS AS CONTESTED TERRITORY

There is no body of historical statistics recording the proportion of immigrants who have arrived in California schools of adult basic education through legal versus illegal means. In terms of adult school culture, there cannot be one. Long-standing and constituitive adult school values of inclusivity, equal educational opportunity, and students' right to privacy make such distinctions culturally taboo.

Adult schools are open to people who—for whatever reasons—have not yet mastered what are taken to be basic functional competencies for adult roles. Traditionally, these schools are open-door institutions that embody the United States maxim, "If at first you don't succeed, try, try again." The national adult education bumper stickers read, "YOU CAN" over their little red schoolhouse logo. They would never say, "ONLY SOME OF YOU CAN." Furthermore, adult schools in California receive state funds based on average daily attendance (ADA). With both their fundamental ideology and their funding based on inclusivity, adult schools try to welcome all new students who enroll. Keeping records of documented versus undocumented students, "legal immigrants" versus "aliens," runs so counter to this mentality that it has simply not been done, except in vague approximations that point to unmet needs. Within California adult schools, legal versus illegal has traditionally been treated as an educationally irrelevant distinction.[5]

This is particularly true in literacy programs. The institutional role of the adult literacy teacher is to initiate new students into the schooling process. The teacher gives encouragement and permission to "come in" to virtually everyone. Entrance standards from graded K–12 schools—instrumental competence in school ways and school subjects, appropriate age groupings—explicitly do not apply. Literacy programs maximize inclusivity in their educational criteria and attempt to ignore immigration criteria altogether.

It is difficult to document this practice, precisely because it is so fundamental to adult school culture as to be transparent.[6] As an ESL/literacy teacher in California since 1977, I was "trained" to disregard immigration status through an implicit process of quiet asides and avoidance practices. In four different adult school districts, I have been instructed to ignore or even to mask over any recordkeeping distinctions between documented and undocumented students. For example, as schools began to computerize their attendance records using social security numbers as identifiers, I was directed in more than one district simply to invent a number for any student who lacked one (the numbers being strictly for internal use at that time). References to legal residency were to be scrupulously avoided during intake interviews and in the classroom, out of respect for the students' right to privacy. I have never even heard it questioned that this was normative adult teaching practice.

Contrast this norm with the regular practice of an employee of another public institution, the Immigration and Naturalization Service. The mission of INS agents is to control and limit the numbers of people who can enter the United States. Legal versus illegal distinctions are crucial; they become evidence of the fairness of regulations that open U.S. borders to some and not to others. INS statistics regularly estimate the numbers of persons residing illegally within the United States as a way of bolstering arguments for increased funding to find these people and deport them. Given the overwhelming numbers of immigrants and refugees seeking

[5]Some states, notably Texas, have had more restrictive traditions regarding undocumented students. See Plyer v. Doe, 457 U.S. 202, 218 (1982), in which the federal courts held that Texas could not prohibit undocumented children from attending free public elementary schools.

[6]Mainstream textbooks to train teachers of adults make no mention of legal/illegal immigration status, even though immigrant education has been central to the development of adult education in the United States; see Knowles, 1970.

entry in recent years, today's INS is driven by the politics of exclusion. The legal/illegal category is alive and central to their work.

It would seem logical and efficient that INS agents would keep a close eye on adult school populations in a state like California. So many of the people seeking free public instruction in English and basic education are poor enough that they would have had a hard time posting the bonds usually required for legal visitor visas. INS could deport thousands of "illegal aliens" simply by raiding the adult schools. However, this has consistently not been their practice. By tacit agreement, INS and adult schools have maintained a healthy distance from each other, even though they often address themselves to the same groups of people. In California, adult schools have traditionally been off limits to INS categories and personnel. This has helped to establish schools as safe places that can serve the constituencies they are mandated to serve, especially immigrant workers from Mexico.

Longtime adult educators at the state level were well aware that, with IRCA, this historical avoidance relationship had begun to change. The officially designated federal monitor for the amnesty classes was the Immigration and Naturalization Service, not the Department of Education. When INS began to exercise its prerogative to visit school offices and classrooms, educational leaders protested and largely succeeded in reestablishing the tacit borders that had traditionally kept INS out of the adult schools in California. However, even these interventions were not able to eliminate the more quiet and persistent ways in which IRCA began to reorient adult schools to operate in terms of legal versus illegal distinctions. Bureaucratic procedures put in place by IRCA have now reorganized adult schools to continue operating in terms of legal/illegal distinctions long after the amnesty program has passed.

In the wake of amnesty by 1990, the schools' capacity and legal responsibility to screen students' immigration status would be consolidated into a formal contract between the Immigration and Naturalization Service and the Department of Education ("INS announces," 1990; Moriarty, 1993; "Privacy Act of 1974," 1990). Not INS agents but adult school and community college personnel would be required to discriminate against potential students who were unauthorized immigrant workers. The penalty for noncompliance would be loss of eligibility for reimbursements through federal entitlement grants, an essential financial underpinning for the chronically underfunded schools. Long after my students had stopped taking IRCA-funded classes, their schools would be left with a fundamentally altered admissions structure.

This possibility is now legally in place; what it will mean for the future of the schools is still being contested. Although the teachers at my research site have managed to ignore the ramifications of the new regulations so far, they report that some adult schools in the surrounding area have begun to use immigration status to set priorities for admission into overcrowded ESL classes. Legal/illegal distinctions have become thinkable within California adult schools, and now seem a "fair" way to deal with the chronic problem of limited school funding.[7] Proposition 187, which passed by a wide margin in 1994, has attempted to deny most social services (including public education) to undocumented immigrants, even requiring teachers to police the immigration status of parents of their students. A federal injunction has blocked implementation of major portions of this initiative, on the grounds that it clashes with superseding federal laws that do not permit state agencies to assume authority for immigration control.

In the face of economic pressures that render the international U.S.–Mexico border permeable, IRCA generated new ways to enforce many small borders around employment and education sites throughout the United States. From an immigration control point of view, "the border" has both failed and multiplied itself. For teachers working in post-IRCA adult schools, a new borderlands has been bureaucratically created; the question is, how do we live in it and continue to affirm core values of equal educational opportunity?

The students already know how to live in the shadow of the Immigration and Naturalization Service. From my literacy students' perspective, INS presence in the schools through the IRCA classes did not present insurmountable problems. By participating in the legalization program, these students realized that they would be submitting to the regulations and scrutiny of the Immigration and Naturalization Service. An estimated 85% even presented their IRCA applications in person at INS offices. Once they had chosen to take that risk, they were neither surprised nor deterred by the penetration of INS recordkeeping and documentation questions into school administrative practices. Undocumented students who had not qualified for the amnesty program continued to be accepted into most adult school classes, although sometimes they were assigned second priority on waiting lists. The same word-of-mouth networks that let adult ESL students know that classes were available also informed them that although the schools could now be expected to ask about their immigration status, students would not be reported to the INS or summarily turned away.

However, the school personnel with whom I worked saw things quite differently from the students. Most of them initially regarded the IRCA/SLIAG monies as a benign and welcome addition to chronically underfunded budgets for adult schools. They worked hard to distinguish

---

[7]Final evaluatory conference with local school personnel, March 1993.

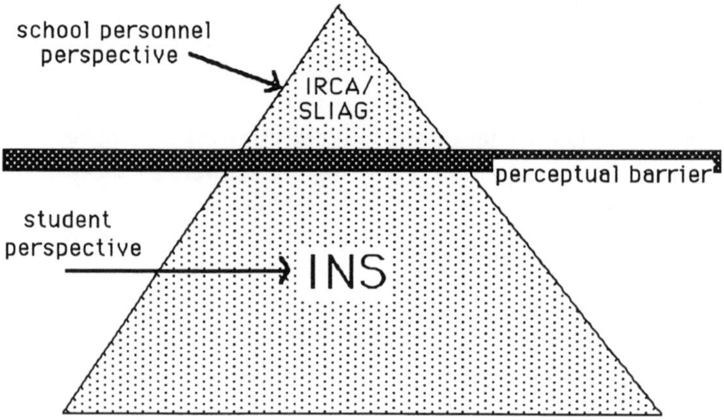

FIG. 2.2. Schematic representation of school/student views of the IRCA program and classes.

the IRCA classes from INS programs by administratively contesting INS on-site monitors, by limiting INS access to student records, and by supporting curriculum that taught students how to defend their civil rights if threatened with deportation. Yet, school personnel did not seem to see the IRCA classes themselves as integrally connected to ongoing INS programs. Figure 2.2 represents the discrepancy between student and teacher perceptions.

On this issue, the students' perspective matches that of the Immigration and Naturalization Service. Both saw the IRCA classes as part of a larger INS program.[8] But where students treated the IRCA classes as established and controlled by the INS, school personnel construed the classes as independently controlled by the schools. Administrators, teachers, and other researchers consistently and repeatedly corrected me when I began to echo my students' viewpoint and refer to INS implication in the classes themselves ("No, it's SLIAG money," "It's Health and Human Services money," "It's IRCA," "It's amnesty," "It's not INS," etc.).

Virtually all discussion of IRCA in educational circles centered around questions of SLIAG appropriations and administration, including record-keeping and curriculum development. Like the students, educators have been working very hard to advance our own priorities by meeting IRCA's requirements. We have been making education out of an immigration control program by agreeing to help administer one of its intermediate stages. This accounts for the "perceptual barrier" in my diagram—it is

[8]INS Commissioner Alan Nelson repeatedly referred to the IRCA classes and citizenship test development as INS projects, "what *we're* doing in education" (emphasis mine; *IRCA Oversight Hearings*, 1989).

essential to the maintenance of the school's identity as school. Teachers have managed to make education out of IRCA by a combination of pragmatic safeguards and strongly held beliefs that it was, in fact, education that we were carrying out, and not immigration control. In so doing, we have dealt in terms of the tip of the iceberg. Recordkeeping by the schools has formed an essential building block toward the students' success in the legalization program. At the same time, it has established a precedent by which INS categories of legal/illegal are beginning to matter in the adult schools.

REFERENCES

Comprehensive Adult Student Assessment System (CASAS). (1992). *Three years of amnesty education in California: Report highlights.* Sacramento, CA: California Department of Education, Amnesty Education Office.

Geertz, C. (1968). *Islam observed.* New Haven, CT: Yale University Press.

Immigration Reform and Control Act (IRCA). (1986). *Statutes at Large, 100* (3359), Sec. 201(b)(1).

INS announces SAVE agreement with Education Dept. (1990, March 5). *Interpreter Releases,* 267.

IRCA Oversight Hearings. (1989, May). pp. 394, 401. Washington, DC: GPO.

Knowles, M. (1970). *The modern practice of adult education: Andragogy versus pedagogy.* New York: Association Press.

Mehan, H. (1975). Structuring school structure. *Harvard Educational Review, 45,* 311–338.

Moriarty, P. (1985). *Codifications in Freire's pedagogy: A North American application.* Unpublished masters' thesis, San Francisco State University.

Moriarty, P. (1993). *Arreglando papeles/Learning to be legal.* Unpublished doctoral dissertation, Stanford University, Stanford, CA.

Moriarty, P., & Wallerstein, N. (1980). By teaching we can learn: Freire process for teachers. *California Journal of Teacher Education, 7*(1), 39–46.

Olson, L. (1989). *Out of the shadows: The IRCA/SLIAG opportunity* (Report 89-10). Sacramento, CA: California Postsecondary Education Commission.

Plyer v. Doe, 457 U.S. 202, 218 (1982).

Privacy Act of 1974 as amended by the Computer Matching and Privacy Protection Act of 1988. (1990, February 20). *Federal Register, 55*(34), 5904–5905.

Rosaldo, R. (1989). *Culture & truth: The remarking of social analysis.* Boston: Beacon Press.

U.S. Department of Justice, Immigration and Naturalization Service. (1988). Form 698. *Application to Adjust Status From Temporary to Permanent Resident (Under Section 245 A of Public Law 99-603),* p. 1.

Wallerstein, N. (1983). *Language and culture in conflict: Problem-posing in the ESL classroom.* New York: Addison-Wesley.

3

The Relationship Between Knowing Our Students' Real Needs and Effective Teaching

Judy Manton
New York City Board of Education

> *Human relationships in the classroom are the foundation of the student's learning. Teachers need to learn about their students so that they can respond to them knowingly and can focus and adjust their instruction.*
>
> —Cummins (1995)

For many years I taught adults without ever doing a serious needs analysis, without knowing them well enough to know what they most needed to learn from me. It was not until Cambodians constituted a majority in my classroom that I realized I had to determine their particular needs and address them through my ESL lessons. When these students began to bring school letters for my help in deciphering the messages hidden within, I began to realize that their children's schools were bewildering places for them.

The need to teach the Cambodian parents school-related English became dramatically clear one day when the usually sweet and shy Phal slammed down a pile of letters on my desk while saying, "Oh, teacher! I collected these from all of my sisters. We can't read them! We just wanted to throw them all into the garbage!"

The more I taught about the schools, the stronger became the bond that was developing among all of us. It was especially strong when I helped prepare the parents for communicating at parent–teacher conferences. This teaching experience came back to me when at the November 1985 conference of the New York State Teaching of English as a Second Language conference I heard Jim Cummins, while speaking about factors related to the teaching of English to immigrant children, say that "Human relations in the classroom are the foundation of the student's learning."

THE RATIONALE BEHIND THESE LESSONS

During 1989 and 1990, research was published showing that children whose parents were involved in their schooling generally scored higher than did children of similar aptitude and family background whose parents were not involved (Henderson, as cited in Glass, 1989). Programs were thus begun that involved the parents more than ever before in their children's education. And in my ESL classroom I began to hold weekly parents' meetings, during which we talked about the problems and progress of their children in school.

The inspiration for my use of the programs, practices, and language of the public schools as a major component of my ESL classes came from the philosophy of Brazilian educator Paulo Freire that education should be used especially to empower people who are oppressed politically, socially, and economically. Because most of my students over the years have been from the Caribbean and Southeast Asia, with an average educational level of sixth grade and with their income coming primarily from the Department of Social Services, I felt that one aspect of their lives in which they could make progress and gain satisfaction was their ability to communicate with the personnel at their children's schools. Additional direction came from Nina Wallerstein (1983), who called on adult educators to employ Freire's approach by listening to the concerns of our students and by designing a problem-posing curriculum based on their daily concerns.

The primary goal of this chapter is to illustrate how we can effectively teach to our students' real needs. The secondary goal is to guide you in helping the parents in your classes along the road to becoming full participants in their children's education and school life.

Limited English Proficiency (LEP) parents may not be as actively involved in their children's education as American-born parents because of cultural differences, lack of understanding of school operations, low self-esteem, and primarily because of the language barrier. In order for LEP parents to be able to participate effectively in their children's education, they must learn how to understand the functioning of the American school system; operate comfortably within the subculture that is embedded in the school system; use appropriate English terminology and phraseology to express their needs and to understand conversations, discussions at parent meetings, and letters sent home from school; overcome cultural barriers; and become politely assertive if the need arises.

FACTORS IN DETERMINING USE OF SCHOOL-RELATED LESSONS

In determining to what extent to use school-related materials in the classroom, there are several factors to consider:

1. *The characteristics of the students:* If the students are Russian engineers or Japanese "education mothers," for instance, they probably had a high input into their children's education in their native country and are probably eager to continue to be active in their adopted country. On the other hand, if they are Liberian farmers or Samoan fisherman, they might not see themselves as their children's first teachers and would have to be convinced through these lessons that they could learn to talk with their children's teachers.

2. *The percentage of the students who have children in school:* Obviously, if the class meets in a public school, interest in school-related lessons should be high. If there are many nonparents in the class, then parent meetings will have to be held to study these materials and the nonparents will have to be assigned other work to do. In order to divide the class, it will be necessary to meet in a large room and work in two groups or, even better, have the groups meet in different rooms. If there are other adult ESL classes in the facility, it might be possible for one teacher to teach the parents from all the classes and, in turn, the other teachers instruct all the nonparents. In order to prevent the nonparents from leaving class early, it is important to give them meaningful work to do and hold them accountable for doing it. At the next class meeting they might share their lesson with the parents.

3. *The length of time they have been in the United States:* If the parents have been in the United States for a number of years, they will have learned quite a bit about how the schools operate and already be involved themselves. New arrivals, however, may feel an urgency to understand the school system and be able to communicate effectively and without embarrassment.

4. *The availability of linguistic and cultural interpreters for each ethnic group in the schools:* If the parents are part of a sizable ethnic group in the community, the schools will probably have bilingual teachers or teachers' aides. In this case, motivation to function at school on their own in English might be less than when no bilingual personnel are available at the school.

5. *The degree of success the students already feel in their ability to communicate at their children's schools:* If the parents feel they are managing their school communications with an acceptable degree of success, they will probably prefer that other material be stressed in class. If, however,

they are frustrated with their inability to understand and communicate, and if that affects their self-esteem, they will be eager to receive help.

6. *The priorities the students have expressed regarding what they want to learn:* The teacher can find out what students want to learn by doing a needs assessment at the beginning of class and at any other time. The students can rank the topics and skills on a list. Note that the needs assessment should contain a few blanks in which students can write their own requests.

7. *The weight the program policy or administrator places on school-related lessons:* If a teacher is teaching an English for Special Purposes class or preparing students for employment, for instance, there may not be much room in the curriculum for school-related lessons.

8. *The strength of the teacher's own commitment:* If the teacher comes from an immigrant background, has taught in public school, or currently has children in school, teaching effective school communication may seem more important than it would to a native speaker or an older teacher.

9. *The number of hours the class meets each week and the amount of other material to be covered:* Again, the focus of the program and the students' expressed needs would determine how much of the class time could be devoted to school-related lessons.

SYLLABUS: FACTORS IN DETERMINING WHAT TO TEACH

The nature of the parent class will determine what will be taught and the level of sophistication at which it will be taught. If the class includes wives of Japanese and Korean businessmen, it can be assumed that many will already know quite a bit about the American school system, and that many are college graduates and have a good knowledge of written English. What such students will need is listening comprehension and practice in speaking with their children's teachers. They should also be prepared for participating in parent meetings at which issues concerning the school community will be discussed.

Russian émigrés may be full of queries and concerns about the schools. Their generally high level of reading comprehension may break down when they come across special school terminology.

Spanish-speaking parents may have lived in the United States for numerous years and, even though they may be in low-level ESL classes, they will know a lot about the schools. They can be relied on to explain school practices to newer arrivals. They can be good sources of information for the entire class. They should be encouraged to contribute as much as possible before the teacher, as a cultural interpreter, provides background information to the class. However, those who had little formal education as children may need to learn a lot about the schools before their self-esteem will be high enough for them to venture to communicate in English.

New arrivals with little education, persons from rural areas, and those from developing countries may require very basic lessons. Some low-level ESL texts include a few pages with school-related lessons.

Therefore, which topics the teacher decides to teach will depend on the sophistication of the students, how much they already know about the schools, and what they are most interested in learning. Topics can be related to the progression of the school year or can be selected according to the expressed interest of the parents at any time.

SCHOOL MATERIALS AS TEXT

Types of Materials

If the class begins at the start of the school year, a supply of the forms, manuals, booklets, and letters that parents confront at this time should be obtained. It will be too late to work with the kindergarten and new student registration forms, because the parents will not enter your class until they have gone through all the necessary steps to get their children started in school, either as new or returning students. As items are obtained, they can be checked off from the following list:

Forms

- Medical examination
- Dental examination
- Free/reduced breakfast/lunch
- Free/reduced milk
- Home language survey
- Emergency contact information
- Textbook responsibility
- Accident insurance
- Authorization for bilingual/ESL participation
- Class trips

Manuals

- Student handbook
- High school course offerings
- Parent handbook

Pamphlets
- ESL/bilingual education
- Special education
- Parent involvement

Letters
- School-to-parent letters can be used throughout the year. The parents can be asked to bring in all letters they receive. The letters are likely to cover all kinds of topics, such as class trips, the parents association, money-raising endeavors, safety, holiday events, class performances, cuts in services, school pictures, parent–teacher conferences, back-to-school night, college night, concerts, international dinners, parent workshops, appointments with school personnel, prom regulations, graduation planning, and so on. These letters can be photocopied for use by the entire class.

Other
- School calendars
- Report cards

SUGGESTED METHODS FOR EACH TYPE OF MATERIAL

The methods that can be used to teach school-related materials are, of course, related to the format and content of the materials used. Following are some suggestions; the skills to be taught are italicized.

Forms

Parents' *reading comprehension* will be challenged as they read the directions on how to fill out medical history and other forms. Writing the correct information on the correct lines will be a *task writing* lesson. Parents can be taught how to ask *informational* and *clarifying questions* to obtain the guidance they may need in filling out the forms. The use to which the school will put the information can be the object of *discussion.*

Manuals

Parent manuals that explain the structure and programs of the schools will be excellent material for *reading comprehension, question asking,* and *discussion.* Advanced students can be asked to *summarize* the information given in certain sections. To check their reading comprehension, a few multiple-choice questions or fill-in-the-blank sentences over the assigned sections of the manual can be used.

High school manuals describing course offerings can be used for *reading comprehension.* The courses offered will reflect certain aspects of American culture (e.g., driver's education, family life, African-American history, etc.). *Information questions* will be put forth by the parents and *discussion* will naturally follow.

Pamphlets

Pamphlets also provide material for *reading comprehension.* If the pamphlet describes the school's bilingual education program, the ground will be set for a *debate.* The parents can be divided between those who are for it and those who are against it. After the rules have been set, a lively debate is guaranteed among students at an intermediate or advanced level of English proficiency.

Pamphlets can also be used for *listening comprehension.* A worksheet can be prepared on which the main points of the program described in the pamphlet can be written. The worksheet can be in outline form with lines to be filled in, made up of multiple-choice questions, or contain blanks for missing information.

Letters

There is a wealth of language and information in the letters that children bring home from school to their parents. Often the language is specialized and sophisticated. However, lessons can easily be designed that follow several basic forms to guide parents to *extract information* from each paragraph to use in answering *reading comprehension* questions. Some letters are suitable for *listening comprehension;* others focus on matters that will lead to group *discussion.*

Other

School calendars lend themselves to *task writing.* First the parents should be provided with blank calendars for the current month. Then the parent who brought the calendar to class should be asked to read the information written on each date. Time should be allowed for the students to write it down in the appropriate rectangle.

Report cards usually contain a lot of language that needs to be clarified. The teacher's comments also need to be explained to high-beginner and low-intermediate LEP adults. The high school report card is likely to be a computer printout: The parents may need guidance in deciphering the meaning behind all those abbreviations and symbols.

Reading Letters From Their Children's Schools

The parents should be asked to bring to class letters that invite them to go to the schools to discuss their children's report cards with their teachers. These letters, once duplicated, will become your texts. Because school letters will probably be utilized throughout the course, a strategy should be adopted that can help the parents extract the most important information from each letter. If the same approach is used toward each letter, after the parents finish the class hopefully they will automatically apply this strategy to each letter they receive thereafter. The strategy I have found to be the most useful is simply to write *wh-* questions (who, what, where, when, why) over the content of the letters.

Letters can be studied in other ways, however, depending on their complexity: *Wh-* questions can be written on the board for the parents to answer as the teacher reads a letter; half of the class can be told to pose *wh-* questions to the other half of the class; a letter can be studied together and then copies of the letter with key vocabulary items to be filled in can be passed out; or the letter can be turned into a cloze exercise. Students should be encouraged to make a continuously expanding glossary of school-related words.

THE TYPES OF CONCERNS THAT MIGHT BE ADDRESSED IN THE CLASSROOM

Once the parents recognize that the teacher is open to their needs and can be approached as a "helping person," they may freely bring their school-related concerns into the classroom. Discussion with other parents may help everyone understand more clearly the nature of the problems; for example, that a lot of problems are shared problems, and that there are school personnel trained to address these problems. Concerns may fall into the following categories.

Subculture Pressures

Although many of the parents may have made significant sacrifices in order to immigrate to the United States in hopes of a better future for their children, they may be dismayed to find that their children have fallen under peer pressure *not* to succeed. Some of the powerful influences on the American high school student are clique membership, social status, sexual relations, and many others. There is peer pressure toward drugs, alcohol, and "bad" friends, and to wear the right brand of sneakers or drive a popular car. In fact, for some teenagers part of the teenage ritual of growing up and breaking away from home is the adoption of indifference toward learning.

Immigrant Problems

Although some parents may give glowing reports that their children are doing very well in school, other parents may express being at a loss as far as knowing what to do because their children's self-esteem is low. As a Korean college student shared with me:

> There I was in school, not being able to understand English, sitting in the chair as if I was a mute. I didn't know anything that ordinary American teenagers enjoy: music, McDonalds, Halloween, dates, proms, and many other things. If someone asked me any question, tears would burst out of my eyes because of my shyness. And the boys would start to tease me and call me a name that's related to my race, just because I couldn't speak any English, and just because I'm Oriental. Those circumstances made it even harder to fit myself into American culture, and I still feel like an alien among them.

At a Teaching of English to Speakers of Other Languages convention, a state education official, originally from Laos, spoke of cultural differences regarding the relationship between parents and the schools:

> Some parents from my country think that American schools can't help them bring up their children. Schools in Laos teach the children traditional ways of good behavior. If our children get into trouble, we blame them. We would never think of blaming the school. But here, if we are unhappy about something at school, we are expected to go there to talk about it. (Phommasouvanh, 1989)

Academic Concerns

The parents may be perplexed about the colorful variety of courses that American high schools offer in addition to those courses required for graduation. High schools in many countries have a fixed course of study designed by that country's Ministry of Education. Therefore, choosing electives to complement required courses in the United States can be confusing. Parents may feel that courses like cooking and woodworking are a waste of their children's time. Some may think that family life courses are intrusive because it's the parents' prerogative to teach their children about sex. Other courses new to immigrants may deal with racism, the gay lifestyle, or substance abuse.

A parent may not want to talk in class about a child who has to repeat a grade. Failure is difficult for anyone to accept, but it may have broader implications for a family that brings another culture with them. For instance, a Korean ESL teacher told me that if a Korean child were retained, that would bring great shame on his or her family within the Korean community. In Korean culture there's a right time in life to do everything, and being held back a grade throws off one's expected timed path through life.

Other School-Related Problems

Parents may receive notices that their children have cut class or not shown up at school, and their reaction may be to punish severely. In order to help the parents understand the school rules, copies of the various schools' regulations can be obtained and studied in class. Parents can practice making mock phone calls and writing notes reporting student absences. The ESL teacher can stress the importance of regular school attendance, and that visits to one's country during the school year can seriously affect a child's academic performance.

The prohibition of corporal punishment in 20 states and the right of children to report abuse by their parents are hot topics of discussion. I have found that parents of various cultures lament the fact that physical punishment is not allowed in the United States. They feel that, as a consequence, lack of discipline is a big problem in some schools, and parental control over their children has been seriously eroded.

I make sure to tell the parents about their right to examine their children's records and appeal school decisions. I teach them to be politely assertive in order to be effective advocates for their children. We study the appropriate language to use. At times, parents may express dissatisfaction with their child's school or program. They may want to move a child, for instance, out of bilingual education or obtain as much help as possible for a child with special needs. One of my parents wrote to her daughter's teacher: "I'm writing this letter to you because I need your help or help from anyone who can help me with my problem. My daughter is in a special education program, but she is not getting the services that she needs. Please call me for an appointment."

Another parent shared in class how he had had his son transferred back from a distant school to his neighborhood school. In order to reward this father's assertiveness and to encourage others to be advocates for their children, I asked Lai to write up his experience. With his permission, I then typed his letter and distributed copies for group editing and discussion. The letter stated:

> The first day he went to school, I felt so sad. The school was far from our house. My son cried when he got into the school bus. I cried also because there wasn't anyone who could speak Vietnamese to translate for him. If

my child had some problems at school, what could I do? My child studied at that school for three months and didn't learn to read or write the alphabet. I wanted to ask his teacher what he did all day in school, but I couldn't because I couldn't speak enough English.

Then I went to see the principal at our neighborhood school and he agreed to transfer my son back next year. I was proud of myself because even though I didn't know much about how the schools worked and even though I couldn't speak English very well, I had been able to help my son get into a better school.

Social Problems

> The cheerleaders take the pill, the band does drugs, and the classroom has become peripheral in the lives of many of our "students." Nearly one out of two of them lives with only one natural parent. For the blacks among them, it's closer to two out of three. Jobs and parties take precedence over education. (Welsh, 1986)

The social problems that have infested this country are felt very deeply in the schools. Almost annually, new programs are designed to try to serve the emotional, social, medical, and educational needs of the students better than before. Some of the problems that might be studied are child abuse, suicide attempts, teenage pregnancy, homelessness, divorce, violence, substance abuse, and racial prejudice. The main sources of information concerning school programs to educate students about these social ills are parent handbooks and letters inviting parents to workshops in which these problems are to be discussed.

In order to encourage parents to feel free to share concerns about their children, the ESL teacher can write lessons that present typical school problems and then ask the parents to suggest steps toward solving those problems. Part of the lesson can be a study of the various roles of school personnel and identification of whom to approach with various kinds of problems.

School handbooks are good references because they detail the services of the guidance counselors who handle matters related to discipline problems, special education, substance abuse, failure, family problems, and academic program and career counseling.

Although I encourage my students who are parents to feel comfortable to bring their concerns into our classroom, I also am careful to set a bright and cheerful mood much of the time. One of my colleagues pointed out that some adults look forward to coming to class to escape from their burdens for awhile and that I shouldn't always be fishing for their problems. Also, it shouldn't be assumed that all immigrant parents are laden down with problems.

PREPARING FOR REPORT CARD CONFERENCES

Of all the units I developed, this one has proven to be the most rewarding to teach, probably because it is very empowering. These lessons enable the parents to express themselves—their inquiries, concerns, and compliments—to their children's teachers. I would like to share what two parents wrote in their compositions after having participated in report card conferences:

> I saw my progress in English when I went to see the teachers. Last year I couldn't say anything.
>
> Teacher, I'm very proud today because yesterday I talked in English with seven teachers at my son's high school. I could understand the secretaries and everything the teacher said. One teacher said my English was good. I told her my teacher prepared all the students to talk with their children's teachers. She said, "Congratulations to your teacher!" I feel good. I feel very good.

Because this unit must be taught prior to the time of report card conferences, the school calendar should be consulted to decide when to begin. That cannot be decided, however, until it is determined how much preparation the parents will need and how much class time can be devoted to that preparation.

This unit should be taught just before report card conferences. First, the teacher should find out how many of the parents have gone to these conferences, if the conferences were conducted in English, and, if so, how the parents feel about their ability to communicate. The parents should fill out a form related to each child in which the name of the teacher(s), room number, and the name, address, and telephone number of the school is to be filled in.

To prepare the class for the expected linguistic interaction between the teacher and the parents, the teacher can write conversations and then cut them into strips. The parents then must assemble them to show that they understand the flow of conversation. Questions and answers or cloze exercises can be used to test their comprehension. Then parents can be paired or grouped to write original conversations.

A large chart of scheduled conferences can be taped to the wall so that the teacher can monitor each parent's attendance. A lot of sentences can be generated with the use of the chart.

In order for the parents to be able to understand their children's progress and problems in school, they will have to understand both the terminology used on the printed report cards and the teacher's handwritten comments. Old or blank report cards can be used to study both the vocabulary and the concepts behind the words.

The most rewarding part of this unit, for me, is the mock report card conferences that I hold with each parent. In preparation, I have the parents write a biography of each child. Then I role play each teacher. Another parent videotapes each conference so that everyone will be able to watch themselves and the parents will be able to critique each other's performance.

During these mock conferences, a parent may sincerely want to consult the teacher about a child's problem. Although the ESL teacher will want to engage in active listening, the most effective way to handle the situation might be to suggest that the parent talk to the appropriate person at the child's school.

When viewing the conferences, the parents can listen critically to assess each other's self-confidence and grammatical correctness. A checklist can be given out to focus their listening on the use of the final *s*, the correct tenses, auxiliaries, using *-ing* correctly with *to be* verbs and the present participle, and so on.

To prepare the parents to report to the class after they have attended the conferences, a dictation using reported speech can be given (e.g., "The teacher said my child was a good student"). Then, as a closure activity, the parents can write short reports on each conference they attended. The teacher or an advanced student can write a model report on the board. The last sentence of each parent's report should be an expression of the parent's feelings about his or her ability to communicate in English at the conferences. This final sentence should be of great importance to the teacher in evaluating the empowerment goal of this unit.

Satisfaction That Can Be Gained by Teaching Effectively to Meet Our Students' Real Needs

Friere put a lot of emphasis on listening seriously to the problems of the needy—a teacher should regularly engage in "active listening." The adult ESL classroom is a safe haven where LEP parents can share their feelings: their pride in their children's accomplishments, as well as their concerns about their children. In the class they will be able to practice problem-solving dialogues that may help them in their own problem solving. They will also be able to learn from each other's experiences.

As the parents are guided through school manuals, letters, and teacher conferences, they will open up more and more because the teacher is showing a personal interest in their families. They will share both their sorrows and their joys as they endeavor to guide their children through the children's school years. I hope that others who teach in this manner will gain the satisfaction that I have from creating lessons out of school publications and situations. Seeing the parents' joy in their increased empowerment is the teacher's reward for having addressed their real needs!

ADDITIONAL RESOURCES

Books

School-related lessons can be found in Mosteller, L., Haight, M., & Paul, B. (1994). *Survival English.* Englewood Cliffs, NJ: Prentice-Hall. See the "School" unit in Levels 2 and 3.

Similar lessons are featured in the "School and Country" unit in all four levels of *Real-life English* (1994), by the editorial staff of Steck Vaugh, Austin, TX.

Other lessons can be found in Blosser, B. J. (1989). Communicating with the school. In *Living in English: Basic skills for the adult learner.* Lincolnwood, IL: National Textbook Co.

Videotapes

"Introduction to American Schools," Newcomer Series (note that this series is geared to Vietnamese refugees, but is suitable for all immigrant adults).

REFERENCES

Cummins, J. (1995, month). *Accelerating academic language learning: Connecting students' pasts with their futures in the ESL classroom.* Plenary address given at the NYSTESOL conference, New York.

Glass, R. S. (1989, September). Parent power. *American Teacher.*

Phommasouvanh, B. (1989). *Title of report.* Report presented at TESOL 1989.

Wallerstein, N. (1983). The teaching approach of Paolo Freire. In J. W. Oller & P. A. Richard-Amato (Eds.), *Methods that work* (p. 196). Rowley, MA: Newbury House.

Welsh, P. (1989). *Tales out of school.* New York: Viking Penguin.

4

Using Journals in Second Language Research and Teaching[1]

Bonny Norton
Department of Language Education
University of British Columbia

In this chapter I describe and analyze my use of journals in a recent research project (Peirce, 1993, 1995) in which I sought to investigate the language learning experiences of adult immigrants in Canada. My study invited participants to reflect on their language learning experiences, not only in the classroom, but also in the home, the workplace, and the community. An important emphasis of the study was on how participants responded to social interaction with anglophone Canadians. In this chapter I first give the background to the study, comparing it to other journal studies in the field of second language acquisition (SLA). Second, I give a detailed description of the methodology I used and how it influenced the progress of the study. Third, I provide an analysis of the study in which I address the progress, outcomes, and limitations of the study. Finally, I examine the implications of the study for classroom teaching.

BACKGROUND TO THE STUDY

In the field of SLA research, a number of researchers have made use of journals to explore the process of language learning. One such type of study is introspective accounts of the learning of a foreign language (see,

---

[1]This chapter is a slightly modified version of Peirce, B. N. (1994). Using diaries in second language research and teaching. *English Quarterly, 26*(3), 22–29. Permission to reprint the article from the Canadian Council of Teachers of English and Language Arts is gratefully acknowledged.

e.g., Bailey, 1980, 1983; Bell, 1991; Brown, 1984; Cooke, 1986; Schumann, 1980; Schumann & Schumann, 1977). In these studies, none of the writers in question was learning the language for the purposes of remaining in the target language country for an extended period of time, most of the accounts were written by the researchers themselves in the process of language learning, and all the accounts were written in the mother tongue. Another type of journal study, which is becoming more common, is studies of the use of second-language learner journals (see, e.g., Hingle, 1992; Savage & Whisenand, 1993; Spack & Sadow, 1983; Winer, 1992). One of the aims of these latter studies is to encourage participants to make use of journals to promote second language writing skills. Spack and Sadow (1983), for example, argued that ungraded, uncorrected journals can provide a nonthreatening way for learners to express themselves in written English. Savage and Whisenand (1993) were interested not only in their learners' writing progress, but also in the learners' use of journals (or what they called *logbooks*) for the purposes of program evaluation. Hingle (1992) focused her research on the changing role of the teacher in dialogue journal writing, whereas Winer (1992) examined how journals can help to change negative attitudes among English as a Second Language (ESL) teachers in training toward teaching writing.

My study shares a number of characteristics with the two types of journal studies outlined previously, but has its own distinctive purpose and outcomes. One of the main purposes of my study was to investigate what opportunities adult immigrant language learners in Canada have to practice speaking English outside the classroom. My research was premised on the assumption that language learning is enhanced if learners have regular opportunities to practice the target language in "natural" or informal contexts, such as the home, workplace, and community (Spolsky, 1989). Furthermore, I took the position that one of the purposes of learning ESL in the classroom is to enhance its use *outside* the classroom. For this reason, I wanted to investigate how opportunities to speak are socially structured in the different domains of an adult immigrant's life, and to what extent an immigrant language learner's social identity influences the extent to which the learner creates, responds to, or possibly resists opportunities to speak the target language.

It was through the use of journals that I encouraged the kind of introspection about language learning characteristic of the first type of journal study described here, while simultaneously providing participants with a nonthreatening way of recording their ideas in the second language, a characteristic of the second type of study outlined. Although I had asked the participants if they would prefer to use their mother tongues for their journals, which would then be translated, they were adamant that they wanted to practice writing in English, and asked for regular feedback on their writing progress.

The distinctive aspect of my study was my interest in using journals to explore the relationship between social identity and second language learning. I use the term *social identity* to reference how a person understands his or her relationship to the social world, how that relationship is socially constructed across time and space, and how the person understands possibilities for the future. Following West (1992), I also take the position that social identity references desire—the desire for recognition, the desire for affiliation, and the desire for security and safety. Such desire, West argued, cannot be separated from the distribution of material resources in a particular society. People who have access to a wide range of resources in a society will have access to power and privilege, which will, in turn, influence how they understand their relationship to the social world and their possibilities for the future. In this view, a person's social identity will shift in accordance with changing social and economic relations across time and space, and will be constantly renegotiated within everyday social interactions.

The use of journals proved to be a particularly powerful tool in helping the participants to analyze their encounters with anglophone Canadians, and to reflect on the extent to which such encounters promoted or inhibited opportunities to speak English. In my study I used such data to critique current conceptions of the individual in SLA research, and to argue for a conception of social identity as nonunitary, a site of struggle, and subject to change (Peirce, 1995).

METHODOLOGY OF THE STUDY

After teaching a 6-month ESL course to a group of newly arrived adult immigrants in Newtown,[2] Ontario, from January to June 1990, I invited the learners in the class to participate in my research project, described in a letter as follows:

> I would like to understand exactly how, when, and where you use English; who you speak English to; what happens when you speak English. The best way to examine this is to ask you to keep a diary (a notebook) in which you regularly make comments about your experiences in learning English. I know that keeping a diary can take a lot of time. For this reason, there will be no rules about what you should write in your diaries or how much you should write. This will depend on what you are interested in and how much time you have. I hope that the project will run for 8 weeks. In addition, I think it will be useful for the people in the project to get together once a week or once every two weeks while the project is in progress. This will give you time to discuss the comments you have made in your diaries. I

[2]Names and places have been changed to protect the identities of the participants.

> hope it will also give you the chance to improve your writing and speaking skills. We can meet at my house, which is in a convenient place for many of you. In addition, if you would like to meet individually at another place, this can be arranged. This part of the project will begin in the middle of January 1991.

Of the 16 learners in the course (9 women and 7 men), 5 women agreed to participate in the study: Eva and Martina from Poland, Mai from Vietnam, Martina from Czechoslovakia, and Felicia from Peru. This approach gave me the opportunity to concentrate my attention on a subset of language learners—immigrant women—who are, as Boyd (1992) noted, "triply disadvantaged" by their gender, ethnicity, and foreign status, and whose experience has been largely unaccounted for because of their silence (Ng, 1981).

It is difficult to determine with confidence how the five women who chose to take part in the study differed from the other learners in the ESL course, both male and female. It is possible that the women in the course were more attracted to the writing of a journal on personal experience than the men were—an observation that is supported by much feminist research.[3] One writer, bell hooks (1990), for example, described how writing is paradoxically both a form of resistance and a form of submission for women who have few means to make their voices heard:

> Writing was a way to capture speech, to hold onto it, to keep it close. And so I wrote down bits and pieces of conversations, confessing in cheap diaries that soon fell apart from too much handling, expressing the intensity of my sorrow, the anguish of speech—for I was always saying the wrong thing, asking the wrong questions. I could not confine my speech to the necessary corners and concerns of my life.

An important aspect of the study was the meetings that were held in my home on a regular basis. The initial meetings were scheduled as a weekly event for a total of 8 weeks. The sessions took place in the evening—Friday nights and Sunday nights were considered the most suitable—and lasted approximately 3 hours. Although our first meeting on Sunday, January 27, 1991, was held in the kitchen around a large kitchen table, our subsequent meetings took place in the living room where the chairs were more comfortable and the setting more intimate. As far as transportation was concerned, Felicia had access to a car; Eva, Katarina, and Martina were driven to my house by Martina's husband, and I gave them a ride home; and Mai was picked up and dropped off by me.

The participants were encouraged to share extracts from their journals at these meetings, so that the audience for their writing included other

[3]See Van Daele (1990) for a comprehensive examination of this issue.

participants as well as me. I hoped that the opportunity to write for an authentic and interested audience would be a motivating factor for the participants in the study. This group approach to writing has proved to be highly successful in other Canadian contexts (see Obah, 1993), and Zamel (1987) wrote persuasively about the importance of social context in writing development.

After nine weekly meetings were over (January 27; February 1, 8, 17, 24; March 1, 8, 17, 24), there was general consensus that the meetings should continue, but that we should schedule the meetings on a monthly basis. We met once a month for the next 3 months, on April 12, May 10, and June 7, 1991. There were thus a total of 12 group meetings between January and June 1991. The discussions that arose from the extracts that the women chose to read to the group were a rich complement to the written journal entries. During the course of the study, I also kept a journal of my reflections on the project.

Establishing a venue, schedule, and transportation for the journal study proved simpler than deciding on a format for the journals themselves. Although all the women had asked me what was expected of them in the entries, I did not want to prescribe a "right" and "wrong" way of approaching the task. However, given my own research questions, I did wish to provide some guidance as to how they might proceed. I did this by articulating my objectives in written form and by responding to the journal entries that the women made.

At the initial meeting on Sunday, January 27, 1991, I gave the women an introductory "letter"[4] that outlined my interest in the project, and provided each woman with a chart on which she could record day-to-day activities that were conducted in English. I indicated that the chart might provide a starting point for further reflections that could be recorded in the journals. (An updated chart was given to each woman at each meeting.) After we had discussed the contents of the letter, I asked the women to consider under what conditions they had used English in the course of that particular day. Martina volunteered to share her experiences. She focused on her experiences of attending church, listening to the sermon, and singing hymns in English. She discussed how strange it was to perform such intimate functions in a second language. I used her discussion as an example of how the journal entries might be made, and I elaborated on this in my letters to the participants in the subsequent two weeks.

During the course of the study, I gave the women regular feedback on their journal entries. Sometimes I asked them to clarify or expand on issues that had been raised. For example, one of my comments to Katarina

---

[4]Copies of the letters and charts I gave to the participants can be found in the appendix of Peirce (1993).

was as follows: "Very interesting, Katarina! It would be nice to know more about some of the conversations you mention. For example, how did you find out about the community service job? Could you give more details about the interview? Who did most of the talking? What precisely did you talk about?"

Similarly, a comment to Eva read as follows: "Very interesting Eva! Please explain why you feel better when you don't have to do the heavy jobs and why this makes you want to talk more."

However, my comments did not only request clarification or amplification. I would often give words of comfort and support—like those I gave Mai: "These are all very interesting Mai! Life is full of ups and downs. Congratulations on getting your drivers' licence!—I'm very sorry that life was uncomfortable this week at work. What has been happening?" Similarly, "You're doing a FANTASTIC job, Mai! Don't let your brother tell you otherwise!"

I would also comment on the quality of the women's writing, and there were times when I would ask the women to give me feedback on my comments. For example, a note to Mai was as follows: "Your comments are very interesting Mai. Is it useful for me to correct your writing as much as I have? Let me know." Within 2 to 3 weeks, each woman had developed a method of communication with which she felt most comfortable.

In some respects, defining my own relationship to the women was even more complex than helping the women develop a format for their journals. I wanted to create a supportive and intimate environment in which the women would feel sufficiently comfortable to discuss their desires, fears, joys, and frustrations. This was one of the main reasons why the meetings were held in my home. I hoped that my home, as a "private" sphere, would facilitate the expression and analysis of personal/private experiences. At one level, I wanted the participants to relate to me as a woman, functioning as a mother, wife, and housekeeper. I did not want my role as researcher to dominate my relationship to the women, because I thought this might create too much distance between us—positioning me as a "public" person in a private space. It was for this reason that I did not use a tape recorder at our meetings; I already had sufficient experience with the use of a tape recorder to know that some of the women felt uncomfortable discussing personal issues in their lives in the presence of such a device. However, I occasionally took notes at the meetings when I wanted to remember direct quotations.

Although I wished to avoid relating to the women as a teacher within the context of the study, it was a relationship that could not easily be ignored because our initial relationship had been structured in an educational setting. Furthermore, I understood that one of the reasons why the women took part in the study was to take the opportunity to improve their oral and written English in a supportive environment. For this reason, I encouraged the women to read some of their journal entries to the group each week. This gave them the opportunity to develop their oral skills, and it gave the group the opportunity to examine and discuss the issues that had been raised. Sometimes, during the course of our meetings, I would discuss vocabulary and grammatical issues with the women when they asked me for comments, or when they were struggling to express themselves. I also undertook to make suggestions as to how they might improve their written expression.

I do not know how well I succeeded in maintaining a balance between my diverse positions as friend, teacher, and researcher. I wanted to apologize on those rare occasions when I corrected the women's pronunciation—although I knew that pronunciation training was what they had requested. Sometimes, when I picked up my notepad in a meeting to record a comment that a woman had made, I almost felt as though I was undermining a friendship—betraying a confidence. Occasionally, I felt that my comments on the women's writing of their sometimes distressing stories were inadequate and trivial. I found myself trying to compensate for what Britzman (1990) called "guilty readings" by helping the women to find employment, prepare resumes, and deal with immigration officials.

ANALYSIS

Progress of the Study

The study was framed as a project about learning English as a second language in Canada. The way that it proceeded, however, was as a project about the complexities of living as a woman in a new and often threatening society, coping with the daily demands of family, work, schooling, housing, unemployment—much of which was conducted in a language that was only just beginning to make sense. It took place at a time when the women were beginning to question the usefulness of formal ESL classes, and were confronting the lack of congruence between their understanding of the world and their experience of it in Canada. It was a time when they saw the need for what Felicia called "practice, practice, practice" in the second language, but also a time when they were beginning to understand that their access to anglophone social networks was compromised by their position as "immigrant" in Canadian society. It was a time when they had a lot to ask, much to say, and a great deal to resist.

Although scarcely articulated at the time, the model of the study that was used in my research had its origins in the consciousness raising groups associated with "the second wave of feminism" that Weiler (1991) described in her work. Through the collective exploration of personal experiences of language learning and social interaction with members of the target language group, I hoped that the participants would come to a better understanding of language learning possibilities and constraints in Canadian society. Although my role within the group remained that of teacher/researcher, my authority was not derived from hierarchical educational structures, but rather from my command of the target language and my history as the former teacher of the participants in the study. It may also have been derived from my position as a professional, White, middle-class member of the dominant anglophone community—a woman with access to symbolic and material resources. However, partly because I had come to know and understand some aspects of the respective histories of each of the women—the talent and resources they had brought with them to Canada—I believe the women felt comfortable in my presence.

It is possible that the very "architecture" of the meetings helped to reduce the power differentials associated with the more formal ESL classroom. We were all located in the private sphere of a home, where the domestic position of a woman as homemaker is more in the foreground than her professional position as teacher/researcher. We sat in a circle, the configuration of which changed each week. The only blackboard was a child's blackboard that was used on rare occasions. As Lavery and Watson (1993) found in their research, changing the configuration of a classroom not only reduces the power differentials between teachers and learners, but reframes the learners' expectations of whose knowledge and experience is most valuable. In the journal study, not only was my status as "teacher" reframed, but so was the status of the "learners." In this context, I was not the guardian of a finite body of knowledge to which the learners had access only through me, nor were the women "learners" who vied with each other for access to my closely guarded resources. This had, I believe, a significant impact on the comfort levels in the group. Given the nonstop discussion that characterized our meetings, I think that the setting was a relatively egalitarian one.

Although one woman's knowledge was not considered more valuable than another's, their experiences as immigrant women were constructed differently across time and space. A fundamental premise of the diary study, reinforced by the architecture of the setting, was that each woman was an expert on her own life. Through the use of the weekly charts, the journal entries, and the feedback to the women, I tried to help each woman explore and articulate in written English her personal experiences of language learning in the home, the workplace, the school, and the community. This approach was a radical departure from the pedagogy that had been used in the 6-month ESL course, where writing was primarily confined to filling in blanks and writing decontextualized sentences.

Outcomes of the Study

During the course of the journal study, the participants made great progress in their writing and appeared to gain confidence in their social interactions with anglophone Canadians. Although such positive outcomes cannot be attributed to the journal study alone, it is possible that the study made a contribution to this progress. The quality and quantity of writing that the women produced, and the range of issues that we discussed in the meetings, were remarkable.[5] Topics included children's schooling, workplace conflict, popular television programs, stories from the women's native countries, the weather, the recession, and the Gulf War. After scarcely a year and a half in Canada, the women were able to make themselves understood in both spoken and written English. This is not to say that their grammar was flawless, their pronunciation perfect, and their vocabulary extensive; rather, they were able to give voice in English to the complexity of their experience.

Of particular significance to my research were those journal entries that highlighted the relationship between social interaction and social identity. Consider, for example, Extract 1 taken from Eva's journal entry on February 21, 1991, and Extract 2, taken from Mai's journal entry of February 8, 1991.[6]

> *Extract 1*
> Situation at work is surprising me, specially today. Usually the manager at the morning tells us, what we have to do. Then the girls (which I wrote about her) pretends, that she is busy all the time. This way I have to do everything. Today the manager gave us the list what we have to do (each of us separately). I was surprised, but the girl was more than me. After that, when I had done everything, she (the manager) asked me to do the order of vegetables, which we needed. Always I had to do the heavy job, this time was different. It made me feel better. When I feel well, than I can talk to the others. Today I was talking more than usually.

> *Extract 2*
> Something's happen at work. it made me felt sad and uncomfortable.
> Today, after we have lunch, Emelia asked two ladies to stay home tomorrow. because there isn't has enough job for everybody. Now my boss decides that he can keep only people who know how to make everything from top

---

[5]Auerbach (1989) noted similar writing progress in what she calls a "social-contextual" approach to ESL literacy for adult immigrants.

[6]The only changes that have been made to these entries are spelling corrections.

to bottom. It doesn't matter how long have they been working here.

everyone in that factory are all have been working there at less 8 months. I'm the only one have been there not so long. then my supervisor keeps me to stay. I know some one else doesn't like that way. But I cannot say anything it is not my fault, even those ladies are very upset. They told in front of me with each other.

One said "that's not fair, how come I am stay here longer, now she lays me off the other one says. Some one else can't does everything why don't lay them off too. then they started to speak they own language Italian or Portuguese by the way they look at some one who is still working it was very strange looking. they said a lot of things I couldn't understand. I don't know what do they think about me. I just have to according to my supervisor.

In Extract 1, Eva described how she is able to talk with greater ease and comfort because she has been given greater responsibility in her workplace (a restaurant), and is no longer simply delegated the "heavy" and undesirable jobs. This increased her self-confidence. The better she felt about herself, the more she could talk to and interact with her fellow workers. Extract 1 stands in stark contrast to Mai's extract, in which Mai described the marginalization she experienced in her workplace (a garment factory) as a result of the preferential treatment she received from the management. Not only did Mai's coworkers refuse to speak to her, but they spoke to one another in languages that were unfamiliar to Mai. Mai had little opportunity to interact socially with her coworkers, and remained silenced in the workplace. As Bourdieu (1977, p. 648) argued, "The most radical, surest, and best hidden censorships are those which exclude certain individuals from communication." However, although Mai was silenced in the workplace, she was able to use her journal to articulate her thoughts and experiences, and develop strategies to resist her marginalization.

Limitations of the Study

Notwithstanding these stories, however, I think the focus of the journals and our meetings was more on the expression of experience than the analysis of experience. Although there was much discussion on how being positioned as an immigrant constrained the opportunities for the women to interact with anglophone Canadians, there was little reflection on the ways in which gender, ethnicity, and class were implicated in larger, inequitable social structures. Consider the following three examples.

First, at our meeting of March 1, 1991, Felicia was expressing concern at her husband's unemployed status, saying "I pity him." Katarina expressed her sympathy for Felicia's plight by saying: "Women can always clean the house, but men must *do* something." There was general agreement with the sexist assumptions underlying this statement: that the work women do in the home is not classified as "doing something"[7]; and that employment is a right for men—and by extension only a privilege for women.

Second, when I was taking Mai home from a meeting on March 1, 1991, Mai was describing the alienation that her nephews experienced as Chinese/Vietnamese people in Canada. For example, the eldest child, Trong, had chosen to change his name from a Vietnamese one to an anglicized one. Mai told me that she said to her nephews that they should not reject their heritage, explaining "With your hair, your nose, your skin, you will never be perfect Canadians." Mai had internalized the racist belief that perfect Canadians exist, and that perfect Canadians are White.

Third, in an interview I had with Eva on January 23, 1991, just before our first meeting, Eva was explaining why her coworkers did not talk to her: "I think because when I didn't talk to them, and they didn't ask me, maybe they think I'm just like—because I had to do the worst type of work there. It's normal." Eva said that it was understandable—"normal"—that a person who has a job with little status should be marginalized by coworkers. Eva never challenged the elitist assumptions underlying this statement.

I did not take up these issues with the women, but instead let them pass. During the course of the study I did not know how and to what extent I should disorganize and challenge the commonsense understandings of gender, race, and class that the women expressed. My desire to maintain solidarity with the women, to create a comfortable space in which they could write and talk about their confusion, their anger, and their joy, kept me silent. I could affirm, but not negate. The danger of remaining silent on such issues, however, became apparent to me in a phone call I had with Katarina in January 1993, long after the study was over. She was telling me that she had moved from her old apartment block to a new one. It was with pride that she said, "There are very few immigrants here. It's mainly old people." It became immediately apparent to me that she was implicated in reinforcing and reproducing the marginalizing discourse on "immigrants" in Canadian society.

Harper, Peirce, and Burnaby (1996) made the point that attempts to incorporate women's experience in the ESL classroom may paradoxically serve to maintain the present status and conditions that women face at work and in society at large. Accommodating women's experience, rather than problematizing it, may not ultimately work in the best interests of

---

[7]See Rossiter (1986) for an insightful analysis of the social construction of homemaking.

women. They stressed the importance of identifying and intensifying the moments in which an opening is created for critical reflection on issues of gender and race.

IMPLICATIONS OF THE STUDY FOR PEDAGOGY

Although I recognize some of the limitations of the study, as noted earlier, I believe that my research has important implications for the use of journals in adult ESL. Although the use of journals in the language classroom is a classic method in communicative language teaching, learners are sometimes discouraged from writing about issues that directly engage their sense of who they are and how they relate to the social world. Thus, Peyton and Reed's (1990) handbook, *Dialogue Journal Writing With Nonnative English Speakers,* although claiming to "individualize language and content learning" (p. 18) simultaneously offered advice on how the teacher can prevent writing from becoming "too personal":

> Some teachers are afraid that leaving the choice of topics entirely open to students encourages them to write about very personal topics or family matters that the teacher is not prepared to deal with, and that the writing can turn into a counseling session. This does occur at times. However, it need not continue. Teachers can gently point out that they are not comfortable discussing that topic and introduce another one. (p. 67)

If language teachers wish to bridge the gap between the classroom and the community, then teachers need to create possibilities for learners to describe and analyze their relationship to the social world. Social interaction, both inside and outside the classroom, impacts on the social identities of all adult learners. Unequal relations of power between interlocutors are not only a function of the relationship between target language speakers and language learners, they are also a function of the unequal relationship between women and men, African Americans and Whites, rich and poor. Through the process of social interaction both inside and outside the classroom, learners of different genders, races, classes, and languages are constantly negotiating their social identities, their expectations, and their hopes for the future. If learners are encouraged to use journals to interrogate such social interaction, reflect on and critique their experiences, and perhaps share some of their insights with other learners, they will develop rich resources as a base for new learning about their schooling, their communities, and themselves. And the study suggests that they may become enthusiastic writers.

Three ways in which the participants in my study used their journals to reflect on social interaction have direct relevance for classroom teaching. First, the participants used their journals to reflect on ways in which social interaction in the classroom impacts on the social identities of learners. In Extract 3, for example, Mai described some of the potential problems with peer evaluation.

Extract 3

Sit beside me in class are a couple Mary and John. They came from England.

Tonight they have to speak with class to introduce their product. John was talking about his camera. Mary had the little box hand made. it use for to put money for save. By the way they speak were slow and very clearly understood everything even the instruction says that they do a good job. every time when someone speak someone else have to mark in the evaluation form for speech to persuade and we have to give some idea, how good the speaker is. the results Mary got from suggestions of someone wasn't very nice. it makes she feels unhappy. She gave to me read that form and I got confused too. one of class mate write.

"Mary! your speech is good, but you look like tired and fall asleep" Also John he got the same person write some bad thing too. I'm going to speak in class on next Monday, I know for sure I can't avoid someone will does the same thing to me like they did before, I don't think it is nice person to be that with classmate.

Second, the participants used their journals to reflect on ways in which social interaction leads to self-assessment of language learning. In Extract 4, for example, written on February 8, 1991, Felicia reflected on the fact that she didn't like to participate in conversations, particularly with strangers, for fear of being positioned as an "uninteresting" person. In contrast, in Extract 5, written on February 17, 1991, Katarina reflected on her progress in language learning by comparing two interviews she had had over a 6-month period.

Extract 4

I listen more English at my work than I have to talk. Sometimes the ladies ask me something about my country or my family, but I think that I'm not an interesting person because my English is limited and I have to think before talking. I feel confidence with them because it is about 8 months that we worked together and I see them every day. They are very nice and patient with my English. I understand almost that they talk, but I sometimes have to guess something. I avoid talking with the children's mothers, because my English is too poor and I don't feel well talking with strangers. I would like to tell the mothers many things about their babies but I prefer to be silent. I only tell what it is necessary.

Extract 5

On Wednesday I had interview in Ontario College in Newtown. I am going to take after [skills course], Computer Programmer Course. I don't have to pass an examination of mathematics. I only have to pass an exam of English. I can compare this interview with another which I have had six months ago. The first interview took place in the Community Service. I wasn't able to tell a lot about myself after ESL course during that interview. On Wednesday I was able to ask and understand about my course, about another course and requirement to these courses.

Third, the participants used their journals to reflect on the discrepancies that existed between what they learned about social interaction in the classroom and what they experienced in the world outside it. In Extract 6, for example, taken on February 17, 1991, Martina explained that her interest in Canadian soap operas grew because she felt that they were a more accurate reflection of Canadian society than that portrayed in the classroom context (my emphasis).

Extract 6

First month in Canada was very difficult, because we weren't able to communicate and understand. When we bought the refrigerator—it didn't work, it warm up. Every second week a repairman came and after one week it stopped to work again. Then we decided to return it and we asked for a small freezer but they didn't have one. The manager told my daughter that she must wait and call every month. I was very disappointed and I wanted to know something about Canadians.

First time we watch "Who's the boss?" or "The Cosby show"—it was funny, but I was looking for something else.

After the ESL course when I had the interview, they asked me very different questions, *the ones that we didn't study in school* and I was very surprised. Then I started to watch "All my children"—not every day and "One life to live". In both soap operas there are stories from actual people's experiences and very few from work. There are different personalities. The life is full of love, hate, danger, and lies. When I told these stories to my children I use some English phrases—leave me alone; what's going on, etc. These phrases sound better in English.

Learner reflection on social interaction inside and outside the classroom is highly instructive for teachers. It gives the teacher insight into the effect of classroom pedagogy on the social identities of learners, and possible reasons for different levels of learner participation. It provides insight into an adult's engagement in the learning process, and the extent to which a learner's social identity is implicated in the kind of interaction that takes place outside the classroom. It highlights discrepancies between formal sites of learning and personal experiences in the wider community.

These insights can help the teacher revise and adapt classroom teaching and course curricula in ways that are directly relevant to learner needs.

My study suggests that the teacher's role is crucial in creating conditions that will promote the use of journals for introspection and critique as well as the communal sharing of ideas. First, teachers need to provide guidance as to the many forms a journal can take, and it should be clear that there is no right or wrong way of recording experiences. The teacher might show learners how experiences have been recorded in the mother tongue (e.g., Bell, 1991) as well as the target language (e.g., Yu, 1990). Second, the teacher might take the opportunity to keep her or his own journal and share extracts with the class (see, e.g., Spack & Sadow, 1983). Such extracts might include samples from the learner's journals, if prior permission has been obtained. Third, the teacher could help learners develop their ideas and their expository writing skills by asking them to clarify or extend particular extracts from their journals. For example, they could encourage learners to explore analytically an experience that has been recorded in a descriptive manner. Fourth, although some researchers advocate that journals be uncorrected and ungraded (Spack & Sadow, 1983), my participants asked me to provide feedback on their grammar and expression. Errors common to a number of learners could be used as the basis for a grammar workshop. Finally, the teacher needs to help create a classroom atmosphere that will encourage the sharing of ideas. The careful organization of small groups might enhance intimacy, and a circular arrangement of desks might help to reduce the power differentials between teacher and learner. If teachers create the conditions that will give learners an investment in what they write, the encouragement to write it, and the opportunity to share it, they may be as surprised as Martina's children were at what the learners produce. It is therefore appropriate that Martina should have the final word:

> The first time I was very nervous and afraid to talk on the phone. When the phone rang, everybody in my family was busy, and my daughter had to answer it. After ESL course when we moved and our landlords tried to persuade me that we have to pay for whole year, I got upset and I talked with him on the phone over one hour and I didn't think about the tenses rules. I had known that I couldn't give up. My children were very surprised when they heard me.

REFERENCES

Auerbach, E. R. (1989). Toward a social-contextual approach to family literacy. *Harvard Educational Review, 59,* 165–181.

Bailey, K. M. (1980). An introspective analysis of an individual's language learning experience. In R. Scarcella & S. Krashen (Eds.), *Research in second language acquisition* (pp. 58–65). Rowley, MA: Newbury House.

Bailey, K. M. (1983). Competitiveness and anxiety in adult second language learning: Looking at and through the diary studies. In H. D. Seliger & M. H. Long (Eds.), *Classroom oriented research in second language acquisition* (pp. 67–103). Rowley, MA: Newbury House.

Bell, J. (1991). *Becoming aware of literacy.* Unpublished doctoral thesis, University of Toronto.

Bourdieu, P. (1977). The economics of linguistic exchanges. *Social Science Information, 16*(6), 645–668.

Boyd, M. (1992). Immigrant women: Language, socio-economic inequalities, and policy issues. In B. Burnaby & A. Cumming (Eds.), *Socio-political aspects of ESL in Canada* (pp. 141–159). Toronto: Ontario Institute for Studies in Education.

Britzman, D. (1990, October). *Could this be your story? Guilty readings and other ethnographic dramas.* Paper presented at the Bergamo Conference, Dayton, OH.

Brown, C. (1984). Two windows on the classroom world: Diary studies and participant observation differences. In P. Larson, E. Judd, & D. Messerschmitt (Eds.), *On TESOL '84.* Washington, DC: TESOL.

Cooke, D. (1986). Learning the language of your students. *TESL Talk, 16*(1), 5–13.

Harper, H., Peirce, B., & Burnaby, B. (1996). English-in-the-workplace for garment workers: A feminist project? *Gender and Education, 8*(1), 5–19.

Hingle, I. (1992, July). *The role of the teacher as interlocutor in dialogue journal writing.* Paper presented at the 12th annual SAALA conference, Port Elizabeth, South Africa.

hooks, b. (1990). Talking back. In R. Ferguson, M. Gever, T. Minh-Ha, & C. West (Eds.), *Out there: Marginalization in contemporary cultures* (pp. 337–340). Boston: MIT Press.

Lavery, R. H., & Watson, M. (1993). Shifting perspectives/shifting practices. *English Quarterly, 25*(1), 4–7.

Ng, R. (1981). Constituting ethnic phenomenon: An account from the perspective of immigrant women. *Canadian Ethnic Studies, 13,* 97–108.

Obah, T. Y. (1993). Learning from others in the ESL writing class. *English Quarterly, 25*(1), 8–13.

Peirce, B. N. (1993). *Language learning, social identity, and immigrant women.* Unpublished doctoral dissertation, Ontario Institute for Studies in Education/University of Toronto.

Peirce, B. N. (1995). Social identity, investment, and language learning. *TESOL Quarterly, 19*(1), 9–31.

Peyton, J. K., & Reed, L. (1990). *Dialogue journal writing with nonnative English speakers: A handbook for teachers.* Alexandria, VA: TESOL.

Rossiter, A. B. (1986). *In private: An inquiry into the construction of women's experience of early motherhood.* Unpublished doctoral thesis, University of Toronto.

Savage, W., & Whisenand, R. (1993). Logbooks and language learning objectives in an intensive ESP workshop. *TESOL Quarterly, 27*(4), 741–746.

Schumann, F. (1980). Diary of a language learner: A further analysis. In R. Scarcella & S. Krashen (Eds.), *Research in second language acquisition* (pp. 51–57). Rowley, MA: Newbury House.

Schumann, J. H., & Schumann, F. (1977). Diary of a language learner: An introspective study of second language learning. In H. D. Brown, C. Yorio, & R. Crymes (Eds.), *On TESOL '77: Teaching and learning English as a second language: Trends and practice* (pp. 241–249). Washington, DC: TESOL.

Spack, R., & Sadow, C. (1983). Learner–teacher working journals in ESL freshman composition. *TESOL Quarterly, 17*(4), 575–593.

Spolsky, B. (1989). *Conditions for second language learning.* Oxford, England: Oxford University Press.

Van Daele, C. (1990). *Making words count: The experience and meaning of the diary in women's lives.* Unpublished doctoral thesis, University of Toronto.

Weiler, K. (1991). Freire and a feminist pedagogy of difference. *Harvard Educational Review, 61*(4), 449–474.

West, C. (1992). A matter of life and death. *October, 61*, 20–23.
Winer, L. (1992). "Spinach to chocolate": Changing awareness and attitudes in ESL writing teachers. *TESOL Quarterly, 26*(1), 57–80.
Yu, L. (1990). The comprehensible output hypothesis and self-directed learning: A learner's perspective. *TESL Canada Journal, 8*(1), 9–26.
Zamel, V. (1987). Recent research on writing pedagogy. *TESOL Quarterly, 21*(4), 697–715.

5

Promoting Gender Equity in the Postsecondary ESL Class[1]

Stephanie Vandrick
University of San Francisco

The field of ESL has been enriched by influences from many different fields. In this chapter I propose that ESL educators can greatly benefit from insights gained from the emerging field of feminist pedagogy. Feminist pedagogy is being practiced in many classes in many fields, and is not limited to women's studies programs or classes. Certainly, ESL instructors are dedicated to promoting equity and justice, and feminist pedagogy has the same goal. More and more women worldwide are participating in higher education, and more and more immigrant and international women students are appearing in college ESL classes. All of these developments provide reasons for consideration of feminist pedagogy in ESL.

Feminist pedagogy itself has been influenced by and has grown out of various other fields, such as psychology, linguistics, literature, education, and composition. Feminist pedagogy needs to be implemented early in the educational process, and there have been many publications about, and much interest in, the topic of gender equity in elementary and secondary school education. The focus here, however, is on postsecondary education.

This chapter traces some of the sources of feminist pedagogy, describes feminist pedagogy and some of its developments and controversies, summarizes gender-related research in ESL, addresses ways in which feminist pedagogy can be applied in ESL situations and, throughout, suggests materials for further reading.

---

[1]This chapter draws on and builds on my two earlier articles (Vandrick, 1994, 1995).

THE SOURCES

Research in the field of psychology on gender differences and on the psychology of women has indicated that women develop differently because of their subordinate position in society. Women are raised to be nurturing, other-oriented, emotional, and passive. These characteristics have been praised and at the same time used by some as evidence that women are less fit for the work world. Women's characteristics are treated as if they are by definition inferior. Women themselves have internalized these attitudes, and have even been so afraid to succeed that they have sabotaged their own success (Horner, 1972). Gilligan (1982) found that females define morality in terms of relationships, whereas males define it in terms of fairness and rules. Belenky, Clinchy, Goldberger, and Tarule (1986) pointed out that male intellectual development has been considered the norm, with its emphasis on rationality, and thus female intellectual development has been considered lacking or inferior because of its emphasis on feelings and connections. These beliefs harm men, too, because men are not allowed to display traits such as gentleness or nurturance without being labeled (or fearing being labeled) feminine. Tavris (1992) stated further that when women are continually judged against the male norm (described as a "universal" norm), they are of course doomed not to measure up, and thus women's development and behavior is "pathologized." Related work in psychology is that of Chodorow (1978), Hancock (1989), and Miller (1976), among others.

The topic of gender differences in language use has become prominent in recent years, and the research in this area is outlined in the work of Lakoff (1975, 1990), Kramarae (1981), Thorne and Henley (1975), Miller and Swift (1976), Spender (1980), and Cameron (1990). This work has been popularized by Tannen (1990). Some of the findings are that women use politer and more tentative language, and that women are spoken about in patronizing and demeaning ways. These differences clearly reflect the way women are treated in society. As was found in psychological research (discussed previously), the male way, here male speech, is seen as the norm, and female speech is thus seen as deviating from and inferior to the male norm. Clearly, educators need to be aware of these differences, and to examine their own biases and behaviors in the classroom and make sure that they are not raising male speech modes to a privileged status.

Over the past 15 years, feminist literary criticism has revolutionized and revitalized the field of literature; this work has immeasurably enriched feminist pedagogy. But it all started with a literary foremother, Virginia Woolf, who in addition to her early feminist literary criticism bravely critiqued the way in which women's colleges and women's education in general were considered second class, and were allocated far less of education's resources than were men's educational institutions. A later pioneer was poet Adrienne Rich (1979), who spoke to and about women students and asked that they take themselves seriously and be taken seriously. Rich still speaks out on this issue, as does Carolyn Heilbrun (e.g., 1990), always an advocate for women in the academy as well as for women's literature. These are only three of the many literary critics and authors who have provided a rich panoply of writing on women's issues and lives, writings that can nourish and assist those who are concerned with feminist teaching.

Postsecondary educators are building on the work of such researchers on elementary and secondary education as the American Association of University Women (1992), Sadker and Sadker (1994), and Orenstein (1994), all of whom have shown, among other things, that girls receive unequal attention in classrooms, are sexually harassed in schools, and are not encouraged in science and math classes. These factors have a negative effect on girls' self-esteem and success. Most of this research continues to apply in the case of adult, especially young adult, students.

The work of theorists in critical pedagogy, such as Freire, Giroux, McLaren, and Apple, has indirectly given feminist pedagogy another context, that of promoting the questioning of traditional educational models and practices. The emphasis of critical pedagogy on education as emancipation and transformation provides a model for feminist pedagogy, and critical pedagogues have given some, although not enough, attention to gender equity.

The field of composition has been a fertile one for feminist pedagogy, partly because that field is already dealing with and focusing on questions of outsiderness and marginalization within the academy. It is also perhaps the closest one to ESL, and therefore the ways in which composition has incorporated feminist pedagogy are of particular interest to ESL educators. Compositionists, who are largely women, have had their consciousness raised by the realization that composition has become "women's work" and is thus treated as "work of lesser value" (Holbrook, cited in Eichhorn et al., 1992). Related to the "women's work" theme is that of regarding the woman teacher as "a caring responsive mother/teacher" (Clark, 1995, p. 109). On the one hand, this can be considered positive, and a celebration of female values; on the other hand, this model may provide ammunition to opponents of feminist teaching or even of women teachers in general. The same question is raised in a different regard: that of students' work. Flynn (1990) and others examined the writings of women students and, confirming the work of Gilligan and Belenky et al., found that compositions by female students show patterns of relational identification and connections, whereas compositions by male students show a preoccupation with individuation and individual achievement. Hays (1995) and others cautioned, however, that instructors should not dichotomize the two types of patterns, because there is much overlap and such oversimplifying thinking can, again, be harmful. Hays pointed out that "The choices are not . . . between, on the one hand, an abstract, excessively emotionless scientific discourse stripped of affective, moral, or personal dimensions and, on the other, an excessively private, affect-based language that eschews hierarchy, analysis, and establishing propositions and is in danger of becoming inchoate and incoherent, apolitical and theory-repudiating" (p. 159). Thus, the question and concern is whether the often-mentioned "feminization" of the field will be a reason for its being marginalized, or will be, as some more optimistic compositionists have stated, an opportunity to "develop democratic research practices and administrative and pedagogical structures" (Flynn, 1995, p. 367) and "work for a transformation not just of the field but of higher education" (Phelps, paraphrased in Clark, 1995, p. 111).

There are other issues regarding the writing of women students that instructors need to be aware of. Annas (1987) and others noted that women writers have been silenced, and have silenced themselves, out of a fear of expressing themselves and exposing themselves. Goulston (1987) found that women often write what they think will please (usually male) authorities such as their professors or bosses. Flynn (1990) concluded that educators must value women's strengths in writing, and must encourage women writers; she stated that "[A]s writing teachers, we have an opportunity—indeed, an obligation—to attempt to rectify . . . inequities by placing women's texts at the center of our curricula and by encouraging our women students to write from the power of their experience" (p. 124).

In addition to this work on women's writing is the work of Fetterley (cited in Peterson, 1991) and others on women's ways of reading; Fetterley labeled as "immasculation" a process by which women readers are repeatedly taught "to think as men, to identify with a male point of view, and to accept as normal and legitimate a male system of values" (Peterson, 1991, p. 175). Feminist educators must counteract this type of conditioning.

FEMINIST PEDAGOGY: THEORY AND PRACTICE

Drawing on the previously mentioned fields and others, feminist pedagogy has become a field of its own. What exactly is feminist pedagogy? It can perhaps best be defined by what it questions: "Feminist educators question the structure of educational institutions, traditional canons of knowledge, women's roles as teachers and scholars, and students' responses to female and to feminist teachers" (Kirsch, 1995, p. 723). There are multiple further definitions and descriptions, but most include the following elements. First, perhaps self-evidently, its proponents are feminists, not only in their educational work but in the broader sense. Second, its adherents believe that the classroom is a place where females are discriminated against, and that it is a place where feminist practices can make a real difference in girls' and women's lives, and thus by extension, in society. Feminist teaching is "engaged teaching/learning," said Shrewsbury (1993, p. 8), in which teachers and students are engaged with the material, with the struggle against sexism and racism and classism and homophobia; they are also engaged with the community and with movements for social change. Shrewsbury further described feminist pedagogy in terms of three central concepts: empowerment, community, and leadership.

In the process of drawing on the fields described earlier, scholars in feminist pedagogy have sometimes criticized the ideas in those fields. Most seriously challenged, although in some ways closest in spirit, has been critical pedagogy. Although feminist pedagogy, like critical pedagogy, advocates emancipation and equal opportunity in education, there is a concern that gender issues have not been a priority for critical pedagogy scholars. It has often been pointed out that Paulo Freire, the leading voice in critical pedagogy, has been sympathetic to women's issues but has not made them an important focus in his own work, and has even seemed to downplay the women's movement (Olson, 1992). Giroux, Shor, and other leading critical pedagogues have also been criticized. Luke (1992) perhaps best expressed the problem in her critique: "The point is this: to grant equal classroom time to female students, to democratize the classroom speech situation, and to encourage marginal groups to make public what is personal and private does not alter theoretically or practically those gendered structural divisions upon which liberal capitalism and its knowledge industries are based" (p. 37).

In a widely read article, Ellsworth (1992) stated that terms such as "empowerment," "student voice," and "critical" can be "repressive myths that perpetuate relations of domination" (p. 91), myths that are based on rationalist assumptions and that posit a universality that is, in fact, "oppressive to those who are not European, white, male, middle class, Christian, ablebodied, thin, and heterosexual" (p. 96). Furthermore, she maintained that theorists of critical pedagogy "have failed to launch any meaningful analysis of or program for reformulating the institutionalized power imbalances between themselves and their students, or of the essentially paternalistic project of education itself" (p. 98) and "critical pedagogues are always implicated in the very structures they are trying to change" (p. 101). Orner (1992), too, was concerned about not only critical pedagogues but also some "Anglo-American" feminist pedagogues, for whom, she felt, "Students/youth are positioned as Other" (p.

74), and who condescendingly assume that students do not already value their own language and background. Furthermore, Orner felt that the stance of these critical and feminist pedagogues assumes, presumptuously, that they themselves are already enlightened and are "empowerers," and not themselves oppressors.

Other problematic issues that feminist pedagogues must grapple with are the difficulties of finding "right" answers about teaching, the opposition that feminist pedagogues and their students often face, and the question of power and authority and how they can and should be shared.

How do these theories and issues apply in the classroom itself? How is a feminist classroom different from any other classroom? There is no one answer, but some of the changes being attempted are as follows. Most generally, all attempt to create more equitable classrooms. Some feminist pedagogues advocate, first of all, systematic observation and feedback in order to honestly evaluate the problems (Sadker & Sadker, 1990). Others explicitly teach "feminist process," focusing on how to participate in a feminist classroom, and teaching such skills as sharing feelings, giving constructive feedback, practicing conflict resolution and cooperation, and integrating theory and practice (Schniedewind, 1993). Note, however, the possible danger caused by "instructors who too globally advocate an ethic of care and thus unwittingly appear to validate the very powerlessness" from which women students sometimes suffer (Hays, 1995, pp. 167–168).

Another feminist focus is on emphasizing inclusiveness of various groups, such as women of color, who up to now have sometimes been "disregarded as participants in the learning environment" (Omolade, 1993, p. 38), lesbians, Jewish women, and "returning" (older) women. Still others focus on exposing students, especially female students, to women's history in all fields. Hoffmann and Culley (1985) recommended including in literature classes the " 'nontraditional' literature of ordinary women" such as letters and diaries (p. 1).

There is now a wealth of material available to assist those who want to make their classrooms more equitable, especially regarding gender. For just a few examples of writings about curriculum planning and teaching suggestions, see Andersen (1987a, 1987b), Cannon (1990), Dill (1994), Fowlkes and McClure (1984), Higginbotham (1988), Howe (1983), Schmitz (1990), Spelman (1985), and Zambrana (1994). Other resources include a special issue of *Women's Studies Quarterly* titled "Feminist Pedagogy: An Update" (Schniedewind et al., 1993), two special issues of *Radical Teacher* (Annas & Maher, 1992a, 1992b) jointly titled "Feminist Pedagogies and Difference in the Classroom," and an issue of *NWSA Journal* with "a special focus, the feminist classroom" (Schweickart, 1995). The journal *Feminist Teacher* is an ongoing resource. Another is the recent book, *The*

Feminist Classroom, in which Maher and Tetreault (1994) described their systematic observations of classes at several universities in which the faculty members aimed to teach with a feminist focus. The classes were in such varying disciplines as literature, history, psychology, education, philosophy, and biology. The feminist practices employed varied widely, thus allowing readers to see various ways feminist teaching can be applied in various fields and various situations; feminist teaching is nothing if not adaptable. Useful for individuals or for use in education classes is a collection of thought-provoking, realistic cases in which gender in the classroom is an issue: *Gender Tales: Tensions in the Schools* (Kleinfeld & Yerian, 1995). The cases are left open-ended, asking the reader to decide on appropriate reactions or solutions. Also especially useful for teacher education classes is *Creating the Nonsexist Classroom: A Multicultural Approach* (McCormick, 1994), which deals with history and classroom practice in a practical yet reflective manner; this book includes an excellent list of resources and references. Resources on preventing and dealing with sexual harassment include recent books by Layman (1994) and Paludi (1996). And for those who would like to get information on their computers, a recent article in *Feminist Teacher* offers a guide to using the internet for information related to Women's Studies, including feminist pedagogy (Warren-Wenk, 1995).

FEMINIST PEDAGOGY AND ESL

As yet there has not been a very fully developed area of research or practice in ESL that could be labeled "feminist pedagogy." Schenke (1991) stated that teaching from a feminist standpoint is "a standpoint that, at present, has little to no currency in (academic) E.S.L. pedagogy and that, aside from linguistic studies of gendered speech patterns and a few token textbook units on 60s style 'women's lib,' is virtually invisible" (p. 47). However, there has been some research regarding gender in ESL pedagogy, and there have been attempts by some ESL instructors to make their classrooms more equitable. There is a small but increasing interest in feminist pedagogy. We know that the consequences of unfairness toward females in the classroom can be very destructive (see, e.g., Orenstein, 1994; Pipher, 1994), not only in terms of self-esteem and potential careers, but also in very immediate behaviors such as eating disorders, self-mutilation, and suicide; there is no reason to assume that female ESL students are immune to these possible consequences. As ESL professionals learn more, they will be more and more likely to investigate and pursue ways to integrate feminist pedagogy into their classrooms.

Research

Sexism in ESL materials was described by Hartman and Judd (1978) and Porreca (1984); both studies found that many ESL texts contained stereotypes about women, underrepresented women, mentioned men first, and made offensive jokes about women. Judd (1983) wrote of the applicability to ESL of sociolinguistic research on gender and language. Gass and Varonis (1986) focused on gender and second language (L2) acquisition. Moody (1986) described problems with instruction and services given to female students in ESL programs.

Specifically regarding the ESL classroom, Markham (1988) described a study that found that students listened more attentively to male speakers. Wolfson (1989) and Thomas-Ruzic, Haney, Monogue, and McGovern (1994) each summarized gender and language research and its possible connections to ESL, and urged further research in and attention to this area. A recent and welcome book dedicated to gender questions and ESL is *Exploring Gender: Questions and Implications for English Language Education* (Sunderland, 1994). It covers language issues, materials, classroom practices, and larger sociopolitical and other issues affecting the ESL classroom and the field of ESL.

Concerns

It is important to note that the tenets and practices of feminist pedagogy clearly cannot and should not be applied wholesale or without thought as to the particular circumstances, backgrounds, and needs of particular ESL students in particular classes. Such application would be ineffective and possibly harmful. Programs and instructors need to look at the specific teaching situation when planning and implementing changes related to feminist teaching.

One major concern for ESL educators who consider adopting principles and practices of feminist pedagogy to ESL settings is the cultural differences that may make such pedagogy less appropriate. Note, however, that as Cochran (1996) pointed out, "The female ESL student is doubly marginalized by virtue of her special cultural and linguistic situation" (p. 159). It is, of course, important for ESL educators to be sensitive to cultural differences, but this sensitivity does not preclude feminist pedagogical practices. Educators must and can find ways to make the two compatible.

Another concern expressed by some ESL educators is that feminist teaching is too political or ideological. However, it has become increasingly clear that, whether we like it or not and whether we acknowledge it or not, all teaching is ideological; there is no such thing as neutral teaching. Benesch (1993) stated that "Educators who do not acknowledge or discuss their ideology are not politically neutral; they simply do not highlight their ideology" (p. 706). Teaching feminist issues may be viewed by some as imposing the instructor's opinions on students. However, the issues do not have to be, and should not be, taught as indoctrination; rather, the instructor should provide information, resources, and a variety of opinions, and should help students evaluate all of these critically and then form their own opinions. Bronson Alcott once said, "The true teacher defends his [sic] pupil against his own influence" (cited in Gardner, 1994, p. 3), and the kind of teaching referred to here allows students to come to their own conclusions, and to do so without negative repercussions in the classroom.

It is also important that when teaching students to identify and avoid bias, instructors not convey to students that they assume students are "more racist, sexist, or ethnocentric, than their U.S. counterparts" (Graham, 1992, p. 586). A particular concern to ESL educators, as well as to educators of those who speak nonstandard dialects of English, is that of honoring and preserving the students' own languages, and not implying that (standard) English is somehow better than their own languages or dialects (hooks, 1994).

Pedagogy

Feminist pedagogy does not prescribe a certain set of practices; each teaching situation is different, and each teacher has to find the practices which work for his or her classroom and students. Feminist teaching requires, first, a consciousness that influences all teaching practices. As Schenke (1996) put it, "Feminism, like antiracism, is . . . not simply one more social issue in ESL but a way of thinking, a way of teaching, and most importantly, a way of learning" (p. 158). Therefore, it is incumbent on ESL instructors to educate themselves about feminist pedagogy and about the relevant research, and then to devise their own ways to integrate feminist teaching into their classes.

Many of the teaching practices described here that apply to classrooms in general (e.g., teaching communication skills and collaboration) can also be applied in the ESL classroom. The lessons from education research such as the AAUW and the Sadker and Sadker studies, mentioned previously, also can be applied in ESL classrooms: Teachers should monitor themselves to see how much attention they give females and males in the classroom, and should be aware of gender differences in learning styles. Holmes (1994) reminded teachers to be aware of and try to prevent patterns of male domination of classroom time, including interrupting and frequent challenges. She stated that male students may need specific instruction in classroom communication skills.

In ESL writing classes in particular, instructors can adopt methods evolved by feminist compositionists, such as using one-to-one tutorials and practicing collaborative learning (Stanger, 1987), both of which are already practiced in many ESL classes; reading works by different types of women authors and discussing many different types of women; and the instructor acting as "a guide rather than an authority figure" (Frey, 1987, p. 99). The process approach to teaching writing, which is now central in most composition classes, can help women students break through their silences and help end gender bias in classrooms (Rubin, 1993).

Materials

A critical feminist practice is to focus on the materials being used in the class. A textbook being considered for adoption should be examined for its inclusiveness of women writers, women subjects, and women's issues. Generally, the engagement with gender issues in ESL texts and classes has tended to be with relatively "safe" issues such as wages; although these are important, we must go beyond the safe issues to such difficult issues as violence against women; sexual harassment; and the roles of government, religion, business, and media in the oppression of women. Some ESL texts address gender concerns, but more such texts are needed; publishers should be encouraged to make this a priority in publishing future texts. Instructors can also supplement ESL texts by including academic or journalistic writings by women and/or relating to gender issues. Keeping a file of clippings on such issues can be very useful. Feminist magazines such as *Ms.* and progressive magazines such as *Mother Jones, The Progressive,* and *Z Magazine* are good resources for such a clippings file.

Providing students with such readings does not dilute or detract from the usual practice in reading, vocabulary building, analysis, discussion, and follow-up writing. In fact, the readings may be more interesting, relevant, and thought provoking than many of the readings done in ESL classes. In addition, the students are learning about U.S. culture and about the kinds of discussions that are going on about culture and politics in the United States and in other parts of the world as well.

The instructor does not have to make a special point of using readings by and about women. These can be used in the same places and ways that other readings would be done. For example, a unit on journalistic writing can include newspaper and magazine articles about gender issues, and can include discussion of ways in which women's news is often relegated to "women's sections" or "people sections." Discussion of advertising can include analyzing the portrayal of women in advertisements. Articles about successful women in various fields can provide helpful role models for young women just planning their own careers and adult lives.

When fiction is taught, stories by and about women can be included, and can be examined both as literature and as spotlights on real women's lives and concerns. Fortunately, there is a wealth of such literature available now. Of course, literature should not be used solely to make social and political points, but students can be shown that such points are one aspect of literature, not only regarding women but regarding other social/political issues such as war, religion, and race. Composition topics too can be related to gender issues, particularly in response to the types of readings described previously.

Another easily introduced type of materials is short, meaningful quotations by women authors, politicians, scientists, and others. These quotations do not necessarily have to focus on women's issues, but quotations on a wide range of topics can serve to show women in roles of expertise and authority. The quotations can also stimulate thought-provoking discussions, and introduce new vocabulary as well as information about well-known people (Vandrick, 1996).

Specific Classroom Practices

In addition to carefully monitoring and selecting materials, an instructor may employ many (sometimes) small but influential feminist teaching practices that can be introduced in the classroom in a natural way, without taking much time and without shortchanging the other pedagogical goals of the class. One can tell students about women's studies programs and classes, and about women professors who are experts in various departments on campus. One can encourage students to attend lectures and films on and off campus about women's issues or women's lives. Such events contribute to students' intellectual, political, and cultural education in general as well as to their knowledge about women's issues specifically. One can cite women as authorities about a variety of topics, and can mention women as examples in various contexts, in a very natural way. Women's names and feminine pronouns should be equally represented in exercises and tests. Even a slight "overcorrection" in favor of feminine names, pronouns, and examples is justifiable, considering the many years during which students have been exposed to instructional materials with an overwhelming bias in the other direction. Tests need to be written in a gender-neutral manner, avoiding questions that are slanted or subject matter that is male oriented. Female students should be called on as often as male students, and should be asked substantive questions, not the merely rote questions that female students are often asked, whereas male students are asked more complex analytical questions (AAUW, 1992).

Research also shows that female students tend to wait a little longer before formulating and giving their answers (AAUW, 1992), so it is important to allow them that time before moving on too quickly to another student or another question. All of these practices need to be followed consistently, not just occasionally.

Wolfson (1989) argued that issues of language and gender should be explicitly addressed in the ESL classroom: "Nonnative speakers need to know which terms to avoid and which are acceptable. . . . As newcomers to American society, nonnative speakers should be made aware of the controversy concerning issues of sexism in language. Such forms as *Ms.* and *Chair* need to be taught and discussed" (pp. 182–183). She also suggested that the " 'he/man' problem" be addressed by the increasingly accepted singular *they*; she feels that students should be told that "Someone left their coat on the chair" is "perfectly acceptable English" (p. 183). Instructors who do not feel comfortable with such a categorical acceptance of a grammar error can still describe and discuss this usage, using the opportunity to explore issues of gender and language with students. Students should also be told of other ways to avoid sexist pronoun usage, such as using plural forms when possible, or using "she or he" or "he or she."

A female instructor should realize that she is or can be a role model for students, a model of a capable, independent woman, who may be balancing a career and a family. She can share the difficulties and the rewards of her situation, if she feels comfortable doing so. A male instructor can share with students his commitment to gender equality, and let students know that men can be feminists too. A male instructor who tells students of his own involvement with his children, and with sharing child care and housework with his partner, provides an invaluable role model and lesson to young people thinking about their own futures. Some may feel that such discussion is too personal, but it can be integrated naturally into the kinds of conversations and examples that occur throughout the semester, as appropriate. Students are generally very interested in such discussion.

CONCLUSION

Most of all, feminist pedagogy involves knowledge about, and attention to, issues of gender and inequity. The methods, the curriculum, and the classroom practices can and should vary, depending on the instructor, the students, and the teaching situation. The common goal is an awareness, a sensitivity, and a will to work toward justice for all students. Although feminist teaching, or at least explicitly and consciously feminist teaching, is still fairly new in ESL and may feel risky, it is important that

ESL instructors educate themselves about feminist pedagogy and about ways in which they can promote gender equity in their classrooms. Because what happens in the classroom is not separable from what happens in the larger society and in the world, it is also important that ESL faculty are aware of and engage with the larger contexts for feminist pedagogy. It is time for ESL researchers and writers to build a body of writing on, and to promote discussion and implementation of, feminist pedagogy in ESL. Feminist pedagogy is not a passing fad; it must be grappled with, and it must be an essential component of the field of ESL in the future.

REFERENCES

American Association of University Women. (AAUW). (1992). *How schools shortchange girls.* Washington, DC: AAUW Educational Foundation.

Andersen, M. L. (1987a). Changing the curriculum in higher education. *Signs: Journal of Women in Culture and Society, 12,* 222–254.

Andersen, M. L. (1987b). *Denying difference: The continuing basis for exclusion of race and gender in the curriculum.* Memphis, TN: Memphis State University, Center for Research on Women.

Annas, P. J. (1987). Silences: Feminist language research and the teaching of writing. In C. L. Caywood & G. R. Overing (Eds.), *Teaching writing: Pedagogy, gender, and equity* (pp. 3–17). Albany: State University of New York Press.

Annas, P., & Maher, F. (Eds.). (1992a, Spring). Feminist pedagogies and difference in the classroom [Special issue]. *Radical Teacher, 41.*

Annas, P., & Maher, F. (Eds.). (1992b, Fall). Feminist pedagogies and difference in the classroom—part II [Special issue]. *Radical Teacher, 42.*

Belenky, M., Clinchy, B., Goldberger, N., & Tarule, J. (1986). *Women's ways of knowing: The development of self, voice, and mind.* New York: Basic Books.

Benesch, S. (1993). ESL, ideology, and the politics of pragmatism. *TESOL Quarterly, 27,* 705–717.

Cameron, D. (Ed.). (1990). *The feminist critique of language: A reader.* London: Routledge.

Cannon, L. W. (1990). *Curriculum transformation: Personal and political.* Memphis, TN: Memphis State University, Center for Research on Women.

Chodorow, N. (1978). *The reproduction of mothering.* Berkeley: University of California Press.

Clark, S. (1995). Review: Women, rhetoric, teaching. *College Composition and Communication, 46,* 108–122.

Cochran, E. P. (1996). Gender and the ESL classroom. *TESOL Quarterly, 30,* 159–162.

Dill, B. T. (1994). Race, class, and gender: Prospects for an all-inclusive sisterhood. In L. Stone (Ed.), *The education feminism reader* (pp. 42–56). New York: Routledge.

Eichhorn, J., Farris, S., Hayes, K., Hernández, A., Jarratt, S. C., Powers-Stubbs, K., Sciachitano, M. M., & Kraemer, D. J. (1992). A symposium on feminist experiences in the composition classroom. *College Composition and Communication, 43,* 297–322.

Ellsworth, E. (1992). Why doesn't this feel empowering? Working through the repressive myths of critical pedagogy. In C. Luke & J. Gore (Eds.), *Feminisms and critical pedagogy* (pp. 90–119). New York: Routledge.

Flynn, E. A. (1990). Composing as a woman. In S. L. Gabriel & I. Smithson (Eds.), *Gender in the classroom: Power and pedagogy* (pp. 112–126). Urbana: University of Illinois Press.

Flynn, E. A. (1995). Feminism and scientism. *College Composition and Communication, 46*, 353–368.

Fowlkes, D. L., & McClure, C. S. (1984). *Feminist visions: Toward a transformation of the liberal arts curriculum*. Tuscaloosa: University of Alabama Press.

Frey, O. (1987). Equity and peace in the new writing class. In C. L. Caywood & G. R. Overing (Eds.), *Teaching writing: Pedagogy, gender, and equity* (pp. 93–105). Albany: State University of New York Press.

Gardner, M. R. (1994). *On trying to teach: The mind in correspondence*. Hillsdale, NJ: The Analytic Press.

Gass, S., & Varonis, E. M. (1986). Sex differences in nonnative speaker–nonnative speaker interactions. In R. R. Day (Ed.), *Talking to learn: Conversation in second language acquisition* (pp. 327–351). Rowley, MA: Newbury.

Gilligan, C. (1982). *In a different voice: Psychological theory and women's development*. Cambridge, MA: Harvard University Press.

Goulston, W. (1987). Women writing. In C. L. Caywood & G. R. Overing (Eds.), *Teaching writing: Pedagogy, gender, and equity* (pp. 19–29). Albany: State University of New York Press.

Graham, J. (1992). Bias-free teaching as a topic in a course for international teaching assistants. *TESOL Quarterly, 26*, 585–589.

Hancock, E. (1989). *The girl within*. New York: Fawcett Columbine.

Hartman, P. L., & Judd, E. L. (1978). Sexism and TESOL materials. *TESOL Quarterly, 12*, 383–393.

Hays, J. (1995). Intellectual parenting and a developmental feminist pedagogy of writing. In L. W. Phelps & J. Emig (Eds.), *Feminine principles and women's experience in American composition and rhetoric* (pp. 153–190). Pittsburgh: University of Pittsburgh Press.

Heilbrun, C. G. (1990). *Hamlet's mother and other women*. New York: Ballantine.

Higginbotham, E. (1988). *Integrating all women into the curriculum*. Memphis, TN: Memphis State University, Center for Research on Women.

Hoffmann, L., & Culley, M. (Eds.). (1985). *Women's personal narratives: Essays in criticism and pedagogy*. New York: Modern Language Association of America.

Holmes, J. (1994). Improving the lot of female language learners. In. J. Sunderland (Ed.), *Exploring gender: Questions and implications for English language education* (pp. 39–43). New York: Prentice-Hall.

hooks, b. (1994). *Teaching to transgress: Education as the practice of freedom*. New York: Routledge.

Horner, M. (1972). Toward an understanding of achievement-related conflicts in women. *Journal of Social Issues, 28*(2), 157–174.

Howe, F. (1983). Feminist scholarship: The extent of the revolution. In C. Bunch & S. Pollack (Eds.), *Learning our way: Essays in feminist education* (pp. 98–111). Trumansburg, NY: Crossing Press.

Judd, E. L. (1983). The problem of applying sociolinguistic findings to TESOL: The case of male/female language. In N. Wolfson & E. Judd (Eds.), *Sociolinguistics and language acquisition* (pp. 234–241). Rowley, MA: Newbury.

Kirsch, G. E. (1995). Review: Feminist critical pedagogy and composition. *College English, 57*, 723–729.

Kleinfeld, J. S., & Yerian, S. (Eds.). (1995). *Gender tales: Tensions in the schools*. New York: St. Martin's.

Kramarae, C. (1981). *Women and men speaking: Frameworks for analysis*. Rowley, MA: Newbury.

Lakoff, R. (1975). *Language and woman's place*. New York: Harper & Row.

Lakoff, R. T. (1990). *Talking power*. New York: Basic Books.

Layman, N. S. (1994). *Sexual harassment in American secondary schools: A legal guide for administrators, teachers and students*. Dallas: Contemporary Research Press.

Luke, C. (1992). Feminist politics in radical pedagogy. In C. Luke & J. Gore (Eds.), *Feminisms and critical pedagogy* (pp. 25–53). New York: Routledge.

Maher, F. A., & Tetreault, M. K. (1994). *The feminist classroom.* New York: Basic Books.

Markham, P. L. (1988). Gender and the perceived expertness of the speaker as factors in ESL listening recall. *TESOL Quarterly, 22,* 397–406.

McCormick, T. M. (1994). *Creating the nonsexist classroom: A multicultural approach.* New York: Teachers College Press.

Miller, C., & Swift, K. (1976). *Words and women: New language in new times.* Garden City, NY: Doubleday Anchor.

Miller, J. B. (1976). *Toward a new psychology of women.* Boston: Beacon.

Moody, L. A. (1986). Women students in our institutions: A response to the U.N. Decade for Women (1976–1986). *TESOL Quarterly, 20,* 347–353.

Olson, G. A. (1992). History, *praxis,* and change: Paulo Freire and the politics of literacy. *Journal of Advanced Composition, 12,* 1–14.

Omolade, B. (1993). A black feminist pedagogy. *Women's Studies Quarterly, 21,* 31–38.

Orenstein, P. (1994). *SchoolGirls: Young women, self-esteem, and the confidence gap.* New York: Doubleday.

Orner, M. (1992). Interrupting the calls for student voice in "liberatory" education: A feminist poststructuralist perspective. In C. Luke & J. Gore (Eds.), *Feminisms and critical pedagogy* (pp. 74–89). New York: Routledge.

Paludi, M. A. (Ed.). (1996). *Sexual harassment on college compuses: Abusing the ivory power.* Albany: State University of New York Press.

Peterson, L. H. (1991). Gender and the autobiographical essay: Research perspectives, pedagogical practices. *College Composition and Communication, 42,* 170–183.

Pipher, M. (1994). *Reviving Ophelia: Saving the selves of adolescent girls.* New York: Putnam's.

Porreca, K. L. (1984). Sexism in current ESL textbooks. *TESOL Quarterly, 18,* 705–724.

Rich, A. (1979). *On lies, secrets, and silence: Selected prose 1966–1978.* New York: Norton.

Rubin, D. (1993). *Gender influences: Reading student texts.* Carbondale: Southern Illinois University Press.

Sadker, M., & Sadker, D. (1990). Confronting sexism in the college classroom. In S. L. Gabriel & I. Smithson (Eds.), *Gender in the classroom: Power and pedagogy* (pp. 176–187). Urbana: University of Illinois Press.

Sadker, M., & Sadker, D. (1994). *Failing at fairness: How America's schools cheat girls.* New York: Scribner's.

Schenke, A. (1991). The "will to reciprocity" and the work of memory: Fictioning speaking out of silence in E.S.L. and feminist pedagogy. *Resources for Feminist Research, 20,* 47–55.

Schenke, A. (1996). Not just a "social issue": Teaching feminist in ESL. *TESOL Quarterly, 30,* 155–159.

Schmitz, B. (1990). *Integrating scholarship by and about women into the curriculum.* Memphis, TN: Memphis State University, Center for Research on Women.

Schniedewind, N. (1993). Teaching feminist process in the 1990s. *Women's Studies Quarterly, 21,* 17–30.

Schniedewind, N., McNaron, T., Chamberlain, M. K., Zandy, J., Swerdlow, A., & Bunch, C. (Eds.). (1993). Feminist pedagogy: An update [Special issue]. *Women's Studies Quarterly, 21*(3 & 4).

Schweickart, P. (Ed.). (1995). [Special issue]. *NWSA Journal, 7*(2).

Shrewsbury, C. (1993). What is feminist pedagogy? *Women's Studies Quarterly, 21,* 8–16.

Spelman, E. V. (1985). Combating the marginalization of black women in the classroom. In M. Culley & C. Portuges (Eds.), *Gendered subjects: The dynamics of feminist teaching* (pp. 240–244). Boston: Routledge & Kegan Paul.

Spender, D. (1980). *Man made language.* London: Routledge & Kegan Paul.

Stanger, C. (1987). The sexual politics of the one-to-one tutorial approach and collaborative learning. In C. L. Caywood & G. R. Overing (Eds.), *Teaching writing: pedagogy, gender, and equity* (pp. 31–44). Albany: State University of New York Press.

Sunderland, J. (Ed.). (1994). *Exploring gender: Questions and implications for English language education.* Englewood Cliffs, NJ: Prentice-Hall.

Tannen, D. (1990). *You just don't understand: Women and men in conversation.* New York: Morrow.

Tavris, C. (1992). *The mismeasure of woman.* New York: Simon & Schuster.

Thomas-Ruzic, M., Haney, C., Monogue, M., & McGovern, C. (1994, March). *Language and gender: Implications and applications for ESL.* Paper presented at the 28th Annual TESOL Convention, Baltimore.

Thorne, B., & Henley, N. (Eds.). (1975). *Language and sex: Difference and dominance.* Rowley, MA: Newbury.

Vandrick, S. (1994). Feminist pedagogy and ESL. *College ESL, 4*(2), 69–92.

Vandrick, S. (1995). Teaching and practicing feminism in the university ESL classroom. *TESOL Journal, 4*(3), 4–6.

Vandrick, S. (1996). Quote/unquote. In V. Whiteson (Ed.), *New ways of using drama and literature in language teaching* (pp. 55–57). Alexandria, VA: TESOL.

Warren-Wenk, P. (1995). Internet literacy: A guide and resources for Women's Studies. *Feminist Teacher, 9*(1), 6–11.

Wolfson, N. (1989). *Perspectives: Sociolinguistics and ESL.* Boston: Heinle & Heinle.

Zambrana, R. E. (1994). Toward understanding the educational trajectory and socialization of Latina women. In L. Stone (Ed.), *The education feminism reader* (pp. 135–145). New York: Routledge.

6

Critical Multiculturalism as a Means of Promoting Social Activism and Awareness

Trudy Smoke
Hunter College, City University of New York

Multiculturalism is one of those areas in education that has become part of the political debate in the past few years. Regardless of one's position in the debate over whether multicultural approaches will save or destroy education, most of us realize that adult ESL classes, either in community or college settings, are inherently multicultural by virtue of the student body. The intentional introduction of multiculturalism into a class can rely on the simple inclusion of foods, holidays, customs, and other cultural artifacts. Yet, although these activities help some students feel accepted and valued, they can be reductive in their presumption of culture as static and benign. Inadvertently, they can reinforce the notion of ESL students as outsiders, as the "other."

What might be needed is a broader view of multiculturalism that goes beyond cultural exposure to include two other perspectives. The first is a focus on identity; the second is an emphasis on social and political literacy. I refer to this combined approach as *critical multiculturalism.*

In using the word *identity,* I am drawing on a feminist and poststructural meaning of it wherein each individual is viewed "in a variety of social sites which are structured by relations of power in which the person takes up different subject positions" (Norton, 1995, p. 15). In a very simple way, this means that an individual may be a daughter, sister, son, brother, student, teacher, taxpayer, and voter. Each of these aspects of identity involves power relationships, some of which are in conflict with others. In this sense, an individual is seen as both subject of and subject to relations of power within a particular site or circumstance (Norton, 1995). The result is the view that identity is not fixed but instead is dynamic and changing, and that it is multiple and contradictory.

The second perspective on social and political literacy derives from the belief that individuals move toward the concept of social justice as they become more politically literate. Through activities in which students do community-based research, read multicultural literature, and participate in political and social events, for example, they may gain some power over their own education and future in the United States (see Ferguson, chap. 1, this volume; Manton, chap. 3, this volume). Freire (1985) wrote, "A political illiterate—regardless of whether she or he knows how to read and write—is one who has an ingenuous perception of humanity in its relationships with the world" (p. 103). This person sees social reality as "a fait accompli rather than something that's still in the making" (p. 103). Freire maintained that individuals should learn to question society and in this process, which he calls "conscientization," they will become enabled to work toward a more humane society.

Thus, critical multiculturalism refers to an educational approach based on broad political and social awareness of issues relating to human difference, social justice, and the form education should take in the pluralistic society of the United States (Sleeter, 1996), at the same time as it focuses on the multiplicity of identity. This concept of critical multiculturalism has been influenced by my readings of the feminist writing that focuses on social identity as a site of struggle and conflict (Belenky, Clinchy, Goldberger, & Tarule, 1986; Benesch, chap. 7, this volume; Ebert, 1991; Gilligan, 1982; Mutnick, 1995; Norton, 1995, chap. 4, this volume; Vandrick, 1995, chap. 5, this volume; Weedon, 1987), and of the critical theorists who focus on social and political literacy (Auerbach, 1991; Freire, 1985; Giroux, 1983; Shor, 1980; Sleeter & Grant, 1994).

To make this concept more concrete I illustrate how critical multiculturalism can work, by focusing on an individual student with whom I have been working for several years. I then present suggestions for incorporating this approach into the adult ESL classroom.

The student, Ming Liang (this is not her real name), was born in a rural area in the Toishan province in the south of mainland China. She was the second girl in a family of four children, three girls and one boy. Like many other rural families in China, her family had no electricity and few amenities. They were not well educated; her father was a minor city official and her mother an embroiderer. Ming grew up speaking only Toishanese and learned about her culture the way her contemporaries did, by listening to the myths and folktales told by the elders of the village. Although she did not begin school until the age of 8, in this way she had begun to learn her culture, its values, and its beliefs through poems, songs, and stories.

School was demanding, and Ming succeeded in this environment—she won awards for her academic performance, even though her family could not afford the extra tutoring that helped many other students in her school do well. Because of her achievements, Ming was accepted into a "status" junior high school miles away from her home. In this school, as in her elementary school, all subjects were taught in Toishanese, and although she did have a math teacher who spoke Cantonese, she remained for the most part monolingual. She moved away from her family to attend the school. There, in addition to spending long hours studying, she had to work each day in the fields planting sugar cane and vegetables or doing manual labor constructing a new dormitory building.

When she was 14 years old, Ming and her family immigrated to the United States, where for the first time she saw non-Chinese people. She knew no language except for Toishanese and a little rudimentary Cantonese. After briefly attending junior high school in the United States, she got a job in a sewing factory that hired Toishanese immigrants. During this time she attended a summer English night school along with her older sister. In the three high schools she attended until graduation, Ming found herself first in a bilingual English–Cantonese setting in which she was an outsider who could not understand nor be understood. Next she transferred to a high school that did not have an ESL program, where she met a Toishanese-speaking student with whom she became friendly. Her parents' move forced her to change schools again, and there she found herself alone and unable to communicate.

As part of my study with Ming, we met and discussed these descriptions of her life. She focused on the multiple sites of her own identity, on the contradictions, and on the struggle. By Chinese tradition the oldest sister should have dealt with family problems, but Ming was the best English speaker in the family, so she became the one who represented the family in public situations. She hated and felt humiliated about her job in the factory, but she could not quit because her family relied on her. In school, Ming was no longer the best or even a good student, but it was even worse for her sister, who was too old for regular high school classes, had to attend night classes, and reluctantly had to rely on Ming to tutor her. Her parents worked long hours at menial jobs and could not learn English, nor could they remain in their relatives' apartments so they moved from place to place. The children had to change schools frequently, which made academic success more problematic, so much so that Ming's brother dropped out of school completely and began to work as a waiter. Ming's disappointment over her family's difficulties, coupled with pressure for her to succeed, resulted in her becoming sick at the same time that her mother suffered a major heart attack. Ming then had to represent the family, meeting with doctors and hospital personnel, making serious decisions that could literally mean life or death for her mother.

Ming's life began to change after open admissions enabled her to be accepted into a special program for financially and academically needy students in a public urban college. There, because of the experience she had gained in negotiating public situations, she was able to secure a Chinese-American counselor to advise her. In addition to becoming a friend, this counselor provided a role model of a successful Asian woman. However, Ming's life still did not improve that much.

A seminal point came after five difficult semesters in the college when, on the advice of her counselor, Ming changed her major from accounting (which her relatives had advised her to take) to education. She also got a job in a college student resource center. These two moves had a consequence in the development of her conscientization and her own critical multicultural awareness.

The next semester she was taking ESL writing for the sixth time when she registered for a writing course that was paired with a social science course taught by Josè Hernández. Hernández described this class:

> My course, "Conquered Peoples in America," describes the consequences of nineteenth-century United States expansion. . . . It expresses the common situation among these groups who lost control over their homelands, describes their cultures, and provides a detailed study of colonization. We examine how these groups have maintained their cultural integrity and are currently struggling to attain equality in American society. We also discuss the roles of women in these cultures, in which women were equal to men before the European conquest. My basic notion is to empower students, most of whom are women, by helping them to recognize their backgrounds and develop self-determination through ethnic and gender identity. (Haas, Smoke, & Hernández, 1991, p. 114)

In this class, Ming read about the history of Puerto Rico and found similarities between Puerto Rican family structures and that of her village in China. She read about the *jibaro* (the farmers), and this helped her recall her experiences farming sugar cane in China. Hernández also helped students to examine critically their failures and difficulties in schools and society, and depersonalize the blame and instead focus it on the institutions and society itself.

In that semester, she passed the writing course, the social science course, and the university-wide Writing Assessment Test, and jumped from a 4.8 to 9.1 reading level as shown on the Nelson/Denny Reading Test. Ming also began a relationship, which would last through the rest of her college career, with a Greek-American student who worked as a tutor in her writing class. She was able to convince her family to accept and even like her non-Chinese boyfriend, but eventually broke off the relationship because she was concerned about the fact that his parents were divorced and that he might not view marriage as seriously as she did.

After discovering that neither her first language nor English would count toward the foreign language requirement, Ming decided to study Spanish, a decision motivated by her good experiences in Hernández's class. Ming also started to make a serious effort to learn Cantonese and Mandarin.

In a composition course she took during her eighth semester, Ming wrote about Maxine Hong Kingston, a writer with whom she strongly identified. She noted that Kingston had felt the "often painful results of radical clashes between American and Chinese cultures." In her paper, Ming also referred to Kingston's refusal to talk, and her "dried-duck voice" as Kingston described it in *The Woman Warrior*. Ming explained that, like herself, Kingston had kept silent at school except for the times she talked with her sister. Kingston's appearance at the college gave Ming an opportunity to meet this woman with whom she had identified. The experience validated Ming's growing awareness of her own identity and her connection with other Chinese-Americans. The encounter with Kingston enabled Ming to link several aspects of her identity—a struggling student and warrior of sorts and a Chinese-American, a believer in filial piety and family honor—with that of Kingston.

In her education classes, Ming found a situation different from any she had ever before encountered in school. The fact that her classes were smaller and, by requirement, participatory, forced her to join discussions and enter study groups. Pressured out of her silent back corner, she began to express herself.

Initially, her friends in the college were other Chinese-American students. At the suggestion of her counselor, she joined an Asian Student Club at the college in which she was eventually elected vice president. The responsibility that came with this position gave her exposure to inequities in the college and the courage to make demands of the institution. Ming learned that Asian students were assumed to be good math students and, because of this stereotype, were sometimes denied math tutoring services. She demanded equal tutoring opportunities for them. Next, she pressed for student teachers to be able to work in Chinatown schools. Despite her insecurity speaking in public, she consented to appear on a panel discussing these and other issues faced by former ESL students as they progressed through the college.

Ming used her art requirement to visit three museums as an opportunity to visit El Museo del Barrio, the Studio Museum in Harlem, and the Whitney Museum. Each visit introduced her to new cultures and art forms. Her response papers show her struggle to deal with these cultures and the problems they exposed in her own identity struggle. In El Museo del Barrio, she saw an exhibit about Columbus that depicted some of the history she had studied in Hernández's class. Of this she wrote, "The title 'One More

Time Columbus' referred to the history of the Tainos Indians and their . . . enslavement which started when Columbus came to their land. In this picture, the eyes were hiding in the dark and behind the trees. Next time when Christopher Columbus comes back, he will never capture them again."

Ming remarked on the cruelty of slavery and the painful history of African Americans in the United States after her visit to the Studio Museum in Harlem. She described a collage entitled "Sauvage" that illustrated the selling of a slave: "Three [white] women are staring at the [black] man with their mouths open. . . . The title "Sauvage" refers to history of the colonial days and how the Blacks were treated by the Whites. . . . The artists in the Studio Museum in Harlem not only emphasize the Black culture, they also talk about the history in the past."

Her response to the Whitney Museum's exhibit of William Wegman's pictures of dogs in human poses and attire was: "The second photo "Dressed for Ball" is insulting to women because a dog dresses in a fancy silk gown and imitates a woman. Moreover, the picture also represent romance, fantasy, and exoticism because the dog in the picture dresses in an oriental gown and stands on the top of the table. . . . I think that this picture is fantasy and is not realistic in American culture." During a discussion about this exhibit, she said that she was offended by the reference to Asian women as exotic fantasy creatures.

What Ming was developing through these experiences was a construct of Latino, African-American, Asian-American, and Euro-American culture and history, and how they are valued in the United States. Requiring her to visit museums helped alter her outlook, and requiring her to write about her experiences forced her to examine her feelings and put them in perspective.

As did all education majors in her college, Ming had to choose a second major, and she chose sociology. In sociology classes Ming was expected to conduct her own research, first observational studies and ultimately broader-based studies. For a project in which Ming was required to summarize a journal article, she wrote not only a critique of the article she had chosen about intergenerational mobility of immigrant families, but also did primary research to back up her criticism of the study (for a detailed description of this paper, see Smoke, 1994). For this paper, she interviewed two African-American people she had met in the college, one a teacher and one a student, to examine their families' intergenerational mobility. In the paper, she also detailed her own family's mobility, leading her to realize that hard work did not necessarily lead to wealth and success for her family or for the African Americans she interviewed. Ming critiqued the journal article by noting that the original study had not examined the roles of women, education, class, or race in intergenerational mobility.

Her increasing realization of the inequities of our society drew her to study the education of young children. This resulted in her using another sociology requirement to examine the college day-care center. She conducted interviews, did observations, and read about other day-care centers to obtain the information for her paper. Her conclusions led her to commend the diversity of the children and the importance of having a day-care center for college students on an urban campus. This experience led Ming to her most involved project—her senior research project.

Her senior research project took more than 6 months to complete and hundreds of hours of interviews and observations. The project was to create a directory of after-school and day-care facilities offered in Chinatown. To do this, Ming went through the yellow pages, English and Chinese, making lists of churches, schools, and community centers. She went to each of these and interviewed, usually in English, the administrators and teachers in the programs. She observed the classes and noted their ethnic make-up, the languages spoken, the condition of the physical settings, toys, art materials, and books that were available for the children. She found out costs, admission procedures, and qualifications for the programs. She ended up writing a 106-page directory that merited her an "A" grade. Because no document such as this one existed, Ming's project became a community source book and led to her being offered a job in one of the centers. She accepted it, and began work the following summer.

Since her college graduation in 1991, Ming has been working in a nursery school where her students are mostly Chinese children (whose first languages are Mandarin, Cantonese, or Toishanese) and Latino children whose first language is Spanish. Her language study has helped her to communicate with the children and with their families, and her experience learning English as a second language has given her insights and understandings into what these children are experiencing. Ming received her Master's degree in early childhood education in 1994 and, as part of her graduate work, wrote an annotated bibliography on multicultural books appropriate for nursery-school-age children.

Entering the United States with a limited knowledge of peoples, cultures, and languages outside of Toishan, Ming used aspects of her college experience to develop her own critical multicultural literacy. This literacy developed partly because of the experience she gained in articulating the identity issues she faced. Her initiative in learning about aspects of the society that were unfamiliar to her was, perhaps, a result of her recognition of the contradictions she faced in her life.

Ming continues to struggle with her own identity issues. She lives at home with her parents who speak very little English. She feels an obligation to take care of them, but would like to be on her own. She likes the power derived from having her own classroom but feels that, with her Master's degree, she should be pursuing a supervisory position in another school, yet she worries that she is becoming too aggressive and ambitious. Ming has almost gotten married twice, but each time stopped because she thought the man in question might prevent her from maintaining her independence and career. At the same time, she is concerned about not being traditional enough and about ending up alone.

Some of Ming's greatest successes in the college came from assignments in which she could write about writers such as Maxine Hong Kingston, or about issues such as immigration or educational opportunities for Chinese children. Her social and political literacy emerged out of encounters with unfamiliar cultures, and helped build her understanding and compassion for others. Offering students the opportunity to focus on the multiple and contradictory aspects of their identities while confronting real societal problems seems to offer a great deal of possibility for their success in becoming participatory and active members of society.

Working with students in this way is crucial today, because we are facing serious problems over the contraction of resources in our ESL programs. Students affected by these political changes need to be prepared to work together and take strong positions to ensure their own futures (see Ferguson, chap. 1, this volume; Moriarty, chap. 2, this volume).

Teaching from a critical multicultural perspective is appropriate for students at all levels. Critical multiculturalism in the adult ESL classroom might include the following methodologies.

1. *Provide opportunities for students to reflect on their own identities:* In their journals; in communications with the teacher, tutors, or peers in person or via e-mail; and in essays, students can focus on the multiplicity of roles in their lives, about when they do or do not have power, where in their community they do or do not feel comfortable, when they do or do not speak English, and when they take an active and when a passive role, and the contradictions that are inherent in their lives.

2. *Introduce a broad range of multicultural literature and art experiences:* Multicultural literature (see Mangelsdorf, chap. 8, this volume)—whether in the form of articles, stories, poems, or novels—will help students find role models and discover how individuals deal with their conflicts. Multicultural literature should also include multicultural art, such as music, painting, photography, sculpture, and theater.

3. *Guide students in doing real research in their own communities and reporting on it to the entire class:* These research projects have as their goal helping students to look closely at their communities and see the role of age, gender, race, ethnicity, and class in child care, community involvement, and work. This can involve using the neighborhood to observe when people go to work, who helps needy neighbors, how children treat

each other, or who supervises and cares for children in their community. In fast-food restaurants, they can observe the patrons and the workers and compare them with the patrons and workers at other establishments. At political events, they can listen to politicians and watch the way they behave with others.

4. *Require participation in the community:* You may require that each student spend 2 hours each term doing something meaningful in his or her community and then report back to the class about the experience. This could mean giving out flyers at school events; writing letters to local newspapers, politicians, and so on (see Ferguson, chap. 1, this volume; Moriarty, chap. 2, this volume); going to meetings and talking to community leaders; and joining clubs in the school. The types of work will vary for each class, community, and school, but they should be relevant to the interests and needs of your students.

The common concept in this critical multicultural approach is that our adult ESL students need to begin to practice democracy rather than just discuss it. They should have opportunities to organize and work collectively for a goal. Also, they need to have the experience of attaining and exercising power, and then reflect on themselves in that role. They need experience in learning how to identify and articulate their own interests. They need to see themselves through the multiplicity of their identities, through their varying levels of power and activism, and above all as dynamic and changing individuals capable of creating change themselves. This approach is based on the idea that education today needs to promote understanding and tolerance of others, social equality, and cultural pluralism; that it needs to provide students with tools that will enable them to make systemic changes in society; and that critical multiculturalism may be an appropriate method for accomplishing these goals.

REFERENCES

Auerbach, E. R. (1991). Politics, pedagogy, and professionalism: Challenging marginalization in ESL. *College ESL, 1,* 1–9.

Belenky, M. F., Clinchy, B. M., Goldberger, N. R., & Tarule, J. M. (1986). *Women's ways of knowing: The development of self, voice, and mind.* New York: Basic Books.

Ebert, T. L. (1991). The "difference" of postmodern feminism. *College English, 53*(8), 886–904.

Freire, P. (1985). *The politics of education: Culture, power and liberation* (D. Macedo, Trans.). South Hadley, MA: Bergin & Garvey.

Gilligan, C. (1982). *In a different voice: Psychological theory and women's development.* Cambridge, MA: Harvard University Press.

Giroux, H. E. (1983). *Theory and resistance in education: A pedagogy for opposition.* Westport, CT: Greenwood, Bergin-Garvey.

Haas, T., Smoke, T., & Hernández, J. (1991). A collaborative model for empowering students. In S. Benesch (Ed.), *ESL in America: Myths and possibilities* (pp. 112–129). Portsmouth, NH: Boynton/Cook/Heinemann.

Mutnick, D. (1995). *Writing in an alien world: Basic writing and the struggle for equality in higher education*. Portsmouth, NH: Boynton/Cook/Heinemann.

Norton, B. (1995). Social identity, investment, and language learning. *TESOL Quarterly, 29*(1), 9–31.

Shor, I. (1980). *Critical teaching and everyday life*. Boston, MA: South End Press.

Sleeter, C. E. (1996). *Multicultural education as social activism*. Albany: State University of New York Press.

Sleeter, C. E., & Grant, C. A. (1994). *Making choices for multicultural education: Five approaches to race, class, and gender* (2nd ed.). Englewood Cliffs, NJ: Prentice-Hall.

Smoke, T. (1991). *Becoming an academic insider: One student's experience of attaining success in college*. Unpublished doctoral dissertation, University of Michigan, Ann Arbor.

Smoke, T. (1994). Writing as a means of learning. *College ESL, 4*(2), 1–11.

Vandrick, S. (1995). Teaching and practicing feminism in the university ESL classroom. *TESOL Journal, 4*, 4–6.

Weedon, C. (1987). *Feminist practice and poststructuralist theory*. London: Blackwell.

II

PEDAGOGY

7

Anorexia: A Feminist EAP Curriculum

Sarah Benesch
The College of Staten Island, City University of New York

The need for greater attention to feminist issues in adult ESL has been highlighted by Vandrick (1995, chap. 5, this volume). According to Vandrick, gender inequality in the workplace, sexual harassment, and sexist language, for example, are discussed in American media and universities and should, therefore, be dealt with in U.S. college ESL classes.[1] Just as feminist issues have been absent from many ESL classes, feminist theory has not yet had a significant impact on second language (L2) theory and practice. One reason for this absence may be the predominance of an ideology of pragmatism in the profession, especially in English for academic purposes (EAP) (Benesch, 1993). This is the notion that English language teaching should provide students with the grammar, vocabulary, and rhetorical forms of particular settings. The goal of pragmatic EAP is to fit students into existing academic and social structures, not to encourage them to question or revise those structures. Feminist pedagogy, on the other hand, assumes a need for greater dialogue across races, classes, and genders to equalize power in society and promote social change (Maher & Tetreault, 1994).

This chapter describes a feminist EAP writing class linked to a psychology lecture course. The psychology course was a biweekly lecture with 400

[1]In this article I discuss an EAP course in an American college. Although EAP courses are taught around the world, my teaching experience has been in U.S. undergraduate institutions. Therefore, I leave it to my colleagues who have taught in other countries to discuss EAP in those localities since the issues vary from setting to setting.

to 500 students, taught by two members of the psychology department, Professors Richter and Allen.[2] Richter, the chairperson of psychology, and Allen, an associate professor, lectured on a variety of topics: history of psychology, research methods, brain/behavior, perception, consciousness, development, learning, motivation and emotion, memory, personality, abnormal behavior, treatment, social psychology, and industrial organization psychology. Students were evaluated by scores on three multiple-choice exams, each of which covered four to five topics. I attended most of the lectures in both the fall and spring semesters with my students, taking lecture notes and observing the students' reactions.

The ESL writing course was the intermediate level of ESL offered by the English department. Of 15 students (eight men and seven women) in the fall class, four were Chinese, three were Russian, and there was one student each from the Dominican Republic, Romania, Cyprus, Nicaragua, Mexico, Pakistan, and France. Of the 10 students (three men and seven women) in the spring course, three were Russian, three were Chinese, two were Bulgarian, one was Dominican, and the other was Argentinean. The EAP course was intended to relate language teaching to the psychology content, provide a more participatory experience than the lecture course, and compensate for the invisibility of women in the psychology curriculum. The pedagogical principles that guided the ESL writing class are presented next, through a contrast of traditional and feminist notions of knowledge construction. Following the discussion of feminist pedagogy, I examine one area of study in the writing class, anorexia, as well as students' oral and written responses to that topic. These responses reveal some of the issues faced by feminist ESL teachers, including possible differences in the ways female and male students react to a feminist curriculum.

TRADITIONAL VERSUS FEMINIST CLASSROOMS

Maher and Tetreault (1994) studied 17 feminist classrooms in universities and colleges across the United States to discover, among other things, the outstanding characteristics of feminist pedagogy and how it differs from traditional teaching. They organized the results into four categories highlighting the differences: authority, mastery, voice, and positionality. Each of these areas is defined here.

Authority in traditional classes is located with the teacher (expert); students are seen as "apprentices in the faculty's disciplines rather than as learners in charge of their own knowledge" (p. 7). Feminist teachers oppose the traditional hierarchy of teacher-expert/student-apprentice, by

[2]These are pseudonyms for the professors who taught the psychology course. I have also used pseudonyms for the students discussed later in the chapter.

accepting student experience as a source of authority and expertise: "We have seen the redistribution of expertise and the widening of sources of authority: knowledge can be produced by all groups in society, including students, rather than solely by the academic disciplines, experts in a field, or teachers" (p. 57).

Mastery has traditionally been measured by comparing student performance to a predetermined standard: "Everyone is measured by the same external standard and is graded in a competitive hierarchy according to their approximation of the standard" (p. 17). Maher and Tetreault believe that this type of mastery silences students who do not meet the external criteria, and that "the material 'master[s]' the students rather than the other way around" (p. 17). In feminist classrooms, by contrast, mastery is not a matter of absorbing information "on the terms of the experts" but of interpreting "knowledge from the new perspectives of students, women, and other marginalized groups" (p. 57).

Voice in traditional classes is the domain of students who feel entitled to answer a professor's question, or ask one of their own. Those who do not speak are not encouraged to do so since listening, not discussion, is the predominate mode of student participation. Voice in feminist classes, on the other hand, is multidimensional. There are the private voices of students whose expression of personal experience is valued as the basis of academic study, and there are students' public voices, theorizing from their own and others' experience.

Finally, positionality is the area of greatest contrast between traditional and feminist pedagogy, because it acknowledges that teachers' and students' subjectivities are socially constructed. That is, *I* is a function of class, race, sexual preference, ethnicity, gender, history, and region. In traditional classrooms, students' subject positions may affect their reactions to the curriculum, but these reactions are unacknowledged. In feminist classrooms, the "multiple positions" (Maher & Tetreault, 1994, p. 164) of students and teachers are the lenses through which material is studied, with the hope that awareness of positionality will create the conditions for pluralism in the classroom and society.

The significant differences between traditional and feminist conceptions of mastery, voice, authority, and positionality revealed by Maher and Tetreault's study show that feminist teachers are interested in pedagogical and social change rather than simply initiating students into established academic discourse communities. The study also shows that feminist teachers view the construction of knowledge as a complex interaction between students and teachers of different races, classes, genders, and cultures (Weiler, 1991).

The psychology lecture course was traditional. The two psychology professors' voices dominated, material was based in conventional disciplinary knowledge, multiple-choice tests were the instruments of evaluation, and students' varying social positions were unacknowledged. Yet Richter was not a champion of large lecture classes—he was distressed that budget cuts in prior years had eliminated recitation sections, making it nearly impossible to help students connect psychological concepts to their lives. He therefore hoped that the ESL writing course would provide an alternative experience: "I'd like you to give as close to hands-on experience as you can, to take what we present here and have it come through another way, through writing, or reading, or speaking, so that they take a topic that's of interest to them and develop it further. . . . I don't think you should become recitation teachers for the psychology department" (Richter, personal communication, June 1994).

My alternative to the lecture course was an experiment in feminist pedagogy. To interrupt the unidirectional flow of discourse from professor to student, I had the students write questions about the psychology textbook and lecture material for the professors to answer. To give students greater authority, I invited Richter to come to my spring semester class for an informal dialogue with students, based on their prepared questions (Benesch, 1996). To balance the psychology curriculum and increase awareness of positionality, I involved students in studying a topic of particular concern to college-age women: anorexia.

ANOREXIA: A FEMINIST CURRICULUM

Feminist teachers redefine academic knowledge by "extending their range of themes and topics" and by "look[ing] at old material in new ways" (Maher & Tetreault, 1994, p. 57). This feature of feminist teaching was especially important in the linkage, because the psychology course highlighted the contributions of men to the psychology canon while ignoring those of women.[3] For example, the developmental theories of Erikson, Piaget, and Kohlberg were presented, whereas the feminist critique of those theories (see Gilligan, 1982; Walkerdine, 1985) was virtually ignored, except for several paragraphs in the textbook which were devoted to Gilligan's critique. The only acknowledgment of a challenge to developmental theories came at the end of a lecture on Freud's psychoanalytic theory of personality, in which the Electra complex had been explained. The students were told, "You can understand why the feminist movement is hostile to Freud." This casual aside trivialized the contribution of Freud's critics, male and female, by painting them with the "hostile

[3]Anna Freud was mentioned, but only in the context of her psychoanalysis of Erik Erikson, whose life and work were discussed during two lectures.

feminist movement" brush. Also, because the lecture on Freud contained so much unfamiliar material, there was no context for understanding why anyone, feminists included, might raise objections to Freud's theory or what the objections might be.

Given the lack of attention to women's issues and women psychologists and the superficial treatment of topics in the survey course, I wanted students to thoroughly examine one area connecting women, psychology, and social issues. My choice was anorexia, a topic mentioned during a lecture on human needs and motivation, and whose definition students were required to memorize in case it appeared on the second multiple-choice exam. Students had not been asked, however, to consider that "[s]ince less than 8 percent of all anorexics [in the U.S.] are male . . . eating disorders are a distinctive form of female suffering" (Chernin, 1985, p. 13). That statistic raises questions not addressed in the psychology class about the place of women in society and the space they are encouraged to take up (Bartkey, 1988).

To introduce the topic, I assigned Levenkron's *The Best Little Girl in the World*, a 1978 fictional case history of an adolescent girl with anorexia whose worsening condition and eventual recovery are described in detail. The strength of this novel is its accessibility; students had no trouble following or understanding the story. However, although the novel offers a clear portrait of one girl's private struggle with anorexia, it lacks a conceptual framework that a more theoretical treatment of anorexia could have offered. Such a framework might have allowed my students to sort out the social and psychological issues that arose during class discussions (some of which I address here). Instead, Levenkron, a psychologist with extensive experience treating anorectics, deals with psychological causes, such as inadequate attention from parents and sibling rivalry, through a narrative. He briefly interjects one social cause of anorexia—the pervasive images of ultra-thin models—without exploring the genesis or purpose of those images. To get beyond a strict psychological interpretation, I had the students do supplemental reading. The different writing and research assignments on anorexia are discussed next.

WRITING AND RESEARCH ASSIGNMENTS ON ANOREXIA

Students were required to take double-entry notes about each chapter of *The Best Little Girl in the World*. These notes were the basis of small-group and whole-class discussions of the book and topic and of student-generated questions, such as the following from the fall semester class about chaps. 1–4:

Why is Francesca unsatisfied with the way she looks?

Why is she comparing herself to thin models?

Does anorexia always lead to death or is there treatment from which you can get help?

Why is there so much hostility between the mother, father, and Francesca?

These questions are 4 of 20 written and edited by students in small groups. The 20 questions served as the starting point for individual research projects on anorexia. To launch the research, I asked students to group the 20 questions into categories, and label each category. They came up with the following categories: psychological causes, environmental causes, treatment, self-image and appearance, perfectionism, outcomes of anorexia, society's role, family influence, attention, and hostility and aggression. After all the categories were put on the board, the students narrowed them down to the following topics, one of which they chose to research: psychological causes, environmental causes, outcomes, treatment, and image. We spent time in the library tracking down sources, to locate articles from both popular and scholarly journals. Each research paper included both types of sources.

MALE RESISTANCE TO STUDYING ANOREXIA

Never having dealt with anorexia as a topic in an ESL writing class, I could not predict the students' responses. Was this a disorder confined mainly to upper-middle-class American teenagers, such as the protagonist of *The Best Little Girl in the World,* and therefore of little interest to women from other countries and class backgrounds? How would men in the class react to a topic affecting women in the great majority of cases? Would the responses to this topic differ along gender lines, with the women being more engaged than the men?

Lewis (1992) discusses how the varying positions and histories of women and men lead to different purposes for feminist teaching, falling along gender lines. Women, she explains, "need space and safety so they are free to speak in order to better understand and act against the violations they have experienced in a social/cultural setting that subordinates them in hurtful and harmful ways" (p. 185). Men, on the other hand, need to examine their "complicity in benefitting from the rewards of the same culture" (p. 186). Regardless of the potential benefits for women and men of feminist teaching, Lewis found that some men in feminist classrooms "find it difficult to engage in the self-reflection required to question the unequal and violent social relations" (p. 178) in which they may unknowingly be complicitous. They might feel threatened and uncomfortable, and therefore attempt to "refocus the discussion in directions that are less disquieting for them" (p. 178). Lewis views men's discomfort in feminist classrooms as an opportunity for the class to explore positionality and inequality, not as an experience to be avoided. She calls these opportunities for self-reflection "pedagogical moments" or "political moments" (p. 169) arising from the course content.

Only a few men in my two classes overtly resisted studying anorexia. However, the negative reactions of these men were simply the most outspoken examples of a quieter resistance on the part of the men to questioning their own possible involvement in women's eating disorders. Therefore, the overt resistance of the men who did speak out is worth examining both in terms of my own response to it (what I did and what I might have done) and in terms of theorizing male resistance in feminist classes.

The first occurrence of male resistance was during the fall semester, the class meeting after the first four chapters of *The Best Little Girl* had been assigned. A young Chinese man, Chen, complained to me, in front of the class, that the book was boring because it had nothing to do with him. He saw no reason to read a book about a young woman starving herself. He said, "I don't have any problems with eating so why should I read this?"

Another challenge came during the spring semester in the double-entry journal of one of the three men in the class, all of whom were Russian. In response to a quote from chapter 8 of *The Best Little Girl*, Sasha wrote:

> I think, think, think and can't get in the inside world of this child. Why did she give up with everything, but not with the starvation? And what is strange, I don't want to know the reason. I'm not interested in the whole topic of anorexia. May be I'll be interested in it later, when I'll may be have a daughter, but for now it is very boring for me. I mean, I'm really sorry for her, but all that girl problems are not my style. Sorry for those words, but at least I'm being honest.

Sasha's classmate, George, called the protagonist "silly" or "crazy," both in his double-entry notes and during class discussions: "Sometimes I think of her as she is a really crazy person because no one should be harmful to one's health." Even after numerous class discussions of *The Best Little Girl* and after watching a television news special on anorexia detailing the social and psychological reasons for the disorder, George declared, "They're crazy!"

These responses share a resistance to studying a problem faced mainly by young women. The three men found it boring to read about anorexia because they did not confront this problem themselves. Yet none had mentioned being bored when reading Axline's *Dibs in Search of Self* (another book assigned in the writing class), even though Dibs' situation, parental neglect leading to severe withdrawal in a 6-year-old, was in no way parallel to their own experience as children. Rather than pointing out this contradiction, I used some of the comments as "pedagogical moments" in which I tried to demonstrate that we are all implicated in the problem of anorexia, whether or not we suffer directly from the disorder.

In response to the first young man in the fall semester who claimed that anorexia had nothing to do with him, I asked, "Do you ever go out with women for lunch or dinner?" "Sure," he said. "What do they order?" I asked. "They're all on diets!" he answered, "All they order is diet soda!" I then asked if he thought the women needed to diet and he answered that they could lose a few pounds. This exchange led to a discussion among the students about why women diet while men are less apt to do so. We also discussed notions of attractiveness, where they originate, and how they are distributed. All the women said they worried about getting fat. Some said they avoided eating in front of men because it is "unfeminine" behavior and therefore unattractive. The men reported that they did not experience this constraint when eating with a woman and were surprised that the women did. The pedagogical moment triggered by Chen's protest over reading about anorexia turned into a discussion, dominated by the women in the class, about the constant "self-surveillance" or "self-policing" to which they subject themselves due to the messages they receive both directly and indirectly about their bodies (Bartkey, 1988, p. 82). Although the men did not acknowledge their possible role in women's self-policing, they noticed that their relationships to food and their bodies were different from those of the women in the class.

George's comments about the craziness of anorexic women were particularly troubling given that he was studying psychology, one of whose purposes is to generate understanding and compassion for people with psychological disorders. I tried to point out this problem by asking the spring semester class to consider what it means to refer to someone as crazy, as George had done. What about calling schizophrenics, hypochondriacs, sociopaths, and those with other disorders they had studied in psychology "crazy," I asked? George was silent during the ensuing discussion, so it is hard to know if it had any impact on him. But those who participated, mainly three women in the class, expressed an understanding of how "crazy" dismisses behavior rather than attempting to understand it.

Sasha's resistance to studying anorexia, in the spring semester class, was ongoing. The issue for him was not only a lack of interest in "girl problems" but also his irritation that the protagonist was turning herself in to an undesirable object. Here are two of his responses to Francesca's decreasing weight:

> Only skin and bones, I guess no breast—is it looks nice for her? She is really crazy. She doesn't even understand the danger of this condition. She is killing herself and she doesn't want help, but she needs it immediately.
>
> I think that when the woman is real thin then she doesn't have anything good in her body. The body has to be shaped in a nice round manner. And the bones don't make it beautifull. I'd like to see someone who says that sceleton is more cute than, for instance, Marlin Monro.

Faced with these responses, I had a few choices. I could have commented on them in writing, discussed them privately with Sasha, asked him to share them with the class, or remained silent. I chose the latter approach because I was unconvinced that questioning Sasha's comments about the proper shape for a woman's body would lead him or other men to connect the objectification of women's bodies to self-surveillance and self-starvation. Of course, I had hoped that the readings would "create the possibility for students to be self-reflexive" (Lewis, 1992, p. 179). Yet Sasha and other men in both semesters did not reflect on their own role in creating the conditions for anorexia, and I was unsure of how to bring about that type of self-reflection.

Having taught the linked ESL/psychology course for two semesters, I can now anticipate the kinds of responses about anorexia I might face from men in the class. Knowing that there could be overt and covert resistance to examining the relationship between women, food, power, body image, and the male gaze, to name a few issues, I would approach the topic differently in the future: I would present it as a debate between the medical model and the sociocultural one. Briefly, the medical model views anorexia as a pathology and attempts to identify psychological and biological causes, symptoms, and treatments.

The sociocultural model, by contrast, examines "a constellation of social, economic, and psychological factors [that] have combined to produce a generation of women who feel deeply flawed, ashamed of their needs, and not entitled to exist unless they transform themselves into worthy new selves (read: without need, without want, without *body*)" (Bordo, 1993, p. 47). The sociocultural, or feminist, perspective does not sharply distinguish anorectics and other women. It claims, instead, that "anorexia represents one extreme on a continuum on which all women today find themselves, insofar as they are vulnerable, to one degree or another, to the requirements of the cultural construction of femininity" (Bordo, 1993, p. 47). While I would argue with the notion of a monolithic "cultural construction of femininity," particularly given the multicultural nature of an ESL class, I found nonetheless that my female students were surprisingly vulnerable to what we might call Western industrial notions of femininity. All were either ambivalent toward food and afraid of gaining weight, or they knew someone who was a compulsive dieter or an anorectic. So, they were able to draw on either personal experience or empathy while studying about anorexia in a way that some of the men were unable. As a result, the women were able "to claim relevance for the lives they live as the source of legitimate knowledge" (Lewis, 1992, p. 187), as I show next.

FEMALE IDENTIFICATION AND EMPATHY

Women in both the fall and spring sections had a problematic relationship with food due to social pressures to be thin, perfect, and in control. In fact, one Argentinean student in the spring semester class, Julia, had been anorexic in high school and continued to struggle with her fear of weight gain. Her journals and contributions to class discussions were poignant testimonials to what Chernin (1981) calls the "tyranny of slenderness." Julia shared her story freely during class discussions, providing the expertise of experience, and theorizing with the students about her experience based on the reading they did for class and for their research papers. Her journal was a detailed exploration of acute episodes of anorexia, including questions about the causes ("As I'm reading this book I realize how ill I was. I feel as though I'm reading my story. How come I became so ill?"), and about whether she would ever be "cured" of what she called her "obsession": "What makes me scared is I still have some habits while eating. . . . Sometimes I go out and ask for a big meal, take two bites and leave it almost completed. In fact, I realize this now after reading this book. It's funny, I thought that I was a lot better and I'm not. I mean sometimes I still lie about eating when in fact I didn't. . . . My problem is mostly with food but everything is related."

While Julia initially referred to anorexia as an illness in her journal, as the semester progressed she began to consider the social, more public dimension. She noted that she had been one of a group of schoolmates in a girls' school in Argentina who stopped eating and that her struggle at that time was, therefore, more communal than personal: "I didn't think I was starving myself to death. I wasn't hungry anymore and that helped to be thinner. Sometimes I wonder how I could have been so blind. Maybe it was because the group of friends with whom I used to hang out were into the anorexia stuff. We thought it was cool not to eat; we were perfect."

Had we been contrasting the medical and sociocultural models as our tool for analyzing anorexia, Julia's experience could have served as a case study to test out these two theories, espiecially given her openness and study to test out these two theories, especially given her openness and eagerness to understand her eating disorder. Without that theoretical framework, we were forced instead to rely on *The Best Little Girl in the World*, with its focus on psychological causes, and a number of articles selected by students for their research papers, most of which also subscribed to a medical model.

Another student in the fall semester class, Su Chang, also identified with the protagonist of *The Best Little Girl in the World*, but in a different and more disturbing way: She wished to have Francesca's willpower in conquering her desire for food, as these two journal entries indicate:

> Somehow I envy the will power that is within Francesca even though it might not be healthy. How could she do anything when she doesn't eats? I could not move if I became too hungry and I think my food is making me fat. I hope I could have the power Kessa has except that I could be conscious about my actions.
>
> I can't believe she considers 98 pounds fat! I wish I am, maybe!

Most of the women in the two semesters, however, empathized with the protagonist rather than identifying with or envying her. Even those, such as Lilliana, who were initially disgusted by Francesca's anorexic behavior, seeing her as spoiled and selfish, became more empathic as the semester progressed. Here is Lilliana's final comment in her journal: "You [teacher] told me that if I think of anorexia as a bad disease rather than bad behavior will let me understand Francesca rather than judging her. And it's true because I thought she was stupid and selfish to kill herself, but I understand that it's not up to you that that can even happen to me. Now I don't judge her anymore. I rather feel sorry for her. I finally like her."

Although I was pleased to see the change in Lilliana's response, and the empathic reaction of most of the women students, I realized when rereading their journals that my own tendency had been to conceptualize anorexia as more of a medical than a social phenomenon. That inclination on my part, coupled with Levenkron's psychological approach (focusing on birth order and family dynamics as the principal causes of Francesca's eating disorder) seem to have skewed the students' responses in favor of a medical approach. As a result, even when female students attempted to address social causes, their analysis was limited. For example, Milena began an entry in her journal on social causes but ended up writing about psychological causes instead: "The society likes and appreciates thin women. People think that really skinny women are more attractive than not so skinny women. The society appreciates women with boy figures, bodies that do not look or function normally. As of Francesca saying, 'Thin is safe,'

I think that something in her world is not right. I think she is not getting a lot of attention at home. That lowers her self-esteem. . . ."

Contrasting the medical and sociocultural models might have allowed Milena and other students to explore anorexia as more than a private problem of self-esteem or family dysfunction. They might have been able to examine cultural constructions of femininity and why women "without need, without want, without body" are appreciated.

Regardless of the shortcomings of *The Best Little Girl in the World* and the predominance of the medical model in the popular and scholarly literature on anorexia, I believe it is a rich and important topic for an EAP class. From a feminist perspective, studying about anorexia accomplishes several things. First, it honors the mainly hidden but highly significant relationship between women and food as a legitimate area of academic study. Second, it makes room for voices that are not always heard in college classrooms, such as Julia's recounting her struggle with food, place, and identity. Third, it challenges the notion that mastery means learning material on the terms of a preselected group of experts whose canonical theories are to be accepted rather than questioned. Fourth, it makes students aware of their varying subject positions as men and women and how those positions can affect their reaction to academic subject matter.

CONCLUSION

Elsewhere I have written about the debate in EAP between basing instruction on the demands of content classes, what I call the "pragmatic stance of traditional EAP," and providing them with an alternative to the offerings of mainstream academic classes, critical EAP (Benesch, 1993, 1996). In this chapter I have tried to show that critical EAP can offer a feminist alternative to students whose academic life is limited by exclusively masculinist content. My EAP students were enrolled in a psychology class that ignored the contributions of women to psychology as well as women's issues. Part of my role, as I viewed it, was to balance that curriculum. The results were instructive. I discovered that in order for students to explore the social dimensions of a particular issue, they must be given tools, a theoretical construct that can frame discussion, along with more accessible narrative accounts. I also found that some men may resist studying an issue that affects women more than men, and that feminist teachers need to be prepared for that resistance, whether or not we decide to respond to it directly. Mainly, I found that we need more reports of feminist pedagogy in a variety of adult ESL settings so that we can begin to develop a greater understanding of the ESL classroom as a site of gender politics that has, for the most part, been ignored. As Schenke

(1991) has pointed out, feminist pedagogy in ESL is "virtually invisible"—"There are no existing curricula, no support groups, no forms of institutional recognition . . . no connections to established women's studies programs" (p. 47).

Reports from other feminist teachers theorizing from their experience would have helped me navigate the difficulties of teaching about anorexia. I wanted to find out, for instance, if others had encountered resistance from men in their classes and, if so, how they handled it. I wanted to know if women in ESL feminist classes had exhibited a greater sense of entitlement, as Julia did. I wanted, above all, to know how hard my colleagues had pushed their students to understand material from a social perspective. Should we be satisfied with initial responses to the materials we provide, or should we try to make students aware of their own role in perpetuating injustice and how to address it? I look forward to reports that could answer this and related questions about the role of feminist teachers in critical EAP classes. That type of exploration will create the support currently lacking for teachers attempting experiments in feminist pedagogy.

REFERENCES

Bartkey, S. L. (1988). Foucault, feminism, and the modernization of patriarchal power. In I. Diamond & L. Quinby (Eds.), *Feminism and Foucault: Reflections on resistance* (pp. 61–86). Boston: Northeastern University Press.

Benesch, S. (1993). ESL, ideology, and the politics of pragmatism. *TESOL Quarterly, 27,* 705–717.

Benesch, S. (1996). Needs analysis and curriculum development in EAP: An example of a critical approach. *TESOL Quarterly, 30,* 723–738.

Bordo, S. (1993). *Unbearable weight: Feminism, western culture, and the body.* Berkeley: University of California Press.

Chernin, K. (1981). *The obsession: Reflections on the tyranny of slenderness.* New York: Harper & Row.

Chernin, K. (1985). *The hungry self: Women, eating, and identity.* New York: Harper Perennial.

Gilligan, C. (1982). *In a different voice: Psychological theory and women's development.* Cambridge, MA: Harvard University Press.

Lewis, M. (1992). Interrupting patriarchy: Politics, resistance and transformation in the feminist classroom. In C. Luke & J. Gore (Eds.), *Feminisms and critical pedagogy* (pp. 167–191). New York: Routledge.

Maher, F. A., & Tetreault, M. K. T. (Eds). (1994). *The feminist classroom: An inside look at how professors and students are transforming higher education for a diverse society.* New York: Basic Books.

Schenke, A. (1991). The "will to reciprocity" and the work of memory: Fictioning speaking out of silence in E.S.L. and feminist pedagogy. *Resources for Feminist Research/Documentation sur la Recherche Feministe, 20,* 47–55.

Vandrick, S. (1995). Teaching and practicing feminism in the university ESL classroom. *TESOL Journal, 4,* 4–6.

Walkerdine, V. (1985). On the regulation of speaking and silence: Subjectivity, class, and gender in contemporary schooling. In C. Steedman, C. Unwin, & V. Walkerdine (Eds.), *Language, gender and childhood* (pp. 203–241). London: Routledge & Kegan Paul.
Weiler, K. (1991). Freire and a feminist pedagogy of difference. *Harvard Educational Review, 61*, 449–474.

8

Literature in the ESL Classroom: Reading, Reflection, and Change

Kate Mangelsdorf
The University of Texas at El Paso

Luis (this is not the student's real name), a 26-year-old student from Mexico enrolled in a developmental writing class, responded in his journal to an autobiographical essay by David Vecsey (1994) called "Old at Seventeen" (I have reproduced the original grammar and spelling):

> I agree with the author of this reading when he says that he felt he was no longer a child and that he knew that he was a teen-ager, because that's the most important thing about growing up. The fact that the author miss his own self as a child it's an idea that makes him think and look older. The story remind me of my old days, it seems as if I was rewritting my own story. I remember when I was a child, a daredevil, nothing could stop me from getting adventure, action, killing, thrilling emotions. The days seem to be endless from day to night all was laughs, fun, and adventure; but one day I woke up with a different actitud, a different view of the world, simply another me. It seems that I was sleep in a dream of pure fun and unexpectally woke up in the middle of nowere. Then I begun to question my self, who am I, what am I doing here, where am I going? what am I going to do? then I realize that I was no longer a child I was a teenager that had to grow older and keep the memories on the past and start to live my own life. Is sad to know that now you are on your own and have to keep moving without looking backwards.

Luis's response to "Old at Seventeen" illustrates how literature in ESL classes can be beneficial. First, his interpretation of the essay took into consideration the writer's rhetorical strategies. For instance, Luis noted that the narrator's nostalgia for his childhood made him "think and look older," an allusion to the narrator's self-consciously mature voice. This attention to rhetorical strategies could help Luis improve his own writing. Also, Luis's reading of the essay led him to construct a version of his own childhood—"it seems as if I were rewritting my own story." In this story, he recreated his younger and older selves. This recreation gave him the opportunity to better understand his own process of maturation.

In this chapter, I argue that we can use literature in ESL classrooms to help students acquire language and the insight into one's self and one's context that language brings. First I discuss the benefits of using literature in ESL classrooms, and then I suggest strategies and texts for using literature in a variety of contexts.

WHY LITERATURE?

Clearly, one advantage to a curriculum that includes literature is that students can be given the chance to read interesting and challenging material. Reading, as a major component of both first and second language acquisition, positively influences speaking, listening, and writing skills. In particular, reading a variety of texts of interest to the reader promotes language acquisition (Krashen, 1993). Through reading, students improve their vocabulary and enrich their repertoire of rhetorical strategies.

But why read *literature* with our students?[1] Given the time limitations of a particular course and ESL students' need to succeed in their other college classes, why not focus entirely on nonliterary texts that students might read in other courses or in their professional worlds, such as textbooks, manuals, or reports? In most teaching situations, this isn't as practical as it might at first seem. For one, students come from a variety of disciplines, each with their own method of creating and communicating knowledge. Such heterogeneity would make it difficult to engage students with texts from each of their disciplines. Even if we were able to deal with the variety of disciplines represented in each class, our own lack of knowledge about the conventions of each discipline would limit our effectiveness. Spack (1988) wrote, "English teachers cannot and should not be held responsible for teaching writing in the disciplines. The best we can accomplish is to create programs in which students can learn

[1]What constitutes "literature" is open to interpretation. In this chapter I'm using the term to mean poetry, fiction, plays, and essays. The range of material is broad, ranging from texts in the traditional literary canon to ones that are marginalized or outside of the canon, including works from popular American culture.

general inquiry strategies, rhetorical principles, and tasks that can transfer to other course work" (pp. 40–41).

Literary texts have the potential to work as Spack suggested: to help students make the transfer from their English classes to their content courses. With literary texts, students can learn to write about other sources by practicing note-taking, paraphrasing, summarizing, and documenting techniques. They can learn library research by exploring, through traditional written sources or on the internet, how other readers have responded to a particular author or work.

Through reading literary texts, students can also better understand the complicated interactions among writer, reader, and text. Zamel (1992) noted that "reading has as much to do with what the reader brings to the text and how the reader interacts with the text as with the text itself" (p. 467). Despite what many reading textbooks still advocate, reading isn't a matter of locating a single, main idea. Reader-response theorists, for instance, locate the meaning of the text primarily in the reader's mind, whereas social constructivists locate meaning primarily in the discourse community in which readers reside. Although such theoretical concerns might seem irrelevant to the ESL classroom, they have generated a richer awareness of the reading process, a process that can be taught to students through particular reading strategies.

One reading strategy is getting students to connect their own experiences and belief systems with the text they are reading. To do this, students can learn to activate their own background knowledge about a topic before, during, and after they read. Having students answer questions about the topic is an easy way to teach students to do this. For instance, the textbook in which "Old at Seventeen" appears, *Interactions* (Moseley & Harris, 1994), contains a series of questions or ideas for students to respond to before, during, and after they read. This strategy is easily transferred to nonliterary texts.

Reading literature can also help students make sense out of texts on difficult or unfamiliar topics. Tierney and Pearson (1983/1988) described how readers (and writers) do this:

> What drives reading and writing is [the] desire to make sense of what is happening—to make things cohere. . . . The reader accomplishes that fit by filling in gaps (it must be early in the morning) or making uncued connections (he must have become angry because they lost the game). All readers, like all writers, ought to strive for this fit between the whole and the parts and among the parts. (p. 265)

The reading process, like the writing process, is recursive in that readers monitor and alter their sense of the meaning of the text as they continue to read. The ambiguity of many literary texts necessitates this type of monitoring, because unlike more straightforward material, such as textbooks, many literary texts demand that readers untangle the meaning as they read. Why does Marguarite, in Maya Angelou's *I Know Why the Caged Bird Sings* (1969), stop talking? Why does Esperanza, of Sandra Cisneros' *The House on Mango Street* (1989), want to change her name? When readers work at understanding texts such as these, they're practicing important meaning-building techniques.

Through reading literature, students can also come to a better understanding of the reading process. Traditionally, reading has been taught as information retrieval. Worksheets and multiple-choice tests reinforce the idea that reading is primarily the decoding of individual words, leading ESL students to approach the text with dictionary in hand. Literary texts can easily explode such limiting notions of reading because they lend themselves to multiple interpretations. By encouraging such multiple interpretations, teachers model for their students a reading process that involves a critical engagement with a text in a collaborative context. As Louise Rosenblatt (1983) explained:

> A free exchange of ideas will lead each student to scrutinize his own sense of the literary work in the light of others' opinions. The very fact that other students stress aspects that he may have ignored, or report a different impression, will suggest that perhaps he has not done justice to the text. He will turn to it again in order to point out the elements that evoked his response and to see what can justify the other students' responses. (p. 110)

By stressing the interpretive, collaborative nature of reading, teachers can help students understand how texts are written and understood in other disciplines.

Literature can be a valuable tool for learning in a participatory, problem-posing classroom. Auerbach and McGrail (1991), drawing on the pedagogical theory of Paulo Freire, defined a problem-posing curriculum: "The teacher poses problems based on students' reality and guides them through a process of dialogue and critical reflection on that reality from which they generate their own group alternatives for dealing with the problems" (p. 101).

Literary texts that reflect students' lives outside the classroom can serve as stimuli for problem posing. For instance, students who are recent immigrants to the United States might read texts about the experiences of other immigrants. By reading texts that are close to their lives, readers' worlds can be validated, challenged, or even transformed. Problem-posing can also occur with texts that don't correspond closely to students' lives, as Luis' experience reading "Old at Seventeen" demonstrates. "Old at

Seventeen" was written from the perspective of a 17-year-old American boy, presumably from an affluent background (a country club is referred to). The boy writes about how he's reluctant to go sledding, seeing it as a childish adventure. In contrast to the narrator, Luis was older (26), from another culture (Mexican), from a lower economic class, and more familiar with the desert than with snow. Nonetheless, this essay precipitated in Luis a growth in self-understanding that resulted from his engagement with the text.

Literary texts can also help students, especially immigrant students, respond to the pressures of acculturation. Rodby (1990) described a "kaleidoscopic" sense of the self, a description that rejects the idea of a unified cultural identity. Drawing on Bakhtin's and Vygotsky's theories of the development of the self, Rodby pointed out that, for ESL students, writing in English results in "a dialectic of identity and difference" as students encounter "an arena of different discourses" (p. 48). To Rodby, students need to create "a self which is made in a world language"(p. 49)—a self created not in the mother tongue nor in English, but one that embraces both languages and cultures. Literature can help students accomplish this by modeling a kaleidoscopic self. Rodby used the example of Tony in *Bless Me, Ultima* (Anaya, 1972), who struggles to come to terms with the Mexican and American cultures. Another example of a kaleidoscopic self is given in Bharati Mulcherjee's *Jasmine* (1989), which concerns an Indian woman's experiences in the United States. Texts such as these demonstrate different ways the self can develop in multicultural situations.

WRITING AND COLLABORATION

Students will benefit most from literature if it's taught in a classroom that stresses integration of skills, in particular writing in combination with reading. To teach literature without the benefit of writing cheats students of the rich connections between these two activities. Zamel (1992) noted that "writing teaches reading" because it allows readers to discover and make concrete their ideas about a text. Indeed, the reading process and the writing process are parallel processes of constructing and communicating meaning: When we read, we compose the text in our head, just as we compose a text when we write.

Reading journals and learning logs are an ideal way to connect writing with the reading of literature. An unstructured reading journal allows students to respond to the reading without specific prompts, enabling them to follow the flow of their thoughts. (Luis' response to "Old at Seventeen" was in an unstructured journal.) Students can be encouraged to write what they liked or didn't like about the material, to connect the reading to their own lives, or to explore a central idea or character. Learning logs are a more structured type of journal in which students use specified prompts or response techniques. For instance, students can be directed to write about a certain passage in the text or to compare and contrast certain characters. Students can also keep a double-entry log in which they record specific passages on one side of the page and react to the passage on the other side of the page (Berthoff, 1981). Because of the double-entry format, students are more conscious of the dialectical nature of reading—the give and take that occurs between reader and writer.

When devising journal assignments, teachers should allow students the freedom to choose the method of responding to writing that suits them best. One way to do this is to assign different types of journal techniques early in the course, and then allow students to select the technique that they prefer. Students could also take turns writing prompts for each other for learning logs. Another method of encouraging student interaction is to have students keep dialogue journals, in which they write about a text to a specific audience—the teacher, another student, or someone outside of the classroom. Dialogue journals work particularly well in classrooms in which students can write to each other online on classroom bulletin boards.

Dialogue journals are an effective way of ensuring that reading literature is a social, not individual, process. We might think of the act of reading as inherently individual because we (usually) read silently, to ourselves. Although the act of reading might not be social, the act of interpretation is. We can make our classrooms interpretive communities in which students generate and exchange ideas about what they have read. To enrich students' experiences with texts, we can provide them with opportunities to talk about their ideas in a noncritical atmosphere. In addition to whole-class discussions, students can form small groups in which they discuss an aspect of the reading and then report to the rest of their classmates about their ideas. Students can also collaborate with each other on written responses to texts, whether informal (as in a journal) or formal (as in an essay).

Activities such as those just described remind us that literature is a valuable tool for enhancing second language acquisition. In my view, we need to *use* literature, not *teach* literature. It's easy for instructors, especially those who were once English majors, to begin discussing literary periods, symbols, or plot devices. Although topics such as these might be helpful in clarifying a particular point, they should not become the center of the curriculum. Instead, literature should be used as a stimulus for inquiry in a classroom that stresses the interconnectedness of reading and writing and the social nature of negotiating meaning.

A SAMPLE LESSON

Here is a sample lesson showing one way that literature can be used for the purposes described previously. The course is a first-year ESL composition class with students from a variety of cultures. About half of the students are immigrants; the rest of the students will return to their native countries once they receive their university degrees. The literary text being considered is a selection from Amy Tan's *The Joy Luck Club* (1989). The narrator in the passage is Lindo Jong, a middle-aged woman who came to the United States from China as a young woman. In this passage, Lindo Jong tells her daughter, Waverly, how she met Waverly's father in an English class soon after they had both arrived in the United States. Lindo has been goaded by her sister An-mei to get married. Following is a section of this passage (the students receive a longer version):

> Sometimes I wonder why I wanted to catch a marriage with your father. I think An-mei put the thought in my mind. She said, "In the movies, boys and girls are always passing notes in class. That's how they fall into trouble. You need to start trouble to get this man to realize his intentions. Otherwise, you will be an old lady before it comes to his mind."
>
> That evening An-mei and I went to work and searched through strips of fortune cookie papers, trying to find the right instructions to give to your father. . . . I knew the right one when I read it. It said: "A house is not home when a spouse is not at home." I did not laugh. I wrapped up this saying in a pancake, bending the cookie with all my heart.
>
> After school the next afternoon, I put my hand in my purse and then made a look, as if a mouse had bitten my hand. "What's this?" I cried. Then I pulled out the cookie and handed it to your father. "Eh! So many cookies, just to see them makes me sick. You take this cookie."
>
> I knew even then he had a nature that did not waste anything. He opened the cookie and he crunched it in his mouth, and then read the piece of paper.
>
> "What does it say?" I asked. I tried to act as if it did not matter. And when he still did not speak, I said, "Translate, please."
>
> We were walking in Portsmouth Square and already the fog had blown in and I was very cold in my thin coat. So I hoped your father would hurry and ask me to marry him. But instead, he kept his serious look and said, "I don't know this word 'spouse.' Tonight I will look in my dictionary. Then I can tell you the meaning tomorrow."
>
> The next day he asked me in English, "Lindo, can you spouse me?" and I laughed at him and said he used that word incorrectly. So he came back and made a Confucius joke, that if the words were wrong, then his intentions must also be wrong. We scolded and joked with each other all day long like this, and that is how we decided to get married. (Tan, 1989, pp. 301–302)

An important reading comprehension strategy is connecting a reader's background knowledge to the text under consideration. This passage lends itself to such a strategy. Many students can easily understand the awkwardness of finding a mate when traditional cultural customs are no longer appropriate, and students learning English can sympathize with the confusion over the word *spouse* that is at the heart of the story. To help them connect their own experiences with the text, students could respond to questions such as the following before, during, or after they read:

- Compare and contrast the traditions for finding a mate in your native culture and in the American culture. Which tradition do you prefer?
- Describe a time when a word in English that you didn't know led to a confusing situation.
- Have you been told how your parents met and married? If so, relate the story.
- Why might family members tell children about how their parents met and married?
- What is your ideal mate? What is one of your classmates' ideal mate? How does your ideal mate compare and contrast with your classmate's? What might explain the similarities and differences?

To enrich the reading process, students could respond to these questions in class or small-group discussions as well as in learning logs.

This passage from *The Joy Luck Club* could also be used to refine students' reading processes. Questions such as the following can strengthen students' ability to make sense of the text as they read:

- As you were first reading this passage, did you ever become confused? If so, what confused you? What was your strategy for dealing with this confusion? For instance, did you reread the confusing part, consult a dictionary, or return to the confusing part after you read the whole piece?
- Is there any part of the piece that you still don't understand? If so, spend 5 minutes writing what you think it might mean. Then show the passage to one of your classmates and explain your ideas about it. Ask your classmate for his or her ideas.
- Write a short summary of this passage for someone who hasn't read it.
- Pick out two or three of the most important sentences in this passage. Explain why they're important.
- Why does the author use so much dialogue in her story?

An important part of this story concerns Lindo Jong's efforts to adapt to a strange culture. In getting the right man to propose to her, she combines a traditional way (the fortune cookie) with an American way (passing a note to her intended). Her Chinese self and her American self are both apparent. Prompts such as the ones in the following list can help students become more aware of their own kaleidoscopic selves:

- In what ways does Lindo seem Chinese? In what ways does she seem American?
- Does Lindo seem to belong to one culture more than another? Why or why not?
- Does Lindo's future husband seem to belong to one culture more than another? Why or why not?
- To which cultures do you belong?
- Which cultural traditions do you abide by when doing the following: picking a mate, preparing a certain meal, talking to different family members, raising a child, being with friends?

In addition to doing informal writing in journals or learning logs, students can extend their responses to Tan's work with lengthier and more complex pieces. Collaboratively or individually, they can write and perform a play based on this passage, compose a story about Lindo and her husband in later years, or write love poems from the perspective of Lindo or her husband. They can compare Tan's piece with other writers' descriptions of finding partners, such as Gary Soto's essay "Finding a Wife" (Soto, 1986), which is about how Soto, a Latino, met and courted his Japanese-American wife. Students can write about their own attempts to find partners. A more academic writing assignment is a report comparing the process of finding spouses in different cultures.

SUGGESTED TEXTS

The list of literary texts appropriate for the ESL classroom is endless. The following suggestions are intended only as starting points.

Some of the most effective texts are an accepted part of the literary canon. Orwell's *1984* (1949) and *Animal Farm* (1946) engage students in issues concerning political power and free expression, whereas Hemingway's *The Old Man and the Sea* (1952) brings out more metaphysical concerns. Willa Cather's *Death Comes for the Archbishop* (1927) raises questions concerning the role of religion in colonial conquest. Sherwood Anderson's *Winesburg, Ohio* (1919) deals with the conflict between societal mores and individual needs. In addition to raising issues relevant to students' lives, texts such as these use simple, clear language that is easily accessible for many ESL students.

Texts dealing with cultural conflicts are quite well suited for ESL students, especially those who are recent immigrants to the United States. Texts about immigrant experiences include Gish Jen's *Typical American* (1991), Gus Lee's *China Boy* (1991), Judith Ortiz Cofer's *Silent Dancing: A Partial Remembrance of a Puerto Rican Childhood* (1991), Julia Alvarez's *How the Garcia Girls Lost Their Accents* (1991), and Jeanne Wakatsuki Houston's *Farewell to Manzanar* (1973). Texts dealing with minority cultures in the United States include James Welch's *The Death of Jim Loney* (1979), N. Scott Momaday's *The Way to Rainy Mountain* (1969), Brent Staples' *Parallel Time: Growing Up in Black and White* (1994), Malcolm X's *The Autobiography of Malcolm X* (X & Haley, 1964), and Sandra Cisneros' *Woman Hollering Creek and Other Stories* (1991).

Many of the most useful resources of literature for ESL students are anthologies with a multicultural emphasis. Some of the best are Gillespie and Singleton's *Across Cultures: A Reader for Writers* (1991); Kirszner and Mandell's *Common Ground: Reading and Writing about America's Cultures* (1994); Wiener and Bazerman's *Side by Side: A Multicultural Reader* (1993); Colombo, Cullen, and Lisle's *Rereading America: Cultural Contexts for Critical Thinking and Writing* (1992); Verburg's *Ourselves Among Others: Cross-Cultural Readings for Writers* (1988); and Divakaruni's *Multitude: Cross-Cultural Readings for Writers* (1993).

THE REAL LITERATURE IN THE ESL CLASSROOM

Using literature in the ESL classroom is an effective way of helping students at different levels of language proficiency to successfully create and communicate meaning. For this to happen, literature should be used as a tool to engage students in critical reading and writing activities. Ira Shor (1992) wrote that "texts [should] enter a student-centered process rather than students entering a text-centered discourse" (p. 245). To accomplish this, he recommended that students have a voice in deciding which texts should be read, have the right to state their opinions about the texts, and have the opportunity to connect the texts to their own contexts. Suggestions such as these remind us that literary texts are a means to an end, not an end unto themselves. Ultimately, the most important texts in the classroom are those produced by the students themselves.

REFERENCES

Alvarez, J. (1991). *How the Garcia girls lost their accents.* New York: Plume.
Anaya, R. (1972). *Bless me, Ultima.* Berkeley, CA: Tonatiuh International.
Anderson, S. (1919). *Winesburg, Ohio.* New York: Modern Library.

Angelou, M. (1969). *I know why the caged bird sings*. New York: Bantam.
Auerbach, E., & McGrail, L. (1991). Rosa's challenge: Connecting classroom and community contexts. In S. Benesch (Ed.), *ESL in America: Myths and possibilities* (pp. 96–111). Portsmouth, NH: Boynton/Cook.
Berthoff, A. (1981). *The making of meaning*. Upper Montclair, NJ: Boynton/Cook.
Cather, W. (1927). *Death comes for the archbishop*. New York: Vintage.
Cisneros, S. (1989). *The house on Mango Street*. New York: Vintage.
Cisneros, S. (1991). *Woman hollering creek and other stories*. New York: Vintage.
Cofer, J. O. (1991). *Silent dancing: A partial remembrance of a Puerto Rican childhood*. Houston, TX: Arte Publico Press.
Colombo, G., Cullen, R., & Lisle, B. (Eds.). (1992). *Rereading America: Cultural contexts for critical thinking and writing* (2nd ed.). New York: Bedford/St. Martin's.
Divakaruni, C. B. (Ed.). (1993). *Multitude: Cross-cultural readings for writers*. New York: McGraw-Hill.
Gillespie, S., & Singleton, R. (Eds.). (1991). *Across cultures: A reader for writers*. Boston: Allyn & Bacon.
Hemingway, E. (1952). *The old man and the sea*. New York: Scribner.
Houston, J. W. (1973). *Farewell to Manzanar*. Santa Barbara, CA: Capra Press.
Jen, G. (1991). *Typical American*. New York: Plume.
Kirszner, L. G., & Mandell, S. R. (Eds.). (1994). *Common ground: Reading and writing about America's cultures*. New York: St. Martin's.
Krashen, S. (1993). *The power of reading*. Englewood, CO: Libraries Unlimited.
Lee, G. (1991). *China boy*. New York: Dutton.
Momaday, N. S. (1969). *The way to Rainy Mountain*. Albuquerque: University of New Mexico Press.
Moseley, A., & Harris, J. (Eds.). (1994). *Interactions: A thematic reader* (2nd ed.). Boston: Houghton Mifflin.
Mulcherjee, B. (1989). *Jasmine*. New York: Grove.
Orwell, G. (1946). *Animal farm*. New York: Harcourt Brace.
Orwell, G. (1949). *1984*. New York: Harcourt, Brace, Jovanovich.
Rodby, J. (1990). The ESL writer and the kaleidoscopic self. *The Writing Instructor, 10*, 42–50.
Rosenblatt, L. (1983). *Literature as exploration* (4th ed.). New York: Modern Language Association.
Shor, I. (1992). *Empowering education: Critical teaching for social change*. Chicago: University of Chicago Press.
Soto, G. (1986). *Small faces*. Houston, TX: Arte Publico.
Spack, R. (1988). Initiating ESL students into the academic discourse community: How far should we go? *TESOL Quarterly, 22*, 29–51.
Staples, B. (1994). *Parallel time: Growing up in black and white*. New York: Avon.
Tan, A. (1989). *The joy luck club*. New York: Ballantine.
Tierney, R. J., & Pearson, P. D. (1988). Toward a composing model of reading. In E. R. Kintgen, B. M. Kroll, & M. Rose (Eds.), *Perspectives on literacy* (pp. 261–272). Carbondale: Southern Illinois University Press. (Reprinted from *Language Arts*, 1983, *60*, 568–580)
Vecsey, D. (1994). Old at seventeen. In A. Moseley & J. Harris (Eds.), *Interactions: A thematic reader* (2nd ed., pp. 51–54). Boston: Houghton Mifflin.
Verburg, C. J. (Ed.). (1988). *Ourselves among others: Cross-cultural readings for writers*. New York: Bedford/St. Martin's.
Welch, J. (1979). *The death of Jim Loney*. New York: Harper & Row.
Wiener, H. S., & Bazerman, C. (Eds.). (1993). *Side by side: A multicultural reader*. Boston: Houghton Mifflin.
X, M., & Haley, A. (1964). *The autobiography of Malcolm X*. New York: Random House.
Zamel, V. (1992). Writing one's way into reading. *TESOL Quarterly, 26*, 463–485.

9

Fluency First in the ESL Classroom: An Integrated Approach

Rebecca Williams Mlynarczyk
Kingsborough Community College, City University of New York

The scene is a classroom in an urban community college a week before the end of the semester. As the students come into the room, they sit clustered in small groups talking intently with their classmates and looking through the papers that other students have written.

Let's take a closer look at some of these student-written projects. Marina, who moved to the United States from her native Russia 4 years ago, has written a book entitled *Songs Which Were Sung by the Ocean.* The book, which is typed and illustrated with black-and-white drawings, consists of seven chapters, each devoted to a different folktale from her native country. In a preface, she explained how she got the idea for this project:

> One day my college teacher gave not regular homework—to write a book. I was very upset. I didn't know what should I write. I never did it before. I broke my head, my brain was in blind alley, so I come to my friend—ocean. I began to complain the ocean.
>
> "Listen"—said my friend—"I could help you. I'm very old, I am old like our planet. So I saw many in my life. I know everything about everybody. I want to tell you few stories. Write about it in your book or use it as you want."

Rosa, who came to the United States from the Dominican Republic less than a year ago, has written an autobiography entitled *My Own Book.* Neatly typed like Marina's, it consists of 11 chapters with titles such as

"My Major Childhood's Fear," "A Special Boy Friend," and "Never Truth in a Beautiful Voice." The book is illustrated with photographs, which Rosa has photocopied from her own collection.

Alex's book, handwritten in a spiral notebook, is the longest project in the class, consisting of 69 pages. Alex was one of three students who decided to write fiction. His book, a novel about life in Russia during the Second World War, is dedicated to "all people who fought in World War II, especially to my grandparents, which went through horrible war and were able to come out alive." Alex, who had immigrated to the United States 4 years earlier at the age of 14, had never written fiction before and insisted that he didn't like reading and writing. But his natural talent for fiction writing seemed obvious from page 1. Here is the beginning of his first chapter, "Sudden Invasion":

> The time was rough, as I was sitting in the kitchen thinking about the old times I remembered the way I used to run through the beautiful, grassy fields. I used to do a lot of work at home, helping my mother in kitchen and I loved it.
>
> But now there was the year of 1941. The Germans attacked my country. They were taking city by city, moving more deeper and deeper inside our territory. I never thought, that the Germans will start the war with Russia. I heard that the countries had an agreement between each other. But on June 21, 1941 my family were listening to a radio and heard this: "Attention, attention. I'm here to inform you that the Germans attacked our borders and began the war with us!"

Although not all of the books in this class were as elaborate as the three described here, every student turned in a final project revealing significant growth in writing during the semester. Besides writing their own books, the students also read three books: Russell Baker's *Growing Up*, Anne Frank's *Diary of a Young Girl*, and a third book that each chose from a list of suggested works, which they read and discussed with a small group of classmates. As in most ESL classes, the students in this class had diverse backgrounds as language learners. Many were in their first semester of college. Some studied English in their native countries, some attended intensive ESL classes soon after arriving in the United States, and some had taken one or two semesters of ESL in the community college before entering this class. For all the students, however, this course was their first experience with Fluency First, a whole-language approach to ESL instruction for adults.

Three factors distinguish Fluency First from more traditional methods of second-language teaching. First and perhaps most important is the massive amount of reading and writing required of students, even those with low levels of English proficiency. Second, the books that students read are authentic texts, not books adapted for ESL readers. Third, grammar is not taught separately but addressed within the contexts of the students' own writing (Rorschach, Tillyer, & Verdi, 1992).

Fluency First is further differentiated from most other ESL programs by the intensity of the students' involvement in their learning. Students participate actively in classroom activities such as discussing their reading with a small group or offering peer response to the writing of a classmate. The teacher is instrumental in planning these activities, but in the classroom he or she functions more often as facilitator rather than as director of learning.

The Fluency First program, which was developed in the late 1980s by Professors Adele MacGowan Gilhooly and Elizabeth Rorschach at City College of the City University of New York (CUNY), is based on the notion that students acquire a second language not by doing exercises and studying grammar rules but by using language for meaningful communication. This approach is not intended for absolute beginners; students are expected to have a basic knowledge of English—a grasp of the fundamentals of English syntax and a vocabulary of about 1,000 words (Rorschach et al., 1992).

Most students and teachers using the Fluency First approach have been surprised by the students' dramatic improvement in reading and writing, and statistics support these judgments. After several years of using Fluency First in approximately two thirds of all ESL courses at City College, the passing rate on the institutionally imposed reading test rose by nearly 100%; the passing rate on the writing exam, an in-class essay written in 50 minutes, rose from around 32% to 69% (e-mail communication from Adele MacGowan Gilhooly, February 6, 1996). ESL students who have participated in Fluency First are also passing the English department's freshman composition course in far less time. The percentage of students who passed composition on the first try rose steadily from 57% in the spring of 1983 to 86% in the spring of 1991 (Rorschach et al., 1992). Before Fluency First, most ESL students had to take this composition course an average of 2.67 semesters before passing; now students pass the course in an average of 1.2 semesters (e-mail communication from Adele MacGowan Gilhooly, February 6, 1996).

THEORETICAL FOUNDATIONS

Fluency First is based on the work of John Mayher, Nancy Lester, and Gordon Pradl (1983). In discussing how children are taught to write in their first language, these authors contended that school programs emphasizing correctness before students have engaged in enough writing to develop fluency are, in effect, stopping young writers before they even get started. A better way to teach writing, the authors reasoned, would be to take our cues from the way children learn to speak, recognizing that "meaning is every writer's first goal" and that even beginning writers should be encouraged to write "complete and meaningful texts, not to copy or fill in the blanks in someone else's text" (p. 54).

In suggesting that teachers focus first on fluency, next on clarity, and finally on correctness, Mayher et al. (1983) recognized that, "Emphasizing fluency first doesn't mean neglecting either clarity or correctness even at the start. Rather than seeing these as independent stages of development, it's probably more accurate to characterize them as interacting aspects of writing ability through which writers cycle over and over as they mature" (p. 54). Although it is essential to understand the interconnectedness of all aspects of language, working within the framework of fluency, clarity, and correctness helps teachers to set priorities.

The Whole-Language Connection

In adapting the fluency, clarity, correctness model for their college ESL program, MacGowan Gilhooly and Rorschach also tapped into the whole-language approach. Initially developed for teaching children to read in their first language, whole language has since become popular in reading and writing programs for learners of all ages and language backgrounds. Whole-language programs are diametrically opposed to traditional language-teaching techniques that start with small bits of language (words or grammatical structures) and gradually expose students to longer and longer discourse segments.

Whole-language teaching also differs from other approaches in that students use language to generate meaning that is relevant to them in the present—not for some need that might arise in the future (Rigg, 1991). Although advocates of whole language insist that students should be personally involved in their learning, they also recognize that knowledge is socially constructed (Rigg, 1991). A true whole-language classroom functions as a collaborative learning community.

Second-Language Theory

Recent research related to language acquisition supports the Fluency First approach. According to Steven Krashen (1982), language "acquisition," in which students conduct meaningful activities in the target language, is much more effective and longer lasting than language "learning," in which students study grammatical structures and rules. Krashen also addressed the affective dimension of language learning. In his view, learning is maximized when the "affective filter"—the tension factor—is low. Students learn more, he reasoned, when they don't have to worry constantly about making a mistake.

Another theorist who influenced Fluency First is Lev Vygotsky (1978). According to Vygotsky, people learn best in their "zone of proximal development"—the area slightly beyond the student's present level of learning—and they benefit from the help of more capable peers.

Finally, Jim Cummins' research (1981) indicated that it takes much longer for ESL students to acquire the kind of language needed for success in school (5 to 7 years for children) than it does to get along in personal interactions. Cummins stressed that certain components are important for acquiring academic literacy: experiential learning, interaction with others, and massive exposure to meaningful content.

From Theory to Practice

Based on their understanding of recent research findings in second-language learning and literacy development, Rorschach and MacGowan Gilhooly developed a whole-language program for adults who are learning English as a second language. They identified two premises as the basis for the Fluency First program: The second language (L2) best develops in ways similar to the first language (L1) and therefore needs similar types and quantities of language; and literacy (in any language) best develops in ways that are similar to oral language development (MacGowan Gilhooly, 1990).

In keeping with these principles, the Fluency First program is holistic, offers massive exposure to English in forms that are interesting and enjoyable, and utilizes language to get real things done. The social context of the class is crucial to the success of this approach; learning is maximized in a supportive, low-anxiety environment where the negotiation of meaning is of primary importance. Rather than stressing correctness (which is often the priority in traditional ESL classes), Fluency First classes emphasize understanding—making oneself understood, and understanding others.

These classes are set up as informal learning communities. Much of the class time is spent in student-led discussion groups (MacGowan Gilhooly, 1990). In a typical 2-hour class, students spend about 90% of the time working in reading groups, in which they discuss the novels; and in writing groups, in which they read drafts of their own writing to one another and exchange feedback, suggestions for revising, and help with editing. The class as a whole spends the rest of the time participating in short discussions about the novels, or in activities designed to generate ideas for writing or to help with revising or editing.

THE FLUENCY, CLARITY, CORRECTNESS SEQUENCE

Because Fluency First was developed for use at City College, the three levels were equated with the three existing courses in that college's ESL sequence (MacGowan Gilhooly, 1991b).

Fluency

The major goal at the fluency level is to encourage students to engage actively with all aspects of English: reading, writing, speaking, and listening. However, students are not asked to read and write difficult academic prose, but rather to read popular works that will pique their interest and to write papers that are personally meaningful.

At the beginning of a fluency course teachers help students to develop a daily reading habit (the guideline is 10 pages a day, 7 days a week). Over the course of a 14-week semester, students read three to six books for a total of 1,000 pages. Books that work well at this level include *Growing Up* by Russell Baker, *I Know Why the Caged Bird Sings* by Maya Angelou, and *Iron and Silk* by Mark Salzman.

Teachers have a great deal of freedom in choosing books they feel their students will enjoy. Some prefer memoirs or autobiographies; others like to work with mysteries or science fiction. Books with movie adaptations work especially well, because seeing the movie motivates many students to keep reading and provides them with necessary background information.

Some teachers ask their students to participate in choosing the course readings by bringing in books they would like to read and negotiating with other students to form a reading group (Mlynarczyk, 1991). The students in the reading groups make up their own schedule of reading assignments, submit a weekly reading journal to their teacher, and meet once or twice a week as a group to discuss the reading.

Reading journals can take a variety of forms. One of the most successful is the double-entry journal (Berthoff, 1981). In this type of journal, students fold their notebook page vertically down the middle. Then, on the left-hand side of the page, they copy a quotation from the book that attracts their interest. On the right-hand side they write their own reactions to the quote. They also use the journals to ask questions and note gaps in their understanding. Additional columns can be added to the journal for responses from peers or teachers.

In addition to reading several books, students in the fluency course write a book of their own. Most teachers give their students a great deal of choice about the nature of this book. Some popular options are autobiography, science fiction, romance, or a magazine including shorter samples of writing in different genres. However, teachers are less flexible about the quantity of writing. By the end of the semester, students are expected to submit a book of 10,000 words—40 to 50 pages, or about 750 words a week (MacGowan Gilhooly, 1996b).

Although students in the Fluency First program at City College are not graded on their writing during the semester, they are assessed at the end of the course to determine whether they are ready to move on to the clarity level. At the end of the semester, teachers meet to assess the students' portfolios, which include all the writing they have done for the course. Students also participate in the assessment process by completing self-evaluations, in which they reflect, in writing, on their strengths and weaknesses as readers and writers, and by selecting three pieces of their own writing that they especially want their portfolio reader to consider.

Clarity

At the next level, where the primary emphasis is on clarity, students begin to read and write in ways that are more traditional for college courses. Students are expected to write expository essays that are logical and complete and that meet the standards for clarity: "a clear main focus, logically connected ideas and paragraphs, sufficient support for main ideas, no gaps or unnecessary material, and effective introductions and conclusions" (MacGowan Gilhooly, 1991a, p. 42).

Although the type of reading and writing required at the clarity level is more difficult for most students, the quantity remains the same: 1,000 pages of reading, a journal responding to the reading, and a 10,000-word writing project. Although the clarity level may appear, at first glance, to be a traditional academic course, whole-language principles still apply. MacGowan Gilhooly (1996a) explained why this is so important: "Abundance of practice leads to automaticity (effortlessness in remembering/doing certain things) and this helps in the attainment of more and more advanced and challenging skills and learning. This is particularly true with language skills. If you read and write and talk abundantly about things you are genuinely interested in, you become more skilled at language" (p. 3).

The clarity course begins with all students reading the same book—usually a work that stimulates thought about important social issues. The book may be fiction such as Harper Lee's *To Kill a Mockingbird*; a nonfiction book with historical implications such as *The Autobiography of Malcolm X*; or an oral history such as Studs Terkel's *Working*. As in the fluency level, students respond to their reading by keeping a journal and by discussing the book regularly with a reading group of four or five students. At the clarity level, discussions often center on the political issues addressed in the reading. At City College, students seem to be especially interested in talking about race relations in the United States.

By the third week of the semester, students begin to select topics for their major writing and research project—not a single sustained piece of writing as in the fluency level, but a series of pieces all related to the student's topic of interest. Students may decide to investigate an issue of importance in contemporary U.S. society, or they may want to choose a topic more closely related to their native country, their career interest, or an important global issue. Students should be genuinely interested in their topics, because these topics provide the focus for a semester-long sequence of reading and writing activities.

The writing project for the clarity level at City College includes eight parts (MacGowan Gilhooly, 1996a):

1. An informal two- or three-page position paper, in which students explain why they chose their topic, what they already know about it, and what they would like to learn in their research.
2. A brief bibliography of sources on the topic, along with a process report about using the library.
3. A 1,000-word book review of one of the books included in the bibliography.
4. Three short point-of-view pieces—fictional first-person accounts written from the perspective of someone who is personally involved with the topic.
5. A taped interview with someone knowledgeable about the topic, including a letter requesting the interview, a list of questions, a transcript of the audiotape, and a report on the interview.
6. The report of a site visit (often combined with the interview).
7. Three library research reports on articles in newspapers, magazines, or journals located in the bibliographic search (see item 2).
8. A term paper of 2,000 words (about 10 typed pages) summarizing the semester-long investigation, reporting what was learned, and asking new questions that have arisen from the research.

One teacher at the clarity level asked her students to participate in an "action plan" as part of the final project; students were required to take some action in the community as a result of their research, and then report on what they did. Most students volunteered in homeless shelters or at soup kitchens. The point was to show how research can lead to positive political action.

The end-of-semester assessment procedures at the clarity level are similar to those used for fluency. Teachers gather to evaluate samples of the students' work, looking particularly for "the ability to write expository pieces that are clear, well developed, complete, and logically organized" (MacGowan Gilhooly, 1990, p. 6).

Correctness

When students move to the final level of the sequence, the focus shifts to correctness in language use, and students are expected to engage in substantial amounts of reading and writing of the type encountered in U.S. colleges. The emphasis in writing is on expository and argumentative essays, although students continue to write informal discussion papers and reading journals. The primary reading material is usually taken from a college textbook in an academic discipline, often supplemented by a work of fiction and articles on related topics.

An innovative approach to the correctness course, based on writing as communication with a responsive reader, was developed at City College by David Tillyer. At the beginning of the semester students in Tillyer's course were given e-mail accounts and access to the college's computers. During the next 14 weeks they used writing to communicate electronically with a variety of partners. In explaining the rationale for this type of long-distance communication, Tillyer spoke directly to teachers: "To be communicative, a piece of writing must have two human beings: a writer and a reader. We want students to communicate but we forget about the reader. We [teachers] end up being the reader, so the purpose of writing tends to be to get a good grade. Nobody can get engaged in writing if the goal is only to get a grade" (Tillyer, 1993).

The correctness course that Tillyer taught in the spring of 1995 typified this approach. Each of the City College ESL students corresponded via e-mail with two different study partners. The first partner was enrolled in a basic writing course at a college in South Carolina. The partners corresponded several times a week (some students wrote daily), discussing the cultures of their respective colleges and expressing their opinions on Tillyer's "Question of the Week," which related to issues encountered in the course reading. One of these questions, for example, was: "What difference does religion make in the lives of individuals within the culture? What is the effect of a particular religion on a society as a whole?" Toward the end of the semester, the ESL students wrote five-page "cultural contact profiles" of their long-distance study partners, detailing what they had learned about the cultural backgrounds of the other students.

The City College students also belonged to a larger e-mail list comprised of both classes and the two instructors. This larger group was described on the course syllabus as "a let-your-hair-down, come-as-you-are party" in which students participate in freewheeling discussions of issues raised in class. All students were expected to contribute, but their writing was not graded.

In addition to the peer partners in South Carolina, each of the City College students had a "teacher" partner in the MA in TESOL program at Central Missouri State University. These teachers in training, under the guidance of Dr. Robert Yates, welcomed the opportunity to correspond regularly with an ESL student. This gave them a chance not only to get to know their ESL partners, but also to analyze the students' use of language. The students in Missouri discussed what they were learning in class and online, using this material as the basis for a class project. The City College students also benefited from the partnership. They welcomed the chance to communicate with graduate students in another part of the country, and they often asked questions they would not otherwise feel comfortable asking. Because of the students' need for privacy in this open-ended correspondence, neither of the instructors involved had access to what the students wrote (Tillyer, 1994).

The emphasis on using reading and writing for meaningful interpersonal communication, which provided the foundation for this e-mail-based correctness course, was a logical extension of Fluency First principles. Even students with no previous computer experience usually became intensely engaged with this new type of reading and writing. As one student expressed it:

> I must admit that in the beginning of the course I was not thrill with the idea of having to work with e-mail. . . . But, to my amazement I found myself . . . actually looking forward to it. . . . I feel like I spend m[o]st of my class time playing with the computer. And in fact this is what I did. . . . But I will not call it playing, I'll call it learning in a playful way. (Tillyer, 1994)

Besides using e-mail for interpersonal communication, students in the correctness phase learn to use the internet for research. They practice accessing information through the Gopher, and consult online sources of information such as Netnews. They also do a substantial amount of "traditional" college writing: a formal essay every week responding to the "Question of the Week," the five-page cultural contact profile mentioned earlier, and a five-page chapter of a class book. Students take a midterm and write a final in-class essay.

As every ESL teacher knows, achieving a high level of correctness in a second language takes a great deal of time and effort on the learner's part. As with all other aspects of Fluency First, students become motivated to achieve correctness by using language for meaningful communication. Most of the students who took Tillyer's course tried hard to make their e-mail messages correct so they would be easily understandable. Sometimes the e-mail partner was instrumental in motivating a student to work harder. One student, for example, refused to make any corrections in her writing, and Tillyer was convinced she would fail the course. But suddenly, about three fourths of the way through the semester, she started revising her essays and writing regularly to her partner in South Carolina, which she hadn't been doing earlier. It seems that the partner, a laid-off factory worker, had warned her that unless she started working hard on her writing and passed her ESL course, none of her dreams for a better life would come true.

Tillyer also used grades to encourage students to work on correctness. He assessed students' second drafts using a scale of 1–10, and regraded the students' corrected third drafts. In order to improve their grades, students had to reduce the number of mechanical errors.

In correctness courses that do not use e-mail, students carefully proofread their expository essays and edit them, usually in small groups. Then they count the number of errors and group them in categories such as "subject/verb agreement," "sentence boundaries," "spelling," and so on. Initially, students edit their writing only for the one or two most common errors. After they have made progress in correcting these errors, they begin to focus on other types. Teachers ask students to reflect, in writing, about why they make certain errors, and then ask them to teach a mini-lesson to the class, explaining the grammar point with which they have had trouble.

Assessment of student progress at the end of the correctness course is similar to that at the other two levels. Teachers meet in groups and holistically assess the students' final essays. These essays are based on a reading that students have been given in advance. Students choose one of five or six possible topics, and have two 90-minute class sessions in which to write the essay. Every essay is read by two teachers as well as the student's classroom teacher. If the two outside readers disagree, a third reader or the faculty supervisor resolves the dispute. Although pass/fail decisions are especially difficult at the correctness level, because passing students exit from ESL into regular freshman composition, most teachers feel that the process of cross-reading student papers leads to fair decisions.

ADAPTING FLUENCY FIRST FOR OTHER CONTEXTS

Writing in 1982, Michael Fullan stated: "Educational change depends on what teachers do and think—it's as simple and as complex as that" (p. 107). In contrast with most other movements for educational change—which tend to be imposed from above by legislators or school administrators—the vast majority of whole-language programs have originated at the grassroots level with classroom teachers. Fluency First, which began with two City College ESL professors, is no exception, and currently the approach is being extended to other educational contexts through teacher education workshops. These are based on a model developed by the National Writing Project and supported by substantial grants from the Fund for the Improvement of Post-Secondary Education (FIPSE).

During the 1991–1992 academic year, I participated in a series of these workshops, which were open to part-time ESL instructors within the CUNY system and offered each teacher a $1,000 stipend provided by the FIPSE grant. The basic goal of the workshops was to provide information and support for teachers who were interested in adapting Fluency First for use in their classrooms and colleges. I still remember the relaxed Friday afternoons when a group of 10 instructors from different campuses met with workshop coordinator Elizabeth Rorschach. We discussed the books and articles we had been reading as a group, experimented with teaching techniques that had been used successfully in Fluency First classes, and shared stories about our own teaching. We kept reflective teaching journals, and twice during the year the workshop coordinator visited our classes and offered suggestions in areas where we had requested help. Participants were not pressured to implement Fluency First, but we were given the support needed to begin the process of change.

When I accepted a job at Kingsborough Community College in 1992, I was pleased to join a group of ESL professors who were interested in experimenting with Fluency First. At Kingsborough we needed to adapt the approach for our 12-week semesters and for students who begin the program at a lower level of English proficiency than do entry-level City College students. Five years later, the majority of Kingsborough ESL instructors have implemented elements of Fluency First. All instructors of courses beyond the beginning level now require students to read two or three books. Several also incorporate the writing component, requiring students to complete a fluency book or a clarity project.

Teachers at Kingsborough have been impressed with their students' progress since they began using these new methods. And most students, even those who didn't expect to like this intensive approach, have been surprised by how much they have learned. As a Vietnamese student in Professor Bailin Song's class wrote: "In your class, you ask initiative and independence from students more than force him to memorize the lessons. . . . I like your method because I feel very independent, I can explain my own ideas. I can agree or disagree with everything if I have support" (Song, 1995, p. 43).

In addition to being used in regular ESL courses at Kingsborough, Fluency First provided the model for the college's Intensive ESL Program, begun in the spring of 1995. In designing this program, Kingsborough's Director of ESL at the time, Robert Viscount, and Program Director, Marcia Babbitt, adapted Fluency First for use in a program that links ESL with credit-bearing academic courses. The goal is to enable highly motivated incoming students to advance quickly into the mainstream. The program includes three levels, roughly equivalent to beginning, low intermediate, and high intermediate. Students attend classes Monday through Friday from 9 AM to 3 PM, with an hour off for lunch. They stay with the same group of classmates for every course, spending 8 hours a week with their ESL professor, 4 hours with Writing Center tutors, and 8 hours in regular academic courses for which they receive eight credits. All faculty involved in the Intensive Program meet regularly to coordinate activities and discuss problems as they arise.

In the lower level, the ESL course is closely linked with two credit-bearing speech courses, and students follow the fluency curriculum, reading at least two full-length books and writing a book about their own lives. In the two more advanced levels, the ESL courses are linked with academic courses such as sociology or history, and instruction is based on the clarity model.

The program developed for the low-intermediate level in the fall of 1995 was representative. In the ESL course, which was linked with the regular college-level Introduction to Sociology course, students read and kept journals on two books with important sociological themes: *Bread Givers* by Anzia Yezierska, which deals with such issues as cultural assimilation, religion, and feminism; and *To Sir, With Love* by E. R. Braithwaite, which introduces issues related to social class, education, and racism.

Toward the end of the semester, the author of the second book, E. R. Braithwaite, spent a day visiting the Kingsborough campus. Braithwaite's visit came about as a result of the letters students had written to him after finishing the book. He was so touched by the students' enthusiastic comments and questions that he volunteered to come to talk with them in person. Much real-world learning occurred as students prepared for the visit. They brainstormed questions to ask during the public question-and-answer session following the talk, and asked about the proper etiquette for such occasions in the United States. Was it acceptable to ask about his marriage or his decision to leave teaching? How does one broach the issue of racism? The student who had volunteered to present Braithwaite with a plaque was especially concerned that his remarks should be appropriate for the occasion.

When Braithwaite addressed the students and faculty of the Intensive Program, he spoke about the great importance of reading and writing in his life. His love of learning inspired him to leave his native Guyana when he received a scholarship to study the sciences at Cambridge University, and he eventually received a PhD from that institution. After his speech, Braithwaite spoke informally with many of the students as he autographed their books. Later, the students wrote thank-you letters, to which Braithwaite responded individually. For the students in the Intensive

Program, this event provided an important lesson about the power of writing—in this case, their letters to the author—to get things done in the world.

In the third week of the semester, students began to choose topics for their sociology-linked writing and research project. During the ESL class, students scanned the table of contents of the sociology textbook, looking for subjects that engaged them personally such as early marriages, causes of teenage violence, assimilation into American life, and problems of infertile couples. Throughout the rest of the semester, the students engaged in ongoing research and writing about their topics, often sharing the results in small groups.

By the end of the semester, only 9 weeks later, the students had learned how to use the college library and had checked out books related to their topics, on which they kept double-entry journals. They had also written an initial position paper, a point-of-view paper, and an essay based on a personal interview. One student interviewed a former member of a teenage gang, another talked with an infertile couple, and another used the internet to interview a lawyer about medical malpractice. By the end of the semester, students could talk and write about their subjects with considerable authority. Significantly, most of their initial positions had evolved or changed entirely—evidence that real thinking and learning had occurred.

Although the sociology professor, Susan Farrell, was not directly involved with these projects, she often talked to the students informally about their research. By the end of the semester, she felt that the students' independent investigations had given them a stronger grasp of sociological principles and an ability to communicate these ideas appropriately in English. Another type of linking occurred when the ESL teachers collected and responded to the first draft of the students' five-page sociology essays on social mobility.

Kingsborough's Intensive ESL Program has been extremely successful. The results for the first semester, which included only beginning and low-intermediate levels, were typical. In the lower level, 33 of 36 students passed at least one ESL level, for a pass rate of 91.7% compared with a rate of 66% in regular ESL classes at this level. Half of these students skipped the next ESL course, based on the regular departmental assessments. In the low-intermediate level, 35 of 36 students, or 97.3%, passed at least one ESL level, compared with the usual pass rate of 66% for regular ESL classes at this level. Of the 35 passing students, 50% skipped two levels of ESL and 36% skipped one level. In both the lower-level and upper-level groups, the pass rate for the credit-bearing speech and sociology courses was 100% (Petrello, 1995). As a teacher in this program, what pleased me even more than the high test scores and outstanding pass rates were the students' increasing comfort and competence in English, which they used not only for their academic work but also in casual conversations with classmates and teachers.

Hoping to make some of the advantages of the Intensive ESL Program available to students whose work and family responsibilities prevent them from participating in a 30-hour-a-week intensive program, we designed a series of content-linked programs, which were first implemented in the spring of 1997. The new programs, which received support from the Kingsborough administration as well as a grant from CUNY's Office of Academic Affairs, use a Fluency First approach and allow students to take their required ESL course in conjunction with a credit-bearing course such as "Introduction to the Internet" or "Principles of Health and Physical Education." In order to work out ways to coordinate the linked courses, participating faculty members spent 12 hours in curriculum development workshops before the semester began. Tutoring was another essential factor in the coordination of courses; Writing Center tutors, who were paid to attend sessions of both the ESL and the linked course, worked closely with the students, providing 4 hours a week of supplemental instruction.

At the end of the semester, participating faculty, tutors, and students were so enthusiastic about the content-linked approach that, beginning in the fall of 1997, all of Kingsborough's ESL courses will be linked with credit-bearing courses in one of the disciplines. One of the most gratifying aspects of the success of the Intensive and Linked programs has been the reaction of the faculty members in disciplines other than ESL. These professors have been pleasantly surprised by the ESL students' active engagement with academic material and superior performance on exams—characteristics that we believe are the result of the Fluency First approach to learning.

APPROACHES TO TEACHING AND LEARNING

Students and teachers who participate in Fluency First courses often discover that this approach to language learning shifts the traditional roles of learner and teacher. In a Fluency First class, students can no longer sit back passively waiting for the teacher to transmit the "content" of the course. Instead, they must assume control of their own learning, actively engaging in meaningful language use.

Teachers—even those who are committed to the pedagogical premises on which Fluency First is based—may have a difficult time adapting to their new roles as facilitators. In an interview, one of the City College instructors expressed her occasional discomfort with student-centered learning:

> I don't go into [the students'] groups unless they invite me. They can also kick me out. If they want to be alone, they can say, "OK, we're through with you." Sometimes I'm just not invited in anymore, so I have nothing left to do. I feel rejected. I know that's good, but I still feel bad. I have had it happen where somebody will come in and say, "Is this a classroom?" (Rorschach et al., 1992, p. 24)

Yet besides the doubts that inevitably come with pedagogical change, there is also a sense of growth. Later in the interview, this same teacher explained:

> I am trying to relinquish more and more of my authority within the classroom. I'm trying to empower my students and to get them to accept responsibility for their own learning—for the direction that the class is going. I do less teacher talk, and they do more writing. I'm finding that groups are very appropriate now.
>
> Negotiating the responsibility of each student in a group provides students with an opportunity to take charge of their learning. Who will speak first? What should they focus on? These are decisions they have to make together. (Rorschach et al., 1992, pp. 24–25)

Another modification that Fluency First teachers often struggle with is how to cope with the huge amounts of writing their students produce. In a whole-language class it is not necessary or even desirable for teachers to read and respond to everything students write. However, finding ways to manage the large volume of student writing is a challenge for teachers new to Fluency First, and is especially difficult for part-time instructors, who may teach two or three writing courses, often at different colleges.

Students, too, may have to adjust their expectations about how teachers respond to their writing. Many ESL students were schooled in countries where correcting errors is assumed to be an important part of an English teacher's job. Thus, some students feel that a teacher who focuses on fluency and clarity before making grammatical corrections is cheating them of the kind of response they need. These differing assumptions about the teacher's role need to be discussed openly and negotiated with students.

Despite occasional problems, however, most students and teachers who have used the Fluency First approach not only experience a more active engagement in classroom activities but also believe that the amount of language learning far surpasses what occurs with more traditional methods. Teachers, especially those who participate in the teacher education workshops, are pleased to be actively engaged in creating new approaches to language teaching. As one teacher expressed it: "For the first time, as an instructor, I felt I got to learn about teaching. The environment, the trust, the exercises, the exchange and the most important thing—the sense of community—allowed all of my ideas to mushroom, to flower. What we are going through here is a real revolution or evolution" (Rorschach et al., 1992, p. 23).

Revolution . . . evolution—these are strong words. But for students and teachers who have experienced the Fluency First approach, they seem appropriate. The challenge—in the present climate of educational budget cutting and denial of opportunities for immigrants—is how to sustain the revolution, how to continue our evolution.

Ironically, at the same time that Fluency First is transforming ESL curricula across the country through its dissemination activities, the program is in jeopardy in the college where it began. Sweeping changes mandated by the Board of Trustees of the City University of New York in June 1995 stipulated that ESL students accepted for the four-year CUNY colleges must finish their ESL instruction within two semesters. This policy resulted in the elimination of the fluency course from the three-semester City College ESL sequence, although the course is still offered during the summer as part of the University's Freshman Year Initiative. At City College, fluency remains an important goal of the new two-semester sequence, and students engage in lots of informal writing and discussion. However, fluency is no longer the primary focus for any level, and students quickly proceed to academic reading and writing. Teachers who have taught in the program see this as a great loss because, in the past, much of the students' success at later levels depended on the enthusiasm and comfort they had developed in the fluency course.

Whether Fluency First will survive in a period of fiscal austerity, attacks on whole-language practices, and demands to emphasize "the basics" is a question that cannot be ignored. The answer may depend in large measure on the activism and commitment of classroom teachers.

Currently, interest in Fluency First is increasing. In the 1995–1996 academic year, for example, faculty development programs for teachers interested in implementing Fluency First were offered at six colleges across the country through a FIPSE Dissemination Grant. And an active online seminar entitled "Fluency First and Whole Language" (open to anyone who has access to the internet; see the Appendix to this chapter for details) provides teachers with invaluable pedagogical support and answers to specific questions about Fluency First.

In pondering the future of Fluency First, we should take heart from the healthy activism underlying this approach to second-language learning. Without spending any more per student than traditional programs do, Fluency First enables ESL students to take charge of their own learning. It produces students who cannot only read books, but who can write them as well. Like their students, Fluency First teachers have an enthusiasm and sense of community that signal strength. Teachers will not easily abandon an approach that they themselves have helped to develop and that works extremely well for their students. With such broad-based support from ESL teachers and students, there is strong reason to believe that Fluency First will not just survive but thrive in the years ahead.

REFERENCES

Berthoff, A. E. (1981). *The making of meaning: Metaphors, models and maxims for writing teachers.* Upper Montclair, NJ: Boynton/Cook.

Cummins, J. (1981). The role of primary language development in promoting educational success for language minority students: A theoretical framework. In *Schooling and language minority students: A theoretical framework* (pp. 3–49). Sacramento: California State Department of Education.

Fullan, M. (1982). *The meaning of educational change.* New York: Teachers College Press.

Krashen, S. (1982). *Principles and practice in second language acquisition.* Oxford, UK: Pergamon.

MacGowan Gilhooly, A. (1990). *The fluency-clarity-correctness model.* Unpublished manuscript, Department of ESL, City College of New York.

MacGowan Gilhooly, A. (1991a). Fluency before correctness: A whole language experiment in college ESL. *College ESL, 1,* 37–47.

MacGowan Gilhooly, A. (1991b). Fluency first: Reversing the traditional ESL sequence. *Journal of Basic Writing, 10,* 73–87.

MacGowan Gilhooly, A. (1996a). *Achieving clarity in English: A whole-language book* (3rd ed.). Dubuque, IA: Kendall/Hunt.

MacGowan Gilhooly, A. (1996b). *Achieving fluency in English: A whole-language book* (3rd ed.). Dubuque, IA: Kendall/Hunt.

Mayher, J. S., Lester, N., & Pradl, G. (1983). *Learning to write/Writing to learn.* Portsmouth, NH: Boynton Cook/Heinemann.

Mlynarczyk, R. (1991). Student choice: An alternative to teacher-selected reading materials. *College ESL, 1*(2), 1–8.

Nelson, M. W. (1991). *At the point of need.* Portsmouth, NH: Heinemann.

Petrello, B. (1995). *Final report on the ESL Intensive Program.* Unpublished report, Kingsborough Community College of the City University of New York.

Rigg, P. (1991). Whole language in TESOL. *TESOL Quarterly, 25,* 518–542.

Rorschach, E., Tillyer, A., & Verdi, G. (1992, March). *Research on ESL composition instruction: The Fluency First approach.* Paper presented at the 26th annual meeting of the Teachers of English to Speakers of Other Languages, Vancouver, British Columbia, Canada. (ERIC Document Reproduction No. ED 350 848).

Song, B. (1995). What does reading mean for East Asian students? *College ESL, 5*(2), 35–48.

Tillyer, D. (1993). World peace and natural writing through Email. *Collegiate Microcomputer, 11*(2), 67.

Tillyer, D. (1994, Spring). High tech/low monitor: An ESL writing course at City College of New York meets multicultural needs with e-mail. *APEX-J (Electronic Journal of the Asian/Pacific Exchange Electronic List).*

Vygotsky, L. (1978). *Mind in society: The development of higher psychological processes* (M. Cole, V. John-Steiner, S. Scribner, & E. Souberman, Eds.). Cambridge, MA: Harvard University Press.

APPENDIX: RESOURCES FOR LEARNING MORE ABOUT FLUENCY FIRST

1. TESLFF-L, an online seminar entitled "Fluency First and Whole Language," is an interactive discussion group on issues related to Fluency First. The seminar is open to anyone who has access to the internet and is led by Marie Wilson Nelson, author of *At the Point of Need* (1991), Adele MacGowan Gilhooly, and Anthea Tillyer.

This is a sublist of the TESL-L list, so to join you must first be a TESL-L member. Your request to join should be sent to LISTSERV@CUNYVM.CUNY.EDU. As the text of your message to join TESLFF-L, simply type:

sub TESLFF-L firstname lastname

Example: sub TESLFF-L Jane Doe

Seminar participants who do not want to receive messages from the larger TESL-L, which is a general list focusing on many aspects of ESL teaching, can designate "nomail" on TESL-L and still receive all the TESLFF-L messages. Another option is to request to receive one or both of these lists in digest form.

If you experience any problems, contact the TESL-L Help Line, e-mail address: TESLHELP@CUNYVM.CUNY.EDU.

2. Student textbooks for use in Fluency First courses:

MacGowan Gilhooly, A. (1996a). *Achieving clarity in English: A whole-language book* (3rd ed). Dubuque, IA: Kendall/Hunt.

MacGowan Gilhooly, A. (1996b). *Achieving fluency in English: A whole-language book* (3rd ed.). Dubuque, IA: Kendall/Hunt.

3. Fluency First consultants. If you would like to hire specially trained consultants to provide on-campus training in the Fluency First approach, contact Adele MacGowan Gilhooly (ADELEMG@AOL.COM) or Anthea Tillyer (ATICC@CUNYVM.CUNY.EDU).

If you prefer, you may contact them at the following address:

ESL Department, R5-218
City College of New York
138th Street and Convent Avenue
New York, NY 10031
Phone: 212-650-6289

4. A 1994 audiotape on the Fluency First approach is available from:

TESOL Publications
1600 Cameron Street, Suite 300
Alexandria, VA 22314 USA
Phone: 703-836-0774
Fax: 703-518-2535

5. For more information on adapting the Fluency First approach, including sample reading lists and syllabi, contact:

Dr. Rebecca Mlynarczyk
Department of English
Kingsborough Community College
Brooklyn, NY 11235
Phone: 718-368-5849
E-mail: rwmkb@cunyvm.cuny.edu

10

Meeting ESL Students' Academic Needs Through Discipline-Based Instructional Programs

Loretta Frances Kasper
Kingsborough Community College, City University of New York

Statistics from institutions across the nation show a dramatic increase in the population of ESL students (Crandall, 1993; Nunez-Wormack, 1993). Yet, at the same time as the ESL population is growing, there have been drastic cuts in programs designed to serve these students. These cuts have been caused by budgetary problems facing colleges and by a political climate calling for a limitation of developmental/remedial English language courses at the college level.

As noted by Sarah Benesch (1993), the political climate impacts ESL instruction in higher education in a number of ways. Factors such as placement procedures, assessment measures, academic credit, and access to content courses are among those that drive the ESL curricula in colleges and universities across the United States. ESL students are often required to meet institutional standards for English language proficiency before they can become fully matriculated into the academic mainstream.

Therefore, their performance on standardized reading and writing tests determines whether ESL students may enroll in credit-bearing mainstream courses, or whether they must take non- or partial-credit ESL courses. In addition, there is at present a movement toward placing a time limit on the total number of semesters a student may remain in these developmental/remedial courses, thus requiring students to meet institutional standards for English language reading and writing proficiency even more rapidly than ever before. Ultimately, then, if ESL students do not pass these tests within the specified amount of time, they will be unable to earn a college degree.

Thus, today, ESL students and educators more and more are finding themselves in a climate of fiscal exigency leading to program reductions compounded by the pressure of constraints in time to meet institutional standards for English language proficiency. For these reasons, it is becoming ever more incumbent on ESL educators to develop instructional programs that will facilitate and hasten the full transition of students into the college academic mainstream. It is no longer enough for ESL programs to teach students the four basic English language skills (listening, speaking, reading, and writing). Rather, we must now put these skills into the context of the academic environment to enable our students to find a place in that environment, so that they will not be isolated nor excluded from it. To accomplish this goal, we must redesign, or transform, our instructional programs so that they better meet ESL students' academic needs.

TRANSFORMING INSTRUCTIONAL PROGRAMS TO MEET STUDENT NEEDS

Many colleges and universities have attempted to meet ESL students' needs by modifying programs within the college mainstream. To this end, they have created interdisciplinary collaborations, in which an ESL course is paired with a mainstream content course. In such an academic course pairing, students are enrolled simultaneously in an ESL course and a mainstream content course, for example, introductory psychology. Instruction is completely coordinated, and the ESL and content instructors work together to develop parallel materials and assignments.

Colleges may also attempt to meet ESL students' academic needs by redesigning courses within the ESL program itself, so that the content of a mainstream discipline becomes the medium of instruction, the medium through which the English language skills are taught. In such a discipline-specific course, the academic discipline (e.g., psychology; see also Benesch, chap. 7, this volume) becomes the core of the ESL course. All materials and assignments are drawn from that discipline. Students therefore use the English language to take in new information, to expand knowledge, and to discuss issues in the context of that academic discipline.

My own research (Kasper, 1994a, 1994b, 1995a, 1995/1996, in press) has demonstrated that discipline-based instructional programs in the form of both interdisciplinary collaborations and discipline-specific ESL courses are effective in shortening the time it takes ESL students to meet institutional standards for English language proficiency. The following sections describe the rationale for and implementation of these programs, and discuss the advantages and problems inherent in each.

INTERDISCIPLINARY COLLABORATIONS

Interdisciplinary collaborations set up a dialogue between instructors from different disciplines. Instructors work together to facilitate the transition from the ESL to the mainstream curriculum by designing instructional activities that will better meet the linguistic and academic needs of the ESL student population. Interdisciplinary collaborations have evolved out of the need to assist ESL students who are taking mainstream courses while still enrolled in the developmental English sequence. Given the sophistication and complexity of the ideas and material presented in these mainstream courses, and the fact that many of them are taught lecture style, a great number of ESL students find themselves overwhelmed and frustrated in these classes.

An interdisciplinary collaboration involves pairing an ESL course with a mainstream academic course. Instruction in both courses is completely coordinated, and ESL instruction parallels the topics that students are studying in the mainstream course. For example, in a collaboration between a course in ESL Analytical Reading and one in Introductory Psychology, students studying the topic "learning and memory" in the psychology class might read the text *Remembering the Forgotten Art of Memory* by Scruggs and Mastropieri in the ESL class. A sample list of parallel content area topics and ESL readings is provided in the Appendix to this chapter.

Interdisciplinary collaborations can significantly improve both content area learning and English language proficiency. My own research (Kasper, 1994a) has demonstrated that academic course pairings have a powerful effect on increasing students' average scores on measures of English language reading and writing proficiency (80.4% vs. 47.8%). Moreover, these paired courses help ESL students perform at the level of native English speakers on measures in the mainstream content area (average scores, 79.9% vs. 79.4%, for ESL and native speakers, respectively). In addition to increasing scores on assessment examinations, collaborative programs also appear to increase student retention. ESL students enrolled in an academic course pairing had a dropout rate from the introductory psychology course 10% lower than the average for the institution (Kasper, 1995b).

Additionally, student feedback on these interdisciplinary collaborations is quite positive (Kasper, 1994a). Students report that academic course pairings lessen both their anxiety and their sense of being overwhelmed by the academic content and the amount of material to be learned in the mainstream course. The overwhelming majority of students say that they would recommend this type of instructional program to a friend. Some representative student responses are: "Pairing ESL and psych is a good idea because ESL opened our mind and completed what we didn't understand about psychology," "I didn't find the amount of work overwhelming because one subject was related to the other," and "I would recommend paired courses to my friend because it's a better way to learn and understand, and it helps us to pass both psych and English class."

What factors lead to the impressive results brought about by interdisciplinary collaborations? Academic course pairings seem to work because they enable ESL students to review content material in the secure, comfortable, supportive environment of the ESL class. Moreover, because instruction is coordinated, students receive multiple exposure to the subject matter at hand. The two instructional contexts allow for greater generalization and consolidation of learning. Finally, focusing on one subject area establishes rich schemata that are continually activated and strengthened throughout the semester.

Although I and many other researchers (e.g., Benesch, 1988; Brinton, Snow, & Wesche, 1989; Smoke, 1988; Smoke & Haas, 1995) have found academic course pairings and other collaborative programs to be very helpful in meeting the academic needs of ESL students, there are several significant problems that often preclude offering such programs on a regular basis. First, collaborative programs require a significant time commitment. Faculty must be trained and willing to devote the extra time and effort required to make these programs work. An effective interdisciplinary collaboration requires that faculty meet regularly and coordinate efforts to develop parallel instructional materials. Moreover, the ESL instructor should have, or should cultivate, some expertise and interest in the content area course in order to integrate the content material into the ESL class effectively and to provide any extra help needed to understand the ideas and concepts presented. Finally, ESL and content area instructors need to attend each other's classes as often as possible.

Collaborative programs also cost money. Colleges must be willing to make adjustments in teaching loads and to provide released time to give faculty the opportunity to plan and prepare materials and activities, to meet to discuss progress and problems, and to attend each other's classes. In addition, colleges must be willing to deal with the administrative and scheduling difficulties inherent in setting up effective interdisciplinary collaborative programs.

In today's climate of financial exigency, it is sometimes very difficult, if not impossible, for colleges to offer interdisciplinary collaborative programs on a regular basis. Therefore, budgetary problems at many times prevent ESL students from taking advantage of this unique opportunity to improve their English language skills. As a result, instructors need to design other programs that will meet ESL students' academic needs. When circumstances preclude offering collaborative programs, we then have to turn to redesigning and recreating the ESL program to make the content of academic disciplines the predominant medium of instruction in individual ESL courses.

DISCIPLINE-SPECIFIC ESL COURSES

I was faced with just such a situation. My 1994 study (Kasper, 1994a) had demonstrated that interdisciplinary collaborations were highly effective in meeting ESL students' academic and linguistic needs. The study, therefore, presented a strong argument in favor of regularly offering such paired courses. Nevertheless, because of administrative and financial concerns at my college, these interdisciplinary collaborations could only be offered on a limited basis. Therefore, I decided to redesign my ESL courses in an attempt to find an alternative form of instruction that might provide my students with benefits comparable to those obtained in the interdisciplinary collaboration.

I created a new ESL course, making the academic discipline psychology the core of the course. I put together a text, *Teaching English Through the Disciplines: Psychology* (Kasper, 1995c), which contained the same reading selections that students in the paired course had used. In essence, therefore, this newly designed course was identical to the ESL component of the interdisciplinary collaboration; the only difference between the discipline-specific and the paired courses was the psychology course pairing.

To test the effectiveness of my alternative course, I conducted a study (Kasper, 1995/1996) in which I compared the performance of ESL students enrolled in an academic course pairing (with Introductory Psychology) with that of students in a discipline-specific course, where both courses used the same psychology texts and materials. As an outside check, I also compared their performance to that of other students in our ESL program that semester who had worked with literary rather than discipline-based texts. The results of my study revealed that on examinations assessing English language proficiency, students in both discipline-based courses performed at statistically equivalent levels (average scores of 73% vs. 75% for discipline-specific and interdisciplinary collaborations, respectively), and both performed better than students enrolled in the literature-based courses (average score of 48%).

As it had been in the interdisciplinary collaboration, student feedback in the discipline-specific ESL course was quite positive. In fact, at the end of the semester students were asked whether they preferred ESL courses to use discipline-based material or literature, and they indicated an overwhelming (86%) preference for discipline-based material. Examples of some student responses were: "This course helped me to understand some psychology problems deeper and better, and enabled me to concentrate on one subject," "I enjoyed this course because it was very specific and I got new knowledge. This course required a lot of thinking and ability to explain things," "The readings and the exercises in this course have taught me to think more logically and enabled me to organize and structure my thinking process," "Academic material is better (than literature) because we can use the knowledge in life and other courses," and, finally, "The articles we read weren't easy, and these articles gave opportunities to prepare ourselves for other courses which I think will not be easy too."

SUBSEQUENT EFFECTS OF DISCIPLINE-BASED INSTRUCTIONAL PROGRAMS

Preliminary results of a follow-up study (Kasper, in press) of ESL students who participated in discipline-based programs indicate that these programs may have beneficial effects beyond a single semester of instruction. When the progress of students enrolled in both the interdisciplinary collaborations and the discipline-specific ESL courses was followed over several subsequent semesters, some important benefits were noted. First, when compared with the overall ESL population, a significantly higher percentage of discipline-based students (69% vs. 41%) was able to complete the developmental/remedial ESL sequence and enter the mainstream English composition course (English 22). Moreover, these students earned higher grades than did the average ESL student in English 22. Eighty-five percent of students from both types of discipline-based courses earned a grade of A or B in English 22, as compared with only 69% of other ESL students taking the course. Second, ESL students who had been enrolled in discipline-based instructional programs were more likely to graduate and earn a degree. In fact, at present, 62% of the graduation rate for ESL students at the college is accounted for by students who have participated in some type of discipline-based program of instruction.

HOW DO DISCIPLINE-BASED INSTRUCTIONAL PROGRAMS WORK TO MEET STUDENTS' NEEDS?

The activities used in discipline-based instructional programs require early on that ESL students use the English language to analyze, interpret, critique, and synthesize information, thereby teaching them the skills they need to be successful in college. The texts and activities used in both types of discipline-based instructional programs foster sophisticated usage of the English language, both spoken and written.

In their efforts to comprehend discipline-based materials, ESL students must use more advanced levels of language processing (Brinton et al., 1989). Working through a discipline-based text, ESL students become aware of how to construct meaning from information stored in memory, how to extract relevant information from the larger text context, and how to filter out redundant or irrelevant information. Specifically, discipline-based texts appear to encourage students to construct schemata, help to increase metacognition of the reading process, and lead to the use of efficient comprehension strategies.

Meaning construction, leading to enhanced linguistic proficiency, is facilitated by incorporating and emphasizing activities that require the ESL student to engage in, to interact with, and to synthesize information from course texts (Kasper, 1996). By creating written responses to a discipline-based text, ESL students articulate their understandings of and connections to that text. Students are encouraged to relate texts to their own experience, knowledge, ideas, and reflections, as well as to view the information presented from a number of different perspectives.

Thus, the instructional activities used in discipline-based courses engage ESL students in a cognitive/intellectual interaction with the course materials. Such interaction helps to develop not only English language proficiency but also critical thinking skills, both necessary for a successful academic experience.

STEPS TO FOLLOW IN DESIGNING DISCIPLINE-BASED INSTRUCTIONAL PROGRAMS

Given the rationale for offering discipline-based instructional programs, how does one go about setting up such a program? Developing a discipline-based instructional program, be it an interdisciplinary collaboration or an individual discipline-specific ESL course, is a challenge. There are several steps to follow in setting up such a program:

1. Choose a subject area that is of interest to both you and your students.
2. Ask students which subject(s) they plan to major in and develop the course to meet both students' interests and their needs.
3. Choose discipline-based materials that are challenging, but not frustrating.
4. Use a variety of textual material to expose students to different styles of writing and vocabulary. Include academic textbook chapters, magazine and journal articles, and books. Have students read topical novels or short stories.
5. Develop oral and written activities that integrate and reinforce the four basic language skills—listening, speaking, reading, and writing.
6. Vary activities to maintain interest, and include audiovisuals whenever possible.

7. Help to consolidate content subject matter and vocabulary by providing visual illustration through the use of topical videos.
8. Allow course content to be flexible, and modify it from semester to semester as necessary to accommodate the needs of students.

Instructors should keep in mind that interdisciplinary collaborations or discipline-specific ESL courses may be built around any mainstream subject area. If desired, individual ESL courses (courses within the ESL program itself) may also be multidisciplinary in nature, so that material from a variety of disciplines is used (see Kasper, 1997). These multidisciplinary courses present students with the same types of activities used in the interdisciplinary collaborations and discipline-specific courses described in this chapter. Multidisciplinary courses may be used with students at the intermediate level or higher. I have found that even ESL students having an entry-level TOEFL score as low as 350 can attain significant gains in English language proficiency from a multidisciplinary course.

TEACHING ACADEMIC SKILLS

An important part of a discipline-based instructional program is teaching ESL students the skills they will need to make the transition to and then to succeed in the college mainstream. These skills include how to listen to a lecture, take notes, read a college textbook, and study and review for an examination. Each of these skills requires that students be able to identify important information in lectures and texts.

Therefore, activities in discipline-based courses should draw students' attention to critical course information by emphasizing context clues, signal words, and rephrasing as ways of identifying important points in a lecture. Activities should also teach students to identify words or phrases that signal definition, explanation, example, or contrast, as well as teaching them how to restate information through paraphrase or consolidate learning through summary. To make it easier to understand lengthy academic texts, instructors should suggest that students use the chapter summary or outline and section headings before reading to establish a knowledge base for the material to be covered in the chapter, and thereby aid in comprehension.

After students have identified and comprehended important course information, they need to be able to demonstrate their knowledge on an examination. Skill in test-taking includes knowing both how to answer test questions and how to study for the test. For this reason, each discipline-based unit should contain an examination activity, so that students learn how to read and answer various types of test questions, including essay and short-answer questions.

Finally, discipline-based courses should be designed to teach students how to conduct themselves in an American classroom. Many ESL students come from cultures where students are neither expected nor required to take an active role in the class. As a result, these students sit quietly and rarely participate in class discussions. To aid their full transition into the college academic mainstream, ESL students need to become familiar with the atmosphere of the American college class by learning how to participate in class discussions and how to ask questions in a lecture-style class. A detailed lesson plan that may be used as part of an interdisciplinary collaboration or a discipline-specific ESL course may be obtained by contacting the author of this chapter.

CONCLUSION

Through carefully designed instructional programs, we can provide ESL students with the linguistic and academic tools they need to succeed in college classes. Discipline-based instructional programs help ESL students meet the standards for full matriculation into the academic mainstream more quickly, and enable them to be more successful once they get there. Students' own comments suggest that discipline-based instructional programs build self-esteem and confidence in their ability to function in an English-speaking academic environment. Moreover, these programs have been used successfully with students from a variety of levels of English language proficiency.

The political and fiscal climate impacting ESL instruction today demands the redesign and implementation of programs and courses that will facilitate and hasten the full transition of students into the college academic mainstream. Thus, meeting the academic as well as the linguistic needs of our ESL student population must become a priority of English language instruction. With their proven record of success, discipline-based programs provide both ESL students and instructors with a highly effective medium through which to meet those needs.

REFERENCES

Benesch, S. (1988). *Ending remediation: Linking ESL and content in higher education.* Washington, DC: TESOL.

Benesch, S. (1993). ESL, ideology, and the politics of pragmatism. *TESOL Quarterly, 27,* 705–717.

Brinton, D. M., Snow, M. A., & Wesche, M. B. (1989). *Content-based second language instruction.* New York: Newbury.

Crandall, J. (1993). Diversity as challenge and resource. In *Proceedings of the conference on ESL students in the CUNY classroom: Faculty strategies for success* (pp. 4–19). New York: CUNY.

Kasper, L. F. (1994a). Improved reading performance for ESL students through academic course pairing. *Journal of Reading, 37,* 376–384.

Kasper, L. F. (1994b). Developing and teaching a content based reading course for ESL students. *Teaching English in the Two-Year College, 21,* 23–26.

Kasper, L. F. (1995a). Discipline-oriented ESL reading instruction. *Teaching English in the Two-Year College, 22,* 45–53.

Kasper, L. F. (1995b). Theory and practice in content-based ESL reading instruction. *English for Specific Purposes, 14,* 223–230.

Kasper, L. F. (1995c). *Teaching English through the disciplines: Psychology.* New York: Whittier.

Kasper, L. F. (1995/1996). Using discipline-based texts to boost college ESL reading instruction. *Journal of Adolescent and Adult Literacy, 39,* 298–306.

Kasper, L. F. (1996). Writing to read: Enhancing ESL students' reading proficiency through written response to text. *Teaching English in the Two-Year College, 23,* 25–33.

Kasper, L. F. (1997). *Interdisciplinary English.* New York: McGraw-Hill.

Kasper, L. F. (in press). The impact of content-based instructional programs on the academic progress of ESL students. *English for Specific Purposes.*

Nunez-Wormack, E. (1993). Remarks. In *Proceedings of the conference on ESL students in the CUNY classroom: Faculty strategies for success* (pp. 1–2). New York: CUNY.

Smoke, T. (1988). Using feedback from ESL students to enhance their success in college. In S. Benesch (Ed.), *Ending remediation: Linking ESL and content in higher education* (pp. 7–19). Washington, DC: TESOL.

Smoke, T., & Haas, T. (1995). Ideas in practice: Linking classes to develop students' academic voices. *Journal of Developmental Education, 19,* 28–32.

APPENDIX: LIST OF READINGS FOR THE ESL PAIRED AND DISCIPLINE-SPECIFIC GROUPS[1]

Reading assignments in both groups correspond to topics discussed in the introductory psychology course. Selections are taken from *Teaching English Through the Disciplines: Psychology* by Kasper (1995c).

---

[1]Note that additional information regarding the design and implementation of discipline-based instructional programs, as well as sample lesson plans, is available from the author. Author's address:

Dr. Loretta F. Kasper
Department of English, C-309
Kingsborough Community College/CUNY
2001 Oriental Boulevard
Brooklyn, New York 11235
e-mail: <DRLFK@AOL.COM>

Psychology Topic	*ESL Reading*
Learning and memory	"Answering Questions" by Donald Norman "Remembering the Forgotten Art of Memory" by Thomas E. Scruggs and Margo Mastropieri
Perception	"Seeing" by R. L. Gregory
Physiological psychology	"Right Brain, Left Brain" by Jerre Levy
Development	"Piglet, Pooh, & Piaget" by Dorothy G. Singer
Personality	"Psychological Hardiness" by Maya Pines
Psychopathology	"Crazy Talk" by Elaine Chaika

11

Democracy and the ESL Classroom[1,2]

Timotha Doane
City College of San Francisco

- Experience is knowledge.
- Authentic presence cannot be disputed.
- Information and knowledge are power.

This chapter is an offering of some experience in which the facilitator and learners endeavored to practice democracy in the ESL classroom and participate in the development of liberatory pedagogy in the United States. We have taken our inspiration for our practice from the work of the learners in our classrooms, spiritual and political practitioners working for the liberation of all beings, Paulo Freire, bell hooks, Elsa Auerbach, Nina Wallerstein, Pia Moriarty, Henry Giroux, and many others. We hope to add something useful to the growing literature and experience of critical pedagogy.

First, and always first, begin with what the learners know. If they think they know nothing, facilitate a problem-posing process through which they can discover what they do know. Then, on reflection and exploration of generative themes, clarify what you need to lead to action. This entire

---

[1]This article is based on a workshop developed in partnership with Clare Strawn. We presented it at TESOL in 1995.

[2]This chapter is dedicated to Jane Slaughter, a spiritual partner who taught us how to be present. If we cannot be present to it (whatever "it" is), we cannot change it. We miss her.

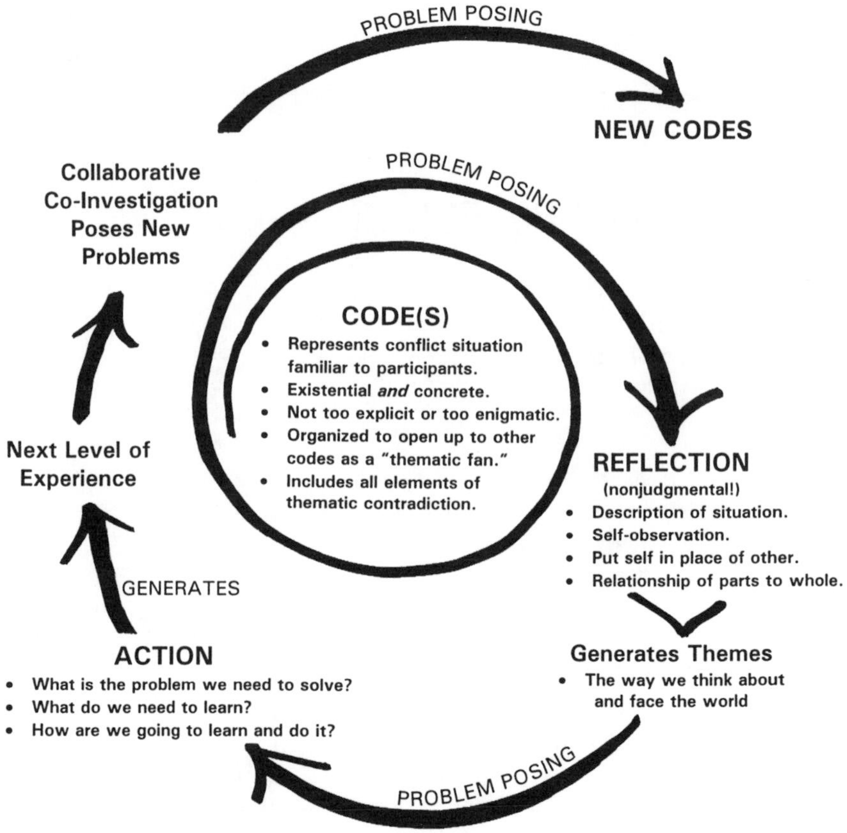

FIG. 11.1. Praxis spiral (conceptual model and graphic representation by Claire Strawn; abstracted from chap. 3 of *Pedagogy of the Opressed* by Paulo Freire, 1970).

process is a transformative one. It spirals infinitely revealing interdependencies. This process, which we will call the *praxis spiral* (see Fig. 11.1), both depends on and develops the practice for authentic presence, which we believe is a necessary step toward democracy in any context.

The key to the practice is in the relationship we create with the learners, because relationship is where we are present with each other. We believe that qualities of learning and society come out of the quality of relationship. In presence, we find intelligence.

Some form of physical exercise during class time is beneficial. It wakes us up and relaxes us. Everything is better and easier with oxygen and when we are actually in our bodies. In class we establish a daily exercise routine, even though many of the learners may be elderly. In one particular class, most of the participants were Chinese and they already knew the benefit of such exercise, because many of them already had a daily habit of practicing

Tai Chi[3] or some other form of healthful movement. What we practiced was usually a combination of yoga and calisthenics. This is an example of building on the experience or knowledge of the learners.

One morning, at 8:15, this class (which was a mixed beginning and literacy level class) was exercising. We finished the usual routine, and suddenly the facilitator noticed that she needed to raise her energy level. She knew it would feel good for herself and the learners, and be helpful in terms of promoting relaxation, wakefulness, and intimacy (which we all know vitally supports language acquisition). The facilitator had the learners vigorously rub their hands together and then bring that energy to themselves by slowly, tenderly moving their hands down over the contours of their faces. When they had finished doing this three times, the facilitator looked at them. They were transformed. Each appeared more present in her or his own body, and more present with themselves and each other. There was less anxiety in the room. The facilitator felt more grounded—her voice had dropped an octave. She felt she could see the learners more clearly. And the learners glowed from this moment of intimacy.

How much do we teachers appreciate, are we sensitive to and mindful of, the intimacy of our relationship with the learners and the acts that occur in the relationship? Out of this moment of intimacy, an elderly Vietnamese woman, who in this class of 45 hadn't been much noticed nor engaged in much interaction, shone out. She was clear and present. She looked at the facilitator with shining eyes and said, "Oh, thank you, teacher. Beautiful!" It is these kinds of moments, which we've all had, in which contact is made and a relationship is established and from which all learning flows. We cherish them. We believe that moments like this reveal our humanity and precisely how we are interconnected. Fostering moments like this—fostering loving kindness between people—is our best hope in the complex, multicultural situation in which we find ourselves in the United States.

As English teachers, we spend our days and nights with the world's people, many of whom carry with them overwhelming trauma, constant change, and the resulting stress. It is difficult but imperative to maintain openness and awareness of ourselves and the people around us. In order to practice and achieve this to the best of our ability, we must find ways to support each other. We can deeply serve ourselves and our students

---

[3]Tai Chi is a form of martial art developed by the Chinese. It involves breathing, movement, centeredness in the body, and power. It is a spiritual practice, as is anything that brings us into our bodies. Being "in our bodies" means being comfortable with who we are—that is, more than conceptualizing heads. Being in our bodies is spiritual because being in a condition of grounded presence is spacious and, therefore, there is greater potential for the generation of compassion. Bringing spirit or language into the body is a spiritual practice, just as bringing health and healing into the body is also a spiritual practice.

with compassion, humor, oxygen, movement, the resources of our communities, and English. We serve by helping them effectively enter our society; and we help our society by bringing the extraordinary knowledge, emerging from the learners' experiences, as part of the solutions to our problems and the continuing struggle for democracy in the world.

How much do we—as teachers of English to speakers of other languages—appreciate the complexities the learners in our classrooms represent and the crossroads we both occupy? In addition to class, economic, political, and cultural analysis that we can provide, we've found that conscious breathing, meditating, and movement help us into our bodies where our voices reside. Such processes mine the wisdom from our experience that we store and carry in our bodies, in our histories, and in our feelings. We have learned that most of us need some daily healing practice to get through the trauma and stress of our lives to reach, and be truly present to, our own voices and the voices of others.

What does this have to do with developing democracy? Democracy depends on the voices of the participants being heard. It depends on people finding and having their voices, and then feeling empowered to use them.

The struggle for a functioning democracy (which we don't currently have) depends on all voices participating. It depends on all voices listening and speaking. As English teachers, we know that these are skills everyone must learn.

We need citizens of authentic presence. This articulation of "authenticity" and the "power" of authentic voice comes from an integration of Freire's (1970, 1973, 1978) work and example, and our own efforts, with Jane Slaughter, to apply this perspective to the classroom as well as to emotional and spiritual healing processes. That means being able to be present in the moment in body, speech, mind, and spirit.

Critical pedagogy is, for us, a spiritual politic. Because we believe that, fundamentally, the problem in the United States is a spiritual one, we have begun to order life and our approach to the tasks of life according to spiritual principles. This does not mean to the exclusion of political principles but, as recovering ultra-leftists, we no longer believe that the ends justify the means. We believe that the ends are now, and that we must now practice being the world we want. We all endeavor to practice this in the classroom as well as everywhere else in life. We don't always succeed—that's why it's called *practice.*

The older we become, the more we notice that there is no time to waste by living inauthentically. Living authentically may propel us into a condition of perpetual "coming out." Of course this doesn't mean becoming reckless, or socially careless, or dropping all professional pretenses. Yet we are more "personal," or spiritually intimate, with learners.

Now, we describe one experience that demonstrates what we are developing in our classroom. The basis of learner-centered, problem-posing education is derived from Paulo Freire (1970), and from principles of critical pedagogy and revolutionary literacy programs written about by others such as Shor (1987a, 1987b) and Auerbach and Wallerstein (1986). These principles assume that human beings have an inalienable right and ability to participate in their own education. Indeed, the continuing struggle for genuine participation in the societies in which we find ourselves is dependent on this understanding.

As we stated earlier, always start with what the learners know. Whether the goals are a single grammar point, a particular competency, a cultural investigation, or the interrogation of a posed problem, find out what the learners know. When we do this, the learners are participating and the information and practice makes more sense to them, because they have a foundation. Such a habit of facilitation also prepares the ground for skill transfer, because learners begin to experience themselves using something they learned somewhere else in a new context. When skill and knowledge transfer does occur, it is useful to point it out to the learners—it helps in the reflection process.

Starting with what the learners know brings them further into the classroom. It creates a foundation for greater participation in their own education and learning, because they experience what they know as being of value. They experience being recognized and more equal to the task, and they engage in a dialogue with the instructor rather than being passively "taught to."

Our experience is with adult ESL students in adult schools, community colleges, and universities. However, a case could be made for applying these principles and practices to teaching ESL at any level, and also in non-ESL classes.

There are many ways to find out about the people in your classroom. A survey is sometimes useful. Besides the usual warm-up questions and vital statistics, ask what their concerns are, what they like, what their problems are, what they want, what's important and meaningful to them, what gives them strength, what they are afraid of, what their prejudices are, and what makes their hearts sing.

We believe that it is important for the facilitator to also participate in any sharing of personal information and experience, or knowledge, along with the learners, because it is important for the instructor to be part of the group. This helps to liberate instructors from the traditional "banking" approach to education in which one person is presumed to have all the knowledge and everyone else is learning from that one individual.

One intermediate ESL class at the City College of San Francisco—composed mostly of Russian, Ukrainian, Chinese, and Vietnamese adult students—complained about feeling afraid of teenagers on the city buses and on the streets. Using the resources in our community, we found a friend, Laurie Antonioli, who worked for a progressive advertising agency in San Francisco. She had noticed that there were very few people of color in the advertising business. At her urging, the agency sponsored a video production project at San Francisco's Galileo High School. Ms. Antonioli asked the students what they would do if they had a 30-second spot on TV. The students got together and decided on the message (or "the problem") they wished to pose. The Galileo students scripted, cast, and filmed the tape with the agency's help. The high school students generated a 30-second videotape called *Hero,* which problematizes what they experience as prejudice from the adult world toward them because they are teenagers.

The problem posed by the high school students in the tape is relevant to all of us involved with ESL classes and more broadly across cultural lines, and especially in immigrant populations in which cultures collide, intersect, challenge, and transform. *Hero* is rich in generative themes. (See Fig. 11.2 for the "clustering," which illustrates the themes generated by one adult ESL class.) The tape is also depersonalized from our students' experiences. A slight distancing allows for an easier sharing of experience, thoughts, and, most important, feelings. The tape lends itself effectively to critical thinking and linguistic activities, as well as to a social values clarification or content approach. The multifaceted usefulness of the tape

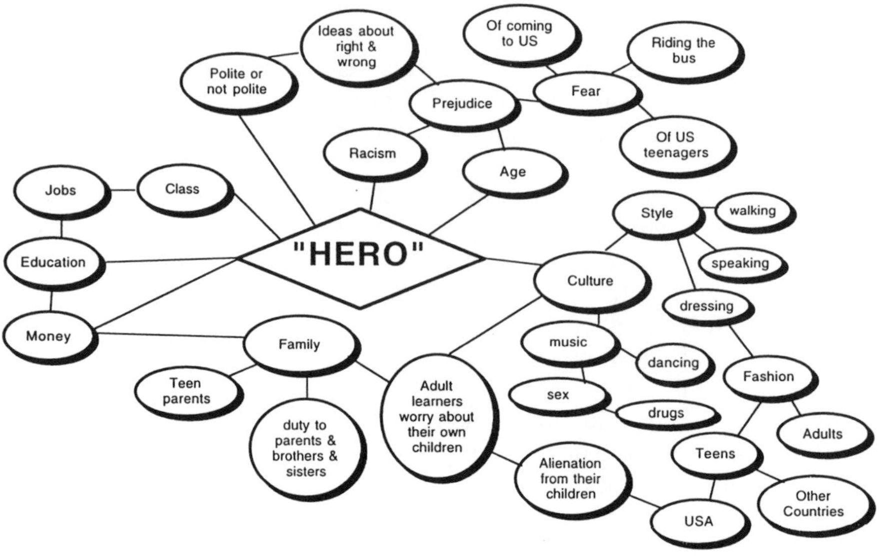

FIG. 11.2. The cluster brainstorm activity shows what the learners know and the generative themes from the code. The code is the tape *Hero*.

contributes highly to our being able to set up a pedagogical situation in which we can practice transferring skills across and through a variety of contexts. We believe that all of these characteristics are part of teaching and discovering democracy in the classroom.

Hero presents three attitudes often projected onto high school students, and responses to these attitudes. It concludes with a poignant question that both problematizes adult prejudice and offers another cognitive option.

The tape is black and white, and lasts for 30 seconds. The three attitudes are expressed by middle-aged people. They are shown in tight, full-front, facial frames that close in on their mouths as they speak. The high school students speak silently with their whole bodies. Their words are printed around them. There is a soundtrack to the text that is a muted but stirring chorus from a popular song.

The first attitude is expressed by a middle-aged European-American woman who says, "You know kids, they don't really care about anything these days." The response is a picture of a teenaged, Euro-American young woman dressed in the current high school fashion looking directly out at the camera. Framing her picture are the words, "Tutors underprivileged kids after school."

The second attitude is expressed by a middle-aged, Euro- or Hispanic-American man who says, "You know, you can spot the drug dealers just by the way they dress." He is answered by a teenaged, Latino-American young man who is dressed in big baggy pants, a plaid shirt, and a white undershirt. He glares into the camera for a moment, then looks away. Around his picture it says, "Supports family while attending high school."

The third attitude is expressed by a middle-aged, Chinese-American woman who says, "You know, most of them, they don't even know how to read or write." She is countered by a teenaged, African-American young woman also dressed in the current high school fashion of jeans and large, baggy plaid shirt. She gazes steadily at the camera, her hands on her hips. She is framed by the words, "Maintains a 4.0 grade-point average."

The final frame is of a teenaged, African-American young man dressed in a tank top and watch cap. He is very muscular and strong-looking. He looks briefly away from the camera and then directly out into it. As the words appear around him, he says, "Do you know a hero when you see one?"

This tape is intense. It is moving and, for some, disturbing. The students have managed to pack an entire deconstruction, confrontation, challenge, and defense of values into 30 seconds. What those values are and how they are expressed offers a rich source of content for an ESL classroom.

These high school students have deliberately thrown our fears back in our faces. They know how most adults perceive and feel about them, and they use these perceptions and feelings in their art. They show themselves unsmiling. They seem resentful and challenging. In their body language and dress, they present the things we find scary or baffling. They present the characteristics that we consider to be the biggest obstacles to communication. They present what they like and how they want to be. They present some values that are different, and some that are the same.

Although it is only 30 seconds long, *Hero* has tremendous generative power. It touches viewers and opens charged issues for us all. It problematizes our society from the point of view of our children.

There are many different ways to approach the content of this video. In our classes, we vary the approach depending on the level and interests of the group. We try to keep each class as experiential as possible by using discussions, group work, role play, transcriptions of group discussions, and activities from the tape itself.

The *Hero* tape works well for critical thinking activities, such as when students use aspects of the tape to identify the differences between fact and opinion. We have made stills of the people in the tape and posters of the script. The learners in our classes classify the script posters as fact or opinion. Then, in small groups, they interview each other about their opinions of the people in the pictures. In this way, the learners not only analyze the facts and opinions in the tape, but their own facts and opinions as well. The whole issue of prejudice is rich territory for these kinds of activities, and is appropriate for adult students who frequently confront problems around this issue.

For one activity, the facilitator brought in a pile of clothes and initiated an exploration of the kinds of judgments people make about other people because of the clothes they wear. We did a similar activity in which we modeled different ways of walking and body language. The groups had to record and report their prejudices.

These activities are particularly useful as preparation for experiencing the tape. They help generate ideas and get vocabulary flowing. This preparation makes the issue more accessible and assures maximum participation.

We practiced this in our adult ESL classes. After the preparation exercises, we showed the tape several times. Then we did a cluster exercise (see Fig. 11.2). The cluster activity brought out generative themes for further learning experiences, including many lively discussions.

For most of the discussions, the groups had some specific linguistic task to complete. Regardless of the particular task, they had to record and report on their small-group discussion to the whole class. This is important for accountability, and to ensure that all learning styles are engaged. It is also important to fulfill the action/reflection of the praxis spiral. These learners also had to record any changes in the way they experienced teenagers that they subsequently encountered outside of the classroom, including any teenagers at home. As well, these learners had to practice at home some of the communication skills we had discussed, and report in class the next day on how things went.

In our classroom we addressed many issues. As mentioned earlier, we discussed our fear of teenagers, especially African-American and Latino-American teenagers. We discussed violence and our expectations of it. Many adult ESL students resent the level of violence in the United States. They thought that when they came to this country they would be free of violence. We talked about the conflict in their families if their teenaged children had been swept up into gangs, drugs, or sex; we also talked about fear of these things, and the attendant communication problems that occur when children begin having lives very different from the ones their parents led. Parents face many difficulties when they experience their children learning English and generally being assimilated into U.S. society much faster than they are.

We talked about high schools. In our San Francisco Bay Area, with adult ESL classes averaging 45 learners, there is a broad variety of nationality, language, religion, and class. Many of the Eastern Europeans are shocked by the low levels of academic expectation in U.S. public schools. Their children often have homework, especially in math, that they did years earlier in schools in their native countries. Other learners who came here from war situations, Moslem women from African countries or Afghanistan, or Central Americans see their children being exposed to education that they themselves never before had the opportunity to experience. Navigating discussion, therefore, takes skill and sensitivity on the part of the teacher or discussion facilitator. It also takes a genuine desire to unlock knowledge for both the learners' and the teacher's use.

Specific to the issue of "democracy," in our classes we have discussed the importance of education. For this discussion, as for all discussions, we drew on our specific experiences, aspirations, and notions of what a functioning democratic society would look like. The groups discussed what they currently saw in the United States and what they would like to see.

We discussed values such as tolerance, competition, cooperation, individual rights, and social rights. These qualities became a lens through which we looked at age, fashion, body language, slang and language in general, style, culture, race, and class.

The groups used pictures from magazines, stories from teen papers, writings from the ESL learners, and other material to support and guide these discussions. Small-group activities in which members of the group had to report on one piece of some written material were great for focusing discussions. If using these activities, a facilitator can lead a whole-group discussion by asking questions, or he or she can give worksheets (what we call *challenge sheets*) to each group to complete. In order to complete these sheets, the learners must negotiate meaning, vocabulary, and grammar. Some particularly useful material can be adapted out of the "Growing up . . ." series published by Avon.

Cutting across all of these generative themes is the one raised by the title of the tape and by the final speaker: What is a hero? We all have many different and some of the same notions of what a hero is. Clustering is a good tool to use for complex themes, because it aids reflection, the generation of further themes, and the design of activities. It's a great activity for brainstorming and organizing.

When we did the cluster activity in our classes, the facilitator wrote the word *hero* on the center of a transparency, and showed it on an overhead projector. Then the learners were asked to state what ideas, concerns, or themes occurred to them while they were watching the tape. The facilitator wrote the ideas down in a loose but logical design, connecting ideas when it seemed appropriate. She also simplified when necessary. Then she drew lines between related issues, so that the learners could more easily identify the generative themes.

All of these discussions were accompanied by ESL and critical thinking activities designed to develop vocabulary, fluency, and accuracy. For example, it proved very useful to teach "reported speech," not only to practice that linguistic form, but also as an aid to communication when participants were feeling threatened, unheard, and angry.

When you use these activities in your own classes, notice the creative tension poised on the shared experience. This tension and the experiential wisdom of the participants create axes of energy. These powerful classroom dynamics fuel our practice of vocabulary, grammar, speaking, listening, and communicating, or sociopolitical-cultural investigation. When it is successful, teachers and students are both empowered and illuminated as they uncover and explore these issues.

In such a dynamic process, ESL items such as indirect quotation of reported speech are more easily learned. The lesson comes from the need to communicate an idea; in this instance, conflicts between different cultures (i.e., those of teenagers and adults) as a social and personal concern. Students seem to find it easier to acquire a particular English form in this type of learning context.

In conclusion, we refer the reader back to the praxis spiral. We start with what the learners know. We can help the learners access knowledge holistically with cognitive, emotional, physical, experiential and kinesthetic, and spiritual processes. In this chapter we have endeavored to show how we have learned to bring authentic presence to the learning/teaching continuum. We are particularly indebted to Paulo Freire, because his methodology invites a dynamic unity of craft, content, and process. Such a process validates the "self" of all participants, and, we feel, contributes to the development of fuller lives for each of us, and genuine democracy for us all.

REFERENCES

Auerbach, E., & Wallerstein, N. (1986). *ESL for action: Problem-posing at work.* Reading, MA: Addison-Wesley.

Freire, P. (1970). *Pedagogy of the oppressed.* New York: Continuum.

Freire, P. (1973). *Education for critical consciousness.* New York: Continuum.

Freire, P. (1978). *Pedagogy in process, the letters to Guinea-Bissau.* New York: Continuum.

Shor, I. (1987a). *Critical teaching and everyday life.* Chicago: University of Chicago Press.

Shor, I. (Ed.). (1987b). *Freire for the classroom: A sourcebook for liberatory teaching.* Portsmouth, NH: Boynton/Cook.

12

The Politics of Pronunciation and the Adult Learner

Angela Parrino
Hunter College, City University of New York

Language most shows a man; speak that I may see thee.[1]

—Ben Jonson

We define ourselves by what we say, but more notably by how we say it. The accents that color the languages we speak impact significantly on our identity. Our pronunciation allies or isolates us from a community of speakers. Even when we whisper, it screams out at our audience. It precedes our intentions and completes our utterances.

It hurts when we are ridiculed for how we sound, because we are intimately connected to our pronunciation and the accent it creates. I remember a certain professor who sarcastically commented on the neighborhood I probably resided in and my ethnic origin after listening to me speak. His response to me might have been appropriate as a phonetics class exercise, but the purpose for our encounter was to obtain information about another professor's whereabouts, not to point out my nonstandard usage of a particular form. Because standard form defines the variety of speech used by the educated people of a community (Stein & Urdang, 1967), his drawing attention to my deviation made me feel somehow deficient. It empowered him and diminished me.

Of course, there are circumstances in which native speakers may *choose* to adopt another pronunciation, another expression of self, for career or

[1]All quotes heading sections of chapter taken from Lederer (1991).

academic purposes. To do so, they will make adjustments in pronunciation using their native language as the basis for variation. An actor may seek to acquire another accent for a role in a movie, or a student might find it useful to speak one way in the academic world and another way at home or with friends. Regardless of the reasons for these adjustments, they are performances born of *choice* and ones over which the speakers ultimately have *control*. Altering pronunciation at times or abandoning the goal of acquiring another way of speaking will still entitle a native speaker to acceptance in his or her own language group, one in which true self finds expression and the stability of belonging to a community of other similar speakers.

This point was made by comedian Fran Drescher, of the TV sitcom "The Nanny," in a recent magazine interview (Stone, 1996). When asked whether she ever tried to rid herself of her nasal twang (a product of the Queens, New York neighborhood in which she was raised), Drescher replied that she had taken lessons to reduce her "whine," but spoke so slowly that she didn't *feel* like herself. To be true to herself, she had to speak as she naturally did, taking her chances that her particular brand of English pronunciation would not interfere with her commercial success. Likewise, Sean Connery, the well-known Scottish actor, related on a late night talk show that early in his career his manager recommended that he rid himself of his non-American English accent. He also took his chances, remaining true to self, for which he has had no regrets.

How do non-native-English-speaking adults figure in this picture? Can they remain true to self while trying to acquire the pronunciation of a language that is not their own? Because sounding nativelike is the green light of acceptance into a mainstream culture, replete with social, educational, and economic opportunities, to what pronunciation standard should the adult ESL speaker be held accountable? When is this standard not about clarity and comprehensibility, but more about maintenance of power and control by the majority culture? How many monolingual native English speakers take the time to consider the emotional, physiological, and economic calisthenics the adult ESL learner is asked to perform to improve his or her pronunciation in what is quite often an intolerant social and political milieu?

Despite a strong determination to master near-native pronunciation of a second language, many non-native speakers find themselves in a losing battle to be seen and *heard* as intelligent, productive, and hard-working members of society. In addition to motivation, factors such as age, first language (L1) influence, L2 exposure, and anxiety affect pronunciation mastery. Can instruction make a difference, then, in perfecting non-native English pronunciation for the adult learner and, if so, which techniques are most useful in promoting such change?

Let's begin to make sense of these questions.

PRONUNCIATION

All the fun's in how you say a thing.

—Robert Frost

Barring neurological impairment, we come to pronounce our native language without difficulty and little conscious effort. Regardless of maturational variance, a native speaker will develop a standard and/or nonstandard form of pronunciation in his or her first language, without consciously seeking to do so.

On the other hand, adult learners often have fossilized errors (those resistant to change) in their second language pronunciation (Klein, 1986). The adult may be fluent, with an excellent command of English grammar, and yet be detected as a non-native English speaker by pronunciation. How frustrating for the adult learner who may sound to the discriminating native speaking ear to be a less than effective communicator! In the movie *A Walk in the Clouds,* a patriarchal figure with a strong non-native English accent from an accomplished wine-making family declares to his daughter's native-English-speaking suitor: "You think because I *talk* with an accent that I *think* with an accent." This is a poignantly powerful statement, yet unfortunately it is often the belief that native speakers entertain of the adult L2 English speaker!

The eradication of such an attitude may not be an easy task, but it is an important one because of the deleterious effect it has on both the learner and society as a whole. The adult learner's pronunciation is not easily disguised, because pronunciation plays such a dynamic role in discourse (Brazil, Coulthard, & Johns, 1980). It allows us to communicate and understand words; the intra- and interrelationships of words in sentences; and the social, cultural, and affective intent of words. Seen in this light, the adult learner's pronunciation is a powerful mediating force in securing a place in the English-speaking society.

Morley (1991) amplified the role of pronunciation in her classroom model of spoken English. She defined pronunciation as both *speech production* and *performance.* In essence, the model marries the traditional view of pronunciation as a collection of discrete points to be mastered with the holistic view of pronunciation as oral communication.

Speech Production

In speech production, pronunciation has a microfocus on the discrete features of voice and articulation. The articulation of consonant and vowel sounds is emphasized here. Attention is paid to syllable structure, linking words, reductions, and contractions. Also included in speech production are the prosodic elements of language—stress, rhythm, and intonation. Rate, volume, and vocal qualities are addressed in this view of pronunciation as well. This microfocus is consistent with a more traditional view of pronunciation.

Speech Performance

Pronunciation in speech performance is defined as oral communication. In this aspect of spoken English, there is a macrofocus on the global patterns of English. Clarity of expression as heard in individual syllables and words of a sentence, as well as the use of particular intonation patterns to express special intentions, are emphasized in speech performance. Facility with discourse and an individual's degree of fluency are also concerns in speech performance. In sum, speech performance goals are those of intelligibility (the degree to which a learner's English is relatively easy to understand) and communicability (a learner's ability to fulfill his or her communicative needs). But what is the value of these terms outside the classroom? Do all employers, landlords, shop merchants, professors—in short, all native speakers of a culture—share a similar notion of what a relatively intelligible and communicable non-native pronunciation sounds like?

REALISTIC VERSUS UNREALISTIC GOALS AND EXPECTATIONS

> *It is obvious that we cannot begin to be citizens in a democracy if we are only partly capable of understanding our own language . . . if we do not realize that language and the word are still more powerful than the atom bomb, that like a weapon it can be used for or against us.*
>
> —Victor Grove

The obvious answer to the last question is no. I taught pronunciation for 13 years at a local college, and found that students arrived demoralized the first day of class (albeit some more than others). Their expectations for themselves were actually expectations that others had for them. These were not expectations based on what was doable for their age, or the time or money they could invest to improve their pronunciation, or the number of errors they actually committed. Rather, they were expectations based on some misguided impression of how they thought they should sound.

At the beginning of each term, I asked my students to share their reasons for improving their pronunciation. Following are some of their responses:

> My boss told me that his wife came from Canada when she was eight years old and that she got rid of her foreign accent. He said that if she could do it, I could too.
>
> My American, English-speaking husband is always correcting my pronunciation. At first, I didn't mind, but I can't get a complete sentence out now without being corrected. It's driving me crazy.
>
> I am ashamed to tell you that I have been living in New York for 23 years now and I still speak like this.
>
> I know my pronunciation is bad. People ask me to repeat so many words over the phone.
>
> My children are always correcting me. They say that they are embarrassed by how I sound.
>
> Can we read children's books as part of the course? I worry so much that I am providing a good model for my children to listen to when I read to them at night. It's really important to me.
>
> I was approached by a large organization to tutor a 60-year-old employee in pronunciation. "Can you rid him of his non-native accent in ten sessions?" they asked. "I don't think that is realistic," I replied. "Well he's up for a promotion and we would like to see some motivation and improvement on his part. A few of his peers complained that they cannot understand him. We told him that he must take classes if he wants to see the raise."

Reading between the lines, we find that many of these adult learners came to improve their pronunciation out of shame and embarrassment. And if not shame, then the reason centered around some deficiency (the parent who wanted to read children's books) or because of pressure from a supervisor and alleged complaints by longtime peers (to get a raise).

They wanted to sound better out of a need for acceptance—at home from their native-English-speaking spouse and native-sounding children, and at work from their employers. I don't remember very many who came just for themselves; most came at the prompting of others.

For the most part, students were functionally intelligible and able to communicate, yet most thought that they were totally unclear. They focused more on what they were told they said incorrectly than on what they *had perfected*. Most were highly motivated, hailing from diverse ethnic and educational backgrounds. Their L1 literacy levels varied, as did their ages, current and/or previous occupations, future career goals, and length of residence in the United States. For 2½ hours, every Saturday morning for 14 weeks, they studied to improve their pronunciation, paying for these non-credit-bearing courses with their own hard-earned money. They were certainly not failures in my eyes, but before they came to believe me, I had to perform an "expectation adjustment." That is, on the first day of class, I informed them that they would not speak exactly nativelike and, therefore, would probably not correct all their errors.

I told them, however, that they would become *aware* of their errors (some knew they sounded different, but didn't know why), that they *would speak somewhat more slowly* (they would be more carefully monitoring themselves), and that they *would start correcting* some errors, hopefully continuing to do so long after the course was over.

Whose English do adult ESL learners believe they must emulate in order to guarantee their fitting in? Had my students really ever asked themselves that question before my class? Was it mine (that of a woman born and raised in Brooklyn, New York) or did they want to speak English with a Bostonian, Californian, or Midwestern accent? Was their dream to sound like TV broadcasters, whose standard pronunciation does not in any way lessen the impact of the nightly atrocities they report? Would British or Australian English make the difference in their becoming part of some amorphous majority with its own collection of dialects and idiolects? Because some non-native English accents may be more favored or, likewise, less tolerated than others by a native-English-speaking community, how learners want or need to sound will be colored by the particular response they percieve their accents to generate.

It is important for the adult learner to realize that there is as much inter- and intraspeaker variation in pronunciation among native English speakers as there is among themselves. I am not proposing that the adult learner should not be held to certain standards for a job, promotion, or admission to an academic program; what I am suggesting is that those entrusted with hiring for such positions would consider the kind of language needed, how it will be used, and what the individual applicant has to offer before making a decision. In addition, we need to keep in mind that the adult learner is set up for failure when we create unrealistic expectations. Morley's notions of intelligibility and comprehensibility are reasonable expectations. They take into account the fact that for "the vast majority of ESL learners, perfect or near-native pronunciation is unattainable" (Morley, 1991, p. 498). The adult ESL learner can achieve a good degree of both intelligibility and comprehensibility without sounding completely nativelike.

VARIABLES THAT IMPACT ON THE PRONUNCIATION OF A SECOND LANGUAGE

Every time a man opens his mouth he says considerably more than he utters.

— Gary Jennings

By no means meant to be an exhaustive list, age, first language influence, degree of exposure to the second language, motivation, time, and anxiety are some of the variables that impact on the adult learner's goals of intelligibility and comprehensibility. Although some may figure more significantly than others in the equation for achieving such goals, it is difficult to generalize with certainty the effect of any of these variables on any individual student.

Age

The age at which he or she begins to acquire a second language has a strong impact on how successfully the adult learner will approximate the standard pronunciation of a second language. The critical age hypothesis posits a critical period for the acquisition of a first language and near-native acquisition of a second language by puberty (Lenneberg, 1967). This is thought to be true because of greater plasticity of the brain cortex and incomplete hemisphere lateralization (Penfield & Roberts, 1959). Seliger (1978) proposed the notion of several critical periods for different aspects of language, explaining why an adult speaker's pronunciation may be resistant to change whereas other areas of the individual's second language acquisition are not. It is not that the adult no longer has access to the sounds, stress, or intonation patterns, but that the ability to do so has atrophied. The musculature has changed, as has the articulatory stance of the speech organs from their position in the first language (e.g., point of articulation or the tensing or relaxing of muscles to produce vowel sounds), and the stress and intonation patterns may vary from those of English (Brown, 1994).

Influence of First Language

By virtue of the similarity of the phonological systems and prosodic elements of some native languages, adult second language learners may be facilitated in their acquisition of the English sound system (Kenworthy, 1987). However, too much focus on such a fact may create a self-fulfilling prophecy of hopelessness for those not fortunate enough to be studying a language that is phonetically similar to their own. Languages whose phonological systems may be dissimilar to English will still have some elements in common.

Exposure to Second Language

Early and maximum exposure to a second language has long been recommended for successful nativelike acquisition. Although Pedalino Porter (1991) talked about the advantages of such exposure for overall acquisition of a second language, exposure alone will not improve pronunciation if the speaker does not accurately hear the second language. This is an important consideration in light of Tomatis' claim that learners can only produce orally what they can hear, and that speakers of different languages hear according to the special band of frequencies of their first language (cited in Wong, 1993). Practice in listening, then, is key to capitalizing on the opportunities for exposure that present themselves to the learner in his or her daily environment.

Motivation

Motivation—the inner drive, impulse, emotion, or desire that moves one to a particular action—is probably the most frequently used catchall term for explaining the success or failure of virtually any complex task (Brown, 1994). Adult ESL learners, who may have age and the accompanying physiological changes working against them, may compensate with a strong desire to sound more intelligible for purposes of obtaining a better job (instrumental motivation) or permanently living in and being part of the second culture (integrative motivation). Although the most recent literature points to both instrumental (Gardner & MacIntyre, 1991) and integrative motivation (Gardner, Day, & MacIntyre, 1992) as having positive association with second language acquisition, the impact of the particular type of motivation on pronunciation will vary from person to person. Among former students who were residing in the United States on temporary work visas and therefore only instrumentally motivated by definition, I found nativelike pronunciation where one would not expect. In contrast, I have heard less perfect nativelike English pronunciation among individuals who planned to live in the United States permanently and who were more integratively motivated.

Time and Relationship to Anxiety

Initial attempts to speak in our L1 are described as "cute" and "adorable." We are given time to perfect incorrectly articulated phonemes; those around us patiently wait for appropriate stress and intonation patterns to work themselves out.

Other than by a teacher or other non-native-English-speaking peers, the utterances of adult second language speakers are not heard as "cute." The adult, by virtue of his or her age, is expected to speak intelligibly in a shorter amount of time.

However, time is of importance for the adult learner for another reason: The adult learner's assimilation and/or acculturation into the larger society is at stake. The longer it takes to become a functioning member of the English-speaking culture, the more difficult will assimilation and/or acculturation be. Schumann (1976) said that the greater the psychological and social distance between the learner's culture and that of the majority (as defined by issues of congruence, ego permeability, length of residence in a country, and language and culture shock), the lesser the chance for the individual's integration into the second language society. Is entry facilitated by possessing good second-language pronunciation, or does one speak well because one is given the opportunity and/or chooses to belong? This is the proverbial "what came first" question, for which there isn't an answer. However, we can say with some degree of certainty that the adult learner's adaptation to a new culture and language will demand new expressions of self, reflecting the changing linguistic, emotional, and social comfort in his or her environment. Changes in pronunciation will also be evident as a part of this process.

THE SIRGA FORMAT (*S*TRESS, *I*NTONATION, *R*HYTHM, *G*RAMMATICAL PRONUNCIATION, AND *A*RTICULATION): SELECTED ACTIVITIES FOR THE PRONUNCIATION CLASS

Mend your speech a little lest it may mar your fortunes.

—William Shakespeare

When I taught pronunciation, I found it helpful to structure each lesson around the following aspects of pronunciation: stress, intonation, rhythm, grammatical pronunciation, and articulation. I engaged students in both speech-production types of activities (concentrating on the elements just cited, with an isolated decontextualized focus) as well as in speech performance activities (integrating the elements in communicatively focused global tasks). Although Stern (1987, 1991; see resource list) recommended exclusive initial focus on stress and intonation, I found that the diverse needs of my students, the length of my classes (2½–3 hours) and the size (15–20 students) necessitated attending to several aspects of pronunciation weekly. Students educated in more traditional school systems welcomed the structure that each session provided. The balance of discrete point work (minimal pair drills, repetitions, and sound discrimination activities; see resource list) and stress and rhythm games (described later in the chapter) kept interest levels high and helped students with varied learning styles to improve pronunciation in both technical and fun ways.

On the first day of class, I introduced students to the meanings of the five elements of pronunciation listed previously through the use of charts and board examples. Dickerson's (1989) graphically simple and clearly illustrated places of articulation and consonant charts were helpful (see resource list), although the rest of his book is advised for the academically and technically oriented student. I especially like his consonant articulation chart, because it does not immediately introduce the phonetic alphabet to distinguish sounds, but instead represents sounds through the English alphabet, with which students are already familiar. I must admit, however, that the vowel articulation chart from the Prator and Robinett book (1985) does employ the Traeger Smith phonetic alphabet (see resource list), whereas other books may use the international phonetic alphabet (Clarey & Dixson, 1975; see resource list). My students worked at making sense of the symbols for the first few classes, and eventually had no problems with them. A certain degree of understanding of these symbols is necessary to be able to use the various published pronunciation books on the market. However, you must determine to what extent your students' needs are best served by a knowledge of phonetic symbols and which system, if any, you will have them use.

Students were also taped reading a diagnostic passage (Prator & Robinett, 1985; see resource list), so as to determine their needs. After taping, I listened to the tape at home and returned to each student a checklist of his or her individual problems (the checklist is also provided in Prator & Robinett, 1985). Students were told to practice one of their problems for each subsequent class by choosing an exercise from one of the books that we used in class, or to practice lists of words, expressions, or passages with which they had had difficulty during the week at home, at work, or while socializing. The first half-hour of each class was then designated to this individualized treatment of stress, intonation, rhythm, grammatical pronunciation, and articulation problems. Five to six students were selected to recite the exercises or other materials they had used to practice. The other students were encouraged to constructively criticize their peers. In this way, all students made gains in critical listening skills, which, as I have already mentioned, are crucial to improving pronunciation. Having the adult learner selectively attend to discrete points, at first becoming conscious of production, precedes the subconscious subsumption of such items in performance activities.

At the end of the 14-week semester, students were again taped reading the diagnostic passage to determine progress. I would also suggest additional means of oral and written assessment.

Selected Activities

In addition to the resource list at the end of this chapter, you might find the following speech production- and performance-oriented activities useful in fostering intelligible and communicable pronunciation.

Stress, Rhythm, and Intonation

Students enjoy acting out 1-inch dialogues and tone poems (Arfa & Kriegel, 1993). The dialogues, as their name suggests, are approximately 1 inch in width, with each line containing one- to three-word utterances.

Typical utterances, such as those found in the Arfa and Kriegel samples (getting a parking ticket and mistaking a plastic snake for a real one) may consist of a noun phrase, verb phrase, or adjective followed by a period, question mark, or exclamation point. At first appearing easier to read or act out than lengthier dialogues, the deleted syntax of these dialogues intensifies the adult learner's need to accurately convey meaning through stress and intonation. These are first modeled by the teacher with one student, and then practiced in pairs and performed for the entire class.

The tone poems, taken from Fleischman (1988; see resource list), are side-by-side poems with selected recurring lines. Students are cued to read the highlighted lines together, which becomes an exercise in rhythm and timing. These are also first modeled by the teacher, but with the entire class as the second voice.

The next stress and rhythm activity was first introduced to me by a former graduate student, Maria Rainey, who applied acting training exercises to the pronunciation class. The class forms a circle and is given a base sentence from which to create other sentences. In the sentence used to demonstrate the activity, "The minister's cat is a/an ______cat," one student at a time supplies an adjective constrained by alphabet order, while maintaining a count designated by the teacher. That is, after the teacher says, "The minister's cat is an angry cat," the student counts out one, two, three, four. The next student must automatically jump in with a new sentence, "The minister's cat is a black cat," lengthening or shortening the stress on the adjective as per syllabification. Several rounds of practice are needed for the students to "get" the rhythm. The last student to remain standing (who never missed a beat!) is the winner. All students find the game an enjoyable way of practicing content word stress (nouns, verbs, adjectives, and adverbs) and function word stress reduction (pronouns, prepositions, articles, and conjunctions), while maintaining the rhythm established by the teacher.

Finally, jazz chants (Graham, 1978; see resource list) can be used to improve stress and intonation, while reinforcing selected grammatical points.

Grammatical Pronunciation

The *-ed* endings to express regular verb past tense endings; final *-s* endings of plurals; third-person present tense singular verbs; contractions; possessives; and the *-ate* endings connoting verbs, nouns, and adjectives are examples of grammatical pronunciation. Practice for this aspect of pronunciation is found in many of the books in the resource list. For a four-part instructional capsule, however, specifically on the pronunciation of the regular verb past tense ending *-ed*, see Cotera-Valencia, Durboraw-Rosales, and Torres (1992; see resource list).

Articulation

There is definitely a glut of ideas for how to improve articulation—the physical production of sounds in the listed resource books. Before having your students practice any of them, you may want to have students warm up with some myofunctional therapy, which I fondly refer to as "articulation aerobics." These resistance exercises—used by speech therapists to build strength in the lips, jaw, tongue, and cheeks—are also used to retrain an infantile or reverse swallow in children. However, articulation aerobics may be an effective tool in improving tongue/tooth ridge and tongue/palate sounds. You may also do these as a contrast to some of the muscle-relaxing exercises on the Stern tapes (see resource list).

lip pop	Pull top lip over top teeth bottom lip over top lip. Pull bottom lip over top lip until you hear a pop.
tongue pop	Put tongue tip on tooth ridge. Press tongue up to roof of mouth. Pull down hard and pop.
slurp and swallow	Put rubber band on tongue tip. Put tongue on tooth ridge. Put teeth together, lips open. Slurp and swallow with rubber band in place.

After isolated work on individual phonemes, you might try some guided role play with your students. One I had success with is "a visit to the doctor's office." Both the "doctor" and "patient" receive cue cards with words containing the sound you might want to review (e.g., voiceless and voiced *th*). The patient shares his or her aches and pains: "My throat hurts" or "I feel like I can't breathe." The doctor responds accordingly with his or her own set of *th* words.

CONCLUSION

We are implicated in our adult students' endeavors to develop intelligible and comprehensible English pronunciation in ways that go far beyond the walls of the classroom. In addition to providing appropriate classroom practice, we must nurture students' self-esteem. Our realistic expectations of them will be a model of what they can expect of themselves. In this way, failure will be diminished and self-worth improved.

In a much broader sense, however, we need to become advocates for all second-language learners in our communities. Mastering another language is a lifelong task. For certain, there is a grammar to learn and a pronunciation to perfect, but there is also a new persona to develop. Being sensitive and sensitizing others to the issues discussed in this chapter may be one of the most important practices for helping the adult learner become an effective second language speaker.

RESOURCE LIST

Books and Articles

Cessaris, A. (1988). *Fluent American speech.* Menlo Park, CA: Key Communication.
Clarey, M. E., & Dixson, R. J. (1975). *Pronunciation exercises in English.* Englewood Cliffs, NJ: Prentice-Hall.
Cotera-Valencia, A., Durboraw-Rosales, C. A., & Torres, M. G. (1992). Stop! Don't look! Just listen! *ESL in Higher Education TESOL Newsletter, 11*(1), 5–6.
Crowell, T. L., Jr. (1961). *Modern spoken English.* New York: McGraw-Hill.
Dauer, R. M. (1993). *Accurate English.* Englewood Cliffs, NJ: Prentice-Hall.
Dickerson, W. B. (1989). *Stress in the speech stream.* Urbana: University of Illinois Press.
Fleischman, P. (1988). *Joyful noise: Poems for two voices.* New York: Harper & Row.
Gilbert, J. B. (1984). *Clear speech.* New York: Cambridge University Press.
Graham, C. (1978). *Jazz chants.* New York: Oxford University Press.
Hagen, S. A., & Grogan, P. E. (1993). *Sound advantage.* Englewood Cliffs, NJ: Prentice-Hall.
Lane, L. (1993). *Focus on pronunciation.* New York: Longman.
Prator, C., Jr., & Robinett, B. W. (1985). *Manual of American English pronunciation.* New York: Holt, Rinehart & Winston.
Sheeler, W. D., & Markley, R. W. (1991). *Sounds & rhythm.* Englewood Cliffs, NJ: Prentice-Hall.
Trager, E. C., & Henderson, S. C. (1983). *Pd's.* Englewood Cliffs, NJ: Prentice-Hall.
Weinstein, N. (1982). *Whaddaya say?* Culver City, CA: ELS.

Audio and Videotapes

Stern, D. A. (1987). *The sounds & style of American English* (Courses #1, 2, & 3). Dialect Accent Specialists, Inc., 606 N. Larchmont Blvd., Suite 4C, Los Angeles, CA 90004.
Stern, D. A. (1991). *Breaking through the accent barrier.* Video Language Products, P.O. Box 30675, Los Angeles, CA 90030-0675.

Equipment

Tok-Back (face band), #136. Incentives for Learning, Inc., 800 W. Van Buren Street, Chicago, IL 60607.
Visipitch (acoustic analysis equipment). Kay Elemetrics Corp., 12 Maple Avenue, Pine Brook, NJ 07058-9798.

REFERENCES

Arfa, S., & Kriegel, H. (1993, April). *Pronunciation? No problem! One inch dialogues and tone poems.* Paper presented at the TESOL convention, Atlanta.

Brazil, D., Coulthard, M., & Johns, C. (1980). *Discourse intonation and language teaching.* London: Longman.

Brown, H. D. (1994). *Principles of language learning and teaching.* Englewood Cliffs, NJ: Prentice-Hall.

Clarey, M. E., & Dixson, R. J. (1975). *Pronunciation exercises in English.* Englewood Cliffs, NJ: Prentice-Hall.

Cotera-Valencia, A., Durboraw-Rosales, C. A., & Torres, M. G. (1992). Stop! Don't look! Just listen! *ESL in Higher Education Newsletter, 11*(1),

Dickerson, W. B. (1989). *Stress in the speech stream.* Urbana: University of Illinois Press.

Fleischman, P. (1988). *Joyful noise: Poems for two voices.* New York: Harper & Row.

Gardner, R. C., Day, J. B., & MacIntyre, P. D. (1992). Integrative motivation, induced anxiety, and language learning in a controlled environment. *Studies in Second Language Acquisition, 14,* 197–214.

Gardner, R. C., & MacIntyre, P. D. (1991). An instrumental motivation in language study: Who says it isn't effective? *Studies in Second Language Acquisition, 13,* 57–72.

Kenworthy, J. (1987). *Teaching English pronunciation.* London: Longman.

Klein, W. (1986). *Second language acquisition.* Cambridge, England: Cambridge University Press.

Lederer, R. (1991). *The miracle of language.* New York: Pocket Books.

Lenneberg, E. H. (1967). *The biological foundations of language.* New York: Wiley.

Morley, J. (1991). The pronunciation component of teaching English to speakers of other languages. *TESOL Quarterly, 25*(3), 481–520.

Pedalino Porter, R. (1991). The false alarm over early English acquisition. *NABE NEWS, 14*(7), 12, 18–19.

Penfield, W., & Roberts, L. (1959). *Speech and brain—mechanisms.* Princeton, NJ: Princeton University Press.

Prator, C., Jr., & Robinett, B. W. (1985). *Manual of American English pronunciation.* New York: Holt, Rinehart & Winston.

Schumann, J. H. (1976). Social distance as a factor in second language acquisition. *Language Learning, 26,* 135–143.

Seliger, H. W. (1978). Implications of a multiple critical period hypothesis for second language learning. In W. C. Ritchie (Ed.), *Second language acquisition research* (pp. 11–19). New York: Academic.

Stein, J., & Urdang, L. (1967).*The Random House dictionary of the English language.* New York: Random House.

Stern, D. A. (1987). *The sounds and style of American English* (Cassette—courses #1, 2, & 3). Los Angeles: Dialect Accent Specialists.

Stern, D. A. (1991). *Breaking through the accent barrier* [Videotape]. Los Angeles: Video Language Products.

Stone, J. (1996, March/April). Frantasia. *Mirabella,* pp. 72–75.

Wong, R. (1993, April). *Teaching pronunciation in large classes.* Paper presented at the TESOL Convention, Atlanta, GA.

13

The Political Implications of Responses to Second Language Writing[1]

Carol Severino
University of Iowa

In her article "Ideology in Composition: L1 and ESL," Terry Santos (1992) portrayed the field of first language studies (composition) as expressly political, and the field of second language (L2)/English as a Second Language (ESL) studies as non- or apolitical, but practical instead—oriented toward teaching language to meet the needs of students and the needs of academia, business, and industry. Yet, L2 scholars have recently recommended that L2 studies begin acknowledging and articulating political stances on second language teaching (Johns, 1990). At the same time, L1 scholars have recommended that composition emphasize the practical over the political in order to address students' socioeconomic needs (Hourigan, 1994). In addition, a pedagogical emphasis on the practical is also a political stance, as this chapter shows.

To acknowledge and articulate how politics are embedded in the entire ESL endeavor, I first discuss the political implications of ESL in general. Then I pose a "continuum of political stances" on response to second language writers and their writing. Finally, I use the continuum to discuss the responses to three writers from different cultural and language backgrounds.

---

[1]This chapter is a slightly modified version of "The Sociopolitical Implications of Response to Second Language and Second Dialect Writing," by Carol Severino (1993), *Journal of Second Language Writing*, 2(3), 191–201. Copyright ©1993 by Ablex Publishing, 55 Old Post Road #2, Greenwich, CT 06831-0504. Reprinted by permission.

THE POLITICS OF ESL INSTRUCTION

The political nature of ESL instruction is apparent in both academic and nonacademic contexts. In academia, ESL curricula—such as English for Academic Purposes (EAP) and English for Specific Purposes (ESP)—should not be construed as simply pragmatic, as Swales (1990) suggested, but instead imply a political stance that is acculturative: the desirability of assimilating quickly into academic, corporate, and U.S. mainstream cultures. Likewise, expressivist L2 writing pedagogies, which emphasize personal experience, growth, and discovery, also have assimilative and Americanizing implications, especially for international students whose home cultures are more oriented to the group than to the individual (Leki, 1992). Emphasizing individualism in writing pedagogy is a particularly Western and more specifically U.S. cultural and political bias; it is neither ideologically neutral nor culturally universal, as North Americans discover when they learn about cultural relativism. Politics are also obvious when ESL teachers avoid discussions of world affairs with students from the wealthy and influential upper classes of their native countries—"the educational and economic elite of the world," as Johns (1993, p. 85) characterized them. These teachers fear the classroom tension and discomfort that might result when students disagree with them and with one another about how nations should be governed.

Outside of academia, the political implications of ESL teaching are even more evident. In community-based ESL programs in large U.S. cities, the dynamics of the curriculum are more obviously assimilative and conservative; such programs promise immigrants and refugees that learning English will increase their chances of acquiring jobs and the good life. Auerbach and Burgess (1985) showed that the ESL "survival approach" curricula common in these programs often encourage passive and subservient social roles in relation to employers, health professionals, and agency bureaucrats: "Language functions in most survival texts include asking for approval, clarification, reassurance, permission, and so on, but not praising, criticizing, complaining, refusing, or disagreeing" (p. 484). James Tollefson (1989) described how the ESL curricula of refugee programs follow the traditions of the Americanization movement by communicating to refugees that their ability to solve economic and social problems depends on their cultural and economic assimilation. Tollefson pointed out that, in contrast to the post-World War I Americanization programs in which immigrants were taught to make sandwiches and pies and salute the flag, today's ESL texts "focus instead on the ethos of the consumer society. Rather than didactic patriotism, texts teach economic patriotism—the importance of proper market behavior and of accepting the principle of starting at the bottom of the employment ladder" (p. 57).

In the Amnesty Program for undocumented workers, ESL pedagogy resembled the Americanization described in *The Education of Hyman Kaplan* (Ross, 1937). In order to stay in the United States, students had to prepare for test questions such as "What were the 13 colonies?" and "How many stripes are on the U.S. flag?" A sample dialogue from the textbook *Amnesty: A Real Life Approach Book 1* (de Valdez, 1990) is:

S1: Why did people come to America?
S2: To be free.
S1: Free to do what?
S2: To live better lives.

Even though this dialogue was for beginners who would find a complex version of the theme difficult to comprehend and imitate, simply inserting the word *most* or *some* before *people* would make the dialogue more accurate, less of an advertisement for the "good life" that not every immigrant finds it possible to achieve.

Many ESL teachers resisted these propagandistic features of the ESL/Amnesty curriculum and encouraged their students to do likewise; they developed a pedagogy based on the thinking of Paulo Freire (1972), specifically adapted to ESL instruction by Nina Wallerstein (1983): to think critically about what they are learning and about their economic and linguistic situations; to choose, as Wolfram (1992) said, the relationship they want to have with the dominant culture in which they find themselves. The very circumstances of these students' ESL classes—learning the host's language in the host's country in order to stay in the United States and increase their economic status—are manifestly political. As Tollefson (1989) and my third student profile demonstrates, it is often the case that U.S. policies in their native countries have contributed to students' immigration to the United States in the first place. The ascendance and dominance of English, contributing to the proliferation of ESL or English as a Foreign Language (EFL) programs both in the United States and abroad, are obviously political, thus causing the situation of any ESL student in any classroom inside or outside a college to be politically charged. To use Frederick Erickson's (1984) helpful terms, the "micropolitics" of the ESL teaching/learning situation inevitably reflect the "macropolitics" of the world situation.

As Santos (1992) predicted, the L2/ESL literature may gradually become more expressly political because, as demographics change and immigrants acculturate, it becomes more difficult to separate L1 from L2 pedagogy and students. As ESL students become harder to distinguish from non-ESL students and as classrooms become more multicultural, the L1 and L2 fields will grow closer. However, what matters is not how we label fields and students, but how we teach—in this particular case, how we respond to students' writing. Whatever our responses, they have political implications, some more subtle than others, that need to be brought out in the open and examined. To examine these political implications, I use three student profiles here to analyze responses to the writing of three college students from different linguistic, cultural, and academic backgrounds: a Japanese graduate student who stayed in the United States to work; and two undergraduate students who immigrated to the United States, one from Korea at the age of 11 and one from Vietnam at the age of 17. The names of the students have been changed to ensure anonymity. A fine-grained analysis of responses and students' texts helps counteract the tendency toward vagueness of much of the ideologically oriented L1 composition theory, which is hard to translate into everyday teaching situations (Santos, 1992), as well as the tendency of L2/ESL pedagogy toward pragmatism without acknowledging political stances (Johns, 1993; Santos, 1992).

THREE STANCES TOWARD RESPONSE TO WRITING

All teachers and tutors, consciously or subconsciously, have a stance on response to student writing, and, in this case, to second language writing. This stance, or as Louise Phelps (1989) called it, the "deep structure of response to writing" (p. 37), is determined by many factors, some more influential than others. One factor is how the teacher's own L1 and L2 writing has been responded to by English and foreign or second language teachers. More influential factors are the pedagogy of the overall writing/language program, the demands of a particular writing assignment, the needs of the writers, and their linguistic and academic situations—their own ideas and feelings about what constitutes helpful responses to their writing. For example, whether international students will be returning to their native countries or entering the U.S. job market affects the way a teacher responds to them and their writing. Teachers' stances are also determined by an even weightier factor: their general political attitude, or their ideology (Berlin, 1988) toward second language writers. This attitude or ideology is about acculturation—how much and how quickly, or even *if* teachers think second language speakers should assimilate culturally, socially, and linguistically into corporate and academic mainstreams, and how much of their cultural and language patterns they can and should retain. According to the degree of acculturation deemed desirable by writing teachers, three stances for responding to writing can be posed: separatist, accommodationist, and assimilationist. These stances comprise a continuum of response represented by the parallel lines in Table 13.1.

Similar models representing different stances toward social, cultural, and linguistic assimilation have been developed in ethnic studies, sociolinguistics, and L1 composition. In ethnic studies, the conflict between the assimilationist or melting pot model and the salad bowl model of cultural pluralism to explain immigration and assimilation patterns in the United States (Chametzky, 1989–1990) was explored by historians Nathan Glazer and Daniel Moynihan (1963) and by Milton Gordon (1964). In sociolinguistics, teachers' different stances toward linguistic assimilation were first addressed by Ralph Fasold and Roger Shuy (1970), who contrasted three approaches to the dialect differences of African-American students: eradication, biloquialism, and appreciation of dialect differences. In L1 composition, Min-Zhan Lu (1992) examined the differences among acculturative, assimilationist, and accommodationist pedagogies used for the basic writers who entered the City University of New York through the policy of Open Admissions; she rejected all three in favor of "a pedagogy of struggle."

Two features on the Table 13.1 continuum distinguish the three stances from one another: the attitude toward culture contact, and the attitude toward linguistic differences. I define the first stance, separatism, as the attitude that cultures, languages, and dialects in contact with mainstream culture should be able to exist almost independently—unaffected and untainted by mainstream culture, languages, and dialects. The second position, accommodation, is the belief that second language speakers can be both a part of mainstream society and apart from it, retaining to some extent their culture and language. Cultures and languages in contact are seen as intersecting. The third position is assimilation—the stance that everyone should blend into the mainstream or melting pot. Table 13.1 must be seen as a continuum rather than as three disparate categories, because writing

TABLE 13.1
A Continuum Representing Political Stances Toward Second Language Writing

	Separatist	*Accommodationist*	*Assimilationist*
Attitudes about cultures	Independent cultures	Intersecting cultures	A blended U.S. culture
Attitude about differences	Ignore differences	Explain differences	Correct differences
Public policy examples	Students' Right to Their Own Language (1974)	Ann Arbor decision (1979)	"English only" movement
Student examples	Susan	Takaro	Thanh

teachers' responses are likely to fall somewhere in between the categories, or teachers may even change response stances for different students or at different points in their careers. If removed from the continuum, these stances might seem like a setup for the classic critical pedagogy essay in which three views are presented, and one of them, usually the third, is obviously the most correct, thereby pointing the finger at those who subscribe to the first and second views. However, like Fasold and Shuy (1970), I believe that valid political and pedagogical arguments exist for each stance, arguments I hope to explain fairly (although my preference is for the accommodationist view, as theirs was for biloquialism).

Assimilationist Stance

The most extreme assimilationist response to second language writing would be to encourage students to write linear, thesis-statement- and topic-sentence-driven, error-free, and idiomatic academic English as soon as possible. The goal is to blend smoothly or melt into the desired discourse communities and avoid social stigma by controlling any features that, in the eyes of audiences with power and influence, might mark a writer as inadequately educated or lower class. The assimilationist position on what Bruce Horner (1992) called the "sociality of error" is conservative. Linguistic differences would be regarded as "errors" or instances of L1 interference—cultural or linguistic—to be eliminated.

At their best, assimilationist responses are practical, bottom-line acknowledgments of the realities and demands of academic and corporate discourses—in short, what many students and their parents assume they are paying for when they register for writing courses. At their worst, disproportionate attention to form and convention over meaning and message either inadvertently or purposely leads to disparaging students for the language, skills, and culture they bring with them into the classroom. Sensitive, moderate assimilationist responses are savvy about discourse conventions, the job market, and promotions; insensitive, extremist ones put students and their cultures down and aim to eradicate linguistic and cultural differences.

Separatist Stance

In contrast, the most extreme separatist view holds that assimilationist responses are unjust and colonialistic, and that language minorities should not have to change or adapt in order to gain educational and economic rights and opportunities. Like those who advocate the third approach described by Fasold and Shuy (1970), which they called "appreciation of dialect differences," separatists believe that the society and the class of employers or educators who disparage and discriminate against second language or second dialect speakers should be challenged and changed, not the second language or second dialect speakers themselves or their discourses. Separatists want to preserve and celebrate linguistic diversity, not eradicate it.

Language policy statements and movements illustrate how the stances and the continuum function. Separatists were more politically influential in the 1960s and 1970s during the Civil Rights Movement. "The Students' Right to Their Own Language" statement (1974) by the L1 profession's Conference on College Composition and Communication can be considered a kind of separatist platform and is therefore placed toward the left on the Table 13.1 continuum. The 1979 Ann Arbor court decision, which held that teachers of Vernacular Black English speakers must educate themselves about their students' language and use this knowledge of language contrasts to teach standard English, is placed in the middle of the continuum, where sociolinguists argue it belongs, not at the separatist end where the media placed it (Farr, 1980). The ideologically conservative "English only" movement is placed at the right (Auerbach, 1992).

At their best and in the most ideal contexts, separatist responses, in emphasizing meaning and ignoring formal differences, permit the ESL writer to work on fluency, development, and communication, freed from what might be distractions and constraints (such as attention to word endings and spelling). Separatists approach the organizational patterns of ESL texts generously, with a "cosmopolitan eye" (Leki, 1992); they are accepting of different culturally influenced logics and rhetorical patterns. As Land and Whitley (1989) maintained, such responders "allow the piece of writing at hand to develop slowly, like a photographic printing shading in the details" (p. 290). They do not demand that the thesis appear at the beginning of the paper and that this strong central argument be obvious throughout. At their worst, separatist responses, forgiving or applauding deviations from Standard English rhetorical and grammatical patterns, inevitably set students up for a shock if the next teacher, tutor, or employer they encounter tends toward an assimilationist stance.

Accommodationist Stance

An accommodationist stance, like Fasold and Shuy's (1970) biloquialism, often called the "compromise" position (Farr, 1990), includes students not giving up their home oral and written discourse patterns in order to assimilate, but instead acquiring new discourse patterns, thus enlarging their rhetorical repertoires for different occasions. In the best of all possible accommodationist worlds, patterns are only gained, not lost; true bi- or tri- or even multilingualism and multiculturalism would be the ideal. At their best, accommodationist responses are comprehensive and rhetorical, emphasizing that certain discourse features are appropriate or inappropriate for certain occasions.

At their worst, they are longwinded, laden with conditions, and hard to process. Accommodationists tell students that in more informal situations, certain features, such as the lack of idiomatic English for ESL students, are acceptable, but that in more formal situations they are unacceptable. "It all depends on how much like a native speaker you want to sound," teachers tell students. At their worst, accommodationists' conditions, contexts, and qualifications may sound like double-talk that may confuse students more than help them; their explanations might even help teachers more than the students, as accommodationists talk themselves into feeling better for not Americanizing their students and forcing them to write "native speaker" prose. However, sensitive accommodationists are, according to their name, accommodating of both linguistic differences and societal conventions. Insensitive accommodationists are overexplainers, whose own agenda (shared by many separatists)—to rid themselves of any association with academic or linguistic assimilation or colonization—can overwhelm their teaching of writing.

RESPONSES TO THREE WRITERS

The enactment of these stances is demonstrated here in actual responses to the writing of three students: Takaro, an international student from Japan, a senior in his mid-20s at the time of the study, who later received his master's degree in Japanese Pedagogy and became a teacher of Japanese in a U.S. city; Susan, an 18-year-old freshman at the time of the study, who had immigrated with her family from Korea at age 11, and has since completed her bachelor's degree in graphics and is attending graduate school; and Thanh, a 23-year-old junior majoring in pre-medicine at the time of the study. Thanh came to the United States from Vietnam at age 17 to join his relatives who had immigrated because of the Communist victory in Vietnam, an example of how a macropolitical situation determined the micropolitical ESL-teaching situation. Takaro had been referred to the writing center by International Student Services; Susan and Thanh by their classroom English teachers.

Takaro and Susan's texts were written at the beginning of the semester in and for the writing center, not for a grade or a class but instead for written and verbal responses to help them improve as writers. After these introductory assignments, however, students can receive help with any of their academic papers for any course. Thanh's text was an academic paper for his basic English course.

The writing center's pedagogy, in keeping with the writing and speaking courses it also serves, is rhetorical: Writers write to communicate rather than to demonstrate proficiency; and meaning, content, and ideas are more important than the formal features of grammar and mechanics (although the latter considerations cannot be ignored, especially when they interfere with the message conveyed). In terms of the continuum, this pedagogy is accommodationist rather than separatist or assimilative. This writing center operates more like an independent study course than a drop-in center; students commit themselves to coming to the center twice a week and work with the same teacher throughout the semester.

The sample texts of all three students are political in content: Takaro's is about the tragedy of a Japanese-American bilingual after WWII; Susan's is about her "binationality" possibly preventing her from acquiring "A Sense of Place," the title of the assignment; and Thanh's is about his mother's death while his family was preparing to leave Vietnam. Such emotionally, culturally, and politically charged themes demand responses that are content-based. Not to address the substance of the students' accounts of political and personal tragedy is reminiscent of the caricature of the insensitive teacher who responded to the sentence "Yestrday my sistr was hit by a truk" by correcting the student's spelling.

The ways I responded all tend toward accommodationist on the Table 13.1 continuum, although my responses to Susan veered more closely to separatist than did my responses to Takaro and Thanh. Because Thanh's writing was for a class, I tended more toward the assimilationist stance with his work. Using my own interactions with students rather than those of other teachers has both disadvantages and advantages; in these combination self- and student profiles, the objectivity that is lost is compensated for by the opportunity for "thick" description (Geertz, 1973) of and critical reflection about the texts and responses to them.

Takaro

Takaro wrote *"Futatsu no Sukoku"* (Appendix A) in 1½ writing center periods. His essay is strikingly relevant to the present discussion in its powerful depiction of the conflicts experienced by a bilingual/bicultural interpreter. In response to a previous assignment to describe his reading interests, Takaro had written that he had recently stayed up all night to finish the book *Two Motherlands*. For his next assignment I asked him to write about the book and why it was important to him. When he finished his piece up to the completed sentence of line 40, he called me over to tell me that he did not consider himself finished because he had not yet written how he felt about the book; he said he wanted to do that in the next lab period.

My response to the text he handed me was as follows: I sat down and with the paper between us, I read it aloud rhetorically and with feeling and meaning. I did not stumble or do doubletakes over non-idiomatic phrases, inconsistencies in tense, or the *l* and *r* confusion. I supplied the missing articles myself. When I read an emotional section, I reacted the way I actually felt. Because I had never seen Takaro's essay or read the book before, it was all new and news; that is, in James Kinneavy's (1971) terms, the text had "surprise value." I was shocked when I read that Kenji, the main character, had committed suicide, and stopped reading to react accordingly. Then Takaro and I briefly discussed the dilemma of being caught between two worlds, two non-accommodating ones.

The following week, during Takaro's next lab period, he took about 20 minutes to write the last three sentences (line 40, "This novel is . . .") about what the book meant to him. Again, I read these lines as an interested reader. When I looked a bit puzzled afterward, he showed me that the meaning of the Japanese characters he had written on the top of the page was ambiguous; they could be translated two ways—into two "ancestral lands" or two "nations." As Takaro said in the essay, being caught between two nation states (two governments or two political entities) was what destroyed Kenji, not being caught between two cultures.

Had I been more separatist, I might have adopted a "hands-off formal features (verbs, wording, spelling) policy" and stopped responding right there. Rhetorically reading for meaning would have been enough; after all, Takaro's text was not only comprehensible, but also powerful, rich, and interesting. I could have ignored its various levels of L1 transfer: cultural, syntactic, and phonological. For example, Takaro's conclusion could be analyzed in terms of cultural transfer—a writer from the reader-based rhetoric of Japanese (Hinds, 1987) expecting an English-speaking reader from a writer-based rhetoric to understand the ambiguity of *Two Motherlands* without more explanation. Syntactic transfer is evident in the missing articles and non-idiomatic phrasing, and phonological interference in the confusing of *l* and *r*, resulting in "interigence" (line 19) and "corapse" (line 23). However, the grammar, wording, *l–r*, and other spelling and pronunciation problems were not serious enough to interfere with the communication of Takaro's summary and evaluation of *Two Motherlands*.

After an error analysis, I discovered that Takaro's most common error was inconsistency of tense. He had two problems with articles and six spelling mistakes—two, as mentioned, from phonological interference. Five problems were in wording/phrasing, some more "global" (causing some cognitive strain to a native speaker) than others (Burt & Kiparsky, 1972). As a separatist might maintain, systematically addressing these errors (first the puzzling conclusion, then verbs, wording, articles, and spelling) could stifle Takaro's desire to write further on this topic and others; such a systematic response would change or interfere with his linguistic choices, some of which resulted in "interlanguage" features

(Selinker, 1972) that, in fact, contribute to the uniqueness and appeal of Takaro's discourse. Such changing and editing often results in what L1 theorists Brannon and Knoblauch (1982) called "appropriation" of the students' texts (p. 158), often construed as an act of academic or linguistic colonization. However, as an accommodationist wanting Takaro to add as native-as-feasible English discourse to his repertoire, and responding to Takaro's requests for detailed corrections, I read the entire paper aloud again to help him edit it.

The more assimilationist option would have been to dispense with a rhetorical reading and do only the second reading to edit. When I read Takaro's paper aloud this second time, I read it more slowly and with less feeling, pausing a few seconds before reading a problematic feature. Takaro had a pen in his hand, and using my pauses as hints and possibly having remembered the changed features from my previous oral reading, he caught most of the verb/tense problems himself. I helped him correct the five phrasing problems and read the smoothed-out phrases aloud in context a few more times so that they would sound natural and he might later have an auditory memory of these phrases; for example, "He had a lot of problems with the camp authorities" (line 15). My last comment to him was the situation-based advice typical of the accommodationist; that is, that one's rhetoric depends on the occasion. If Takaro were writing the paper for a class, he would have to explain in the paper what he told me orally about the ambiguity of the Japanese words and characters to make sure that his conclusion had the proper impact. The common spelling errors that even native speakers make, such as "exsistence" (line 31) and "goverments" (line 42), I ignored in order to focus on more important areas.

Susan

Susan, the second student, was not an international student like Takaro, but had immigrated from Korea at the age of 11 with her family. She is a good example of someone who is neither L1 nor L2 but close to bilingual. She attended a U.S. junior high and high school in a school system with an excellent reputation for its language arts programs. Susan had also been through the university's ESL program. However, her fluency in speaking English was far ahead of her fluency in reading and writing, as can be seen from her brief piece in response to a writing center assignment called "A Sense of Place," which asked students to recall in detail a place that was important to their emotional development (see Appendix B).

As with Takaro's paper, my first response was rhetorically based, but in the form of written marginal and end-comments that simulated a conversation. I wrote the comments rather than reading aloud and commenting orally as I had with Takaro's essay, because Susan had not completed the piece until the very end of the lab period. To Susan's comment that she did not have a significant place "to show the part of me," which at the time struck me as sad and self-deprecatory, I wrote what I thought was an upbeat comment—that maybe her significant place was here in the United States in the Midwest. In retrospect, I realize this comment could be interpreted as a kind of push toward stronger emotional identification with the United States, in other words, toward assimilation. It seems that Takaro, Takaro's subject Kenji from *Two Motherlands*, and Susan all have one foot in each land.

My other marginal note was a "me-too" comment, common in responses in the lab and the writing/speaking program that train teachers to respond to discourse as an act of meaning-making. I wondered why in the United States the game is called "Red Light, Green Light," but in Korea "Red Light, Blue Light." My two endnotes are also me-too comments focused on childhood games ("Playing with friends under the street light is a great memory"), but the second endnote introduces an error pattern intimately attached to meaning that I wanted her to work on in the following session ("Is there a special place in the Midwest that you can write about today? Also, we could edit this paper for tenses to make sure it shows your games happening in the past").

I chose tense/time as a focus because it seemed like the easiest feature to work on successfully, and it was the most frequent error, as in line 13 ("want" vs. "wanted" and "should come" vs. "had to come") and line 24 ("tomorrow" vs. "the next day"). Susan had one article problem ("the part of me" vs. "a part of me" in line 5) and a faulty word form (the adverb "well" instead of the adjective "good" in line 29). During the next session, after we chatted briefly about childhood games, I reiterated the point about events happening in the past, and had Susan read the paper aloud slowly, pausing where something did not sound right, so she could make corrections. She experienced dissonance when reading over a few features and proceeded to correct them herself with some prompting. In the first few lines, for example, she deleted the words that did not belong—both instances of the word "in" (lines 1 and 2). She also added words that were missing—"little girl" (line 3) and "close enough" (line 6).

An assimilationist response could have been to circle all the errors and/or correct them myself, a strategy that could backfire and contradict the assimilationist goal to write in Standard English as soon as possible, because Susan would not be participating in the process of finding and correcting problems. A more separatist response would have been to avoid mentioning matters of form such as tense and omitted words, in the interest of working on Susan's fluency and development, clearly the discourse matter she needed to address first. Yet, I was concerned about Susan's success in her English class and therefore veered to the right on the response continuum. In the course of the semester, I discovered she was unsure about when and how to use relative clauses. In Korean, relative clauses are used before rather than after the head noun, as they are in English (Celce-Murcia & Larsen-Freeman, 1983).

Thanh

Thanh immigrated from Vietnam at the age of 17 to join his relatives who had come years earlier. He took 3 years of ESL classes in high school and 2 years in college before placing in a basic writing and speaking class for which students received no credit toward graduation. (This course is no longer offered.) Writing lab was a corequisite for this course. That is, students enrolled in the course were required to attend the lab twice a week. During these lab hours, they would work on in-lab writings such as the assignments Takaro and Susan did, but they would also discuss papers for the basic writing and speaking course. The classroom teachers often asked via conversation with lab teachers or marginal comments on students' papers that lab teachers address sentence-level concerns for which they lacked the time. Because the basic English class also involved making speeches and reading essays aloud to workshop them, it was particularly important to reduce the number of non-idiomatic features so that Thanh, who had difficulties with English pronunciation, could make himself understood to his classmates when he read his essays aloud.

Unlike Takaro and Susan's papers, which were written by hand in the lab, Thanh had written his paper on a computer in his dormitory. His "Awake to Reality" was a response to his first English essay assignment: "Write a personal narrative about a major event in your life that now seems to have some sort of larger meaning for you. Choose an event that is somehow connected to social or life issues. Based on your lived experiences, what insights into human behavior, feelings, or social problems can you offer?"

Several days before the essay was due, Thanh brought in an eight-page draft (see the excerpt in Appendix C). My strategy was an assimilationist one of reading the essay aloud with a pen in my hand and then helping Thanh "native-speakerize" the prose. He was especially interested in correcting his problems with word forms that his former ESL teacher had alerted him to—adjective versus verb versus noun. In between explanations of grammar and expression, we discussed the numerous personal and political issues in his papers; hence, language and content issues were discussed simultaneously. Unlike my more accommodating twice-through reading strategy with Takaro, I read Thanh's essay only once and did not prioritize which errors I wanted to correct and which I wished to leave as is, but addressed them as they occurred in my single oral reading. There was simply too much text and too little time.

For many reasons, including the interests and needs of Thanh, his teachers, and his classmates, my stance with his writing was generally more assimilative than my stance with Takaro or Susan, with whom I had worked 2 years earlier than Thanh. The entire academic year, after only three writing lab assignments, we worked on papers for Thanh's courses—English, History, and Biology. A writing-across-the-curriculum perspective, emphasizing the needs of an audience and adherence to the conventions of each discipline, contributed to this stance. The pedagogy of the lab and the writing and speaking program is moving in this assimilative writing-across-the-curriculum direction.

Thanh was also taking a course on the History of the Vietnam War. Because three of his four English papers and all of his history papers were about Vietnamese–U.S. relations and politics, we spent most of the semester discussing these issues from our differing but somewhat complementary perspectives. Thanh had lived through the Vietnam war and been educated about the U.S. role by the Communist government, even though his family was on the A.R.V.N. side supported by the United States. He was taking the history course to get a more complete picture of what had happened in his country and why, to try to distinguish the truth from propaganda on both sides. My more limited perspective was that of a U.S. anti–Vietnam War activist from the 1960s and 1970s educated by leftists who supported the Vietnamese Communists. Both of us had heard that some American GIs in Vietnam had been "baby butchers," but from different sources. Thanh needed to come to terms with the fact that, according to his teachers in Vietnam, he was now living in "the belly of the monster." Like Takaro and Kenji, politically and emotionally he was in the process of accommodating and synthesizing the politics and cultures of two motherlands.

In helping Thanh edit his paper, if he could not change a language feature himself (usually idiomatic expressions or more complex verb forms: "should be" to "should have been," line 60), I changed it for him, explained the change with a rule or principle, and went on to read the next sentence, unless he or I felt there was a matter of content or organization we had to discuss. The first lab period we worked on the first few pages of "Awake to Reality," changing features such as the direct to an indirect question in lines 5 and 6 and "from one of my ear to another ear" to the idiom in lines 21–22. The next period, we finished the sentence-level changes and we discussed the sudden death of a loved one. I expressed empathy with Thanh as my mother had also died without much warning. We also discussed the differences between Buddhist and Christian teachings. Like Takaro's essay, Thanh's was about a traumatic and devastating experience.

During the second lab period, I noticed that his essay, like many first drafts, was composed of two different stories—the death of his mother and the reform of his attitude toward schooling. The strands were related because his mother always encouraged him to educate himself. I suggested that he choose one story and develop it, even though the paper was due the next day. I told him that I preferred the story about his mother, because the story about discovering the value of education was a common one, especially for American students who comprised the majority of his class. The story of his mother's influence on him, however, would be unique and appeal more to his classmates and teacher, I thought. His English teacher, also a lab teacher, was in the lab preparing for the class at the time of our tutoring session, so I sent Thanh across the room to talk to her about which story to develop. They chose to focus on the mother's death. The next day Thanh handed in a significantly revised narrative, so powerful and beautifully written that the teacher wrote, "I feel educated by this essay. I don't often say that I feel honored to read a student paper; however, I do sincerely feel honored to read this one." Thanh told me that when he is upset he reads the essay over and over to comfort himself.

Had I only given feedback on the choice of story and not on grammar and expression, my stance would have veered toward separatist. An error analysis of the excerpted section shows that Thanh's errors occur in four categories. His most common error, and the one on which we concentrated for 2 semesters, was confusion between word forms, for example, the present progressive *-ing* form versus the root form ("wasting money" vs. "waste money" in lines 6 and 7); between an adjective and a noun ("hardworking" vs. "hard work," "modest" vs. "modesty" in line 71); an infinitive versus a gerund ("I regretted not listening to her," line 73); between a predicate adjective and a noun ("reincarnated" vs. "reincarnation," lines 78 and 79); and between a predicate adjective and a verb ("terrified" vs. "terrify," line 44). These are first language transfer problems, because Vietnamese does not have such categories.

Also common in Thanh's writing were syntax problems, such as the two phrases with "besides," lines 1 and 14; double subject, lines 53 and 82; tense problems—"now" instead of "then"; and numerous omissions of past tense markers ("feared," "died," "struggled," "deserved"). He also had several omitted articles, plurals, and incorrect prepositions ("in my neighborhood," "in bed"). He had few spelling problems except for the confusion of "stared" versus "started" (lines 1 and 64) and "quite" versus "quiet" (line 44). I did not recommend major changes in sentence patterns in "Awake to Reality," such as sentence-combining with subordination, changes that would have had more assimilative implications. Thanh tended to write in series of short sentences that induced a calming feeling and rhythm that reinforced the essay's theme of coming to terms with his mother's death and finding peace.

THE POLITICS OF RESPONSE TO WRITING

Responses to L2/ESL texts, such as those by Takaro, Susan, and Thanh, have political implications that can be acknowledged and explained; the nature of a particular response to a text and a writer suggest a stance toward linguistic and cultural assimilation. Indeed, the entire ESL teaching and learning enterprise, both inside and outside academia, is as politically charged as L1 teaching and learning; it is just that the political implications need to be openly articulated and discussed, as I have begun to do. ESL teachers need to be aware of the politics of their stances toward ESL writers and realize that a continuum of choices is available to them. They can choose responses based not only on the L2 development of ESL students, but also on the kinds of political messages their responses invariably suggest to students—messages about acculturation. Because it is impossible to separate language issues from their political contexts, and because the international and national macropolitics affect the micropolitics of the relationships among teacher, student, and text, it is important for L1, L2/ESL composition, or any endeavor concerned with English language teaching, to acknowledge and make explicit the political implications of responses to writing.

REFERENCES

Auerbach, E. (1992). Review. The challenge of the English Only movement. *College English, 54*, 843–851.

Auerbach, E., & Burgess, D. (1985). The hidden curriculum of survival ESL. *TESOL Quarterly, 19*, 475–495.

Berlin, J. (1988). Rhetoric and ideology in the writing class. *College English, 50*, 477–494.

Brannon, L., & Knoblauch, C. (1982). On students' rights to their own texts: A model of teacher response. *College Composition and Communication, 33*, 157–166.

Burt, M., & Kiparsky, C. (1972). *The gooficon: A repair manual for English.* Rowley, MA: Newbury House.

Celce-Murcia, M., & Larsen-Freeman, D. (1983). *The grammar book: An ESL/EFL teacher's course.* New York: Newbury House.

Chametzky, J. (1989–1990). Beyond melting pots, cultural pluralism, ethnicity—or deja vu all over again. *MELUS, 16*, 3–38.

de Valdez, D. D. (1990). *Amnesty: A real life approach, book 1.* Austin, TX: Steck Vaughn.

Erickson, F. (1984). School literacy, reasoning, and civility: An anthropologists's perspective. *Review of Educational Research, 54*, 525–546.

Farr, M. (1980). *Reactions to Ann Arbor: Vernacular Black English and education.* Arlington, VA: Center for Applied Linguistics.

Farr, M. (1990). Dialects, culture, and teaching the English language arts. In J. Jensen, J. Flood, D. Lapp, & N. J. Squire (Eds.), *Handbook of research in teaching the English language arts* (pp. 365–371). New York: Macmillan.

Fasold, R. W., & Shuy, R. W. (1970). *Teaching standard English in the inner city.* Washington, DC: Center for Applied Linguistics.

Freire, P. (1972). *Pedagogy of the oppressed.* New York: Herder & Herder.

Geertz, C. (1973). *The interpretation of cultures.* New York: Basic Books.

Giroux, H. (1983). *Theory and resistance in education.* South Hadley, MA: Bergin & Garvey.

Glazer, N., & Moynihan, D. P. (1963). *Beyond the melting pot: The Negroes, Puerto Ricans, Jews, Italians, and Irish of New York City.* Cambridge, MA: MIT Press.

Gordon, M. (1964). *Assimilation in American life.* New York: Oxford University Press.

Hinds, J. (1987). Reader vs. writer responsibility: A new typology. In U. Connor & R. B. Kaplan (Eds.), *Writing across languages: Analysis of L2 text* (pp. 141–152). Reading, MA: Addison-Wesley.

Horner, B. (1992). Re-thinking the "sociality" of error: Teaching editing as negotiation. *Rhetoric Review, 11,* 172–199.

Hourigan, M. (1994). *Literacy as social exchange.* Albany: SUNY Press.

Johns, A. (1990). L1 composition theories: Implications for developing theories of L2 composition. In B. Kroll (Ed.), *Second language writing: Research insights for the classroom* (pp. 24–36). Cambridge, England: Cambridge University Press.

Johns, A. (1993). Too much on our plates: A response to Terry Santos' "Ideology in Composition: L1 and ESL." *Journal of Second Language Writing, 2,* 83–88.

Kinneavy, J. (1971). *A theory of discourse.* New York: Norton.

Land, R., & Whitley, C. (1989). Evaluating second language essays in regular composition classes: Toward a pluralistic U.S. rhetoric. In D. Johnson & D. Roen (Eds.), *Richness in writing: Empowering ESL students* (pp. 284–293). New York: Longman.

Leki, I. (1992). *Understanding ESL writers: A guide for teachers.* Portsmouth, NH: Boynton/Cook.

Lu, M. Z. (1992). Conflict and struggle: The enemies or pre-conditions of basic writing? *College English, 54,* 887–913.

Phelps, L. (1989). Images of student writing: The deep structure of teacher response. In C. M. Anson (Ed.), *Writing and response* (pp. 37–67). Urbana, IL: National Council of Teachers of English.

Ross, L. (1937). *The education of Hyman Kaplan.* New York: Harcourt Brace.

Santos, T. (1992). Ideology in composition: L1 and ESL. *Journal of Second Language Writing, 1,* 1–15.

Selinker, L. (1972). Interlanguage. *International Review of Applied Linguistics, 10,* 209–231.

Severino, C. (1993). The sociopolitical implications of response to second language and second dialect writing. *Journal of Second Language Writing,* 2(3), 191–201.

Students' right to their own language. (1974). *College Composition and Communication, 25,* 1–18.

Swales, J. M. (1990). *Genre analysis: English in academic and research settings.* New York: Cambridge University Press.

Tollefson, J. W. (1989). *Alien winds: The reeducation of America's Indochinese refugees.* New York: Praeger.

Wallerstein, N. (1983). *Language and culture in conflict: Problem-posing in the ESL classroom.* Reading, MA: Addison-Wesley.

Wolfram, R. (1992). Toward a feminist shift in the ESL classroom. In M. Hawthorne & T. Williams (Eds.), *Essays by the feminist foreign language teaching collective* (pp. 1–14). Unpublished collection.

APPENDIX A: TAKARO'S WRITING

"Two Motherlands"

1 "Futatsu no sokoku"

"Two mother lands" is the most impressive novel I've read recently. The scenes are U.S., the pacific islands, and Japan. The main character is Kenji Amous, who is a second gneration Japanese immigrant. He was born in California, and his parent send him to Kagoshima, Japan, where they came from, for learning Japanese spirit and culture. So, Kenji became a complete bilingual. This character put him in a difficult situation in coming war between U.S. and Japan. Kenji got a job at a local Japanese news paper for Los Angels area, but the war broke out and he was sent to a kind of concentration camp only because he is a Japanese though he has an American citizenship. However, his attitude is always reasonable though he made a lot of dispute with the camp authorities. A U.S. interigence officer sees through his talent and reliability, and persauded Kenji to join the U.S. military as a Japanese teaching instructor, translator, interpretator, and interigence officer.

He is distressed about what his identity is and he joins the U.S. army after all. He knows Japan will lose sooner or later, he wanted to prevent Japan from its total corapse. He was assigned to the front of Pacific islands, and then, after the victory of the U.S., goes to Japan as a monitor of the translation of the Tokyo trial, which judges war criminals. From Kenji's view, this trial is not fair, and the American authority who occupies Japan try to use this trial politically to carry out the occupation. Kenji's distress and fatigue make him kill himself, at last.

The exsistence of such Japanese-Americans are not known well. Their role during the war was tremendous because they are the bridge and they know both sides. This extreme situation is not occuring in today's U.S.–Japan relation, but I guess some element is existing all the time. The concept or notion of "nation states" *separate* the people and their thoughts. The nations' borderlines are clearly on the map, but actually today's big multinational enterprises activity is crossing those lines all over the world. This novel is tragic because the main characters so clinged the notion of "nation" or "two governments." I prefer the world "mother land" to "state." This novel's title, two mother lands" don't tear him apart, but "two states" do.

APPENDIX B: SUSAN'S WRITING

"A Sense of Place"

My native soil could be Korea since I was born in there and raised in there; a beginning of my childhood. Since I was a little, I haven't been to any places except around seoul, and mostly around my neighborhood. I don't have a significant place to show the part of me. Maybe I haven't paid close attention to where I was and how it might have affected me.

I lived in a neighbohood with a lot of kids around my age. Without very much separation between boys and girls, we all gathered around and played active games, like hide and seek, tag, blue light, red light, etc.

Usually our playing time was set, after dinner. Around that hour everybody who want to play should come out by the post, which was close to my house. I remember with my brothers, I used to hurry up with the meal to be on time for a game. Even though, it was pretty dark, the electric light on the top of the post helped us to see where we were going. We could not go very far, for the safety that we always drew the line to never go over that line or else one is one of the game.

Each game, we had a policy, but it was fair enough to enjoy the game.

After the game, everybody would go back home and ready for school tomorrow.

The reason we set the time of playing at night was, everybody would be free by then. Finish school work or other things during the day and enjoy the free time after dinner while adults watched television for themselves. It was a pretty well neighborhood.

APPENDIX C: THANH'S WRITING

Excerpt From "Awake to Reality"

. . . When I stared third grade besides I went to public school, my mother sent me to private school to learn English, mathematics, physic, and chemistry. She kept sending me to private school until I got into high school. One day I asked my mother a stupid question that why she sent me to to Private school? and I said that she was waste money. She got angry and explained to me that I was luckier than her. When she was a young girl, ten years old, she really wanted to go to school, but my grandmother did not let her go to school. Instead my grandmother forced her to stay home to do the house work and took care of her sisters and brother. My mother told me that life would be misery and struggle if I did not want to learn. Besides going to school, My mother said to me that if I did not learn about life, other people would hurt me or fool me. She told me her stories when she was fifteen years old, how she reacted to her neighbor friends when they tried to beat her up. She tried to teach to me her experiences and how to react to friends and strangers. She always told me her stories over and over again, I just listened but I never thought about what my mother said. Whatever my mother said, it seemed to go from one of my ear to another ear. I did not care what my mother said because that time I was a young, stupid, innocent child. I did not care anything about how she had struggle in her life. I liked to have fun rather than just listen to my mother stories . . .

By the time I was seventeen years old, I still used to hang around with children four, five years old in my neighborhood. One day, the day was the most frighten in my life, I was playing game "cat catch mouse" with some four or five small boys at my neighborhood in the evening. My mother suddenly came to me, and told me that I had to follow her to the hospital to sign some papers. My father and brother were gone. I followed my mother to the hospital to see the doctor. The doctor told me that my mother had stomach cancer in the third state. She needed surgery in the next few days; if not, she would die very soon. The doctor explained to me that he could not tell my mother that she had stomach cancer because he fear that my mother might have a nerve break down that made her life more dangerous. When I talked to my mother, I guessed she already knew she had stomach cancer. I guessed by looking at her face; she was sad and very quite. I felt terrify, the color of my face had become white like corpse. I thought that if my mother died who would take care me; everything in the house she took care of it. From now on, my mother had to be in the hospital and waited for surgery. I could not eat, sleep, and I prayed for my mother. I visited her every other day. My mother understood my feeling. She tried to be happy but I knew she was very sad. After she had surgery, I thought my nightmare was over, but my mother day by day she got weaker and weaker.

Two weeks after surgery, she could not walk, she stayed on the bed waiting to die. My father and my aunt went everywhere try to find good herb medicine for her such as Chinese herbs, but it did not help my mother to recover. In the meantime, my family was ready to leave Vietnam for refuge in the United States. I should be happy but I felt said and worried. I skipped school almost everyday. I did not want to stay home to see my mother die . . . She passed away a few days later.

Since the day my mother died, I stared to think about why she died suddenly, why she had this fatal disease. I thought my mother should deserve to live because she was a hard-working mother, modest, lovely (she waited for my father seven years in the concentration camp and did not remarry). She raised my brother and me in a good care, and taught me many moral and virtues such as discipline, respect, patience, hardworking, modest, helping poor people, and so on. I recalled what my mother said to me when she was alive. Now I regretted about not to listen to her. I saw many good people died early but bad people live longer. My family believed in Buddhism, so I had learned some virtues and moral of Buddha's philosophy. Buddha said that life is struggle, people are born to get sick, to get old, and die like a circle, and people are reincarnation. Depending on what they do when they alive, if they practice good virtues, they will go to another world, enjoy a happy life and there is no suffering. Those who live without virtues and commit sins, they will pay their consequences such such as becoming a animal, living in a poor family, having a life of struggle. Is that true that in previous life I committed sins? I just wondered about myself, who I was, why I was born in the family that had too much trouble and struggle in life. My father was in a concentration camp when I was two years old. Somehow I remember about Buddha and his philosophy. I went to my mother's friend's house. I borrowed Buddha's book and read. I hoped that I would understand more about my life through Buddha's philosophy . . .

III

PARTICIPATION

14

Building on Community Strengths: A Model for Training Literacy Instructors

Elsa Auerbach
Joanne Arnaud
Carol Chandler
Ana Zambrano
University of Massachusetts, Boston

> *I love it. . . . After working as a housekeeper all day, working with cleaners and mops and things like that, it's like a refreshment to go to the school and teach and be with the students and offer something from myself, something that is not my strength, my legs. . . . For me, this is a refreshment.*
>
> —Estelita Matute, Intern,
> Bilingual Community Literacy Training Project

The refreshment that Estelita was talking about in this quote was her work teaching ESL to other immigrants who, like her, were struggling to make a new life for themselves in the United States. She was a participant in a project designed to train immigrants and refugees to become ESL and literacy instructors in their own communities. The project, which took place between 1989 and 1993 in the Boston area, was a university–community collaboration premised on the notion that the communities of adult ESL and literacy learners are rich with untapped resources. It was based on a "from the community–to the community" model in which community needs were addressed with community resources.

That there is an enormous need for adult literacy and ESL services within immigrant and refugee communities in the United States cannot be disputed. Adult education centers across the United States confront long waiting lists, overenrolled classes, inadequate resources, and pressure to move students through programs quickly. As an increasing number of adult students come with little prior education or first language literacy, teachers who are not familiar with students' languages and cultures often feel overwhelmed and underprepared.

At the same time, immigrant communities are rich with people who have strong educational backgrounds in their own languages and a desire to contribute to their communities. Because they have shared the experiences of coming to a new country, they are intimately familiar with the needs and concerns of literacy students as well as with issues of cultural and linguistic transition. Yet, they are often unable to make use of their strengths because of limitations in their English ability or lack of formal credentials; even as their English improves, it is difficult for them to find meaningful work or to access higher education. Thus, it is not uncommon for skilled, community-minded newcomers like Estelita to find themselves working on assembly lines or cleaning houses.

The project that Estelita participated in was based on the principle of drawing on the strengths of this group of immigrants and refugees to address the needs of those with minimal prior education, ESL, or first language literacy. Through a collaboration among three adult education programs, the University of Massachusetts/Boston, and the Boston Adult Literacy Fund, immigrants and refugees were trained to teach either first language literacy or ESL in their own communities following a participatory, Freire-inspired approach to literacy instruction and teacher training. This chapter describes the context of the project, its underlying philosophy and training design, as well as an assessment of what did and did not work.

THE CONTEXT

> *In the daytime, I felt like a robot, but at night I was a human being.*
> —Felipe Vaquerano, JMCS Intern and later HCC Mentor

The idea for the project was a response to realities confronting Boston community-based adult education sites, and was based on their long-standing commitment to promoting community leadership. The three participating sites were the Harborside Community Center (which serves a mixed, but largely Spanish-speaking population in East Boston); the Haitian Multi-Service Center (which serves Boston's Haitian community); and the Jackson-Mann Community Center (which serves a mixed ESL population in Allston-Brighton).

The most striking characteristic of the context of the Harborside Community Center (HCC) is the rapidly changing demographic situation in East Boston, where it is located. Over the past 10 years, 7,000 new Spanish-speaking residents have arrived in East Boston. According to the 1990 U. S. census data, over 25% of the population of East Boston are refugees and immigrants, many of them recent arrivals from Central America with limited English language abilities and few economic resources. In East Boston alone, 60% of the Hispanics responding to the 1990 U.S. census had not completed high school; an estimated 20% of the Hispanic adults seeking educational services had less than a fourth-grade education and had minimal Spanish literacy proficiency. Of the over 200 adult literacy students enrolled at Harborside annually, 54% are Spanish speaking. Thus, although the learner population at Harborside is a mixed one, it is the central place in East Boston where Spanish speakers go for educational services.

The HCC Adult Literacy Program has been offering basic education services since 1983. It provides several levels of ESL classes, as well as reading, writing, and math for native English speakers, from basic literacy levels through high school equivalency. The HCC has long been committed to training, hiring, and promoting staff from the communities of the learners. Its staff has included several language minority ESL teachers as well as bilingual aides and bilingual volunteer tutors. In addition to ESL, the HCC identified the need for first language literacy classes in the late 1980s. A Khmer literacy program was initiated in 1989; furthermore, a previously hidden population of immigrants with limited educational backgrounds (many of whom were Central American) began to enroll in classes in order to meet requirements for amnesty. Thus, Harborside saw the need to start a Spanish literacy component for the growing numbers of learners who might otherwise have been relegated to the waiting lists or never come for classes at all. This need set the stage for the HCC's participation in the collaboration described in this chapter.

The Haitian Multi-Service Center (HMSC) has a long history of providing human and education services, as well as promoting community development and leadership in the Haitian community. Its mission is based on a "Haitians serving Haitians" model. Over the past decade there has been rapid growth in the number of Haitians living in the greater Boston area, making it presently one of the largest Haitian population centers in the United States. Current estimates place the Haitian population in the state of Massachusetts at over 60,000; the majority of Haitians—up to 25,000—live in the Dorchester and Mattapan areas of Boston. The HMSC, located geographically in the heart of this community, is the largest human service agency serving Haitians in Massachusetts.

The HMSC provides a broad range of services; in addition to adult education, it provides preschool services, prenatal care, AIDS outreach and education, refugee resettlement, legal services, family counseling, and translation services. Adult education is its largest component, providing morning, afternoon, and evening classes with two levels of Kreyol (Creole) literacy, four levels of ESL, and a high school diploma program. The HMSC has been committed to the hiring of bilingual/bicultural staff since its inception. In the mid-1980s, the Adult Education Program established a 2-year Bilingual Teacher Training Project to address the need for increased recruitment, training, and hiring of bilingual Haitian adult education teachers. In addition, the HMSC has worked extensively with local colleges and universities to recruit Haitian undergraduates for internship and work-study positions.

The primary difference between the Jackson-Mann Community School (JMCS) in Allston-Brighton and the other project sites is the incredible diversity of ethnic and linguistic groups represented in its classes. According to the Boston Redevelopment Authority Boston Household Survey for 1985, 20% of households in Allston-Brighton identify a language other than English as their primary language; early indications from the 1990 census suggest that this percentage is growing. The population served in Allston-Brighton is predominantly low income, including local public housing residents, AFDC recipients, and the working poor.

Classes at the JMCS reflect the diversity of the area's population: The program serves students from 25 to 30 different ethnic groups. An estimated 5% of the adults in the ESL classes received less than a fourth-grade education in their home countries. Because classes are so linguistically mixed, ESL is the only viable instructional option. The program has four components: ESL, ABE (Adult Basic Education), GED, and EDP (an external degree program for high school equivalency). Like the other sites, the JMCS has promoted leadership from within the learners' communities for many years, training students as community advocates as well as hiring language minority teachers and teaching assistants.

Based on the conditions at each of the sites and their histories of developing community leadership, the idea for a university–community collaboration arose in the late 1980s. At that time, the HMSC and UMass/Boston worked together to write a proposal for a collaborative project to train bilingual community literacy instructors, drawing on a model already established at the HMSC. The collaboration was funded from 1989 to 1992 by the Office of Bilingual Education and Minority Language Affairs of the U.S. Department of Education as the Bilingual Community Literacy Training Project (BCLTP); and, from 1992 to 1993, by the National Institute for Literacy as the Community Training for Adult and Family Literacy (CTAFL) Project.[1]

[1]The Boston Adult Literacy Fund (BALF), an organization that secures funding for the Boston adult literacy community, was the grant recipient and fiscal administrator for the CTAFL. The project coordinator was a faculty member at the University of Massachusetts at Boston (UMass/Boston).

The basic design of the project was to train interns to teach literacy in accordance with the needs identified at each site. Thus, the project trained interns to teach Spanish literacy at the HCC, Haitian Creole literacy and ESL at the HMSC, and ESL at the JMCS. At each site, there was a mentor who coordinated the program, modeled the instructional approach, and mentored the interns. In addition, all of the project participants came together for regular training workshops at UMass.[2] The mentors were experienced ESL teachers from the communities of the learners who had been ESL learners and gone through many of the same kinds of experiences as their students. The interns, likewise, were people from the communities of the learners who came from a range of backgrounds: Some had been teachers in their home countries but had no U.S. credentials and were doing menial work; others were advanced ESL students from the sites who had demonstrated leadership qualities or were undergraduate students from UMass/Boston who wanted to give something back to their own communities. Most held other jobs, working as security guards, office workers, and assemblers, or delivering pizzas, cleaning houses, washing dishes, and, in some cases, working at the adult learning centers (as receptionists, etc.). Interns worked 10 hours a week, generally 8 hours in the classroom and 2 hours in training, and were paid a stipend of about $9.00 an hour. Details of the training design are elaborated next.

PHILOSOPHY AND RATIONALE

> *The students' lives are the curriculum.*
>
> —Intern, HCC

The project had many aspects: administration, training, teaching, evaluation, and collaboration. Underlying our work in each of these areas were certain common underlying philosophical principles—an implicit set of beliefs that guided our work. The key word here is *implicit*: Because each of the project participants began with different backgrounds and experiences, we had different philosophical starting points. Thus, the principles described here emerged from and were forged through our work together. These beliefs underlay the rationale for both the training of interns and the literacy instruction; yet, although the rationale arose directly from the concrete conditions, needs, and initiatives at the sites, we were by no means alone in arriving at these perspectives. There is substantial justification for each of the key tenets of the model from a wide range of other sources—

[2]During the BCLTP, these were monthly workshops that met for 3 hours on Saturday mornings; during the CTAFL, they were biweekly 2-hour Friday afternoon sessions.

from adult learning, language acquisition, and literacy theory and research, as well as from the work of other practitioners and projects both nationally and internationally (see Auerbach et al., 1996). Here we briefly sketch some of the support for our beliefs without including specific references.

The starting point for working with adult learners is respecting their knowledge and their experiences; students learn best when content is related to their own experiences. When adults come to ESL or literacy classes, it's uncomfortable for them, at their age, not to know how to read and write, or not to be able to express themselves in English. It is important to show them their own capacity to learn by drawing out what they already know and using their stories and experiences to teach them. This view of literacy is congruent with recent perspectives from adult learning theory suggesting that adults learn best when instruction is contextualized in their life experiences, related to their real needs, and when they are involved in determining instructional goals and content. They are able to do more when learning builds on what they know. This means that the curriculum comes from within the classroom and draws on learners' cultural and personal histories; as such, it may include telling, writing, and reading stories about their own countries and cultures. Thus, it is critical that instruction be meaning centered rather than mechanical, and that content be relevant to the life experiences of learners.

The relationship between teachers and students must be one of mutual respect in which they each learn from each other. This means breaking away from the traditional approach in which the teacher knows everything and it is his or her job to give this knowledge to the students. If the teacher is seen as the only one with something to offer, learners will feel less comfortable. In order to implement this goal, the traditional concept of curriculum development must be changed; in the traditional model, the teacher identifies what is to be covered in a course (e.g., skills, grammar, competencies) before coming in contact with students; instruction, then, is a process of finding the most efficient way of transmitting this information from teacher to students. In place of this model, the concept of learner-centered and emergent curriculum development is becoming increasingly widespread. The new model involves collaborative discovery of learners' goals and concerns, with constant dialogue and negotiation at every step of the way. This participatory model for adult ESL literacy offers a systematic process for building curriculum around learners' lived experiences and social realities.

Literacy practices vary according to cultures and social contexts. Because literacy is more than just a set of discrete, mechanical skills or functional competencies, teaching must take into account culture-specific literacy practices. It must focus on socially significant literacy uses in learners' lives. This belief is supported by the theoretical paradigm, which views literacy practices as varying according to cultures, contexts, purposes, and participants. Because learners' familiarity with the content and forms of texts shape their reading processes, culture-specific aspects of language and literacy use must be taken into account in curriculum development, and teachers must be aware of learners' culture-specific discourse practices and literacy uses.

Literacy education means more than just teaching students to read and write. Newcomers face many problems: being unable to find work, dealing with discrimination on the job, raising children in a new country, maintaining communication with their families at home, and more. Education should enable participants to understand the social nature of these problems (rather than seeing them as personal problems or inadequacies) and to work together in finding ways to address them. Current literacy theory suggests that literacy is meaningful for learners to the extent that it enables them to better understand and shape their world. In the approach proposed by Freire (1970), instruction starts with learners' social reality, providing a context for analyzing and taking action on it. If literacy acquisition is linked with this kind of critical analysis, it can enable learners to challenge the social conditions that disempower them. Thus, literacy instruction should invite learners to explore the social issues they confront.

Students' first language should be seen as a resource, not an obstacle, for literacy or ESL acquisition. Beginning literacy students can use their existing oral language as the basis for learning how to read and write; they can use first language (L1) literacy as a bridge to ESL. There is increasing evidence that adult ESL students with little prior education or L1 literacy often have difficulty in ESL classes; the existing studies of L1 literacy programs suggest that L1 literacy is a critical stepping stone to ESL. Starting with the L1 reduces anxiety and enhances the affective environment for learning, takes into account sociocultural factors, facilitates incorporation of learners' life experiences, and allows for learner-centered curriculum development. Most importantly, it allows language to be used as a meaning-making tool. This means that teachers must be able to draw on learners' linguistic resources.

People who share the culture, language, and life experiences of the learners are uniquely qualified to teach them. Although the idea of hiring community teachers who may not have either traditional higher education or teaching credentials may seem unusual in the U.S. context, it is not uncommon in other parts of the world. Preliminary work in the United

States suggests that this model is highly relevant for this context as well; centers participating in this project have found it to be a successful model for more than a decade. Taken together, the previously discussed principles suggest why community teachers are particularly suitable for ESL or L1 classes: Their shared linguistic and cultural background can enable them to draw on culturally familiar discourse forms; their common cultural, political, and historical knowledge base can be integrated into learning; and their experience as immigrants or refugees, struggling with issues of transition to the new culture, can be a powerful tool for participatory curriculum development. Furthermore, their own experience facing linguistic and cultural challenges enables them to act as role models for students and resources for colleagues trying to understand the issues facing language minority communities. As one of the mentors in our project said, "It is very important that we speak the learners' language and we have suffered all the problems they have, because in a way, they can come to us and tell us their problems and we will understand because we have passed by them. We have suffered them."

TRAINING DESIGN

Training was a chain: We saw things that happened in the classrooms and we talked about them in the training meetings.

—Julio Midy, Mentor, Haitian Multi-Service Center

The most important underlying principle guiding our approach to training interns was that it should model our approach to teaching adult learners. This meant that training, like teaching, should be participatory. The knowledge and experience of interns should be valued; mentors and interns should learn from each other, and training should emphasize dialogue, sharing, and investigation rather than transmitting knowledge or prescribing teaching practices. Again, this approach to training is supported by models of leadership training internationally, particularly in the popular education movements of Asia, Africa, Latin America, and Canada. In order to implement this approach, the training design included three components: classroom-based mentoring, during which interns observed and worked alongside experienced mentors; site-based teacher sharing meetings, during which the mentors and interns at each site shared planning, issues, and concerns; and university-based workshops, during which project participants developed a conceptual framework for teaching, explored classroom tools, and shared experiences with participants from other sites as well as with facilitators. These components were closely related, starting with and going back to what was happening in the classrooms. The teacher-sharing meetings focused on what the interns and mentors were doing with students; the issues that arose in the teacher-sharing meetings were, in turn, brought into the training workshops. Throughout, we attempted to model the participatory process as follows:

- We started by trying to make interns feel comfortable in the training.
- We didn't tell interns what to do. We tried to challenge their idea that training meant learning techniques. Our goal was not the transfer of skills.
- We tried to let the interns participate or talk more than us.
- Most of what happened in the workshops came from the interns. We incorporated their concerns and used their experiences as examples.
- We tried to debunk the myth that, we as "trainers," were experts who had all the answers. Our view was that everyone teaches, everyone learns.
- We didn't give solutions to problems, but instead created space for figuring them out.

In practice, applying these principles meant developing the training workshops through interaction with interns, rather than predetermining a curriculum that specified skills, competencies, or topics. Of course, we started with an overall sense of the direction, content, and processes for the workshops. By the end of the workshops, we hoped that interns would have a conceptual framework for participatory literacy/ESL instruction as well as a sense of how to develop curricula based on themes from learners' lives. We hoped they would be comfortable with the following steps of this participatory curriculum development process, which we modeled in the development of the workshops:

- *Investigation:* Assessing needs based on the lived experience of participants, not on the analysis of outside "experts."
- *Dialogue and reflection:* Sharing experiences and relating them to an analysis of the broader social context.
- *Problem-posing:* Addressing problems or concerns from participants' day-to-day reality through a collective sharing of strategies.
- *Action:* Taking action based on strategies developed through dialogue and problem-posing.
- *Evaluation:* Reflecting on what was and was not productive, and why.

To implement this process, we always tried to begin workshops with participants' experiences, eliciting what they had done in the intervening weeks since we had seen each other. We then introduced new information or concepts through a presentation, creating space for participants to relate it to their own experiences. We went on to do some kind of hands-on, participatory activity to demonstrate a tool that interns could use with students. We then discussed how the interns might use what they had learned at their sites (an action plan). Finally, we elicited feedback and suggestions for future workshops.

Possible topics were determined in a number of ways. Right from the start we tried to get interns' input about their own needs and goals by asking them why they were participating in the project and what they hoped to get out of it. As we proceeded, we also listened for specific issues, requests, or problem areas that came up during the course of workshops and follow-up evaluations. In some cases, interns themselves identified problems (e.g., they wanted to focus on finding materials for native language literacy). In others, we identified issues through our own observations of their practice; for example, mentors noted at one point that interns needed to refine their approach to responding to errors; at another point, an intern cut off a heated dialogue among students because he didn't know how to integrate it with literacy work. Thus, subsequent workshops focused on responding to errors and facilitating dialogue.

Once the topic for a workshop had been selected, we discussed objectives in greater detail. The bottom line questions were: Why is this workshop important? What do we hope that interns will come away with from this session? The answers to these questions then helped us determine activities. After developing some objectives, we brainstormed activities that would allow us to get at the topic interactively and to model the process or tool being presented. If we weren't sure how to begin planning, we sometimes started just by talking about our own practice as teachers in dealing with the topic at hand. We then tried to generalize and identify aspects of the topic that we should explore in the workshop. Later, we specified the order of activities and logistical details. Following this process, some of the topics that workshops explored were: the conceptual framework (what is a participatory approach?); listening for themes in learners' lives ("Ways In" to student issues: photos, charts, and maps); the language experience approach; dialogue journals; making and using codes; theater and sociodrama; photostories; games; linking literacy with action; finding, using, and developing materials; and assessing student progress.

TAKING STOCK: WHAT WORKED AND WHAT DIDN'T

> *I feel much more strongly than I felt before about having people from the communities themselves be part of the staff—and not on a volunteer basis!*

> *For myself, the project has opened up a whole new panorama, but it has also made me realize how little we are really appreciated.*
>
> —Ana Zambrano, Mentor, JMCS

It is not possible to summarize the richness of experience that this project yielded in a few short pages. In the remainder of the chapter, we focus on three things: first, some of the issues we struggled with in both training and teaching; second, the impact of the project as expressed by the participants themselves; and third, some of the challenges entailed in promoting this model.

A cyclical recurrence of training issues emerged in the workshops. Some of these issues pertained to the general approach to teaching adult literacy, some to the workshops themselves, and some to the relationship between training and teaching. These issues can best be characterized by questions that interns asked as they moved from traditional, teacher-centered, and mechanical conceptions of teaching to a participatory one.

"What method are we supposed to use?" Some interns started out wanting us to tell them exactly what to do in the classroom: They were looking for a method or techniques that could be applied directly from the training to teaching. Although they expected us to tell them the "right way" to teach, we wanted them to experiment, discover, reflect, adapt, and figure out for themselves what would make sense in their own contexts. We had to find a balance between establishing a guiding conceptual framework and providing practical, hands-on content that they could use immediately.

"Where's the curriculum?" Similarly, some of the interns felt strongly that the project or the sites should have given them a curriculum or a list of what was to be "covered" at each level. At the same time, their accounts of successful lessons often involved not following a preplanned sequence of activities, but instead responding to student issues that arose spontaneously or as a result of a trigger activity. Thus, there was a tension between the legitimate need of new teachers for a guiding curriculum and the notion that the most effective curricula are those that integrate ongoing student issues and emerge through negotiation with students.

"What do the experts say?" A related issue was the sense, among some interns, that outside experts had the "answer," that there was some external body of knowledge about how to teach literacy the right way. At times, some felt that the information of an outside expert was more valuable than that constructed by the group. Yet, very often the workshops that the interns were most engaged in were the ones in which they shared their own experiences and practices with each other. Thus, one of our tasks became demystifying our role and challenging the idea that "experts know better."

"Why are we talking about unemployment? This is not a job agency." Because many of the interns had experienced only a very traditional, teacher-centered, and skills-based approach in their own education and had learned to read using a decontextualized, bottom-up phonics method, there was some resistance to a meaning-centered approach, particularly for teaching initial literacy. It was a struggle for some interns to see dialogue about student concerns as relevant to literacy education or as a possible context within which to teach skills. A central issue was how to make the transition from mechanical to participatory approaches.

Teaching Issues

Many of the issues we dealt with in training were mirrored in the classrooms with adult learners: Just as interns had started by expecting a methods-oriented training, students started by expecting a mechanical, teacher-centered approach to literacy and a grammar-based approach to ESL. Some of these teaching issues are characterized here by quotes from students:

"What are we going to do with these pictures?" Many of the initial issues centered around students' expectations of schooling and the transition to a participatory approach. Students often had the idea that school meant sitting in rows, having a textbook, doing exercises from worksheets, speaking only when called on, listening and copying, taking tests, and so on. Responding to pictures, for example, seemed inappropriate to them. Some interns as well felt that until beginning literacy students had "mastered" the basics of decoding (through a rote learning approach), they could not do meaningful work. Mentors addressed this by slowly demonstrating what could be learned by integrating mechanical and participatory approaches.

"Why don't I have an American teacher?" Some students (especially ESL students) were disconcerted to find that their teacher wasn't a North American native speaker of English. They felt that they could learn better from someone whose English was "perfect." Interns and mentors responded to this in a variety of ways: by inviting students to try the class with the option of changing if they didn't think they were learning, by inviting native speakers to class on a regular basis, by explicitly discussing variations in dialect and pronunciation, and by discussing when "correct" pronunciation is and isn't important.

"Where's the book?" A key issue was the desire of both interns and students for textbooks. However, most of those available, especially for L1 literacy, were not appropriate in terms of content or level: They were often geared toward a non-U.S. context, were too overtly political or too mechanical, too elementary or too advanced. Mentors and interns developed a variety of other strategies to address the need for materials: We had two workshops focused on authentic materials for adults; interns used learner-generated materials as they became more comfortable with the participatory approach, and tools like the language experience approach and dialogue journals. Even so, both the Spanish and Creole literacy teachers continued to feel the need for good Ll texts.

"You're the teacher—you're supposed to tell us what to do." Students often initially viewed the teacher as the authority who was supposed to transmit information, ask questions, correct students' errors, enforce discipline, and have the answer to any question. Some students were initially uncomfortable with the idea of helping to select topics. They felt that a good teacher should know what to do without having to ask. As interns developed more structured ways of eliciting themes and issues, students became more comfortable about contributing their ideas and experiences.

"What's the right answer?" A related issue concerns students' notions of what counts as "real" knowledge. Often students didn't see their own knowledge or opinions as valid; they thought the teacher was the only one with the "right" answers. This meant that some were uncomfortable with dialogue or helping each other. At times, tensions arose when students answered each other's questions or corrected one another—some students were uncomfortable with disagreeing, or debating ideas, having come from political contexts where stating one's true beliefs was dangerous. Teachers addressed this by explaining that they didn't have all the answers, by talking about the participatory approach, and by turning students' questions back to the group.

"Homeless people are lazy." Once interns felt comfortable facilitating dialogues, they began to wonder whether they should give their own opinions or keep silent. For example, if students made statements with which they strongly disagreed (e.g., that homeless people are lazy or that women who are abused deserve it), should they intervene? Some mentors felt that our responsibility as teachers is not to express our views because it will silence students. Others said that sometimes you have to participate as a person, not a teacher, and this means saying what you think. Strategies that the mentors suggested were to express one's views without imposing them, and to ask questions that prompted people to think more deeply about their own statements or views.

"Let's stop talking and do our work." Although dialogue was seen as conversation practice in ESL classes, in L1 literacy classes students sometimes felt that open-ended discussion was not "real work." It was seen as a diversion from, rather than part of, the lesson. Interns, too, sometimes saw it as outside the curriculum, and didn't always know how to link it to literacy acquisition. A related dilemma was whether to stick to lesson plans or go with the flow when something interesting came up. As interns learned to connect discussion with more structured learning activities and acquired tools for responding to spontaneous dialogue, students began to see these diversions as legitimate.

"I can't concentrate. I'm too distracted." Often students come to class preoccupied with worries that blocked their participation. Some interns initially tried to get students to leave their problems outside the classroom door (telling them to stop talking about things unrelated to the lesson). Later, they became increasingly skilled at integrating these concerns into the lessons, asking questions like: What makes it hard for you to come to class? What makes it hard for you to concentrate? From these questions, they developed LEA stories, journals, and so on.

"It's embarrassing to talk about breasts." In some cases, the issues themselves were difficult to talk about because of cultural taboos. For example, as students began to talk about health care, the reproductive system, and breast cancer, the interns found themselves having to explain vocabulary and concepts that were embarrassing in mixed gender classes. In many cases, they dealt with this by laughing and using humor to dispel tensions.

"If we wanted to learn about war, we would have stayed in El Salvador." An additional dilemma concerned how to connect literacy work with the social or political context of students' lives. Students often explicitly resisted political discussions when they were initiated by teachers; however, over and over, our experience was that they became very engaged when discussion of the same issues emerged spontaneously or in the context of language work.

There were several key processes that helped us to address both training and teaching issues. The first was combining traditional with innovative approaches: In the training sessions, we included both presentations by "experts" and modeled participatory approaches, reflecting on both; likewise, in classes, more mechanical approaches to literacy instruction were combined with more meaning-centered participatory ones. Second, we did problem-posing with participants about issues that arose in training or teaching, involving the learners in figuring out how to address the issues. Third, we involved participants in curriculum development: We invited interns to help select topics for workshops, and invited students to identify themes they wanted to explore in class. The fourth strategy was modeling: The facilitators modeled participatory tools, giving interns and/or learners a chance to participate in using and evaluating them. Finally, we incorporated explicit discussion about ways of learning, so that interns and learners could compare various learning experiences and their responses.

THE IMPACT OF THE PROJECT

The project gives you a ladder; it opens doors.
—Felipe Vaquerano, JMCS Intern and HCC Mentor

The impact of our work cannot be assessed only by looking at "outcomes" or quantifiable changes. Our assessment took many forms, from detailed documentation of training to qualitative assessment of changes among students (see Auerbach et al., 1996). Among the most revealing indications of the impact of the project were interviews with participants and observation of their practice at various points during the project. The following discussion presents selected quotations from these interviews to give a flavor of how interns and mentors themselves saw the impact of project.

One of the biggest changes among interns was their gradual appreciation for the participatory approach not only to teaching, but to the training process itself. One of the interns said at the beginning of the project, "I want to get techniques"; however, gradually interns began to embrace a participatory model of training, as the following quote indicates:

> To tell you the truth, in the beginning, when I started to go to the training, I was expecting that you—would give us the materials and show us the way to teach. That was my idea. When I started going, I thought, gee, this was different. Why did they come with these different ideas, why didn't they tell us "you have to do this and that"? . . . The more I went to the trainings, I really enjoyed it. I saw the different ways you were introducing . . . not the way we are used to doing it: you do this and you follow. You gave us the opportunity to grow—not to depend on somebody else. The workshops gave us the ideas and we wanted to apply them. At least they give you the ideas, and it's up to you. . . . So, I think it works better that way. In my opinion, it's been wonderful. I look through the notes and when

> I read them, I know I can apply them. If I think it would be too difficult, I try to do it another way where it would be more simple and they [the students] would understand. But the ideas are great. . . . I didn't expect that in the beginning.

Changes in interns' views of the training (their own ways of learning) led to changes in their views of teaching. They no longer saw their task as one of transmitting skills or knowledge to learners, but began to see the ways in which they could draw knowledge from students and work in a relationship of mutual respect. As one intern said, "My job is not to give them knowledge, they're not empty—here is some knowledge in them which is not conventional knowledge that we need to develop." Another put it this way:

> I feel like family with them. It's like I belong to them. It's not like, "I'm here to teach you and you have to learn." I think they feel comfortable with us too. You can tell the way they express themselves. . . . You don't go over there and say, "Well I'm here just to teach." No, you tell them, "If you think that we're not teaching right let us know; that's what we're here for because YOU people are the teachers," I tell them. "I'm the student, I'm learning from you guys." And it is true, you learn from them. They learn from you, but you learn from them too because their ideas sometimes work more than your ideas.

The interns began to see their role as one of posing rather than solving problems: "[The students'] judgment is good; they might not be able to read and write, but when they talk, their logic is good. . . . You learn that you can't impose on adults, you have to exchange with them."

Interns' conceptions of themselves as teachers changed as well; rather than seeing their job as one of implementing a predetermined curriculum or following a lock-step method, they began to see themselves as teachers who develop curriculum through interaction with students:

> You cannot transplant, you cannot think, "Hey, E. tried this, and I am gonna try it in my class because it worked for her." No, it doesn't work like this. You have to know your own students . . . to really get something good out of them. There aren't any specific tools that will always work because each learner has his own problem and I am supposed to find it. What I learned from all those workshops—here is a problem and you as a teacher are like an investigator—you have to find it and once you get it, then you say, "This is how I'm going to work." The context of the students is very important.

Interns began to adapt training activities to their own contexts, taking the initiative to develop lessons and introducing new activities. The following excerpt from workshop minutes shows how one intern developed her own tools for learner assessment:

> The dialogue journal is a good process of teaching because you get in communication with the students. You develop ideas from them. You are on the same level with them, and when you are on the same level with the students, they feel comfortable to express their ideas or their thinking. If they write and you only correct, without giving them any response, it will be like STOP—no more ideas. When you respond and tell your students to respond, then you keep on going, getting ideas from it.

Similarly, interns became more comfortable both with developing their own plans and with going with the flow. "Now I have more tools. I can have a topic and I can take it in any direction I want. At the beginning, no, I just got the book and did it the way it was. Now I have this new skill because of the experiences that we have shared. I don't even have to look at readings or books. I just get the topic and I can change it the way I want."

The project also led to changes in interns' confidence about their own skills and their views of possible job futures. Several who had been working in factories or as housekeepers decided to continue their education and enrolled as undergraduates at UMass. Some who had started this project as a sideline were surprised at its impact. As one said:

> I didn't think I would be so involved. Just to think about further education or to change my field—I didn't expect that. I thought that it would be something on the side. I thought I might pursue another field, but not education. . . . But I'm really pleased that I participated in this project because it helped me in myself to find a career. . . . I tried what I learned in the project and it really worked. And that left me with the feeling "All right, I'm going to try other things. . . ." That brought me confidence.

Another said: "I think my plans have changed because I feel like I want to learn more things. I want to go back to school. I have to see other alternatives because this whole project made me realize that I need to know a lot of things that I don't know, explore things that I haven't explored."

One of the most powerful changes concerned interns' sense of connection to other people and to their own communities, as the following quotation indicates:

> [The teaching] makes me change in my relationship with other people. By listening you think more, you think more of other people, you become more a listener, you listen more to people . . . that does change me in a sense

> that I'm always encouraging other people to be more involved in the Haitian community. At first I didn't care, but now I take time just to get people to volunteer and to speak with them about the project. . . . And it not only changed me but other people told me, "I can see that you are doing something useful or something wonderful" and that is really encouraging.

It was not only the interns who developed a stronger sense of their own leadership capacities. The new roles that mentors took on during the project shaped their views of themselves and their relationships as well. In the following quotation, Ana Zambrano revealed how she became a more reflective teacher as a result of her work as a mentor:

> Before I was a mentor, I wasn't as conscious or rational in what I was doing as a teacher. I think the best way to learn about something is by trying to teach it. When you try to teach somebody else, you have to be clear in what you are doing and you have to have a way of explaining it. I've gotten more reflective about what I do. When you reflect on just about anything, there is a change, a change in attitude, a change in style. By attending those workshops, I always have something new that I learned. Eh—that doesn't mean all of them work; some don't work, but most of them work. . . . What's important about it is—from one thing you learn, you can create another thing.

Another mentor, Julio Midy, spoke about learning how to provide leadership without being a boss:

> In a sense, my participation in this project is a continuity with my life, but at the other side, it's also a change because it gives me what we call the sense of responsibility because I am the person in charge. I have to think about the project, I have to think about what the interns are doing. I don't want to sound bossy, but what's important, I have to keep contact with them, to know if they have any problem, if there's anything that they need. This gives me an opportunity to evaluate myself as a responsible person, to evaluate myself if I can deal with people without letting them feel that I am their boss, which I don't want.

Mentors also came to appreciate their own ability to train other people, as Ana said:

> The workshops gave me the framework for solving the problems and also for guiding interns. To some extent, I think before you enter this kind of project, there are certain mystiques, a certain mysticism, and as you get into it, as you participate, you understand and get at peace with it, less afraid. For me, the project demystified the training part. I have learned to be a supervisor without being a boss. I come forward more with ideas. I

> think that the way I demystified the training was that I understood that there were things that l knew that had some value.

For Felipe Vaquerano, who had started as a learner at the JMCS, then became an intern there, and was later selected as a mentor at the HCC, the project not only led him in a new career direction, but allowed him to become a role model for others:

> For me, being a factory worker when I began, I thought that was the job that I would do for the rest of my life. I didn't know anyone to help me. Since then, my life has changed. The project gave me the opportunity to use my skills, not just my hands. This is the other me. I can be a role model for people who want to do something. People look at me and say, "Well, if he did it, why can't I do it?" They see role models and they want to improve, to get better in their lives.

CHALLENGES

> *This model has the potential to be a powerful model, but it can only work if it is adequately supported.*
>
> —Ana Zambrano, JMCS Mentor

When we started this project, our goals were to develop and implement a participatory training curriculum, to promote native language literacy instruction, and to provide meaning-centered, culturally sensitive ESL and literacy instruction. The key to achieving each of these goals was to enhance the leadership of community literacy instructors. Our project might be called a success story in many ways: It was a story of growth and transformation for many of the interns and mentors, and it was a story of inspiration and hope for many adult learners.

Yet, it was also a story of struggle. As one of the interns said, "This project is like a flower. We have planted the seed, the flower is starting to grow, and now we are cutting it." The single biggest obstacle, not only to our efforts, but nationally in terms of adult literacy provision, is inadequate and unstable funding. We were funded as a demonstration project, and lauded for the work we did; yet, securing ongoing funding to continue the work, extend the model, and implement its positive features has been an uphill battle. As is the case with many demonstration projects, once the funding ended, finding support to institutionalize the model became an enormous burden for the centers. In the case of our project, the native language literacy components have been able to piece together funding to continue in a scaled-down way; many of the interns have continued teaching or proceeded to other leadership positions within their own communities. But the sites continue to struggle to ensure the survival of the positive aspects of the model.

Another struggle that should not be minimized was that of working collaboratively. Collaborations are often seen as cutting-edge initiatives, favored by funders. Yet, it is important not to romanticize them. There are enormous institutional pressures that make collaboration difficult. Each participating agency needs to safeguard its future, and agencies are often pitted against each other in the competition for scarce resources. The need to survive in a climate of cutbacks and reduced support makes it difficult for agencies to find the time to work together. On top of this, of course, are the inevitable conflicts among differing agendas, personalities, and priorities. As with our struggles in addressing training and teaching issues, a great deal of learning has come from struggling with these issues of funding and collaboration.

Thus, our project lies somewhere between a story of success and a story of struggle: It is, most of all, a story of possibility. Clearly, the project has demonstrated what can be done when the rich resources of language minority communities are recognized and promoted. The project started with needs and initiatives that originated in the participating community-based organizations, and perhaps one of its most powerful contributions is the fact that participants have gone back to their communities, not only with skills, but with the commitment to make changes. We end with a quote from Estelita, thinking back on what she had gained from the project and where she wanted to go with it:

> Now I would like to do more things—I feel more motivated to do things for women, for Latina women, because now I see that there are not barriers if you want to do something with all your heart. I think our women need hope, they need to set up goals. I feel like a kind of role model. I feel so angry that young women could do so many things, but they don't have this hope, they don't have this motivation. Especially when we are in a strange country that's very hard, new for us, we have to try to shine in a new world. Maybe someday we can change the world. . . .

REFERENCES

Auerbach, E., Barahona, B., Midy, J., Vaquerano, F., Zambrano, A., & Arnaud, J. (1996). *Adult ESL/literacy from the community to the community: A guidebook for participatory literacy training.* Mahwah, NJ: Lawrence Erlbaum Associates.

Freire, P. (1970). *Pedagogy of the oppressed.* New York: Seabury.

15

Language and Authority: Shifting the Privilege[1]

J. Milton Clark
Carol Peterson Haviland
California State University, San Bernardino

Immersed in postmodern literary and cultural theory and committed to educational openness and equity, most basic writing faculty are far less elitist than some of their colleagues in other literature and composition fields. These basic writing faculty members tend to select more varied, representative, and relevant reading and writing topics; to incorporate the richness of their students' experiences; and to be quite open to linguistic diversity. However, most instructors have continued to insist that language sharing be largely one-way, with faculty members as the purveyors of standard written English, which they hope their students will acquire quickly enough to survive as writers of academic English.

As we considered our philosophical and theoretical commitments to inclusiveness and collaboration, we began to recognize how limited that inclusiveness and collaboration were, particularly with the non-native speakers we have in our fairly typical Southern California basic writing classes: a mix of White, African American, Latino, Asian, and American Indian native speakers, as well as Latino and Asian non-native speakers who have scored in the lower half on California State University's English Placement Test and are enrolled for one, two, or three quarters of pre-freshman composition instruction. We recognized that although we chose texts that might appeal to a multilinguistic and multicultural group, the texts themselves remained singular—standard academic English—and that although we had welcomed linguistic diversity, we had not really embraced it or attempted to see what value that diversity might have for all

[1]This chapter is a slightly modified version of Clark and Haviland (1995), "Language and Authority: Shifting the Privilege," *Journal of Basic Writing, 14*, 1, 57–66. Permission to reprint the article is gratefully acknowledged.

our basic writers. Even though we agreed with Hannah Arendt's observation that "for excellence . . . the presence of others is always required" (1958, p. 49), we often allowed ourselves to use others' presence to highlight individual excellence or, more benignly, simply to be content with the others' presence, forgetting how much more we could gain from reciprocal activity. We remained stalled at the level that Henry Giroux (1992) describes as tolerating differences but not engaging them.

We decided to test the value of using other languages in our teaching, not because we rejected the value that a common language might provide or because we advocated bilingual basic writing instruction, but because we wanted to work toward creating more truly shared language communities. From our classrooms in San Bernardino, California, this meant including some Spanish, French, and Chinese or other Asian language texts as part of the readings in our basic writing classes, which were 2 of the 20 basic writing sections offered each quarter.

Certainly, one response to such a choice might be alarm—alarm that in reading Chinese or Spanish texts we would neglect English and create even slower entrance into the academy for students who already feel behind in some respects. However, this response rests on the assumption that to value one language is to devalue the other. Such an assumption grows out of the thinking of the traditional order, an order that tends to view sharing as diminishing its own share of privilege or authority.

However, a second response grows out of postmodern and feminist theorists who suggest that sharing power increases power. Thus, rather than worrying that sharing language might involve relinquishing language, we chose to believe that sharing language would be generative, multiplying that language facility so that we could embrace the linguistic richness residing in our classes and gain, while losing nothing.

With these commitments to greater diversity, inclusiveness, and collaboration, along with a desire to use the linguistic variety in our classes as the context, we describe here a composite of 18 basic writing classes in which—in addition to our usual reading of English language essays, poetry, and short stories—students used magazines written in Spanish, French, and Chinese as stimuli for writing. We hope to demonstrate how this choice embraced the classes' linguistic diversity; how it shifted or expanded privilege in the class, giving voice and authority to often silent students; and how it led students to read and write texts more globally and collaboratively. In addition, we propose other locations in which this same choice can embrace rather than merely tolerate the diversity that many groups of ESL and adult learners bring to university classrooms.

Our aim in our basic writing classes was to use texts written in a language other than English so that we could tap the linguistic diversity in each class and allow everyone in the class to benefit from that diversity in as many ways as possible. Thus, on the first day of class, we polled students for non-English reading competence. In each of our classes, we had students who reported some level of reading comprehension in Spanish, French, and Chinese, as well as in English. Based on these self-reported competencies, we purchased contemporary magazines in the three languages: *Imagen,* published in Spanish in Puerto Rico; *Le Figaro,* published in French in Paris; and *The Observer* and *Commonwealth,* both published in Chinese in Taiwan.

To prepare the class for using these texts, we began by discussing how readers from other countries might gain different information and perspectives about the United States through reading the magazines they might find either at an airport or a typical mall bookstore. For example, we had students put the names of as many different magazines on the board as they could recall. As we grouped those magazines by subject matter, students were readily able to see that readers would get very different impressions of the United States from looking at *Mother Earth News, Better Homes and Gardens, Time, GQ,* and *Architectural Digest.* If the magazines happened to be *Soldier of Fortune, The National Enquirer,* or *Wrestling USA,* the impressions would shift radically again.

Following this exercise, we arranged students in groups of five. In each group, we placed two or more ESL students who had reading competence in the target language. The remainder of each group was a mixture of abilities and languages. We considered writing ability and assertiveness as well as a number of other factors in trying to create productive work groups. We then gave each group one of the three texts, asking that they designate group leaders and recorders and that they rotate those roles each class meeting.

Their assignment, which occupied 3 weeks of the 10-week quarter, was to investigate collaboratively what they could learn about the country the magazine represented, creating as rich a communal database as possible, and then to write papers responding to the question, "What can you know about this country from the magazine we've given you?" In some classes, we had students write individual papers, and in others we had them write group papers.

Following their normal strategies, students wanted to gather information by reading text. Some were annoyed, others embarrassed or inhibited, by their inability to read the text. As the groups turned to those students who could read the text, some students were startled as they realized that students who had appeared to struggle the hardest with their writing and speaking in English (the ESL students) were best equipped for this assignment. The tacit assumption that those students were not as academically able had to be reevaluated in light of their obvious competence in this new arena. The privilege visibly shifted as the more capable writers of English realized that they needed their peers in order to do this assignment.

In addition to reading text, they developed a second strategy, approaching and defining reading in a larger sense, and some groups began by "reading" the ads, the cartoons, and the photographs, noting that even the advertisements (BMW, Jaguar, Rolex) revealed socioeconomic information about the French readers of *Le Figaro*. The large number of ads for wedding apparel along with pictures of debutantes, weddings, baptisms, and family reunions in *Imagen* suggested the importance of the family in Puerto Rico. Students could "read" the Chinese-captioned cartoons in *Commonwealth* because they could see how the caricatures of American, European, and Asian politicians illustrated Taiwan's political concerns.

By the second day of collaboration, most groups began to pull together. This was a pleasant surprise because, in many collaborative assignments, students merely size up the tasks, divide them, and then work individually. This assignment, however, required real collaboration, and our students began to recognize that when each of them contributed different observations, together they could write richer, fuller papers than any of them could produce individually. The joining of forces enriched rather than diluted their efforts. For example, we were intrigued as we watched Peggy and Michele, a Taiwanese and an African American, read together, translating Chinese into English, creating language and knowledge about marriage in Taiwan, as they pieced together the story of an elderly tycoon who left his first wife to marry a younger woman. Neither student was sympathetic to the tycoon, and both expanded their thinking about marriage relationships, family, and language as they worked together to understand and explain the story.

We then set students to using their collected observations to create generalizations about the countries represented by their magazines. These generalizations reflected the particular magazines each group used. *Imagen* and *Le Figaro*, both upscale magazines, led students to generalizations about the wealthy in Puerto Rico and France. *The Observer* was largely political, and thus the students in that group spoke about the Taiwanese as being very sober and male-oriented.

Once the students had collected and shared data, they began to draft their papers. These drafts then moved through a series of usual workshop activities involving peer review and response, finally emerging as finished papers that we reproduced for the entire class to read.

We have observed a variety of outcomes from this assignment for our students, for us as teachers, and for the linguistic community. Among the results for the students, the social implications are of considerable importance. First of all, our ESL students gained stature in the class. They became leaders in their groups because they were the literate ones. Often, these were the same students who previously had spoken only when directly called on. As we watched the groups explore their magazines, we saw native students asking questions of the ESL students about matters outside the scope of the magazines. The ESL students responded very positively to their new roles, and some of them participated in the class in ways we had not seen before.

Another outcome is that students engaged in real, not pseudo, collaboration. As we noted earlier, this full investment is difficult to generate. Initially, students felt constrained by efficiency, fear of exposure, and individualism. They were wary of trusting their peers—even in a small class. Those writing individual papers worried that if they contributed to the communal databank, some other writer would "take all their good stuff." However, most came to see working with others as community interaction, not dependence, to see that they were members of a large club who also feared others looking at their writing, and to see that, even though they sprang from a shared text, their papers were surprisingly different. Those writing group papers noted that they had fewer problems generating text; rather than having to pad their papers to fill enough pages, they were able to be selective as they edited. Thus, they experienced real collaboration and ound it productive.

A third outcome for the students was a greater use of their imagination and resourcefulness. Many of our students had learned to suppress their personalities and ideas in order to survive in writing classes. Urging them to call on other skills to unravel the meanings of the assigned material boosted their beliefs that they could do college-level work, even in a writing class. For example, when we watched students solve the puzzles that emerged as they composed on computers and experimented with different printers, we saw the quality of their imaginations at work. In this assignment, we wanted to invite students to use as many means as they had at their disposal to solve the puzzles we had set out for them. When they widened their repertoires, they "read" texts in a variety of ways.

Fourth, the native students learned things about their ESL peers that they might not otherwise have been interested in learning. We overheard discussions about language and customs. The students talked about the geographical, political, and social differences they saw in other countries. Not all of what they learned was significant, but much of it was eye opening. For example, one quarter it took most students several minutes to discover that they were looking at the Taiwanese magazine backwards. What they considered the front of the magazine was, of course, the back because, as the Taiwanese students gently told them, the text was printed in the opposite direction from English. This discovery generated a thoughtful exploration of the left to right and top to bottom American print conventions, particularly as students debated what makes text readable and "right." In another class section, students argued vigorously about representations of women, basing their assertions on the clothing women wore in the advertising and other situations in which they were pictured. As students interpreted these drawings and photographs, they examined the differing cultural perspectives they and the text brought to the debate.

A final sensory-rich outcome from one of the classes extended the process of learning from the text to the potluck lunch table. Each student brought food typical of his or her country; we had Jordanian, Thai, Chinese, Mexican, and American food, everything from spring rolls to mole to peanut-butter-and-jelly sandwiches. Students were particularly interested in the ingredients common to so many different diets (flour, tomatoes, nuts, cheese, and greens).

Finally, student writing improved. In the nine quarters that we have used this writing project, the grades for these papers, whether group or individual, uniformly have been among the highest of the term, very often fully one letter grade higher than their earlier assignments. Papers have responded clearly to the writing assignment, have supported generalizations with details, have been visibly organized, and have been carefully edited. And at no stage have the groups' best writers simply taken charge; rather, the papers represented the groups' best joint efforts as the students drew on diverse abilities. For example, in the several stages of paper production, we saw students clustered around a single computer, arguing about details, coherence, and verb endings. With few other assignments have we seen students challenge each other about whether a paragraph hangs together or whether a string of words is a sentence or a fragment or, even more surprisingly, whether they have fully and fairly interrogated the text, whether they have explored conflicting viewpoints and been faithful to the observations of all group members. In one class, four group members spent several class sessions arguing whether their conclusions about Taiwan were drawn from their magazine or from two of the group members' experiences in Taiwan; one member was Taiwanese and another had visited on a band tour. Their exchanges produced important self-discoveries about the difficulty writers experience as they bring existing opinions or data to an assignment or writing group that challenges their ideas and beliefs. The Taiwanese student, particularly, had difficulty allowing her group to write what she saw as an inaccurate representation of Taiwan because she was offended by the magazine's picture of her country; as a group, however, they were able to write a paper that focused on the magazine's perspective but ended with a well-articulated assertion that the magazine presented only one view. At the end of the quarter, the Taiwanese student contributed an additional Taiwanese magazine to our supply, urging us to let the next term's students see a more balanced picture. Her group's willingness to let their ideas clash allowed them to think carefully about assignments, using rather than silencing oppositional discourse. Thus, in addition to meeting traditional grading criteria, our students have shown us what engaged voices can produce: lively prose, full of detail and energy, contextualized within the writers' lives and yet generalized to their readers' worlds.

Yet, this assignment did more than benefit our students—at a greater level than ever before, we began to share power and privilege with our students. With most reading assignments, the text is wholly familiar to us. We have read it before, and both we and the students know that any questions we ask about that text are questions more for them than for us. In this assignment, we were not the experts; like most members of the class, we did not read Chinese. Our skills in French and Spanish certainly were weaker than our ESL students' skills in English. We were, therefore, also collaborators with our students in making meaning. The classroom became, for this assignment, a Bakhtinian dialogue, a place where everyone, the teacher included, could learn.

Equally important, this way of teaching writing has begun to change our writing practices as well as our students'. Four years ago, as we set out jointly to author a paper, we responded just as our students had to such tasks: We divided the writing and went off to our respective computers to write, hoping the seams would not be too obvious. To compose this chapter, we, too, hunched together over a single keyboard, arguing, interrupting, amending, despairing, and dancing when our single text began to emerge. And, we believe that our text, as our students', is richer for this fuller collaboration.

Thus, this assignment takes a step toward the kind of wider inclusiveness that composition teachers have long advocated. It acknowledges that all of us belong here and that each of us can contribute in valuable ways to the whole. It models that thinking and provides one enactment of it.

In addition to offering an extended description of this one basic writing class enactment, we would like to note briefly three other enactments in which we have worked with colleagues using the same model in other disciplines: marketing, nursing, and education.

First, we worked with marketing faculty members in whose courses students develop international marketing plans. Together we set up classroom work groups that mixed international students who knew the target markets, cultures, and languages with native students who knew American business customs, law, and languages. For example, Indian or Taiwanese natives were able to help American-born students see the flaws in their literal interpretations of trade agreements or their aggressive get-to-the-point sales approaches. And students who had spent their entire lives as consumers in the North American economy could help their counterparts negotiate the thickets of business English and American definitions of profit.

With nursing faculty, whose students prepare many community health presentations, we helped group ESL students who knew the community culture and language, adult returning students who had had years of health-care experience with their own extended families and communities, and 22-year-olds who were freshly immersed in academic nursing. In these groups, students read current research on immunization alongside community norms against outside interference and preferences for native healers. They tempered the ideal of the newest therapies with the experiences that mothers caring for five children and elderly parents could contribute. They discovered how to translate both medical terms and emotional responses into local dialect, and they learned to listen both to their research-based instructors and to their community-based patients.

Finally, we have used this model with education colleagues whose students are preparing to teach in Southern California's enormously diverse public schools. There, the workshops included experienced teachers returning to update their credentials, bilingual teacher aides preparing to be credentialed classroom teachers, and both native-speaker and ESL students who themselves were only 4 years out of the classrooms in which they were preparing to teach. The diverse groups allowed students to formulate teaching theory enriched by multiple sources, each with essential knowledge to contribute.

In each of these enactments, as well as in a continuing variety of other collaborations, students can discover each other's strengths as well as the value of collaboration. And, as faculty members, we can extend not only our understanding of collaborative models for student classrooms but also of how we can learn from our colleagues' and students' cross-disciplinary differences. Indeed, although creating successful writing experiences for our composition students as well as for students using writing in a variety of disciplines is important, we are equally concerned with expanding the boundaries of our own terms and assumptions, particularly those cutting-edge terms and assumptions that seduce us with their currency. *Collaboration* and *welcoming diversity* are such terms. Collaboration appears to be widely accepted and practiced, clearly occupying a place in the educational spotlight; indeed, in the last several years' CCCC (Conference on College Composition and Communication) sessions, nearly 100 titles refer to collaboration. Equally clear, however, is the dramatic variation in the meaning of collaboration.

Similarly, welcoming diversity was the theme of the 1990 CCCC annual convention, and diversity has been included in a large number of subsequent session titles. However, welcoming can be little more than the perfunctory plastic smile and handshake of tolerance that people receive at obligatory social occasions or students receive as they enter classrooms, and it can remain stalled at toleration rather than growing into engagement.

As we pushed our own definitions of collaboration and welcoming diversity, we saw that both were thin; we saw that collaboration must entail giving and learning and changing ourselves as much as we expected our students to change. We recognized that welcoming diversity was more than smiling warily at it; it meant greeting diversity expectantly, hoping that it would shape our lives and praxis as well as our students' lives. Nan Johnson, a keynote Young Rhetoricians' Conference speaker, eloquently told how, as teachers of writing, we change students' lives and buttressed her assertion with powerful illustrations of students' writing. We would like to press that a step farther, suggesting that although what we do with our students is critical, our understanding of the theories that underpin these choices is equally important. We begin to understand collaboration, authority, privilege, and diversity not when we direct others in those activities but only as we participate in them ourselves. We begin when we insert ourselves, along with our students, into the rich unknown of Mary Louise Pratt's (1991) contact zone, "where cultures meet, clash, and grapple with each other, often in contexts of highly asymmetrical relations of power" (p. 34), and when we acknowledge and participate in the struggles that their oppositional discourses produce (Miller, 1994). We begin when we recognize the truth of Jean Lave and Etienne Wenger's (1991) definition of situated learning, in which students and teachers are equally transformed. We begin when, as Shyh-chyi Wey, one of our ESL tutors, puts it, we make our classrooms and offices "environment[s] where right thinking is not the possession of one and merely the aspiration of others" (1993, p. iii).

ACKNOWLEDGMENT

This chapter is a slightly modified version of "Language and Authority: Shifting the Privelege," by J. Milton Clark and Carol Peteson Haviland (1995), *Journal of Basic Writing, 14*(1), pp. 57–66. The authors gratefully acknowledge permission to reprint it here.

REFERENCES

Arendt, H. (1958). *The human condition*. Chicago: University of Chicago Press.

Giroux, H. (1992). *Border crossings*. New York: Routledge.

Lave, J., & Wenger, E. (1991). *Situated learning*. New York: Cambridge University Press.

Miller, R. E. (1994). Fault lines in the contact zone. *College English, 56*, 389–408.

Pratt, M. L. (1991). Arts of the contact zone. In P. Franklin (Ed.), *Profession 91* (pp. 33–40). New York: MLA.

Wey, S.-C. (1993). Frontispiece. *The Compost HEAP, 3.1*, iii.

16

An Orphan at the Table: The English Language Fellows Program

Richard Blakely
Rhode Island School of Design

> *The foundation for a successful undergraduate experience is proficiency in the written and the spoken word.*
>
> —Ernest Boyer (1987)

If this statement is true, then the United States is systematically condemning to failure between 10% and 20% of its first-year college students every year. We are doing this consciously, and yet with a good conscience, telling ourselves that those students who come to the university speaking a native language other than English have just as much chance of becoming successful members of society now as our immigrant grandparents did a century ago. But in saying this we are deceiving ourselves, and ignoring a problem that has almost grown out of control.

The English Language Fellows Program was designed to address the problem of nonnative-speaking (NNS) students in the United States, who, by the time they graduate from college, are for all intents and purposes illiterate.[1] The idea for the program came to me while I was attending a conference on content-based language learning. The conference was hosted at Brown University, the home of a Writing Fellows Program (WFP) that, since its creation by Tori Haring Smith, has been replicated throughout the country. I was already familiar with this program and, during the conference, it occurred to me that a possible way of solving the ESL problem at the University of Rhode Island (URI) might be through a peer tutorial

[1]The problem is also discussed in Blakely (1995).

program similar to the WFP at Brown, except that in this case the fellows would be native speakers and the people they would be tutoring would be NNS classmates in courses both happened to be taking together. The whole program would be content based in that the language learning would take place while focusing on other academic subjects—geology, literature, economics, and so on.

Thanks to a grant from the Fund for the Improvement of Postsecondary Education (FIPSE), this idea was realized at the University of Rhode Island as a 3-year pilot project, from September 1, 1992, to August 31, 1995. The first year was spent creating and eventually getting approval of two new courses; a three-unit course (ELS 200) to train the native speaking (NS) students who would become peer tutors, and a one-unit language study section (ELS 201) that qualifying NNS students could take in conjunction with another three-unit content course. These one-unit English-learning sections were to be organized and conducted by the fellows in the program, under close supervision of the program staff. Multiple sections of this course would be offered every semester, depending on the number of fellows and the number of courses they were taking in which there were nonnative speakers. Each of these one-unit study sections could accommodate up to three NNS students, and these students would be allowed to continue taking these special sections as long as their English continued to need improvement.

By the end of the third year of this pilot project, 56 fellows had successfully completed the training course, 79 sections of ELS 201 had been offered in conjunction with 74 content courses ranging from African American Studies to Zoology, and 75 to 80 NNS students had participated in the program, many of them several times. Retrospective self-reports from participating students and faculty were overwhelmingly positive, some saying the program had changed their lives for the better, and corrected misperceptions they had had about immigrants and ESL. Hard data collected at the beginning of Semester 6 corroborated this positive subjective feedback by showing a dramatic increase in the rate of retention of NNS participants and a significant improvement in grades, both of NNS students and of the fellows.

What follows is a brief history of this program, based on a final report compiled for FIPSE in December of 1995, including recommendations to others who wish to set up similar programs at their own institutions.

PURPOSE: DESCRIBING THE PROBLEM, AND OBSTACLES ENCOUNTERED ALONG THE WAY

The ELF program was originally designed as a solution to a local problem at the University of Rhode Island—increasing numbers of graduating students who were unable to get jobs for which they were supposed to qualify, because of their limited English. But while setting up the program, my teaching assistant (T.A.) and I realized that it was an inextricable part of a much larger, tangled web of problems that has come to be popularly known and generically referred to as "the ESL problem" (Zamel, 1995). One need only mention the phrase to anyone involved in public education in this country, at any level, to receive a nod of recognition, or a sigh of despair.

Because of the awesome complexity of this problem it is difficult to discuss it in a logical fashion, laying out the causes one by one. Instead, I attempt to identify some of the threads and knots that my T.A. and I discovered—sometimes much to our surprise—in hopes that our discoveries will be of use to others, and will eventually lead to the web being untangled and the problem resolved.

The most surprising obstacle we encountered in putting this program together was at the beginning of the second year, when we opened our first sections of ELS 201, in conjunction with several heavily enrolled content courses, and hardly any NNS students came forward to enroll in them. In the end we were able to convince 10 non-native speakers to participate (and later they were glad they did), but it was a hard sell!

What those students told us, once they realized we were on their side, was that they were reluctant to get involved with the program, notwithstanding the extra credit, because they "didn't want anything to do with ESL." As one of the students in an advanced English literature course said that semester, when offered the opportunity of studying with a native speaker (she herself had been born and raised in Guatemala, and had spent the last 10 years in the United States), "I never had to take ESL and I don't intend to start now."[2]

This aversion among non-native speakers to ESL, despite the fact that it was what they needed most, became the subject of an article that was published the following year in the *Providence Journal*, arguing that it would be wrong to assume that "the ESL problem" was strictly a problem of higher education, "or strictly its fault":

> The root of the problem lies in the way these students are perceived and treated long before they apply to college. If we really want to solve it we must correct these misperceptions and change the policies that issue from them.
>
> In Rhode Island, as everywhere else in this country, most non-native-speaking children are "mainstreamed" out of English language classes well

[2]Ultimately, this student did enroll in the one-unit study section, and she and the professor both agreed afterward that if she had not done so, she would not have done nearly so well in the content course. This student, a senior who was hoping to become a teacher, went on to enroll in another section of 201 the following semester, and ended up a firm supporter of the program.

> before they have attained the necessary skills to perform successfully in school. The assumption (blessed by theories that are now being questioned) is that they will pick these skills up along the way. Unfortunately, they don't. A ninth grader with "third grade English" who is told in her college prep English class to read *Macbeth* and write a paper on it, simply panics. If she does manage to write a paper (often with a lot of help from her friends) it is liable to be returned to her with one of two opposite, and to her equally mystifying reactions. Either it will come back covered and criss-crossed with angry "corrections" and a note saying she is in the wrong class, or there will be no marks on it whatsoever, save for a few lines at the bottom that say she has good ideas and expresses them well, considering.
>
> On papers students have shown to me I have seen both extremes. Those who get enough of the first usually give up hope of ever going to college, or even of completing school. Those who receive the second and manage to get into college by virtue of good grades and exemplary behavior arrive at the University hoping they'll be able to hide their limited English for the next four years as well as they hid it in the past. And many of them do. (Blakely, 1994, p. A14)

Another aspect of the ESL problem that makes it more complex and even more urgently in need of a solution is the number of students involved. Between 1985 and 1991 the population of K–12 students in the United States with certified limited English proficiency rose by 51.3%, to a total of 2.3 million children. By the year 2000 this population will have grown two and a half times as fast as the overall student population in those grades (Waggoner, 1995). According to data now being released by the 1990 census, over 30 million people living in the United States at that time were non-native speakers of English (Waggoner, 1995).

However, even these figures are problematic. It is common knowledge that large numbers of "illegal aliens" went uncounted during the last census, either because they did not want to be counted, or, as some have claimed, because certain politicians did not want them counted. In any event, any effort to get accurate information about numbers of immigrants or non-native speakers in this country leads into foggy terrain. Until 1992, at URI there was no attempt to count or keep track of students for whom English was not their first language. They literally did not count. One of the first accomplishments of the ELF program was a revision in the letter of acceptance that prospective students were to send back to the Admissions Office, so that it included a little box that they could check off if they spoke a language other than English at home. Probably half of the incoming NNS students, including those with very limited English proficiency and therefore at great risk of failure their first year, refused to check the box. When we got to know them better and asked them why, the invariable response was that they were afraid they would have been forced to take ESL. They were also afraid of being labeled outsiders—which leads to another knot in the web.

Because ESL is usually considered remedial, or worse, because in the United States people unable to speak English fluently are often considered cognitively deficient, programs designed to provide support for these people tend almost always to be marginal. If courses taken by native speakers are "mainstream," then courses designed specifically to help NNS students master English must exist in a stagnant backwater from which one is wise to escape as soon as possible, in the interest of good health. This perceived marginality of most ESL programs in schools and colleges means that those programs are often homeless, not fitting into any pre-existing academic program or department, and the first to be cut when the budget gets tight. It also saps morale within the program at every level, resulting in resentment and lack of motivation of students who are forced to take these courses, to inferior salaries and absence of job security for teaching staff.

There seem to be two reasons for the marginal status of ESL in the United States—two attitudes that overlap and interact and can be seen as typically American.[3] They could in fact be called the original American sins. They are arrogance and ignorance. The first is aggressive and belligerent, stemming from the belief that because the United States has won every war it ever fought (almost) and is the richest, most developed country in the world (or used to be), anyone from another country, speaking another language, is by definition inferior and deficient. One finds this arrogance in the wording of laws proposed by advocates of "English only," and in angry editorials written in frustration at picking up the phone to call the hospital and getting a receptionist who speaks with a foreign accent and "can't understand plain English" ("Push them into English," 1994).[4]

Ignorance is more benign, a kind of national provincialism, that is rooted in America's historical self-image as a huge physical and economic island, cut off from the rest of the world and sufficient unto itself. One finds this attitude in the naive but deep-seeded conviction that anyone

---

[3]In EEC countries, on the other hand, courses and programs designed to help new immigrants learn the language and the culture of the adopted country are considered a vital link in the educational network, and their staff are treated the same as other colleagues.

[4]The hostile tone of the first paragraph of this editorial, maintained throughout the article, is indicative of the paranoid belligerence one often encounters these days in discussing the issue of recent immigrants in this country: "Too many of us have experienced the frustration of calling a bank, hospital or government office, only to find that we need an interpreter to speak to the switchboard operator, whose English is so minimal that he or she cannot understand third-grade English. It's irritating enough when the operator cannot comprehend English well enough to spell the name of the person or office that you may want to get through to. It's infuriating and even dangerous in an emergency" (p. A16).

can learn English in a few years, *if they really want to*, and in its corollary (sometimes devastating to ES/FL programs) that anyone who does speak it can teach it, obviously. The opinion also seems to suggest that students who do not speak fluent English do not belong in an American university. This pervasive ignorance helps us to understand the continuously embattled status of foreign language programs in the United States—in a crisis they're the second thing to go, after ESL. It also helps explain an utter lack of comprehension of what it is like to be a foreigner in this country (strange, because most of our parents or grandparents were foreigners), and of the fact that learning English for a Cambodian can be just as just as daunting and time consuming as learning Cambodian would be for a native speaker of American English.

One would not expect to find these benighted attitudes at a university, but they are there, sometimes at the highest levels. One day the president of a state university in the northeast calls a special ceremony to announce that despite the budget shortfall he has approved plans to build a large new multicultural center in the middle of campus. A few days later the local paper quotes him as saying that any non-native speakers who are not yet fluent in English should not even apply to the university, but should go to the community college instead, where they will be better served.

Thus, if one wants to untangle the ESL problem at one's own campus the first thing to do is educate one's co-educators about the existence and complexity of the problem, and to convince them that the problem is urgent. Perhaps the best way to do this is to have them recognize that it is directly linked to overpopulation, which is the major crisis of the end of the century. As the world population grows, so will wars and famine and economic instability and so, as a result, will hordes of refugees fleeing one country into another, either by invitation or by force. Proponents of "English only" and of restricting immigration should make no mistake. The problem they are obsessed with is not going to go away. It is just beginning.

BRIEF HISTORY OF ESL AT URI, HOW THE ELF PROGRAM CHANGED THINGS, AND GETTING THE NAMES RIGHT

Twenty-five years ago there were so few NNS undergraduates at URI that their presence was hardly noticeable. Most of them were visiting this country on student visas and planned to return to their homelands after a year or two, or after getting their degrees. To accommodate the English language needs of this small group, two special courses were designed and offered as part of the new writing program: WRT 112 and WRT 122.

These courses were an ESL option for those international students who would have difficulty passing the two writing courses required of all NS undergraduates, and they could be taken in their place. Thus, the original purpose of these courses was to accommodate international students and *to attract them to the university*. In the interest of "global awareness" it was considered good to have a certain number of foreign students on campus (often thought of as "exchange" students), and of course these students, many from oil-rich countries, paid full tuition.

By 1992, the situation had completely changed. Fewer and fewer international students were coming to URI at the undergraduate level, and more and more students signing up to take WRT 112 and 122 were children of immigrants who had fled war and economic hardship in their own countries. In Rhode Island, the majority of these students at that time were from Southeast Asia. The English language needs of these immigrant students were far different from those of the original customers of WRT 112 and 122. Although immigrant students come to the university with fairly good oral skills (speaking and listening), their writing and reading are often woefully deficient, perhaps because they never had any explicit training in the rules that govern English syntax. Most international students come to the university knowing more about English grammar than their NS classmates. Because of the way English is usually taught in mainstream "college preparatory" classes, immigrant students arrive knowing next to nothing.[5] The end result was another twist to the ESL

[5]For many mainstream English teachers, and many ESL teachers as well, grammar has become a dirty word. When dealing with native speakers of English, there are good reasons for this. In order to get his thoughts on paper, a native speaker doesn't need to know the difference between a gerund and a participle. But for the non-native speaker of English, at least at the earlier stages of learning the language, knowledge of grammar is one more useful tool that she can use in gaining fluency. In fact without it, the English language learner is at a loss, severely disadvantaged in comparison with her native-speaking classmates. Imagine being forced to write a paper on Moliere, in French, and not knowing how to conjugate a verb, or even to locate the verb in a sentence. When they first arrive at the University, more and more of our non-native speakers are unable to do just that: locate a verb in a simple sentence; explain the difference between a noun and a verb; say whether "a" or "the" should come before a noun, or whether it needs no article. When we point out to them that an "s" is added to the end of a verb in the present tense, 3rd person singular (I write, you write, but she *writes*), they are amazed. No one ever told them that before.

I am not saying these students do not belong at the University. . . . They would be much better off, however, if their English language training before they got here had been deeper and more sustained. By the time they arrive at the University many of their non-standard or "faulty" patterns in speaking and writing have been "fossilized," set and reinforced by years of usage, because they were never corrected, or not corrected enough. Breaking these habits and learning new ones at twenty is much harder than it would have been at nine or ten. For some college students, this process of correction is just as long, and in a way just as painful, as breaking bones that have been badly set and having them set anew. (Blakely, 1994)

problem and is another good reason for the ELF program. In an ESL classroom it is almost impossible to balance the course so that it is equally beneficial to both types of students. But when a trained peer is working with an international student from Japan and another who immigrated to the United States from Cambodia 7 years ago, she can divide her attention between the two and give both of them what they need most (Blakely, 1994).

Although the kind of students enrolling in 112/122 had drastically changed by 1992, what we found when we were setting up the program was that most members of the faculty, even faculty in the English Department where those courses were housed, were unaware of that change. For them, students who needed ESL were foreigners, and the new FIPSE-sponsored project was going to increase enrollments of foreign exchange students at URI.

We knew that as the program spread throughout the university over the next 3 years, this misperception would gradually be corrected. More and more faculty, through contact with the fellows (advocates of their NNS classmates), would learn the truth about growing numbers of NNS students in their courses and would become more sensitive to their needs. But we also knew it was essential, from the outset, to clearly describe what the program was and whom it was designed to serve. By providing for two new courses to be added to the curriculum, the EFL program posed two questions that needed to be answered: Where should those courses be offered, and what should they be called? Because I was a member of the English Department and the courses had to do primarily with English, it seemed logical at the time to include them among the offerings of that department.[6]

The second question, what these courses would be named, was harder to answer. Although writing was going to be an important component of both courses, it was certainly not the only, nor even the main component, and thus it would not be appropriate to put them in the Writing Program, where ESL had been lodged, rather uncomfortably, until then. The English Department had no separate rubric for ESL, and even if it

---

[6]This is a decision I now regret. At the time, the two other options were for the courses, and the entire ESL program, (a) to be an autonomous unit, answerable to the provost, or (b) to be housed in the Department of Foreign Languages. In hindsight, I think it would have been better for the program, and more appropriate all around, to have chosen the latter option. As an autonomous entity, this program would not have the support of an established structure, and would be vulnerable when money got tight. In the English Department, as it turned out, it also lacked support because hardly anybody understood what it was all about, or, frankly, cared. Faculty in the English Department were primarily interested in literature or in writing. Colleagues in Foreign Languages, on the other hand, understood the program implicitly, and provided valuable input throughout its life.

had, I felt this wouldn't have been appropriate either. Even before the project began and before I learned of the deep aversion NNS students have for anything to do with ESL, I myself had not found the acronym appealing or even accurate.[7]

In the fall of 1992, because of the attention focused on ESL by the ELF program, the Dean of Arts and Sciences at URI formed a special committee to explore "the ESL problem" at the university and come up with recommendations. The first recommendation called for the creation of a new course designation, called English Language Studies (ELS), under which all existing ESL or EFL courses, and the two new courses created by the FIPSE-sponsored project, would henceforth be grouped. After some discussion, this recommendation was approved by the English Department, and went on to final approval by the Dean. Hence, the ELF program was a catalyst for changing the name of all courses designed to serve NNS students at the university, and, as far as I was concerned, a change in what you call something is the first necessary step in changing how you see it.

Two other names were changed that year, as a result of looking more closely at what we were naming. The first was the name of the program itself, which in the original proposal to FIPSE, was called, "A Peer Tutorial Program in Content-Based English as a Second or Foreign Language." While walking around campus, talking to students and faculty about what we were hoping to do, this title became a heavy burden. It was also not quite accurate. The first thing to change was that cumbersome term "peer tutor," as shown in the Annual Report to FIPSE, Year 1:

> The word "peer" pops up so often in academic language these days that it has become another meaningless buzz word. Also, the deeper I got into planning for the "tutor training seminar," the more clearly I saw that we did not want to train these students to become tutors. The word tutor brings to mind an image of an individualized teacher, an authority on some subject who is usually paid to help someone else catch up on that subject, often

---

[7]As I said in my annual report to FIPSE for Year 1 (1992–93):

> One of the major obstacles ESL teachers face every day is the widespread perception that their profession is marginal to mainstream academics, and I am convinced that the term "second" helps maintain this image of marginality in people's minds. It is also, in many cases, a misnomer. Many people learning English are fluent in other languages as well, and for others, English is the first language in which they have achieved a degree of literacy. In the interests of de-marginalizing the profession, "English as a Foreign Language" is hardly better, and at any rate it is the title generally used nowadays to designate teaching English in countries where another language is dominant. And so I decided that if I were going to make a case for improving the situation of NNS students on campus, . . . I had better dump the terms "second" and "foreign."

> by doing remedial work. Tori Haring-Smith [founder of the Writing Fellows Program at Brown, and consultant to the project during the first year] helped me understand the dangers in having our trained undergraduates perceive themselves, and therefore having them be perceived by their classmates in the study groups, as authority figures. And in fact it is not simply a matter of skillful semantics, of choosing the right word to camouflage or diminish an aura of authority. These students will be taking the courses right along with their NNS classmates in the study sessions, learning the course material with them. Hence, . . . they should see themselves "not as teachers, nor even as tutors, in the strictest sense, but as **active collaborators in learning**, whose knowledge of English as a native speaker will help [their] non-native speaking classmates to improve their English while studying course content."
>
> And so, taking the lead from the program at Brown, we decided to call this group of students not peer tutors, after all, but "fellows," and the subject they would be helping their NNS classmates to master, while studying other courses, would not be ESL or EFL, but simply the English language. Hence: The English Language Fellows Program. (pp. 3–4)

Of course, as several people have pointed out, *fellow* does have unfortunate sexist connotations. In the latest edition of the *American Heritage Dictionary*, the first definition is "A man or boy," and then, heaven forbid, "A boyfriend"! But what else in English is there: *Colleague? Associate? Friend? Cohort?* Because of its association with images of work and collaboration, *comrade* was a tempting alternative, but in attempting to get corporate funding for the program at a later date it would certainly have proven to be an even greater burden.[8]

So finally, after consultation with the students in the first training course, we decided to stick with *fellows*. After all, they had been learning that languages are constantly evolving organisms. Lexicons change not only by new words being added to them but by existing words being

---

[8]Some have also suggested Vysotsky's "more capable peer" (Vygotsky, 1978), but in terms of leveling the terrain between the NS and the NNS participants, that would put us back at square one, and be even more cumbersome than *peer tutor*. One can imagine a student jumping up from his or her table in the cafeteria and saying, "I've got an appointment with my more capable peer."

Another argument against using Vygotsky's term is that "more capable" might well apply to a higher "actual developmental level," but would it apply to someone who had more knowledge of the native language, but not necessarily of the subject matter? Indeed, if the NS classmate were Vietnamese, and our peers were studying at a university in Vietnam, it is the class mate who would be more capable.

Bruffee (1993), although keeping the terms *peer tutors* and *tutees*, took pains to stress their equality. "In peer tutoring this equality means, first of all, that the students involved—peer tutor and tutee alike—believe that they both bring an important measure of ability, expertise, and information to the encounter and, second, that they believe that they are institutional status-equals: both are students, clearly and unequivocally" (p. 83).

stretched to fit new meanings. We were willing to bet that within the decade *fellow,* thanks in part to our program, would come to lose its strictly masculine overtones. The eventual degenderization of *fellow* was to be one of the program's extra benefits. In the meantime, there was always *fella.*

The other name that changed that year, before the program actually got off the ground, and again in collaboration with the students in the first training course, was the designation of the students with whom they were going to be working the following year. For reasons previously discussed, calling them ESL or EFL students was not desirable. Even less so, of course, *immigrants* or *internationals* or *foreign students.* The most common designation, *non-native speakers,* which I have used here so far and elsewhere in talking about the program (mainly because of its recognizability), did not seem satisfactory either, once we started thinking about it. Why define a person by something he or she is not? Native American-speaking students in the training course, who had spent time abroad, said they would have found it strange, as well as tiresome and discouraging, to have constantly been referred to as non-native speakers, as outsiders, in a word. And so we decided on the term English-Learners, or E-Ls.

PROJECT DESCRIPTION, THE TWO NEW COURSES, AND UNDERLYING ASSUMPTIONS

The main features of the ELF program at URI were the fellows training course, ELS 200, and the special study sections for the English-Learners, ELS 201. The key assumption underlying the content-based language sections (ELS 201) was that they were worthy of academic credit and therefore should bear at least one unit *that would count toward graduation.* Otherwise the program would be flawed from the beginning. Good reasons for awarding credit for ESL at any level had already been articulated before the program began (Benesch, 1988; Blakely, 1989), and, as mentioned previously, in the formal course proposal for 201 we restated those arguments as convincingly as we knew how, and came up with a few more:

> First, one must bear in mind that the language material to be learned in the supplementary sessions is not remedial. Their purpose is not to reinforce deficient study habits or go back over something a student was taught before but never learned. It is to improve her mastery of a foreign language—in effect to help her learn language through content. In recognition of the value of combining the study of language and content, "Language Across the Curriculum" programs are springing up all over the country.

In all of those programs, language combined with content study is either an integral part of a credit-bearing course or *is awarded extra credit towards graduation*, as well it should be. At St. Olaf College, for example, a native-speaking American student who takes a course in Religious Studies, taught in English, and at the same time attends an additional discussion section of the same course in French, will receive additional credit for the work she does in the extra session. Most would agree that this is simply granting credit where credit is due. Now, since we give credit to native-speaking American students for learning a foreign language at an intermediate level, shouldn't we also award credit to non-native speakers, who, while taking university courses native speakers find difficult, continue to develop their English language skills at a level that is very advanced?

Another reason credit should be awarded for the supplementary study sessions is that this will help make them academically meaningful and give them genuine scholastic status, so that both the Language Fellow and the NNS student, as well as the campus at large, will take them seriously. A common weakness of many supplementary instruction programs that do not give credit is that after the first few weeks, or during periods of intense study, such as mid-terms or finals, when students *especially need* the services offered by those programs, they stop attending. And who can blame them? Many of these students are putting themselves through college, so they must work long hours in addition to carrying exceptionally heavy course loads in areas such as science and math. When their schedules get too tight for everything to fit, it's only normal that they drop the course they're not taking for credit. But again, one must make a distinction between more traditional supplementary instruction programs, designed primarily to review course material and sharpen students' study skills—a task which may well be considered remedial—and the English Language Fellows Program, which in addition to reviewing course material, requires study of language features that the student has never done before. It is for this additional language study that the extra credit is to be awarded.

A student who comes to URI not knowing how to play the piano very well, but with a strong desire to learn, is allowed to repeat a 2-unit course in piano performance, for credit, as often as he wishes, and as long as his instructor thinks he can continue to make progress. This makes perfect sense, since learning to master a musical instrument takes years and years of diligent practice. Furthermore, in gaining mastery of the piano, this student is learning a skill which he may use, for profit, throughout the rest of his life—as a teacher, for example.

Gaining fluency in a foreign language also takes many years, and when it is the dominant language of the country in which one is going to spend the rest of one's life, learning it is not a luxury, it is a necessity for survival.

At the end of Year 1, both ELS 200 and 201 were provisionally approved as "X" or experimental courses. At URI, an X course can be offered twice before being reconsidered as a permanent curricular offering or rejected. Based on the success of these two X courses the first 2 semesters they were offered, both were accepted as permanent offerings by the beginning of Year 3.

ELS 200

The prerequisite for admission to ELS 200, and therefore as a potential fellow, was "permission of the Program Director." That permission was granted on the basis of a two-page application form, including space for a short essay on why the applicant wanted to become a fellow, three letters of recommendation from faculty or employers, and a 20-minute interview. The interviews were conducted by a panel consisting of the project director, the graduate assistant, and one or two experienced fellows, and they were held during the last 2 weeks of classes, so that letters could be sent out in time for students who were accepted in the program to make the necessary changes in their schedule to accommodate the training course.

As the program evolved, we found that one of the best resources for recruiting students was the network of faculty who either had already participated in the program, or who understood it clearly and were committed to its success. Foreign language faculty were especially helpful in this regard, for obvious reasons. About halfway through the semester we would send a memo to these professors (the list kept growing; by the end of the third year it included over 200 names) asking them to send back the names of one or two students in courses they were currently teaching who were truly outstanding. To these students we would send a special invitation to apply to the program. Similar letters were sent to incoming students with exceptionally high SAT scores (1200 or higher), and to students who made the honor role (with a GPA of 3.5 or better) during their first semester at the university.

What we discovered, predictably, was that high SAT scores or GPAs were not always a reliable indicator of what it took be a good fellow. What it did take is not easy to answer. One of the most timid students I ever met went on to become one of our most effective fellows. Another candidate whose grades were certainly not impressive and whose written English left much to be desired turned out to be one of the most helpful and accommodating to her E-L classmates, who all became devoted to her. But although such anomalies will always crop up, and help make running such a program so rewarding, it is possible to summarize certain factors that we came to look for in reading the essays and conducting the interviews.

The first consideration was the applicant's year at the university. Obviously it made more sense to accept students in their first, or possibly second year, because they would be around longer. Also, NNS students were more in evidence, and their English language needs more immediately apparent, in the large "gen ed" courses that students tend to take in their freshman and sophomore year. The further a fellow majoring in Communicative Disorders progressed toward his or her degree, the fewer E-Ls he or she was likely to have in those increasingly specialized courses. To offset this tendency we did advise the fellows to save some "gen ed" courses for their junior and senior years, and those who were not locked into a rigidly structured curriculum, such as Pharmacy or Electrical Engineering, were usually able to do so. But as a general rule, as the program grew and we were able to become more choosy, we tended only to choose students in their freshman year, or those who still had lots of "gen eds" to take.

Something else we looked for in potential fellows was a proven interest in other cultures, and better yet, a degree of fluency in another language—another reason many of our fellows came from the Foreign Language department. The reasoning, which tended to hold true, was that if you were going to help someone learn your own language it was important to understand what went into learning a language—to know, for example, that it would be extremely difficult, if not impossible, to "pick up" a second language simply by rubbing elbows with native speakers for a couple of years. In other words, they needed to appreciate the amount of work and perseverance that goes into learning a second language, and to want to make that work as enjoyable as possible for their E-L classmates. Students interested in becoming fellows did not have to "know grammar" as they often asked, timorously, before applying to the program. We knew that their understanding of the complexities of their own language would grow as they gained experience trying to explain those complexities to E-L classmates. Nor, for that matter, did they have to be native speakers. A few of the fellows were still English-Learners themselves, although at a very advanced level. Their insights proved very valuable to others in the training course, and their understanding of problems faced by other E-L classmates was built in.

Finally, we were looking for something we referred to rather vaguely as "intellectual and emotional maturity." Listing the qualities we grouped under that heading would make this sound like the *Boy Scout Handbook* ("A Fellow is reliable, resourceful, adaptable and articulate. S/he is diplomatic and self-confident, . . ."). But what we meant, basically, is that in setting up and conducting those sections of 201, fellows took on a lot of responsibility; therefore, they had to be responsible. Those few students who were admitted to the training course and who started missing a lot of classes or arriving late for no good reason were encouraged to drop the course, or their absence resulted in a low grade that prevented them from becoming fellows. (To become a fellow one had to receive at least a B– in the course.)

As for the training course itself, ELS 200 had three stated objectives: to give students an awareness of problems and patterns of immigration in the United States and an understanding of what it was like to be an immigrant in this country; to provide an introduction to the theory and practice of second language acquisition, especially as they applied to learning English (pointing out specific features of English pronunciation, grammar, etc., that were particularly difficult for certain non-native speakers, and explaining why); and to show students how to use this knowledge in small collaborative groups while studying the content of other courses—that is, having them define their role as future fellows. During this last third of the course, fellows currently working in the program would come to class and talk about their experiences and unexpected challenges. The last time the course was offered, when we had a large enough pool of active fellows, students in the training course were paired with fellows who were actually conducting sessions. As one of their "practical activities," all "fellows in training" were to observe one of those sections for two weeks, then report back to the class on what they saw and learned.

Most of the students who took this course found it difficult. In their evaluations, they said that the amount of reading was substantially heavier than in most other courses, even advanced literature courses, and some of the texts (especially in the second phase of the course, devoted to language acquisition) they found excessively technical and scholarly and therefore hard to read, particularly for first-year students. But most of them also said that the course had brought about a change in their world view, and thus in their lives, because it had brought them into contact with people and problems of which they'd had no knowledge previously (see the example of "Murray" in Blakely, 1995).

Thus, it seems fair to say that even if nothing else resulted from the program (and it is true that as many as one fourth of the students who took the training course did not go on to participate as active fellows, for a variety of reasons), something very positive had been accomplished. But, as we always told the students at the end of the course, that was just the beginning.

ELS 201

Four to five weeks before the end of the semester, the students in the training seminar and all the other fellows submitted a list of courses they were planning to take the following term. A master list of all these courses was then compiled (excluding those in which there were not likely to be any students in need of help with their English, such as a senior seminar in German), and this list was distributed throughout the campus. NNS students could consult that list and pre-enroll in any of these courses, knowing they would probably be able to enroll in the accompanying section of ELS 201. The master list for fall 1995, distributed the previous spring, consisted of 134 courses, and more courses would no doubt have been added, as some of the 39 fellows had not yet chosen all of their courses.

At the top of the master list we always stated that "supplementary English language study sessions *may* be available for the following courses," because before opening those sections we had to receive permission from the instructors, which was the next step. In the first few days of the ensuing semester the fellows were again polled about the courses they were taking, the apparent absence or presence of E-Ls in them, and whether or not they would feel confident about offering concurrent sections of 201 (fellows were never forced to conduct sections of 201—encouraged, urged, cajoled perhaps, but never forced), and the master list was revised accordingly. To each instructor on that list we sent a personal letter introducing the fellow in their course and asking if they had any objection to this person offering a section of ELS 201 "for up to three non-native-speaking classmates," based on the content of their course. In four semesters, sending out this letter to over 200 faculty members, we only received one negative response. The reason this professor gave for not wanting to participate in the program (handwritten in a full-page letter to the program director) was that he didn't need anyone else to help teach his course, thank you (it was a large, introductory physics course), and that if an undergraduate did undertake to do this, the professor was sure that student would not "get it right," and would only mislead "the students he was tutoring."

The letter was interesting for two reasons. First, it was typical of a kind of response produced by other peer tutorial programs and one that we had been warned to expect. Because programs like ours were often perceived as turning over responsibility for teaching to students (when in fact they were involving them as active participants in learning, rather than as vessels to be filled), some members of the institution were sure to see the program as a threat to their authority (Bruffee, 1993, had a lot to say about peer tutors as agents of subversion). But the letter was also interesting because it was the only one of its kind we ever got. On the whole, faculty at URI were much more favorably disposed to the program than we had thought they would be.

The next step for the fellows, and in some ways the most delicate phase of the program (for reasons stated earlier), was identifying E-Ls in their content courses, and then convincing them that they *were* English-learning students (and not just non-native speakers), that they could benefit by continuing to learn English while studying the course content, and that such a thing was in fact possible. The E-Ls had to be convinced, contrary to deep-seated impressions that might have been implanted in them years before in school, that they could still make progress in their English. Many NNS students remained doubtful, but we had three incitements for encouraging them to enroll in 201. The first was the unit of credit. Second, there was the fact confirmed repeatedly once the program was up and running, by E-L participants and course instructors, that enrolling in these sections increased their chances of passing and doing well in the content course. Third, the sad truth that more and more NNS students who had recently graduated from the university were now checking out groceries at a supermarket, rather than designing bridges or computer programs, because of their limited English.

To ensure that these sections remained truly collaborative and did not become mini-courses taught by the fellows, enrollment in each was limited to three. (In fact, only about 20% of the sections of 201 ever offered actually had the maximum enrollment. Another 20% had two students enrolled, but the majority had only one, which was in some ways ideal for both the fellow and the English learner. In those few instances when more than three students wanted to enroll in one section and they could not sort it out among themselves, the project director made the decision, based on seniority and need.) The first meeting between the fellow and the E-Ls was to decide where and when they would continue to meet throughout the semester. Ordinarily, those meetings were to take place twice a week and would last at least an hour. At this first meeting the E-Ls also filled out a questionnaire that would help the fellow determine each E-L's needs and desires in studying English. The questionnaire also contained a brief contractual statement, to be signed by the E-Ls, that made it clear that they understood the purpose of those sessions and that they agreed to attend them regularly and do the extra language-related study that would be required. (Attendance at less than 80% of the sessions resulted either in not being awarded the extra unit of credit or in having it recorded as a "fail.")

After each meeting with their E-Ls, throughout the semester, fellows were required to fill out a brief "course report" summing up what went on in that session. As soon as they started coming in, these course reports became the lifeblood of the program. Originally intended to keep the project director and graduate assistant informed of the day-to-day progress of each section so that they could monitor the sections and intervene if any problems arose, the reports also became instrumental in helping the fellows themselves understand what it was they were doing and prepare for future sessions.

And problems did arise. E-L students would stop showing up. Fellows would stop sending in course reports. Personality conflicts would develop. Cultures would clash. A woman conducting a section of 201 for an older male student originally from Southeast Asia was shocked speechless one day when he told the woman he thought it was perfectly natural and appropriate for a wife to be beaten by her husband from time to time. (Ironically, the E-L had been moved to express this view because of his sense of confidence in the fellow.) Even more shocking to this fellow was that the subject of the content course was the history of women's liberation.

One can easily imagine that, as the program grew, so did the burden of the project director and the graduate assistant to keep it running smoothly. To alleviate this increasingly heavy administrative burden, two very important reforms were launched.

The first, thanks to a small grant from the URI Foundation, was the establishment of two computer networks, one for all the active fellows and the other for the fellows training course. From then on, fellows conducting sections could send in their course reports via e-mail (and they were strongly encouraged to do so), getting immediate replies when problems arose, or even before they arose. Common problems that could be discussed openly were posted on the ELF electronic bulletin board, and fellows helped one another find solutions. Teaching the fellows training course was also facilitated and enhanced by a computer network. For every text the students read in that course, they were required to write a short summary and critique. Now those summaries were posted on the network for everyone in the course to read and, if they wished, respond to. Other written work as well—reports on "practical activities" and other exercises—were also posted on the course bulletin board for everyone to share.

This in itself did not result in less work for the project director. During the spring semester I was actually spending as many as 5 or 6 hours a day in front of the computer, communicating with program participants via e-mail. However, it did mean that this time spent was much less dispersed and more densely concentrated, and thus more effective. It also meant that I could continue to do much of what was required to run the program from my office at home, which led to the second great reform of Year 3.

One of the problems of this program, a flaw built in from the beginning and referred to previously, was that the further some of the fellows progressed toward their degrees, the fewer occasions they had to practice the talents they had been acquiring, because there were fewer and fewer E-Ls in their courses. This was especially unfortunate because of the natural tendency of most of the fellows to get better and better at what they did the more they did it, and to enjoy it more.[9] Another basic flaw was the ever-increasing amount of time required to monitor the sections

---

[9]This was not true across the board. A few of the fellows did burn out after a couple of semesters, or decide to take a semester's leave of absence—which was the case of the fellow in the Women's Studies course, referred to earlier.

of ELS 201, which were multiplying every semester. If, as originally planned, 40 to 50 fellows were conducting sections of 201 for two of their courses, the project director would be receiving between 160 to 200 course reports every week. Setting up a computer network revealed that those sections receiving immediate feedback via e-mail were much more effective and progressed much more smoothly; hence, the need to respond to each course report as it was received. Properly monitoring those sections also meant sitting in on each of them from time to time, especially at the beginning of the semester. Those sections were being held at all hours, all over, in sorority living rooms, hidden corners of the library, dormitory lounges, even living rooms of private houses far from campus (fellows were strongly advised *not* to hold sessions in their rooms). Keeping track of all of them, even for two people doing nothing but that, would have been physically impossible. But in addition to monitoring the sections of 201, there was the fellows training course to teach (which changed every semester), more and more letters to be sent out to faculty, more and more students applying to the program, longer and longer payroll forms to be filled out every two weeks, purchase orders to be completed, announcements to be posted, master lists to be compiled, E-L lists to be updated, and on and on.

There was a simple, one might even say organic solution to both problems. In the fall semester of 1995, three fellows who had conducted sections of 201 in the past but had no E-Ls that term were hired to take over a number of administrative tasks: helping to set up the new computer network, taking over some of the accounting and paperwork, recruiting NNS students into the program and NS students as future fellows, and occasionally helping monitor some of the sections of 201.

The idea proved so successful that it evolved into the concept of the senior fellow—someone who would not necessarily be conducting a section of 201 him- or herself, but by virtue of past experience would be eminently qualified to help other, less experienced fellows in conducting theirs. During the following semester (spring 1995), seven senior fellows worked with the project director in helping to monitor sections of 201. In some ways these senior fellows were more effective monitors than the project director or graduate assistant, because their presence was perceived as less intrusive and their input more in keeping with the cooperative spirit on which the program was based. Because I was now spending most of my time running the program from my office at home, via e-mail, I was able to turn over my office on campus to a staff of senior fellows who came in at regular hours and were constantly on hand to answer queries over the phone, consult with fellows and E-Ls who stopped by with questions and minor problems, and conduct their own sections of 201 (if they had any). One of these senior fellows, an advanced pharmacy student who enjoyed doing clerical work and did it well, was able to take over the increasingly heavy burden of record keeping and accounting. Another, a major in computer engineering, took charge of maintaining the two computer networks and was available to conduct mini-workshops and help other fellows, even the least computer-literate, to get on line. Finally, a Cambodian student who had taken several sections of 201 with many different fellows and was a fervent supporter of the program was also hired as a staff member who would provide liaison with NNS students on campus. This student's job was to recruit other E-Ls into the program and "talk it up" with campus ethnic groups such as the Asian Students Association and the Latin American Students Association.[10]

For fall semester 1995, on-campus management of the entire program was set to be taken over by a core staff of 9 or 10 senior fellows. In addition to continuing to fulfill the tasks described previously, each would be in charge of two or three other fellows, reading and responding to their course reports and monitoring their sections of 201, reporting directly, when there were problems they could not resolve, to the program director. Thus, the responsibilities of the project director would be gradually taken over, in a natural process of evolution, by the fellows themselves, and the ELF program would not only be genuinely student centered, it would also be student run.

It does not seem an exaggeration to say that the English Language Fellows Program in this last phase—students working together to solve the ESL problems day to day, course by course, individual by individual—would have set a stunning example for others grappling with this problem, and could even have become a landmark in American higher education. Unfortunately, however, this was not to be.

EVALUATION AND PROJECT RESULTS

In 3 years, what did this program accomplish? When one considers that sections of ELS 201 were only offered for 2 of those years, once the two new courses had been put in place and the first group of fellows trained, the accomplishments are remarkable. In spring semester of 1994, the average grade of E-L students in courses in which they were working with fellows was 2.92. This compares to an overall average in those courses, *for native*

[10]One might worry that this increased activity would prove to be too costly, but in fact all of this was done while staying well within the limits of our budget. In the third year $30,000 had been allotted for fellows' salaries, but in fact we ended up spending only two thirds of that amount. Moreover, providing the same type of English language support to the same number of students through more traditional means—full- or even part-time faculty—would have cost much more.

and nonnative speakers alike, of 2.34. Confirming our expectations that conducting sections of ELS 201 would have a beneficial effect on one's own grades, the average grade for fellows in those same courses was 3.62. Both the grades of the fellows and those of their E-L classmates in those courses were significantly higher than their overall GPA.

In the fall of 1994, the average grade of the 34 E-L students in courses for which they were taking concurrent sections of ELS 201 was 2.80. The overall class average in those same courses was 2.49. The average grade for fellows in those same courses was 3.45.

Another goal of this project that can be judged qualititatively was increased retention of the E-L students on campus. As of the end of fall semester 1994, 42 E-L students had participated in the program.[11] Of those 42, 1 had by then dropped out; the rest were still pursuing their studies at URI. These figures give the program a retention rate of 97.6%. The average, *overall* retention rate at the University of Rhode Island is 54%. Based on figures supplied by the Public Information Division of the Office of Educational Research, *the estimated rate of retention of linguistic minorities nationally is between 30% and 35%!*

One normally tends to give more weight to the hard data than to more subjective feedback but, because the ESL problem at its origins is a problem of attitude, I think it is important finally to focus on the latter. The overwhelmingly positive feedback from NS students in the training course, and from E-L students during the first year sections of 201 were offered, was amply documented by Glenn Erickson, Director of the Instructional Development Program at URI and on-site evaluator of the 3-year pilot project.[12] The fact that the fellows training course had a profound and lasting effect on the NS students who took it, even if they did not go on to become active in the program, was discussed at length in the December 1995 issue of *College ESL*. What follows is a brief summary of subjective data received in the third year of the program, from both the fellows and their E-L classmates, in the form of evaluative questionnaires handed out at the end of each semester.

Of the 23 fellows who responded, 7 said they did "much better" in the content courses as a result of conducting concurrent sections of 201, 9 said they did "better," and 7 said they probably would have done "about the same," that is, received the same grade. These last seven all said, however, that preparing for the sections had a beneficial effect on their study habits

[11]Although the program serves both "immigrant" and "international" non-native speakers, this number includes only immigrant students who plan to remain in the United States, and it does not count more than once those students who have taken multiple sections of ELS 201. Hence, the number might seem lower than one would expect.

[12]Dr. Erickson's reports were included in the appendix of my annual reports for Year 1 and 2 and are available from the Fund for the Development of Postsecondary Education.

because it prevented them from procrastinating, helped them formulate ideas about papers and tests, forced them to take better notes, and so on. In discussing what they liked most about the program, the great majority spoke of the close relationships that developed between them and their E-L classmates, whom they would never have gotten to know otherwise, and of the "good feeling" that comes from being a fellow, and which therefore added another dimension to the traditional undergraduate experience. Following is a sample of some of the fellows' responses:

> "Participating in the program makes you feel like you're doing something special."
>
> "The personal contact involved with being a Fellow has made the experience valuable. This program enables people to come together and share their ideas. I have made a friend and an excellent study partner this year. . . ."
>
> "Participation in this program has impacted my academic performance the most. Secondly, this program has made me a little more outgoing, as the Fellow must earn the trust of the E-L. To do this, one must pay attention to people and be aware of them. . . ."
>
> "I have realized that ESL is not remedial at all . . . that it involves learning a new way to think along with a new language, that it involves an immense amount of courage, having an open mind and a strong hold on your own values."
>
> "I learned how to LISTEN."
>
> "I felt it was a great learning experience. It has taught me a lot about teaching and understanding."
>
> "[I experienced a] nice feeling to help E-Ls and make friends with them. My grades were better because of the study sessions. The E-Ls' grades were better also. This showed me that the program was working. I learned a lot about the different cultures and customs outside of the U.S., the E-Ls learned a lot more about the U.S. and the language. Everyone had fun while learning."
>
> "I have learned so much about the E-Ls and now they are my friends. We will be able to keep in touch with each other, even though we may not have a class together anymore. . . . I've learned that being a fellow goes beyond the classroom. . . ."

Of the 36 E-Ls who handed in questionnaires, 2 said if they had not participated in the program, they would have done "about the same" in the content courses, 20 said they did "better," and 14 reported "much better." As for the effect they felt the sessions had had on their English language skills, 2 said their English had stayed "about the same," 14 that it had gotten "a little better," and 20 said that because of that one-unit study section their English had gotten "much better." Asked if they intended to participate in the program again in the future, 32 said they did (several adding "absolutely!") and 4 said they did not—3 because they were living off campus and did not have the extra time, and 1 because she was graduating. All 36 respondents said they would recommend the program strongly to their NNS friends. For them, as for the fellows, an important side benefit of the program was the personal dimension, and the feeling that they were not alone. Clearly, it was also changing the way they saw themselves. Here is a sample of some of their responses:

> "[The program] tells you that there are people out there to help you, you're not alone. It takes me a long time to read, and this helps me to know I'm not dumb, or illiterate."
>
> "I like studying with F. She so helpful, so wonderful person. . . ."
>
> "The program is able to most important thing, build the confidence in us. We have low confidence, low self-esteem. . . ."
>
> "I never like to have other read my writing because I feel embarrass, but I've learned from this and made me realize that this class was helpful."
>
> "It's good because I can ask S. anything I want, without being afraid. It helps to know someone."
>
> "I could never do this class without this work together."

In preparing the proposal for a follow-up dissemination grant, some of the faculty who had had firsthand experience with the program were asked to write letters of support. I end this section by quoting from those letters, because they show the extent to which the program had taken hold, and begun to have a positive effect, in terms of faculty development, in 2 short years:

> I am an academic counselor for a special admission and retention program for students projected to be at risk at the university. . . . My students were nurtured and encouraged by the individual outreach and attention. They were helped immensely by the specific content work done with Fellows and felt the language work was building proficiency and confidence. Many of my students have felt isolated and marginalized in the classroom, . . . and this program opened doors and built skills like no other I've seen. . . . I have run tutoring programs for over twenty years. I have worked with at risk populations in higher education for over twenty years. This Fellows program combines the best elements of content work and language acquisition.

> Students who are non-native speakers of English [at URI] have benefited enormously from the Fellows Program. In my own [philosophy] classes this past term I witnessed the development of academic skills and confidence in a young Laotion woman who possessed a strong intellect but an uncertain mastery of English, and the breathtaking achievements of a Vietnamese-American student who eventually surpassed her Fellow's performance on an exam! . . . Prior to the inception of [the ELF program] I sadly watched motivated NNS students drift behind or become discouraged in some of my courses; despite my most earnest efforts, I could not attend fully to their individual language needs. The Fellows Program has rectified this situation. . . .

> I am a 53-year-old white male tenured full professor with 27 years experience teaching in the English Department at URI. . . . The young Vietnamese woman in my lower-division [literature] course this spring had a strong work ethic but a heavy schedule of classes and work. Her English Language Fellow kept her focused and working efficiently. . . . The Vietnamese student earned a B+ in the course; the Fellow earned an A; I felt great satisfaction in seeing both succeed in a challenging course. But the benefits were more far reaching than reflected in these superior grades. . . . The Fellow freed me from the frustration of trying to work with the non-native speaker on tasks and in ways that I had no preparation for. . . .

> In the past two semesters, I have been pleased to have [Fellows] working with their nonnative speaking classmates in my introductory physical anthropology courses. . . . Predictably, the difficulties are compounded for nonnative speakers, with the result that many do not make grades commensurate with their intelligence or their overall academic record. The ELF Program has worked wonderfully to eliminate the disadvantages experienced by nonnative speakers and allow them to maximize both learning and grades.

CONCLUSION

At the beginning of Year 4, 39 fellows were poised to conduct sections of ELS 201 in as many as 134 content courses for over 150 E-L classmates. Thus, the program was on the verge of living up to its promise to provide ESL instruction to more students, in a more relevant manner, than traditional courses in ESL per se.[13] By this time many ESL professionals throughout the country had learned about the program and had expressed an interest in replicating it in some way on their own campuses. In the spring of 1995, extensive plans were made between URI and six other U.S. colleges to apply for another FIPSE grant under a special competition designed to "dissemi-

[13]By then, the average number of E-L students accommodated by these more traditional courses every semester at URI had dwindled to 25 or 30.

nate proven reforms." Receiving the grant would have provided seed money to establish similar programs at each of the six institutions.

Unfortunately, at the very last minute, the president of URI decided to withdraw his support for this proposal. Moreover, when FIPSE funding ran out in August 1995, the URI administration decided not to continue supporting the program at its current level, and in fact to cut it so drastically that it could no longer exist in the form that is described here. The position of the project director was terminated, and I was replaced by a part-timer who agreed to take over directing the program in return for compensation for one course. Funds for the fellows were slashed to a fraction of what was needed. Instead of getting paid, fellows were encouraged to conduct sections of 201 on a volunteer basis, or were told they could receive academic credit instead of cash as an Independent Study Project, two "solutions" put forth by the administration that I had vehemently opposed for a number of reasons.[14]

The URI administration said it had no choice in making these cuts. Like many other public state universities, URI was faced with severe budgetary shortfalls and was forced to make painful decisions. Still, these

---

[14]When I learned about the proposal to substitute credit for cash, I said that it raised serious questions, and that, if adopted, would subvert the spirit on which the program was based. Because this proposal *was* adopted (over my strong objections), and because other people interested in establishing similar programs have asked me what I thought about the idea, I briefly summarize some of those questions here:

1. Much of the work that the fellows do is administrative in nature—making copies, filling out course reports, looking through texts for appropriate exercises in grammar, pronunciation, and so on. A lot of it is also repetitive—going back over the same pronunciation problem again and again throughout the semester until the NNS student begins to get it right, pointing out the same error in articles or verb tense in weekly writing assignments, and so on. Wouldn't giving credit for this type of activity run the risk of devaluing academic credit at the institution, and of alienating other faculty concerned about maintaining academic standards?
2. My own experience with independent study projects is that they require a lot of extra work, and that faculty are wise not to take them on too readily, certainly not more than one in any given semester. Would this nontenure-track part-timer, in addition to everything else he or she would have to do to keep the program running, also be expected to monitor 35 to 50 independent study projects every semester, and make sure that they were academically sound?
3. Many of the fellows, students in Engineering, Pharmacy, or Education, are already taking the maximum allowable number of credits every semester. At URI they are allowed to add to that load, but they must pay for it. Thus, instead of being paid for conducting those sessions, were some of the fellows—and some of the most dedicated ones—now going to have to pay for that privilege?
4. Giving people something you can manufacture in unlimited quantities, in exchange for their doing something for you, indicates either that you don't take what they are doing very seriously, or, if you do, that you hope they do not realize that what you are "paying" them is worthless. In either case, the ploy seems pretty cynical.

decisions imply a political dimension that is impossible to ignore. Last summer, after learning that my own position was being terminated and that the entire English Language Studies program was being decimated, effectively wiping out the progress we had made in the previous decade, I had lunch with a member of the faculty who had always been a friend and supporter. The way he saw it, ESL at URI was like a poor orphan in a Dickens novel. "You may be more deserving, more capable and qualified than other persons who came after you, but because ESL was an orphan you had no one to stand up for you, and in the end when there was not enough money to buy food for everyone, it was your plate that was removed from the table." After a year thinking about what happened, and why, I think this person was right, and unfortunately I think that what he said holds true for a lot of other people besides myself, going to the heart of the ESL problem throughout the country.

Looking back, one can say that in the end the English Language Fellows Program at URI fell victim to the very ignorance it had been created to dispel, because despite a loudly proclaimed policy in favor of "multicultural diversity," the administration made it very clear, when push came to shove, that its priorities did not include improving the plight of NNS students on campus, all of whom, however, were from different cultures. In this respect, the decision of the administration to cut academic support for these culturally diverse students reveals attitudes about language and "foreignness," discussed at length previously, that one would not expect to find at a university.

Still, the people who spent 4 years helping to put this program together know that it is only a matter of time before those attitudes are recognized for what they are. In the meantime, we are confident that the English Language Fellows Program will serve as an inspiration and model to others, and that the programs those others create will take root and prosper.

A NOTE ON FUNDING AND ADMINISTRATION, AND A FINAL WORD TO OTHERS

The total amount of support from FIPSE, spread out over the 3-year life of this pilot project, was $187,000 (approximately $47,000 in Year 1, $63,000 in Year 2, and $77,000 in Year 3). The great bulk of that funding went into three main areas: 50% of the salary for the project director; full tuition, benefits, and salary for a graduate research assistant; and, in Years 2 and 3, matching funds to pay the fellows. Fellows were paid $6.00 an hour the first semester they conducted sections of ELS 201, and every semester thereafter in which they continued to be active in the program they received a 50 cent raise, up to the allowed maximum for undergraduates at URI of $8.00 per hour. Active fellows spent an average of 5 hours a week on each section of ELS 201, including time spent preparing, reading their classmates' papers, and so on, for which they were also paid. This works out to an average of 55 to 60 hours per 15-week semester, per section of 201. Our budget in the second year included $20,000 for fellows' salaries, and in the third, $30,000, but in both years we ended up spending only half the allotted amount.

People wanting to set up similar programs at their own institutions should bear in mind a few very important considerations:

1. Getting such a program up and running is a full-time job. In addition to a project director, staff for a similar-sized program should include some sort of research or teaching assistant, and secretarial support to help process the increasingly heavy weight of paperwork.

2. The study sections conducted by the specially trained native speakers *must be credit bearing,* and that credit must count toward graduation. There are many strong arguments to support this, and these arguments should be clearly understood by the administration before the groundwork is laid.

3. Once the program is running, communication is the key to success—communication between the director and the fellows; between the fellows and the content faculty; and among the fellows, the director, and all participating NNS students. For this reason, weekly or bimonthly meetings should be a built-in feature. Half- or full-day workshops are also a good idea, and attendance at the meetings and workshops should be obligatory. Direct communication among all participants is now greatly enhanced by the possibility of establishing a computer network, something that became a vital feature of the ELF program in its last year.

4. In order for such a project to succeed and prosper it must have, a priori, the unqualified, enthusiastic support of the administration; and that support, including guarantees of employment security, must be in writing.

REFERENCES

Benesch, S. (Ed.). (1988). *Ending remediation: Linking ESL and content in higher education.* Washington, DC: TESOL.

Blakely, R. (1989, October 18). We must learn to deal with foreign students' language problems. *The Chronicle of Higher Education,* p. B2.

Blakely, R. (1994, March 18). Drowning in the mainstream. *Providence Journal-Bulletin,* p. A14.

Blakely, R. (1997). The English Language Fellows Program. In D. Brinton & M. A. Snow (Eds.), *The content-based classroom: Perspectives in integrating language and content.* White Plains, NY: Addison-Wesley Longman.

Boyer, E. L. (1987). *College: The undergraduate experience in America.* New York: Harper & Row.

Bruffee, K. (1993). *Collaborative learning: Higher education, interdependence, and the authority of knowledge.* Baltimore: Johns Hopkins University Press.

Push them into English. (1994, March 18). *Providence Journal-Bulletin,* p. A16.

Vygotsky, L. (1978). *Mind in society.* Cambridge, MA: Harvard University Press.

Waggoner, D. (Ed.). (1995). New language information reveals differences by English-speaking ability. *Numbers and Needs, 5*(4), 1–4.

Zamel, V. (1995). Strangers in academia. *CCC, 46,* 506–521.

17

The Creation and Development of a Community-Based English Program: The Riverside Language Program, Inc.

Leslie Robbins
The Riverside Language Program, New York

The Riverside Language Program is a not-for-profit school that teaches English to newly arrived refugee and immigrant adults. The program was started in 1979 by three teachers: Phyllis Berman, Anne LeLan, and Leslie Robbins. We knew that there was an enormous need for literacy and ESL classes for refugees and immigrants in our community, and to meet the needs of these students we wanted to develop a program that was designed by experienced teachers, not by administrators with little experience in the classroom. We wanted a program that put students first—a school in which the administrators served the teachers, so that the teachers could serve the students. In the past 17 years we have taught over 25,000 students from all around the world and quadrupled our budget. Still, with all our success, we are faced with an uncertain future because of recent anti-immigrant feeling that has gripped this country.

CORE VALUES

Hierarchy

When we began the school, we had each worked in settings in which politics, funding, or other needs drove the programs. Participants were considered last. We wanted our school to be different. We planned Riverside's hierarchy as an inverted triangle—a place where students were at the top. Student needs came first, and they were to drive the program.

Next in order of importance came teachers, because they directly serve students. We wanted to find people who viewed teaching as their career. We were interested in people who were open to new ideas but not without ideas of their own. Most of all, we looked for people who listened to students.

At the bottom of the triangle was administration. Its primary function was to make it easier for teachers to do their work with students. Each administrator believed that direct service to students is the most important aspect of any school. In the beginning we spent at least one third of our time teaching, and we knew from our own experience how important it was to have the mimeograph machine working or sufficient chalk on hand. Teaching concerns were not viewed as an interruption in the office but as its *raison d'être*.

STAFFING

Job Design

We were determined to create a setting in which teachers could grow professionally. By offering core staff full-time jobs with the attendant benefits (which is unusual in adult education), we were able to give our teachers the luxury of time. Teachers who must rush off to other part-time jobs in order to pay the rent cannot be expected to form an attachment to a program; those who can support themselves from one job in one site often have time to share their successes and failures with one another and time to devote to institutional needs. As a result, we have attracted staff who are truly exceptional.

A full-time job at Riverside means teaching the same group of students from 9:30 AM to 3:30 PM 5 days a week, with a 1-hour lunch break, and being available for meetings between 3:30 and 5:00 PM. Although meetings are only held about twice a month, we do not want to hire teachers who have another job that requires them to leave regularly at 3:30, because we value the informal time spent with colleagues after class for professional growth. Many teachers come early or stay late to prepare for class. Salaries in the full-time program are annualized. Built into the system is that teachers may be absent for 1 day in a 30-day class cycle with no effect on their pay. If, however, a teacher is not absent, the monies that would have been paid to a substitute are instead given to the teacher as a bonus. This ensures that our teachers are not penalized for providing consistent coverage for their students.

When we are unable to offer full-time jobs, we do our best to offer as many teaching hours as possible so that we have fewer staff teaching more hours. In our off-site program, classes meet 2 evenings a week for 2½ hours a session; hence, scheduling makes it difficult to offer more than 10 hours a week. Part-time teachers are paid on an hourly basis. We do try to hire full-time teachers from our part-time staff, when feasible.

Hiring

At Riverside we make every effort to hire people who view the teaching of English as their vocation. We look for people who have solid educational training in ESOL, with a background in linguistics and language acquisition among other subjects—people who are able to present the regularities of English grammar and pronunciation as well as who are knowledgeable about the latest research and pedagogy in our field. Full-time teachers must have a master's degree in TESOL or a related field.

We want our teachers to have first-hand experience of several methodologies (i.e., teachers who have studied foreign languages with practitioners who used different methods). There is no single methodology that we espouse as a school; we encourage our teachers to develop their skills in whatever ways they feel suit their personal styles. We would expect teachers to have some familiarity with the Silent Way, Community Language Learning, Total Physical Response, and Suggestopaedia, whether or not they choose to teach using these methods. We would, however, expect from all our teachers student-centered teaching.

Although we think that different kinds of experience can have different values, we are in the enviable position of having more qualified applicants than positions, so we also look for people who are experienced with adults and groups the size of our typical class. Of course, as Caleb Gattegno said, 20 years of experience can mean that a teacher has repeated his or her first mistakes for 19 more years. Therefore, we look for a combination of experience and openness.

Finally, although we value training and experience, we believe that teaching is an art as well as a skill. In interviews, we look for one characteristic over others: an ability to listen. We believe that despite the stress of an interview, a prospective employee who does not answer the question asked, or who needs to have something repeated several times, will display the same lack of focus in a classroom. If you are to teach to the needs of students and to capitalize on the "teachable moments" when students are truly open to learning, you must be tuned in to your students. No amount of training or experience makes up for the personal qualities that lead to good listening.

Salary

When we apply for a grant, we are competing against other programs. Sometimes another program can offer the same services less expensively, because they do not hire full-time teachers and/or they do not pay benefits and/or their hourly rates are low. Because funders seem to look at the bottom line first, this helps to keep salaries in adult education far below what they should be, despite the dedication and training of the practitioners. Although our salaries, for example, are competitive with other adult education programs in New York City, they are about one third lower than salaries at city and state universities. The problem may be rooted in the assumption that most adult education teachers do something else as their primary source of income. We have tried to be as fair as possible with regard to salaries; it has been our policy to pay all teachers at the same rate—regardless of their amount of time with us—for two reasons:

1. A new teacher must spend much more time in preparing than must an experienced one.
2. We didn't want to be in the position of needing to let experienced teachers go because they were more expensive than newer ones.

However, we do offer experienced teachers on our staff special projects that come with extra compensation: Our teachers have worked as and been paid for acting as "master teachers," for developing curriculum, and for doing supervisory work in our part-time program. The working conditions, the skilled colleagues, and the extraordinary students are the things that make low pay at Riverside tolerable, although we do not consider it acceptable.

Staff Development

At Riverside, we think that one of the best ways to learn about teaching is to observe other teachers at work. Unfortunately, this has historically been a privilege reserved for supervisors. Several years ago, one of our teachers, Jim Roth, when talking about the value of peer observation, suggested that if each teacher had a free period during the week while other teachers were teaching, more peer observations could be scheduled. On this suggestion we redesigned our program. Instead of teaching from 9:30 AM to 3:30 PM 5 days a week, each teacher is free for a different hour and a half each week. This allows the teacher to observe any of the 13 other full-time teachers whose classes are in progress.

We encourage practitioners of different philosophies (integrative learning/suggestopaedia, silent way, counseling/learning) to give language-learning demonstrations in foreign languages at our school. This ensures that our knowledge of the methods is not abstract—that we have experienced the methods personally. Feedback sessions help us learn how our colleagues responded, and we remember how we personally felt about working with colleagues who learned more quickly (or more slowly) than we did. Thus, our own experiences can inform our teaching.

We also encourage our current and former staff to provide professional development experiences for the rest of us. These are scheduled into staff meetings, offered after 3:30 on weekdays or held on weekends. For example, a staff member who has explored alternative ways of assessing student language proficiency might present a workshop to other staff members. Someone who has worked on developing respect for other cultures in the classroom might make a presentation. In the past we read together *Hunger of Memory* by Richard Rodriguez and *Lost in Translation* by Eva Hoffman, and met at lunchtime to discuss their implications for our teaching. Each activity serves to make us more aware of the learning process and, we hope, better teachers. But lest this sound too sanctimonious, we also like one another and enjoy spending time together.

Representation

To ensure that teachers' concerns are voiced and that there is a clear interchange among teachers and administrators, we have monthly staff meetings led by staff members. The responsibility for facilitating revolves, so that everyone on the full-time staff has the experience of running the meeting. Facilitators are asked to check in with other staff members and to incorporate their concerns in the agenda. In this way, each meeting reflects the particular style of the facilitators, whereas also responding to the needs of other staff members.

ENTRANCE LOTTERY

When we began the school, we accepted students on a first-come, first-served basis. As our reputation grew, however, our classes filled earlier and earlier, until we began to see hundreds of prospective students who wanted to study at Riverside. Because of funding limitations, we could accept fewer than one fourth of the candidates. Hopeful students began sleeping at our site to ensure a place in the class. Not only was this heartbreaking, it was also clearly untenable; we needed a creative solution. We decided to institute a lottery system that would treat everyone equally. Although there was some initial concern that a lottery for education was undignified, the equity of the system won out.

Currently, all eligible people who are present at a particular time place a self-addressed postcard into a lottery box. When all the postcards are in, we pull out and mail the number of postcards equivalent to the number of spaces we have. The rest of the cards are marked "Sorry, no space available" and mailed. Students receive immediate feedback about whether they have secured a place in the class, and are not placed on waiting lists that serve only a public relations value. If people have not been accepted, they know that they must actively search out another program.

Our classes are scheduled so that we hold a lottery every month and take in about 150 new students each time. The remaining 150 spaces are filled by students who are continuing in the program from a previous class.

PART-TIME CLASSES

In 1985, we were approached by the New York Public Library to run ESOL classes in several of its branches. We worried about whether, in a part-time off-site program, we would be able to sustain the professional atmosphere and standards that we had established for our intensive program. We were concerned because where there is one teacher at a site and little administrative support, it is extremely difficult to be as excited about your teaching experiences as when there are colleagues with whom to share your experiences, and administrators to share the problems.

Over the years, we think we have developed some ways of making teachers in these libraries feel less isolated. First, we never run fewer than two classes concurrently. This ensures that each teacher will have at least one colleague on site, and it allows us to divide the students into at least two levels. Second, teachers from our intensive program work as administrators in our part-time program. This ensures that our philosophy and ideals are brought to our off-site teachers. It also provides our full-time teachers with an opportunity to develop their supervisory skills. This practice is in keeping with our philosophy that administrators who are also teachers are most likely to keep students' needs at the core of the program.

LANGUAGE WORKSHOP

The Language Workshop had its birth because we wanted to free teachers to observe one another, and from its inception it has been very popular with both teachers and students. In the workshop, students select the materials with which they want to work. Teachers or the workshop staff can make recommendations, but the final choice rests with the students. Because we want students to take responsibility for their own learning, this system helps to develop their skills and to emphasize our respect for their ability to make appropriate decisions about their own language-learning needs.

Students may choose to listen to popular songs with headphones. We have several tape recorders, cassettes of popular music with words, and typed song sheets. Students may choose to read current magazines or newspapers in English. *The New York Times* classified ads, *Newsweek*, *New York Magazine*, *People*, and *Consumer Reports* are some of the most popular.

We have Language Master machines on which students can hear a word or sentence, then tape themselves saying the same thing and listen to the differences in pronunciation. We have a variety of card games created by teachers that encourage students to match words and pictures or verb tenses, and so on. We have paperback copies of classic and popular novels in the original and abridged versions. Students may choose to work with any of our commercially prepared materials, both texts and cassettes, all of which are self-correcting. As long as the material being worked on is in English, we feel it benefits our students.

Some of the most popular places in our workshop are our conversation tables, where students have an opportunity to talk with college students, retired people, or other neighborhood volunteers. Our students often say that school provides their only opportunity to meet Americans. Our conversation partners often provide them with the cultural insights for which they are looking, not to mention the language and social skills.

There are also six typewriters in the room. With nothing more than a sign-up sheet, some blank paper, and some touch-typing practice charts, we are always surprised at how many students choose to spend their lunch hours or after-school time here. Students actually compete for space so they can learn to touch type. They view keyboard skills as the route to clerical and computer jobs.

MODEL SCHOOL PROGRAMS

Observation Days

For many years we have opened our doors to people who are interested in our approaches to teaching or administration. Some of our visitors are policymakers, some are teacher trainers, and some are teachers. We designate one day a month on which we are open to visitors and, as part of formalizing the visits, we now charge for them. Visitors must reserve a place in advance by sending in a check for $25. Adult education teachers working in New York City not-for-profit agencies can attend free of charge, thanks to a short-term grant we received.

We begin promptly at 9:00 AM with an hour of orientation to the school. During this orientation we hope to provide visitors with a context in which to observe, so that they need not disturb the teacher with questions during the class. We are also explicit about our expectations of how visitors will behave in the classroom; we ask them to be as "invisible" as possible. We request that they participate only if specifically asked by the teacher. Armed with this information, visitors create less of a distraction and do not interfere with teachers focusing on students' needs. Visitors may observe as many as three teachers during their visit, and end the day at 4:30 PM after reflecting on the experience in a small-group setting. These observation days have proven to be extremely popular in the New York City adult education community.

Internships

We also offer internships for graduate students, in which they can work with a "master teacher" for 6 weeks. These cost $1,000 and are paid for by the institutions granting the degree or by the students themselves. Initially interns observe the "master teacher," and gradually they take more responsibility, starting with small-group activities and building to planning and taking responsibility for the whole class. Teachers and interns meet together on a daily basis to plan activities, discuss the class, and evaluate their successes and failures.

Workshops

We also offer monthly workshops by staff members that are open to non-Riverside faculty. These subjects range from "How to Get Authentic Feedback and What to Do With It" to "Large Groups, Small Groups, Pairs: When to Use Which and How," to "Incorporating Workplace Skills at Each of the ESOL Levels." Workshops are 3 hours long and are offered on Friday afternoons. We charge $50 per person for attendance, and places must be reserved in advance by sending in a check.

ADVOCACY CONCERNS FOR THE FUTURE

We have always seen ourselves as advocates for both the profession and the people we serve. As such, we attend a variety of meetings and conferences concerned with both teaching and immigration, at which we try to advance the concerns of both groups. We have by now developed a reputation for being outspoken. (Although perhaps not everyone would use that euphemism.)

In reissuing the Adult Education Act, Congress called for the states, by the summer of 1993, to develop plans that would detail the indicators and measures of program quality. Riverside's directors have played an important role in the debates that have focused on such questions as how to quantify quality (e.g., how to document adult education clients' "growth" in ability) and what instruments should be used to measure that growth.

Issues of program success are even more acute for recipients of "performance-based" contracts, which have become increasingly popular. The outcomes for which programs receive payment are often unrelated to what practitioners consider success. For example, although we are funded to teach ESOL, on one of our contracts the largest amount of money comes to us for students who get jobs or are accepted into training programs.

We are also at odds with funders about the most basic measure of "success" of ESOL students. We are required to use a test whose authors say emphatically is not designed to measure progress. The funders, however, have required entry and exit scores on this test to measure "growth." The test takes great time and expertise to use well, even for placement. As a measure of progress, it is totally inadequate.

To assess the quality of our program, Phyllis Berman created the following list:

1. Are our classes full, with a reasonable ratio between students and teacher (15 to 20 students to one teacher)?
2. Are there enough students who show interest in the program to let us know that the need for instruction exists and that our reputation draws people to our classes?
3. Do students stay in class for a reasonable amount of time (at least 75% of the class hours) to indicate their satisfaction with the instruction?
4. Do students make progress in English? (We have designed a portfolio that contains tapes of students speaking and samples of their writing to document growth in English language skills, to substantiate what our teachers know about their own students' progress. These portfolios are far more authentic assessments than a "standardized" test.)
5. Does student mastery of English lead to greater participation in American life? (We telephone and write to students after they leave the program to know what other steps they have taken toward full entry into American life.)
6. Do we provide appropriate out-of-classroom services (e.g., counseling, life skills workshops, conversation practice, and help in taking the next steps after ESOL) to support the teaching/learning relationship?

7. Do we find and retain staff who are well trained, experienced, and committed to working with ESOL adults?

8. Are we able to provide an environment of respect and growth for our staff that makes it worthwhile for people to continue to work with us despite the general inadequacy of pay for adult education professionals?

9. Do we see positive movement in the attitude of funders, legislators, and the general public toward non-native speakers of English, immigrants, and refugees in general, and ESOL instruction in particular?

10. Do we manage money responsibly so that we neither overspend nor underspend, and utilize our resources wisely?

11. Do we get feedback at every level of our program and remain flexible to needed changes?

We believe that if programs and funding agencies asked similar questions, programs could be serving participants rather than having to spend their limited resources on meaningless responses to bureaucratic questions. We would assume that answers to these questions would not be "yes" or "no," but instead would fall onto a continuum (perhaps a range from "rarely" to "frequently"). Programs would be expected to improve their performance regularly—rather than to begin as perfect.

18

Cooperative Links Energize New Jersey ESL/Bilingual Professionals

Jessie M. Reppy
Kean College

Elaine Coburn
Union County College

This chapter outlines the story of a vision and the project that developed from it. Creating the Resource Center for Language Minority Students (RCLMS) enabled educators in New Jersey to work collaboratively to better serve the adult ESL and bilingual education (BE) students of our state. We hope that the ESL professionals who read this chapter will be inspired to create their own statewide resource centers, and that our writing of this chapter may in some way be instrumental in the re-funding of our RCLMS.

Jessie M. Reppy and Elaine Coburn were director and assistant director, respectively, of the RCLMS at Kean College of New Jersey from its inception in 1992 until it was defunded by the state of New Jersey in 1994. The center served any professional working with limited-English-proficient (LEP) students in New Jersey's 2- and 4-year colleges and universities, both public and private.

No one knew the needs of college-level ESL students better than Dr. Jose Adames, presently associate dean, School of Liberal Arts, at Kean College in Union, New Jersey. Bilingual himself and with many years of teaching and administrative experience in Kean's ESL Program, Dr. Adames saw immediately the advantages inherent in the 1991 offer of $40,000 from the New Jersey Department of Higher Education to begin a statewide resource center that would support the professionals in New Jersey's 2- and 4-year colleges and universities, both public and private. Also, he saw immediately that Kean, a 4-year state college that draws its students from Newark and Elizabeth's multi-ethnic populations and is easily accessible from anywhere in the state, would be a perfect location for such a center. Kean's commitment to serving the needs of ethnic and language minority students was another factor recommending it as the site for the proposed center.

THE VISION

Marta Carbral, director of the Office of Bilingual Educational Issues (OBEI), New Jersey Department of Higher Education, discussed the vision of a statewide center with Dr. Adames and the Dean of Kean's School of Liberal Arts, Edward Weil. Such a statewide center, she held, would involve all ESL–Bilingual coordinators in the state. Ms. Cabral also suggested that such a service, which she named the Resource Center for Language Minority Students, would gather data, conduct and support research, and create a mechanism to establish policy for the LEP students. The significance of her vision should be noted: In 1991, the New Jersey ESL–BE college population was invisible and needed advocacy.

In retrospect, Dr. Adames noted, "The RCLMS was the fruit of the collaborative effort of ESL–BE coordinators to meet the needs and make visible the LEP population. It re-energized ESL–BE practitioners because they saw a new opportunity to do good work for the students."

Ms. Cabral's vision took form with the planning grant written for 1991–1992 under the supervision of Dr. Adames. This grant provided for an assessment of the needs across the state, and for a testing survey to be carried out by two teams composed of ESL–BE coordinators from different regions in the state. The testing team was to ascertain which tests were being used in programs and to investigate the possibility of using other measures. The needs assessment team designed and sent out a questionnaire to survey statewide needs. From the work of the needs assessment team, grant writers determined that a center would work best if comprised of separate components: a materials bank, an ongoing database, research, professional development services, technical assistance for program development, and information dissemination.

Under the planning grant and during the first year of the center's operations, researchers discovered that there were 9,700 ESL–BE students actually sitting in the state's college and university classrooms, up from 8,200 in 1988 (*CELMS Report*, 1992). New Jersey's experience was consistent with the national trend at that time. According to the U.S. Department of Education (1992), enrollment of non-White and foreign-born college students in the United States rose with only the White enrollment declining over a 1-year period. Asian enrollment was up 9.4%, Hispanic enrollment was up 10.1%, and foreign-born enrollment was up 9.9% (*The Chronicle of Higher Education*, 1994).

Given the growth in the language minority college student population, and understanding that this population and their instructors have requirements that are somewhat different from those in the mainstream, the need for a statewide resource center was obvious. No one had done this before; however, the country was experiencing the largest tide of immigration since the early 20th century. Thus, Kean became home to the Resource Center for Language Minority Students.

While working on the planning grant, Dr. Adames and Ms. Cabral designed the center. Dr. Adames remarked, "Marta had the vision, but needed people to bring about something that would work in the real world. She wanted a mechanism that would continue to advocate for the LEP population."

THE REALIZATION

From the work of the planning grant came the implementation grant in 1992. First, Dr. Reppy was appointed the director of the RCLMS. Next, there was a search committee for assistant director composed of ESL–BE program coordinators from various institutions around the state. The committee selected Elaine Coburn as assistant director. Her qualifications included a master's degree and considerable classroom experience in ESL, as well as a background in graphic arts—a combination that proved invaluable to the center.

After taking on a graduate student and a student aide, the director and assistant director equipped the office. The director made appointments to staff the various components, and established an advisory council composed of representatives from the business and academic communities. Elaine Coburn assumed responsibility for information dissemination.

Drawing on a network built over 25 years in the profession, Dr. Reppy secured coordinators for professional development, technical assistance for program development, materials bank, database, and research to join the coordinator for dissemination (see Fig. 18.1). Coordinators received a small stipend or, in the case of Kean faculty, released time.

Materials Bank

A program coordinator from an area county college agreed to establish a materials bank. Kean's Curriculum Library would be the repository for the holdings. The coordinator not only solicited several publishers, but also purchased materials. At the end of 2 years, the collection boasted

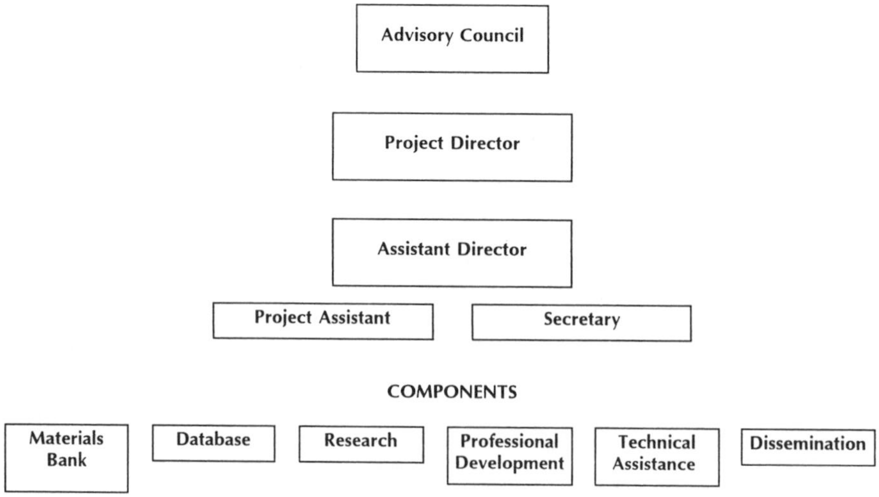

FIG. 18.1. Resource Center for Language Minority Students.

over 500 pieces, including books, audiotapes, and videotapes. The center also offered a collection of language tests that were kept in the office for security reasons. This was not a circulating library, but anyone interested was free to enjoy the collection on site.

Michael Pekarofski, ESL teacher and advisor from Essex County College, stated, "The value of having hands-on access to so much teaching material cannot be underestimated. This is a great service, one that I hope to take advantage of more often."

The growing importance of computer-assisted learning prompted us to devote a portion of the materials bank to software for student use. The center and ESL–BE coordinators at Jersey City State College (JCSC) contracted to review, select, and make available language-learning software at the computer center at JCSC. As a part of this agreement, the faculty at JCSC offered free workshops for ESL–BE professionals. The RCLMS advertised the workshops, handled the registration, and provided printed materials necessary for the presentations.

The RCLMS published a brochure of the software holdings and made its availability known through its newsletter and workshops. Because the center was online, the materials bank inventory was posted on the electronic bulletin board New Jersey Intercollegiate Network (NJIN), out of Rutgers University. The listing was periodically updated. The staff determined that this, in addition to the newsletter, *Newslink*, would keep ESL–BE professionals current with the holdings.

Database

The need for a database was unquestioned, and the coordinator selected to manage it was a survey and data analysis specialist from Kean's psychology department. Under her direction, the center staff, with the cooperation of the state's ESL–BE program administrators, began a multipronged effort to gather information on the LEP population, including their needs, numbers, programs, and staffing. In the past, the data on this population had been gathered sporadically and were not available from a central location.

The consultant recommended a core survey and a 3-year matrix, with a focus on a special item each year. The items for each of the 3 years were, respectively, program assessment, support services for ESL–BE students and faculty, and faculty background and development. These items targeted information that, although important, did not need to be gathered yearly. The consultant recommended 3 years as the amount of time necessary to determine trends in the population.

The center published database information yearly for 2 years. OBEI was very pleased to receive the two publications, *Program Profiles* and *Program Profiles, Year II*. These publications represented the first time that this data had been professionally gathered and published. The publications were free and available on request. Coordinators of programs found the volumes valuable for comparing their programs with others around the state. For example, if coordinators wished to approach their institutions about credit for ESL courses, the publications enabled them to see what other individual institutions across New Jersey were granting, thereby saving numerous phone calls and much time.

In an era of growth, data are indispensable. In an era of increasing numbers and diminishing funds, a database is critical in designing individual programs and making strategic plans for the future. Such information is also very useful in advocating for this population in the political arena, whether it is on an individual campus or in the state capitol.

Research

The director appointed two representatives from two different institutions in the state to lead a research consortium. Both appointees had expressed an interest in doing research. They, in turn, formed a small consortium whose charge was to survey program administrators and carry out research projects on issues deemed important in the field in New Jersey. The consortium members also solicited input from the Office of Bilingual Educational Issues, DHE, and the Council for the Education of Language Minority Students (CELMS). CELMS was a policymaking body composed of volunteer members from the academic community and organizations with concern for LEP students, and was established by DHE during the period of the planning grant. During the existence of the center, consortium members carried out research on the New Jersey Basic Skills Placement Test, a replacement for this test for LEP students, and the adjunct population in the field in New Jersey. In 1993, the director of the center formed a research review committee that reviewed the research done and returned the reports to the authors for adjustments. The center made final research reports available on request to those who wished to read them.

In the field nationwide, there are issues that require research before they can be addressed. These issues may vary from state to state, but it is universally accepted that time and individual institutional support for such research are hard to secure. The research component at the center supplied the talent, time, and means to address issues of critical importance in the field of ESL in higher education in New Jersey.

Professional Development

Professional development opportunities for ESL faculty in higher education were a real concern. Many professional opportunities in the state were geared for K through 12. Added to this situation was the reality that many ESL–BE faculty were adjunct, and the cost of professional development was often prohibitive for them.

With this in mind, the director appointed coordinators to lead the professional development component. They polled program administrators and responded to their needs for regional workshops. This component presented a total of eight regional workshops across the state over 2 years. There were workshops for content area faculty, and workshops on topics requested by individual ESL programs such as oral communication skills in the classroom and process writing for a multicultural student body. The director, with the consultants, networked both in and out of state to secure the presenters for the workshops. The center staff prepared flyers, mounted publicity, and provided evaluation forms for the workshops.

A chair of the professional development component, Professor Nancy Brilliant (an ESL teacher trainer at Kean College) maintained, "Only with the support of the upper-level administrators such as academic vice presidents would work with content area faculty be fruitful." With this as her rationale, she visited the associations of academic vice presidents of 2- and 4-year colleges in the state. She informed the groups about the center, particularly its capacity to give professional development assistance to content-area faculty on the instruction of students.

Three statewide conferences were offered over a 3-year period, funded by the planning, implementation, and continuation grants. The director and staff of the center took over the running of the first conference from the planning grant personnel; they, with the collaboration of the professional development coordinators and input from other component coordinators and program directors, designed and carried out the second and third conferences.

The conferences explored the practical concerns of the ESL–BE professionals in higher education. They included individual workshops and plenary sessions with internationally known speakers; the third conference included a round table for authors. The keynote speakers included Dr. Jim Cummins, Ontario Institute for Studies in Education; Dr. Jodi Crandall, University of Maryland and Center for Applied Linguistics, and former president of TESOL; and Dr. Teresa Pica, University of Pennsylvania. Workshop presentations were by invitation, and presenters received a small stipend.

Technical Assistance

Under the component for technical assistance for program development, the director divided the state into three regions—north, central, and south—and assigned a coordinator to each. The charge to each coordinator was to ascertain the needs of the programs in their region. Based on the input from the regional coordinators, the center organized workshops for administrators over 2 years. They included workshops on ESL–BE program assessment, working with content-area faculty, how to handle program expansion, and "Wending Our Way Through Trenton" (a talk on how to work with DHE and the state legislature on issues relating to LEP students).

In addition, the regional coordinators proved invaluable for regional promotion of the center's events and input regarding professional development needs of the personnel in their regions. Under the auspices of this component, the coordinators discovered that the needs of the southern part of the state were not the same as those of the north, even though New Jersey is a relatively small state geographically. In this case, a workshop was set up in which the northern program coordinators shared their experiences of program expansion with the coordinators from the south, whose programs were entering a period of growth. This growth was due, in part, to the burgeoning employment in the gambling industry, located in the southern part of the state. Immigrants working in this industry sought to improve their skills and further their educations by enrolling in ESL–BE programs.

Dr. JoAnn Bouson, director of ESL at Rowan College in southern New Jersey, said, "The resource center was a wonderful help to all the teachers and program administrators in the state because it provided information on a statewide basis on who the ESL students were, what they were doing, and gave us some hard data to work with. The fact that the activities were regionalized was particularly helpful to those of us in the south, who have to travel a considerable distance to statewide activities [that] are usually held in the central and northern part of New Jersey. Most important was the access to a central location for information."

Finally, none of the work of the center would have been successful without advertising the service. The responsibility for information dissemination came under the aegis of the assistant director. In managing this component she promoted the activities and services of the center, and nurtured an information network of the college ESL–BE programs throughout the state. These tasks were accomplished through an "inaugural" open house, contacts with the general press and professional publications, a triennial newsletter, dissemination of brochures, presentations at professional conferences, and use of the electronic bulletin board. The center was a TESL-L subscriber and promoted its conferences, other professional development opportunities, and its general services and materials through this means.

The electronic connection was suggested and implemented for the center by a computer consultant hired on the suggestion of the RCLMS advisory council. John Coburn, of Rutgers University, assisted the center in going online. This was accomplished by participation in a newsgroup, njin.esl, generally known as pilot.njin.net. Newsgroups are collections of messages posted for all to read and answer that often lead to discussion with wide-ranging participation. The center staff used njin.esl to announce upcoming conferences and workshops and to carry updates to the RCLMS printed materials bank. Indeed, the center's entire materials bank holdings were posted on listserv. Anyone who had a computer with a modem and a log-on account could access this information source and tap into resources of other networks.

The pilot.njin.net computer is on the Busch Campus, Rutgers University in New Brunswick, and is managed by the Rutgers University Computing Services (RUCS) under a state grant. It is primarily for the use of faculty and staff at all higher-education institutions in the state. RUCS provides log-on accounts and support to the entire njin community at no cost.

Because the pilot.njin.net is on the internet, connection is also available directly through campus computers without the need for a modem (use telnet). The internet connects to countries worldwide, providing mail access not only within New Jersey, but also to the broadest community of ESL professionals.

During the life of the center, access to the electronic community was invaluable. Because of it the center was connected to the free flow of ideas in the ESL–BE community, and enjoyed a medium to promote services and resources. If this was important in 1992–1994, it is even more important now, when virtually every professional has access to the information superhighway.

Initially, the assistant director produced a brochure explaining the mission, organization, and components of the center. Staff included this brochure with much of the routine communication, and distributed it at conferences. The brochure was fundamental in publicizing the center.

The press and professional publications received releases about the center's opening and subsequent offerings, but perhaps the best means of disseminating information was the center's newsletter, *Newslink*, published three times a year. Every New Jersey ESL–BE college and university instructor, whether full-time or adjunct, received a copy of the newsletter at home. The *Newslink* mailing list also included administrators, heads of all English departments, legislators, editors of all ESL–BE professional publications, and newsletter editors of organizations with related concerns. By the end of 2 years, the mailing list numbered 712, and was reaching ESL–BE professionals outside New Jersey.

Newslink covered center activities and news and activities from programs around New Jersey. Often there were research reports and descriptions of new programs in the state. Legislative issues were a regular feature.

Readers called the center about some of the articles, which gave the staff a good indication of the networking effect of the publication. The newsletter was the main channel for making known the availability of the center's research reports, software bank, and database publications. *Newslink* also served as the brochure and means of registration for the center's annual conferences and workshops.

A state newsletter such as *Newslink* has a special significance for the classroom teacher. In particular, *Newslink* helped classroom teachers find out which programs were successful in other institutions, and offered the advantage of actually phoning the center or institution with questions about adapting news ideas, programs, or policies to their classrooms or institutions. *Newslink* was also the venue for finding out the availability of regional (and free) professional development opportunities, software, and print materials.

Of *Newslink*, Dr. Karen Medina, director, ESL Program, Hudson County Community College stated, "The newsletter the center produced, called *Newslink*, was not only of superior quality, it also provided a sense of continuity and purpose, keeping us informed about important issues and activities in the field."

The center's grant paid for the printing, and the host institution, Kean College, underwrote the cost of mailing. *Newslink* was a very good use of funds; it fostered and maintained the ESL–BE network on many levels from the classroom to the board room.

The assistant director also handled publicity for all the events of the center: annual conferences and workshops, promotion of RCLMS publications, and the materials bank.

What has been presented in this chapter represents an amalgam of 3 years' work. With each project, the staff learned new and better ways to deliver the "product."

The first change came with the realization that full-time staff was absolutely necessary to maintain the service network, which was the main objective of the center. In addition, work sometimes lost its continuity with part-time staffers. In order to maintain a reliable presence for the people working in the field, the assistant director became a full-time employee, and a full-time secretary was hired. Because the database and research components needed so much support, a half-time professional specialist joined the staff. Student workers worked part time for special projects such as the annual conference, telephone surveys, and data inputting.

Because there is a difference between start-up work and maintenance work, in the second year some components required reconfiguration. The materials bank, for example, required a coordinator for the first year, but in the second year the need was for maintenance. At that point the center's professional specialist took over and updated the collection. Also, less money was appropriated for the software bank in the second year. Some new pieces were acquired and workshops for faculty were added.

Each year of operation gave a sharper picture of the needs of the programs throughout the state, as well as opportunities for meaningful responses on the part of the center. Flexibility is important; the needs of a state vary with each passing year.

Basically, seven steps to designing a state resource center evolved:

- *Connect:* Good communication and organization of ESL–BE program administrators in a state are indispensable.
- *Assess:* Determine what the state's needs are, and start thinking about how the resource center will meet those needs.
- *Acquire funding:* The necessity for funding is obvious. State, federal, and private sources should be investigated.
- *Investigate:* Similar operations can spark ideas and give new insights into meeting the needs of the state.
- *Organize:* Draw on local talent, clarify the mission, and design the structure of the center.
- *Implement:* Choose coordinators, staff, and advisory committee members; equip the office; and sell the service. Public relations become very important now.

- *Tune:* Make adjustments in the organization and operations as more is learned and the LEP population changes.

The Resource Center for Language Minority Students served 38 2- and 4-year public and private institutions of higher education, their administrators, their faculty, and therefore their students. This was accomplished on a budget of $100,000 each year with a minimal staff, a modest cost when one considers the widespread effects of the center's operations. From 1991 throughout 1994, RCLMS obtained valuable demographic information about language minority students and programs in the state, forged cooperative links between and among programs, assisted programs throughout the state, and provided free professional development for faculty on a regular basis. The overall result was a strengthening of the programs and services for limited English proficient students and their faculty in New Jersey's colleges and universities.

It was with sadness that we watched the doors of the RCLMS close in December 1994 due to lack of funding. There was cataclysmic change in the state when the Department of Higher Education was dissolved under Governor Christine Todd Whitman. With it went the Office of Bilingual Educational Issues, which experienced downsizing through the years of the grants. Governor Whitman appointed a new Commission on Higher Education. Despite testimony before the commission by users of the center and a petition of signatures supporting it, the funding for the RCLMS was not renewed. The memory of the energy, collaboration, and good work that the center generated among those who worked with LEP students in the state lingers on.

> Conferences sponsored by the RCLMS were among the best I attended. In addition to memorable keynote speakers the conferences offered informative and practical workshops. A unique feature of these conferences was that they were well attended by professionals across disciplines, affording ESL and content professors and administrators a rare opportunity to discuss common concerns in meeting the needs of LEP students. RCLMS was invaluable as a resource center by identifying key issues and compiling research findings throughout the state. Its demise due to lack of funding is a great loss.
>
> —Lynn Meng, associate professor,
> Intensive English Institute, Union County College

REFERENCES

Gratz, Z., with Luna, C. (1992). *English as a second language: Program profiles.* Compiled for the Resource Center for Language Minority Students at Kean College of New Jersey, Union, NJ.

Gratz, Z., with Luna, C. (1993). *English as a second language: Program profiles, II.* Compiled for the Resource Center for Language Minority Students at Kean College of New Jersey, Union, NJ.

Report of the New Jersey Council for the Education of Language Minority Students. (1992, September).

Women and minorities led the way in a year of slow enrollment growth. (1994, January 26). *The Chronicle of Higher Education, 40*(21), A32.

19

Electronic Communication, New Technology, and the ESL Student

Keming Liu
Medgar Evers College, City University of New York

The internet has been hailed as one of the most democratic advances of the late 20th century. Never in human history has information been made more readily available to so many people at such a low cost. The impact of digital technology on all aspects of life is not immediately measurable, but the inevitability of its penetrating education is and will be a sure thing. Thus, important questions include:

- What new strategies should we as ESL educators develop to accommodate a new learning environment?
- How can we best take advantage of advanced knowledge resources to make them useful for our adult ESL students?

To answer these questions, we need to look beyond the astigmatic topic of computers in education to the question of what we can and should accomplish as educators, making full use of digital tools. Educational change is not and should not be technologically driven; instead, it is technologically enabled. Changes in the way we teach have been made, and technology is only going to result in faster and better results. It is true that faith in technology can run head on into faith based on tradition and authority. Fast-moving technology represents an alien ideology to many educators. This chapter demonstrates how I have used the emerging digital technology, and suggests some possibilities for incorporating digital technology into the adult ESL classroom and into our professional lives. At a time of educational change, digital technology offers teachers a tool to communicate with colleagues and students.

A CASE STUDY

A Relationship Achieved Via E-Mail

Face-to-face communication is often threatening, especially when it involves an authority figure and, worse yet, when the other interlocutor is still developing language skills. Such is the situation many of my ESL students encounter in college when they need to interact with the teacher and other classmates. Chances are that many ESL students would remain silent until they had no other choice but to speak. During a semester at Hunter College, where I was teaching an ESL writing course, I introduced my students to electronic mail. Yes, it took awhile before my students became comfortable using it, but once they finally got the hang of it, I was bombarded with so many e-mail messages that I could hardly respond to all each week. I gave many assignments via e-mail to force everyone to use the system, and used e-mail to answer school-related as well as personal questions. It was during that time that I started to realize what a valuable tool the internet was.

Cathie.[1] A shy and very quiet girl in class, Cathie stood 5′2″ and weighed no more than 100 pounds. Every day, she was the first person to get to class, carrying a cup of tea or coffee and a sweet. She never attempted to volunteer answers, and when asked she'd respond with a smile. I never knew what was really on her mind, but was sure that she followed her classwork. When I first introduced my class to the computer and the internet, many students were curious but intimidated at the same time. They did not grasp the concept of communicating with each other via e-mail right away because no traditional learning tasks necessitated the need for interaction. Not until I assigned group work did most students find e-mail to be a handy tool in coordinating their group projects. Once they got the hang of it, they became quite inventive. I did not need to tell them to "talk" to each other on a daily basis—the next thing I knew I could hardly get their attention once they were online. Like her classmates, Cathie started to show signs of great interest and always managed to complete my e-mail assignment first, often with a friendly greeting at the end of each message. She'd ask questions regarding grammar and sometimes ask personal questions. Like others in the class, she was curious and wanted to know more about

[1]The student's real name is withheld to protect her identity.

me. To quench their thirst, each day I would tell them a bit more about myself and share with them my feelings about what was going on around us at the time. One day, Cathie did not show up in my class; I thought she must have fallen ill. Another day went by, and Cathie still failed to come to class. A week later, I received an e-mail message from Cathie in which she told me what had happened to her. She said she felt ashamed about something and wasn't sure if she should tell me about it. I answered her message immediately and reassured her that it was okay if she did not want to tell me something; but I mentioned that I was concerned about her absence. Before the next class session, Cathie wrote to me and told me that she had been raped the week before when she and her boss had been closing the store where she was working as a cashier. When I finally saw her in class, Cathie avoided looking into my eyes. I knew I should not confront her and instead I wrote her back. In my message I acted as both a teacher and a counselor. After that, Cathie allowed the dam to open and wrote to me every day. I did advise her to report the incident but she declined to do so, due to various reasons that are not necessary to discuss here. However, through our e-mail exchanges, Cathie did finally get over her shame and collected herself together enough to successfully pass the class and the CUNY WAT exam.

Cathie's story is just one of those I was able to collect while teaching the class. This story demonstrates a merit of e-mail: It facilitates less inhibited behavior and better student–teacher communication.

Magnitude of Writing

During the course of a semester, my ESL students wrote an average of 20 pages more than they would usually have done. Most of the extra writing was accomplished through e-mail, and was not requested as a class assignment. The extra writing included messages to each other, to the teacher, and to partners. Because it was not always convenient for the students to get together for group projects, I encouraged them to communicate among one another via e-mail. They divided their tasks and went ahead working on their own. They then "talked" to one another and sent their writing to other group members for critique. The group leader's task was to collect every member's e-mail writing and download it onto his or her diskette for printing. Not only did the students write more in this way, but they also learned how to cooperate and execute team work.

DESIGN A DIGITAL LEARNING COMMUNITY

By *digital learning community* I mean learning via the employment and exploitation of electronic media. Why? Reasons abound. Consider what fundamental differences digital technology can make in redefining the nature of learning and knowing, note interactions between information technology and educational practices, and recognize the far more powerful and flexible possibilities of electronic media for cultural exchange in comparison with the printed media.

Learning and Technology

Theory is transient. What was sensible in a print-based context is perhaps vestigial in our digital context. Thomas Kuhn (1970) contended that scientific discoveries are not results of sequential buildup but instead emerge from an explosion of new ideas.

In print-based schooling, knowledge is acquired exclusively through access to verbal-mediated ideas and information. Advanced learning is both facilitated and enhanced by verbal ability, and yet, in the case of the failure to understand verbal information, hindered by it at the same time. The ability to employ verbal semiotics for adequate comprehension is not equally distributed among all human beings, and verbal semiotics in a new language creates additional problems. Digital technology greatly extends the power of multiple representation of ideas and information, as McClintock (1992) expressed:

> Multiple representation had its most significant effect, not on how people received ideas, but on how they found them, activated them, and then apprehended them. Pictures, icons, sounds, and gestures came to rival written expressions as means of accessing ideas. With that change, the resources routinely usable in the curriculum blossomed—pictures, films, performances, recitations, diagrams, graphs, animations, simulations, [and] maps lost their merely "illustrative" character. People began to make arguments with them, to explain things through them, discovering how to give images apodictic, declarative, propositional power . . . in our electronic culture visualization enhances the verbalization that characterized the print culture. (¶28)[2]

Because theory is transient, learning is continual and cumulative. The old, compartmentalized learning experience has to be changed. A particular textbook for a particular class/course and semester breaks up knowledge as a whole into discrete domains of subject matter, and leaves students to tackle bits and pieces of information with minimal access to the materials used in prior or coming years. Learning is made sequential instead of cumulative. Digital technology, however, makes access far easier, and storage of old and new materials far less cumbersome. For

[2]The author uses numbered paragraphs as the means of referencing locations to accommodate digital technology and its hypertext nature.

hands-on examples, visit sites on Netscape offered by the Institute of Learning Technology (ILT) at Columbia University. Its URL[3] is as follows:

http://www.ilt.columbia.edu/academic/classes/index.html

This site gives you a panoramic view of all course materials that students can surf through while engaged in current learning. You are also welcome to visit my home page, in which many sites are linked with the courses I have taken at the school and which addresses certain issues discussed in the course during and **after** the semester. (Notice that I emphasize the word *after*—much learning is unfinished, and the process is cumulative.) Having a site on the internet allows me to receive feedback from classmates and experts who visit my site, and it is possible for me to constantly go back to my incomplete thoughts and premature perceptions to make revisions. My home page URL is:

http://www.cc.columbia.edu/~kl84

Education and Technology

As the information infrastructure shifts from print to digital network, the previously limited and scarce educative resources are expanded and increased to a point where a strategy different than that of simple instruction starts to make sense, and a different approach to learning is developed. Advanced information technologies make construction of integrated learning far more feasible, due to the fact that digital technologies expand personal potentialities and function as a means for augmenting our human intellectual skills. Word processors red-flag anomalous spellings; writing software such as *Writer's Helper*, *Grammatik*, and *MLA Editor* help beginning writers get ideas, reorganize semantic units, and conform to conventional formats; spreadsheets and SPSS allow anyone to perform complex statistics quickly and accurately; databases permit us to manage large quantities of information; Netscape[4] takes you to sites that are thousands of miles away at one click; and Yahoo[5] performs your search

---

[3]URL is short for Universal Resource Locator—a system that provides a unique address for every resource (such as a home page) on the internet. For example, the URL http://www.hunter.edu is what you must furnish to Netscape (or another internet client) to enable it to find and retrieve that resource.

[4]Netscape is a web browser, a program written for web users to navigate among World Wide Web servers and retrieve and display information from them. Netscape is the standard district browser. For further information, go to the last section of this chapter.

[5]Yahoo is one of the search engines that help you find resources on the internet. To learn more about Yahoo, go to the last section of this chapter or surf the cyberspace using the URL provided.

for information as if you had dozens of researchers at your personal disposal. These and many other new specialized tools greatly lower the skill levels needed for anyone to participate effectively in wide ranges of cultural activity. What are now considered basic skills vital for success in college may not pertain under the learning and knowing conditions that are emerging with the digital augmentation of human intelligence.

Electronic Media Versus Printed Media

A Chinese saying goes, "traveling a thousand miles is better than reading 10,000 books." The wisdom within conveys that "a picture is worth a thousand words." Although we and our students may be able to afford a flight to Beijing, Paris, or London, none of us can physically get to all three capitals within a matter of minutes. Even if we could, we'd be breathless or, worse yet, have a heart attack. However, digital technologies have made it possible for us to visit all three places within minutes via virtual reality. You may argue that books can do similar things by taking your mind's eye there, but print media takes longer. Take the 1996 summer Olympiad, for example: One had to wait at least 12 hours for the results of any game to appear in the paper. But telecommunications made it possible to get the results right away (live). In the case of adult ESL students, printed media often prove to be formidable as well.

Take again my class as an example. During the summer Olympic games, I was teaching an ESL writing course that ran for 6 weeks. Because the last week was reserved for the finals, we actually had only 5 weeks to accomplish all the objectives: writing to convey meaning in the narrative mode, understanding the basics of English grammar, learning to organize an essay, and writing a research paper on the Olympics. With all the objectives at hand, researching on the Olympics seemed far-fetched. My students were leery of this task, and so was I. I was not sure whether my students would be able to get all the resources they needed for the group project. Nor was I confident in the internet's depth on this particular subject. I had simply taken for granted that the internet would have such information when I assigned the project, and my students were completely naive about this digital tool. To avoid total disaster, I first provided lots of URLs on the current games in Atlanta, and my students were fascinated by what they stumbled onto. They were thrilled to learn about the medal winners of their preferred venue and participated in e-mail interactive activities, such as responding to questions about their feelings for the U.S. women gymnasts. They felt quite privileged to be able to write to experts in the sports world or news anchors, and were candid in giving their opinions because they could remain anonymous in their responses.

The most valuable experience for my students seemed to be that they were not intimidated at all in using the English language to convey their feelings, and they were able to use authentic vocabulary in their responses because they had just read about the topic they were responding to or because they were able to click a GO BACK key to fetch the word they wanted to use in their response. In roughly 1½ week's time, all five groups came up with very impressive papers about the history of the Olympic Games and the changes that have taken place in the past 100 years. When we surfed the information superhighway, we were led from one site to another and before we knew it we had accumulated more than we needed for the project. This is not to say that the library cannot effect such a result, but one would have to spend much more time to find what we found so easily on the internet.

During the summer, my students constantly wrote to inform me about the new sites they had found, and I would forward all new URLs to the whole class. I also taught my class what *cc* meant on e-mail, and the group members used the cc function to its maximum. Students and teacher became a web-of-information network, and the instantaneous connection produced unheard-of results. In big group instruction at any college or community setting, one problem often lies in the lack of teacher–student interaction and student–student interaction. Writing notes to each other via paper often proves impractical and less efficient than does e-mail, and pen and paper often present an unwanted formal tone to interaction. Because learning does not necessarily occur in formal settings, the adaptation of a medium that poses no threat and no intimidation is probably a welcome tool for adult ESL classrooms.

Digital media will inevitably effect change in education that years later will be taken for granted. What new approaches should be implemented to make learning more meaningful? What educational changes can be made, and what new strategies can be developed employing electronic media? What are the advantages of using them? These questions are answered sequentially later in the chapter, with regards to what best facilitates learning.

APPROACHES

Learning Through Research

Research involves inquiry, study, and problem solving. Educators have often praised these modes of learning, but they have also often found it hard to mobilize the diversity of cultural resources to withstand open-ended inquiries that may require a substantive period of time to sustain cumulative information. To design such an inquiry, educators may want to try the following:

1. Viewing themselves with a renewed role—fomenting questions, doubts, and uncertainties.
2. Presenting scaffold or model strategies.
3. Guiding students in their inquiry and facilitating autonomous work.
4. Offering feedback and critiques rather than criticizing results.

The procedures taken for an open-inquiry design should be laid out as a guideline that materializes these principles. The following model was designed for a basic writing course; it is general enough for you to modify to fit your own needs and subject:

1. Identification
2. Collaboration
3. Interpretation construction
4. Contextualization
5. Knowledge organization
6. Knowledge consolidation
7. Knowledge transfer

The steps are each organized into three parts that follow the progression of the writing process: planning, composing, and revising. Figure 19.1 illustrates the relations among the subject, writing, the process of writing, and the execution of the process under the principles.

1. IDENTIFICATION

In this stage, teacher and students work together to identify students' interests through sharing and discussion. Writing itself does not become an anchor of interest until there is something about which to write. Before there is a theme or topic of writing, it is best that students are encouraged to "identify and define their own issues that are related to the anchors and to then seek relevant resources" (Lin et al., p. 5). This phase is vital to the later development of the course, because it builds the basis or foundation for the content to be pursued in the process of writing. In order for students to become interested in writing, the materials should be relevant. When students are writing about something relevant, they are more likely to be able to communicate the meaning of their world to their audience.

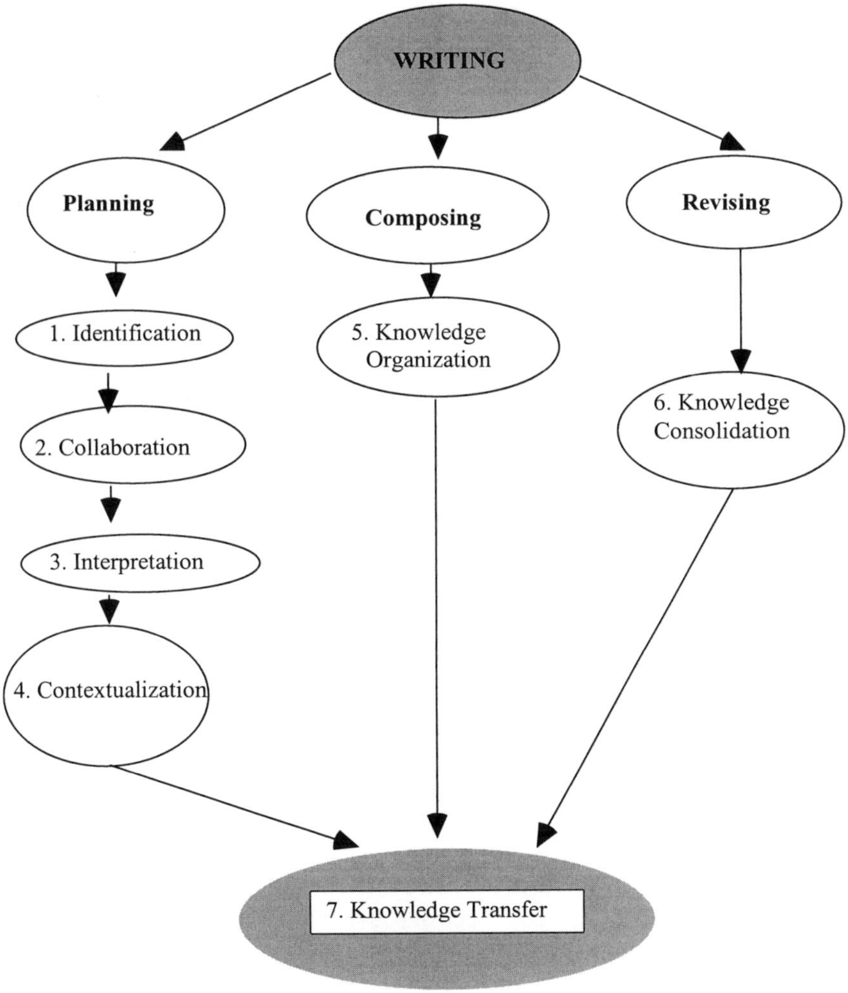

FIG. 19.1. Graphic representation of relations.

Planning for Identification

You are preparing to start your semester working with a group of 25 or so college ESL students to accomplish a common goal: write to communicate one's feelings and understandings successfully. Your goal is for your students to identify the possible interests and themes or topics that are meaningful to them and that lend themselves to developing a literature (literary readings: poems, stories, novels, etc.; multimedia readings: the internet—World Wide Web) and composition unit. To do this, you need to have focused questions for students to start with, so

TABLE 19.1

What I Know About the Topic	*What and Where I Have Learned About the Topic*	*What Is Still Confusing for Me About the Topic*
1. 2. 3.	1. What? 2. Where? 3. Call # of the book: 4. URL of the site:	1. I don't know when and where the first immigrants settled in the United States. 2. 3.

they are guided to move onto finding their own themes through sharing and discussion. The following activities may help you and your students reach that goal.

Activities

1. Group your students in threes or fours and have them interview one another following this guideline:[6]
   a. Where are you from?
   b. When did you or your family come to the United States?
   c. What do you perceive as the most difficult aspect of living in a foreign country?
   d. What education did you receive in your native country?
   e. What do you know about immigration issues in this country and/or in your native country?

2. Join two small groups together to identify some common responses to the questions.

3. Make knowledge construction overt by asking students to fill out a questionnaire on the three categories (see Table 19.1).

4. Plan what you need to do to clear up what is still confusing for you. In this activity, you can show students how to set up deadlines for themselves and what to find out through researching in the library and online. For example, you can write this on the board as a model for your students (scaffolding/modeling):

Goal: To carry out the tasks I set for myself by XX date:
1. Learn how to research in the library and on Netscape.
2. Find out when and where the first immigrants settled in the United States.

[6]The guideline is a series of questions focusing on possible themes, such as immigration, the Olympic Games, or technology. You may design your own set of questions with a purpose or goal of identifying topics.

3. Find out when and where immigrants from my country settled in the United States.

You may offer to guide a tour to the library and show your students how to search for materials germane to the topic, and provide the URLs listed next for students to go online for materials. You may also ask if professors from the History Department would not mind fielding questions on the topic by allowing your students to write to them via e-mail. The following URLs address the topic of "immigration," and many of them may lead your students into other inquiries:

- European immigrants:
  http://www.itp.berkeley.edu/~asam121/1948.html
- U.S. Border control:
  http://www.usbc.org/homepage.htm
- The American immigration home page:
  http://www.bergen.gov/AAST/Projects/Immigration/
- Current debates on immigration:
  http://www.aclu.org/news/mararc14.html
  http://www.rand.org/publications/RRR/RRR.fall94.calif/immigration.html
- Useful links:
  http://www.walpole.ma.us/web%20site%20folder/Library/lreferencehistimmigr.html
  http://www.sandiego.sisna.com/drww/drww/david/links.h tml
  http://av.yahoo.com/bin/search?p=immigation&b=21&d=a&hc=0&hs=0
- Getting involved with the immigration issue:
  http://www.itaa.org/govtaffr/smtpltr/smtp01.htm

The planning stage may be a lengthy one, because your students need this time not only to investigate but also to learn how to go about using the library and the internet. The URLs look formidable when you think of tying each address into the Netscape locator box, and, with only one tiny error, not getting where you or your students want to go. To minimize the potential difficulties and unnecessary frustrations, you may be advised to designate one student who is good with details to type the URLs and save them as a document. That way, everyone can copy the URLs onto their own disks and keep them for personal use.

Another question is *how*? Following is how you can make your and your students' lives much easier. When you surf on the internet you can also go to other applications, such as your word processor. Most computers now have enough memory to allow you to run two, three, or more windows at the same time. For example, if you want to visit one of the sites provided earlier, all you need to do is the following:

- Open the document your student or you have saved on Microsoft Word, Word Perfect, or another program.
- Select one "http://" site by highlighting it.
- Go to "edit" on the menu and choose "copy."
- Open Netscape located on the hard drive.
- At the URLs location, highlight the current URL, click "edit" on the menu, and then choose "paste."

Your own URL now should be at the locator—hit the "enter" key. Voila! To save labor once you are at the site, tell/show your students how to save that site to access the next time. Simply click "bookmark" on the Netscape menu and choose "add." The next time you want to visit this site, go to "bookmark" and click on the one you desire.

Your Thoughts After Your First Trial With Identification

Here are some issues related to identification that you may wish to consider:

- What questions or concerns do you have about having students identify their own interests in relation to the interests you provided?
- What went well and what did not?
- What do you think you need to do differently next time?
- In what areas do you feel you need to do more modeling for your students?

To effectively reflect on what you need to improve for the future, and to become more informed, you can get feedback from either your students or other professionals in the field via e-mail. Because distance is not a concern with digital technology, you can also talk to colleagues far away online, and get your students online with e-mail pals.

2. COLLABORATION

In this phase, students collaborate in searching for information either online or in the library, developing/selecting appropriate materials, and taking charge of decision making. During this stage, e-mail is most recommended. Collaboration takes advantage of the human resources in the classroom. A study of concept formation in educational setting led Vygotsky (1986) to the dialogical character of learning. He argued that a child achieves progress in concept formation through cooperation. The place where that progress is made is termed as *zo-ped*, "the zone of proximal development." Collaboration constitutes the zone of proximal development, where students come face to face with each other and with the teacher, and where disorganized spontaneous concepts "meet" the systematicity and logic precipitated by the collaborative setting.

During collaboration time, you as the teacher/facilitator should make it clear to your students that knowledge gaps should be viewed as something positive because "knowing what one does not know is a vital kind of metaknowledge" (Scardamalia, Bereiter, McLean, Swallow, & Woodruff, 1989, p. 57). More important, each individual possesses unique capabilities at different times and in different situations: Everyone has something to offer, big or small. To effectively motivate students to collaborate, you may first identify those who are familiar with either library research or computer search, and those who are not familiar with any information-searching systems. The following instructional strategies may help you organize activities for students to collaborate on.

Strategies for Activity Organization

1. *Reciprocal teaching (RT):* Reciprocal teaching is a process in which student-led groups master the use of strategies to pose expert-level questions, learn to summarize the material, pinpoint confusing areas for clarification, and predict. During the search for information, you may group the "student-experts" in information searching with novices. Modeling of certain learning strategies is important; you may use Table 19.2 as a guide for what students should model.

2. *Jigsaw grouping (JG):* Jigsaw teaching is analogous to the jigsaw puzzle, in which each piece is a vital part of the whole picture. The jigsaw model, originally envisioned by Aronson et al. (1978), was designed to recognize other human resources in the classroom in addition to the teacher. JG allows multiple answers to one particular question (multiple perspectives), and aims at increasing each student's emotional well-being and self-esteem, which have great impact on a student's learning. In jigsaw groups, students treat each other as resources rather than competitors, and they learn to teach and to listen to each other: "A jigsaw classroom is not a loose, 'anything goes' situation. It is highly structured. Interdependence is required. It is the element of 'required' interdependence among students which makes this a unique learning method, and it is this interdependence that encourages the students to take an active part in their learning" (Aronson et al., 1978, p. 28).

TABLE 19.2
Learning Strategies for Information Searching

Metacognitive Strategies	
Organizational planning	What's my purpose for the search? How do I begin and end? Should I take notes of what others in my group did to aid my memory and my individual search?
Selective attention	What are relevant materials for the theme at hand? Among all the materials we've found, which ones are better to start with? Can the title and table of contents help me decide which one to start with?
Advance organization	Can the title and chapter headlines help me get a general picture of what the text is about?
Self-monitoring and self-assessment	How am I doing in the group? Should I be more assertive or more of a team player? What personal questions do I have for the teacher that would help me out?
Cognitive Strategies	
Elaborating prior knowledge	What do I already know about the topic, and what experiences have I had related to what I am searching?
Note taking	Should I write down what I already know in order to help me focus on what materials my group or I should be searching? How should I record what I know, do not know, and want to know—using charts, tables, maps, diagrams, or something else?
Social/Affective Strategies	
Questioning for clarification	Who should I ask for more information about online searching? How should I ask?
Cooperating	How can I work with my group to accomplish the objectives? What can I do to ease our group work?
Self-encouragement	Yes, I can do this. All I need is to spend more time in the library and the lab to practice.

After information searching, you may try JG with your students. You may ask your students to break the theme, "immigration" in this case, into manageable subproblems to be researched by a small group. For example, possible subproblems may be "when did African Americans come to the United States?" You may alert students to the set of questions you developed for their identification of themes, and have them follow it as a model (modeling).

Your Thoughts After Your Trial With Collaboration

Answering these questions may help you clarify your thoughts about collaboration:

- What questions and concerns do you have after this phase?

- What do you think needs modifications? Record your thoughts, and keep e-mailing correspondence.

3. INTERPRETATION CONSTRUCTION

In this phase, students construct interpretations of the materials researched and construct arguments for the validity of their interpretations. Black and McClintock (1995) posited that although students construct interpretations of the materials related to the theme, they are actually developing and declaring ownership of their work. Lin et al. (in press) maintained that ownership enhances and motivates learning. The activities designed for interpretation construction will cultivate learning strategies by calling on students to identify and deal with confusion, problems, insights, critical judgments, and information.

Activities

1. Have students form groups based on similar interests. Write the names of the students in each group. If one group is too big, break it into two. If one student ends up the only member of a group, ask him or her to join another group. Table 19.3 shows a sample form.

2. Assign the rest of the class the following activities while you are with a reciprocal teaching group:
   a. Make a journal entry using *The Amazing Writing Machine* (Broderbund, 1994).
   b. Silently read a text related to the group interest.
   c. Continue group research in the library and online.
   d. Work with your group using learning strategies such as selective attention to important parts of the reading materials, taking notes, sharing ideas with others, and so on.

3. Introduce and model the RT strategies during the reading process; students take turns leading a discussion during this time, as shown in

TABLE 19.3
Sample Form

	Group 1	*Group 2*	*Group 3*	*Group 4*
1.				
2.				
3.				
4.				
5.				

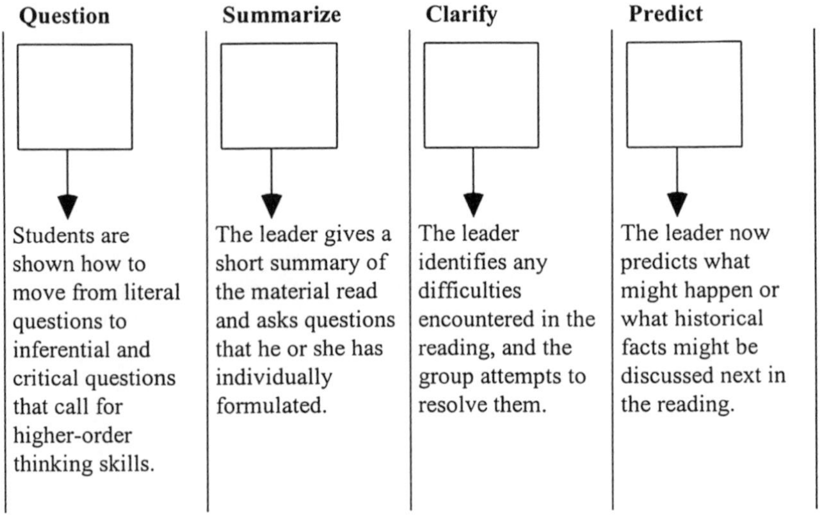

FIG. 19.2. Steps in modeling RT strategies.

Fig. 19.2. This activity allows you to introduce reciprocal teaching for the first time. Your goal is to introduce the strategies and model their appropriate use. When giving directions for reciprocal teaching, name the four different strategies.

While the group is performing the RT, multiple interpretations of the same material should be encouraged and students should be taught to be tolerant of others' opinions. Learning growth is like theory growth, which follows a "positive-negative-positive" cycle (trial and error).

Your Thoughts

Record what was successful, unsuccessful, and why. Again, you may join online discussions on related topics with colleagues, graduate students, and/or counselors in this field.

4. CONTEXTUALIZATION

Contextualization is a process through which knowledge starts to solidify, expand, and mature. Students access background and contextual materials of various sorts to aid interpretation and argumentation. Some specific Netscape searches may be recommended for contextual information. For example, students in a group might visit a site in a particular neighborhood and investigate its changes, throughout the years, with old immigrants leaving and new immigrants arriving. To contextualize is to make connections between virtual reality and reality. When researching the topic of immigration, students are working in a sort of virtual reality because the materials they read or access are still not necessarily their own experiences. For better and fuller understanding, students are encouraged to use their own experiences as immigrants to help them understand and interpret materials at hand. One way of contextualizing is to ask students to interview their relatives, parents, or neighbors and construct an oral history of their communal immigration. This process allows students to put their feet on solid ground and truly understand the policies and politics of immigration. The community immigration changes offers a vantage point for students to arrive at valid and mature interpretations. You can assign RT groups to do further research based on their discussions while you work with another group. You can also provide access to videos, movies, and other sources that depict what the students have read. Then allow other groups to engage in CSILE (computer-supported intentional learning environment), which provides a setting for quiet, reflective thinking that precedes the next round of group discussion. Students can pose and answer questions anonymously during this time. The rationale here is that any style of learning is valid. This activity offers a chance for those who do not prefer face-to-face discussion to voice their opinions. This is a self-reflecting process, during which students store rough notes while other ideas are pursued.

By now, most students should have a direction for their projects. Students should share useful URLs they found while surfing the net; some possibly related URLs are given in the list that follows. When typing in the URLs, be sure that upper and lower cases are clearly and correctly typed exactly as they are given, because the internet is case sensitive. Informational and practical locations include:

- http://www.excite.com/Subject/Politics_and_Law/Law_and_Lawyers/Practice_Areas/Immigration/s-index.msn.html
- http://www.pcworld.com/annex/features/immigrant/pg03.html
- http://epn.org/sage/rsdefr.html
- http://www.pcworld.com/annex/features/immigrant/pg02.html

5. KNOWLEDGE ORGANIZATION

In this step, students organize their knowledge in writing. This is the actual composing phase in the writing process. By now, students have had adequate preparation for formulating their knowledge in writing. Before

Name: ____________________

Topic: ____________________

Who: For whom am I writing?

____

____

____

Why: Why am I writing this?

____

____

____

____

What: What do I know? (Brainstorm)

1. ____
2. ____
3. ____
4. ____
5. ____
6. ____

How: How can I group my ideas?

How will I organize my ideas?

• Comparison/Contrast • Explanation • Problem/Solution • Other

FIG. 19.3. Plan "think-sheet."

the actual writing commences, you may use the "Plan 'Think-Sheet' " shown in Fig. 19.3 (Chamot & O'Malley, in press) to get students started. Again, students should not have to conform to one way of representing their knowledge. They may implement into their writing alternatives that include maps, pictures, or codes. CSILE and *The Amazing Writing Machine* (AWM) provide access to the different tools that students may employ in their knowledge organization.

6. KNOWLEDGE CONSOLIDATION

In this phase, students assemble the full picture of the jigsaw puzzle and take responsibility for explaining and sharing their portions of the whole picture with the rest of the group and class. Although cooperative task performance is comparatively easy to orchestrate, cooperative learning is not always easily syndicated. Taking and "sharing responsibility is perhaps the most important principle for achieving the overall objectives" (Scardamalia et al., 1989, p. 65) and goals. All students should be given access to e-mail and take time to respond to other students' requests for information and ideas, their confusion, and so on. Scardamalia et al. (1989) suggested that teachers base their evaluations of students on the helpfulness of such responses. Students also use this time to help one another evaluate and revise their writings by attaching personal comments and reflections to their peers' writings. A convention for comments and reflections can be established, such as using pencils to write on the margins of hard copies or using the boldface feature on the computer and/or bulletin board for open debate.

7. KNOWLEDGE TRANSFER

At this stage, students use the learning strategies in a second research project and internalize the principles they've picked up throughout the assignment. You can use this principle when assigning group projects for final/summative evaluation. Students apply the principles introduced to them earlier to new contexts, and to see the manifestations of the principles behind what they are doing.

Knowledge transfer is a principle serving as off-line assessment. The active use of knowledge calls for measures of transfer of learning. Then *how* and *what* to assess become the designer's problem.

TERMS AND URLs[7] YOU MAY WANT TO KNOW

The Internet Dictionary

The e-mail address of the internet dictionary is: http://nisus.sfusd.k12.ca.us/resources/glossary.html.

Browser

A browser is a program written to navigate among World Wide Web servers, and retrieve and display information from them. Netscape is the standard district browser.

---

[7]You may go straight to the sites mentioned in this section, or learn about the terms here. Most of the following definitions are do·:nloaded from the sites, with minor changes.

Netscape

Netscape is an internet client or the standard district web browser that is used by more than two thirds of the internet. It is free to schools, students, and teachers, and has versions for Mac and Windows computers. If you have at least 8 MB of RAM, you may want to use version 2.01. It is recommended that you not use versions labeled with "b" for beta (test), because they are less reliable and may not work properly.

URL

URL is short for universal resource locator—a system that provides a unique address for every resource (such as a home page) on the internet. A URL is used by web browsers to locate a web page, and the location of a site is like a home address. When you want to visit a friend, you need to know his or her home address/location. The same is true with online visits. All URLs start with "http://" and most start with "http://www." For example, "http://www.hunter.cuny.edu/" is what you give Netscape (or another internet client) to enable it to find and retrieve that resource. If you desire to learn about the following terms, surfing the net is the best way to do so.

World Wide Web

The World Wide Web is a program for sharing text, images, and multimedia files across the internet via hyperlinks, or nonlinear links to related information. This is the fastest-growing area of the internet.

The Internet

- http://www.cis.ohio-state.edu/htbin/rfc/rfc1206.html
- http://ntia.its.bldrdoc.gov/~bing/fs-1037c/_internet.html

The internet is a worldwide interconnection of individual networks operated by governments, industries, academia, and private individuals. Note that the internet originally served to interconnect laboratories engaged in government research, and has now been expanded to serve millions of users and a multitude of purposes, such as the web and e-mail. It carries many kinds of traffic, of which Usenet is one (and the internet is only one of the various networks carrying Usenet traffic). The internet is a large collection of networks (all of which run the TCP/IP protocols) that are tied together so that users of any of the networks can use the network services provided by TCP/IP to reach users on any of the other networks. The internet started with the ARPANET, but now includes such networks as NSFNET, NYSERnet, and thousands of others. There are other major wide-area networks (such as BITNET and DECnet networks) that are not based on the TCP/IP protocols and thus are not part of the internet. However, it is possible to communicate between them and the internet via electronic mail, because of mail gateways that act as "translators" between the different network protocols involved. (Note that you will often see *internet* with a small *i*. This could refer to any network built based on TCP/IP, or might refer to networks using other protocol families that are composites-built.)

E-mail

The *e* stands for "electronic," and you often see the word now without the dash in between (i.e., *email*). People now also use it as a verb, as in "Please e-mail me a message." You can apply for an e-mail account the same way you apply for telephone service at your home. Once you are online, you can access almost everything, including your bank account. Big banks such Chemical or CitiBank encourage their customers to use their online services as a means to cut down expenses and as a strategy to make their businesses more convenient. As an electronic transfer of messages between computer users, the district uses three types of e-mail: a regular internet mail server—muse—which most users access with Eudora; cc:Mail, which is on the zeus server; and a bulletin board mail system for students and parents on hc (see the next section for an explanation of hc). All three have access to internet mail. Netscape will send out e-mail (e.g., the feedback button at the bottom of the page) if you have given it your e-mail address by going to options—preferences—mail.

hc

This is a bulletin board system (BBS) set up to provide e-mail to students and parents at schools distributing home computers, as well as in other schools to support planned educational projects. The internet address for hc users is <username>@hc.sfusd.k12.ca.us.

Telnet

- http://father.dental.upenn.edu/Documentation/CompSvcs/LLab/teln.html
- http://www.mediawest.com/ver2/def/mwstdf23.html

"Telnet" is an internet protocol that allows a local (or client) user to log on to a remote server or host as if it were just another terminal to that server (terminal emulation). Telnet allows the manipulation of executable files. For example, say that you want to access your e-mail messages and you are not physically where your host is. All you need to do is to click on the Telnet icon and type in your complete host address. If your host is CUNIX or SHIVA or HEJIRA, all you do is type the following (this is an example of my host): "cunix.columbia.edu." In other words, Telnet is a program that lets internet users log onto computers other than their own host computers, sometimes on the other side of the world. If you wish to learn about Telnet in other languages, visit the following site:

> http://av.yahoo.com/bin/search?p=definition+of+telnet&y=y&e=77085&f=0%3A74294%3A75192%3A76539%3A77085&r=Computers+and+Internet%02Internet%02World+Wide+Web%02CGI+–+Common+Gateway+Interface

Usenet

- http://www.tezcat.com/~abbyfg/faq/what-is-usenet.html

Usenet is the set of people who exchange articles tagged with one or more universally recognized labels, called "newsgroups" (or "groups," for short). There is often confusion about the precise set of newsgroups that constitute Usenet; one commonly accepted definition is that it consists of newsgroups listed in the periodic "List of Active Newsgroups" postings that appear regularly in news.lists and other newsgroups. A broader definition of Usenet would include the newsgroups listed in the article "Alternative Newsgroup Hierarchies" (frequently posted to news.lists). An even broader definition includes newsgroups that are restricted to specific geographic regions or organizations. Each Usenet site makes its own decisions about the set of groups available to its users; this set differs from site to site.

Yahoo

- http://www.rescribe.com/v1/yahoo.htm

Yahoo is one of the web search engines. Major search engines include Yahoo, Webcrawler, and InfoSeek.

Gopher

- http://ntia.its.bldrdoc.gov/~bing/fs-1037c/_gopher.html

Gopher is a menu-based information-searching tool that allows users to access various types of databases, such as FTP archives and white pages.

FTP

This is short for file transfer protocol. FTP is a program (built into Netscape) to transfer files between networked machines/computers. Before uploading a file, you should make sure that the file is saved as text and not as a Word Perfect or Microsoft Word document.

REFERENCES

Aronson, E., et al. (1978). *The jigsaw classroom.* Beverly Hills, CA: Sage.

Black, J. B., & McClintock, R. O. (1995). An interpretation approach to constructivist design. In B. Wilson (Ed.), *Constructivist learning environments.* Englewood Cliffs, NJ: Educational Technology Publications.

Chamot, A. U., & O'Malley, J. M. (in press). *The CALLA handbook: Implementing the cognitive academic language learning approach.* New York: Addison-Wesley.

Duffy, T. M., & Jonassen, D. H. (Eds.). (1992). *Constructivism and the technology of instruction: A conversation.* Hillsdale, NJ: Lawrence Erlbaum Associates.

Engel, B. S. (1990). An approach to assessment in early literacy. In C. Kamii, M. Manning, & G. Manning (Eds.), *Early literacy: A constructivist foundation for whole language* National Education Association.

Kuhn, T. S. (1970). *The structure of scientific revolutions.* Chicago: University of Chicago Press.

Lin, X. D., et al. (in press). Instructional design and the development of learning communities: An invitation to a dialogue [special issue]. *Educational Technology.*

McClintock, R. O. (1992). *Power and pedagogy: Transforming education through information technology.* New York: Institute for Learning Technologies.

Scardamalia, M., Bereiter, C., McLean, R. S., Swallow, J., & Woodruff, E. (1989). Computer-supported intentional learning environments. *Educational Computer Research, 5*(1), 51–68.

Vygotsky, L. (1986). *Thought and language* (A. Kozulin, Trans.). Cambridge, MA: MIT Press.

20

Making Connections Through the Internet

Trudy Smoke
Hunter College, City University of New York

What do a 23-year-old cosmetology student in Peru (Sims, 1996), a child in a Croatian refugee camp (Cummins & Sayers, 1995), and immigrant students in Keming Liu's (see chap. 19, this volume) ESL writing class have in common? They are all on the internet: in one case to find out about new hairstyles in Paris; in another to tell the world about the atrocities and suffering taking place in a refugee camp; and in another for an ESL student to tell her teacher about a rape and for other students to find out more about the 1996 Olympic games. Individuals worldwide are using this powerful tool to inform and be informed about the human condition, from the benign to the vile.

Hailed as the "brave new world" of our future, the internet offers great possibilities for communicating nationally and internationally at the mere touch of a few keys, and with that in mind we need to know a little bit about how the whole system works. The three basic systems of global digital communication are: e-mail, the internet, and the World Wide Web. To participate, you need a computer (most schools and many libraries have them) with a modem—a device to attach your computer to a phone line. Internal modems are about the size of a credit card or small calculator, and fit inside your computer. External modems are placed outside your computer and are connected via cables. In each case, your modem comes with software—a computer program that tells your computer of the modem's existence and sets up the connection.

E-MAIL

E-mail (or electronic mail) is a method of sending messages from one individual to one or many others very quickly. In order to communicate with someone by e-mail, you each need an e-mail address. My address is: tsmoke@shiva.hunter.cuny.edu.

The first part of the address is the user id, the name of the person; in some systems case is important, so make sure that you type the address exactly, using either lower or upper case as it has been given to you. After the @ (at) sign comes the domain that tells you the particular computer that receives and sends the message. In my case, my message is sent through the shiva system, at Hunter College, in the City University of New York. The .edu indicates that it is an educational institution. Some other endings for e-mail addresses are: .com, a commercial site; .gov, a government site; and .org, an organizational site.

Most schools (and many libraries) provide inexpensive or free access to e-mail for their faculty, staff, and students. However, they sometimes impose a charge if the e-mail is done from home. You need to check with your institution.

There are many commercial providers such as America Online (aol), Prodigy, MCI, and others that offer competitively priced internet access. Once you have an address and access, you can write to anyone by using the appropriate address.

Many teachers are now using e-mail to communicate with their students through dialogue journals, daily or weekly notes, and responses to student writing. Students are also in easy communication with their teachers. Students can write to other students in the same class, or can write to students in other classes. The possibility of bringing about faster and more frequent communication with your students is enormous.

Once you are using e-mail, you will find methods for sending letters to groups of individuals (e.g., a whole class), forwarding letters received from one person to someone else, and transferring whole files. Most access services provide guidebooks to help you do these things.

You can also join LISTSERVs or discussion groups in your areas of interest. One extremely useful discussion group for the topics related to this book is TESL-L, a discussion group of around 4,000 ESL educators all over the world. TESL-L was started by Anthea Tillyer of City College of the City University of New York, and, through a FIPSE grant, she administers it with Susan Simon (also of City College) and Tom Robb (of Kyoto-Sangyo University in Japan). To join TESL-L, send an e-mail message to the following address:

> listserv@cunyvm.cuny.edu (If your e-mail address ends in "bitnet," send your message to listserv@cunyvm.bitnet.)

In the body of your message write:

sub TESL-L yourfirstname yourlastname (e.g., sub TESL-L Trudy Smoke)

Once you have joined, you will receive a welcome message that has information about how to read and reply to TESL-L messages, and how to gain access to many of the other TESL-L services. You will probably want to print out this welcome message or download (save) it on your computer.

THE INTERNET

In addition to the many uses of e-mail, the internet itself can be a great source of information for you and your students. One internet tool is the Gopher (search tool), which is easily accessed in most systems by typing the word "gopher" into your computer at the system prompt line, pressing return, and waiting for a menu to appear telling you about the services offered by the Gopher.

One Gopher that you may find very useful is connected to the Teaching English as a Second/Foreign Language archives at the City University of New York. These archives contain magazines, journals, abstracts, conference information, TESL-L archives, and announcements of employment and exchange programs. To reach this site, type the message:

gopher.cunyvm.cuny.edu

at the system prompt line and then select "Teaching English as a Second/Foreign Language."

Using a Veronica makes the Gopher service even better, because the Veronica allows you to type in the exact words or exact reference you are trying to locate. This makes it much easier to track down information quickly. You get to Veronica through the Gopher path:

Other Gopher and Information Servers/
  Searching GopherSpace using veronica/
    Search GopherSpace (veronica) in ——

Then you type in the word or words you are interested in finding out more about.

Another important internet site is Telnet. Telnet allows you to log on to a computer in a distant site and access communication there without having to dial a long-distance number. You simply log onto your own system, and at the system prompt, type "telnet" and skip a space and type the name of the system of the computer you want to reach (the right-hand side of the computer address). To reach my system, you would type:

telnet shiva.hunter.cuny.edu

You can use telnet to check your own e-mail when you are out of town, and you can use it to get material for your students from the Electronic Newsstand, which contains a wide variety of articles from newspapers, magazines, and journals. To reach the Newsstand at your system prompt, type:

telnet.enews.com

When you are asked for a login name, type "enews." You will be automatically connected to the electronic newsstand and can choose what you want to read.

File transfer protocol (FTP) is a special internet tool for transferring information or files from one computer to another. There are an enormous number of files and materials that can be accessed and stored through FTPs. There are several steps involved in using an FTP, and most guidebooks for the internet spell out the one most appropriate for your particular service. However, the FTP also has a search tool like Veronica, called Archie, that will search through anonymous FTP files to look for information. To access it, at the system prompt, type "archie" and the name of your institution (e.g., archie.hunter.cuny.edu), and begin your search. For this and all of the previously described internet services, you need to experiment and be willing to make a few mistakes, but if you do this you will soon find some of the many great resources available through the internet.

THE WORLD WIDE WEB (WWW)

The Web is for many the most exciting new source of communication and information on the internet. You need a special connection or browser, such as Netscape, to "surf the web" (travel to different sites). The Web is a single integrated system that includes both Gophers and FTP sites. Its graphical interface enables you to look at full-color pictures, listen to voices and music, and watch videos, as well as read text. The Web uses hypertext (highlighted features in the text) to enable you to search through vast troves of information to explore your interests in creative and often unexpected ways.

Most addresses or uniform resource locators (URLs) on the Web begin with http://. This translates into hypertext transfer protocol (the protocol on which the Web is based). Some interesting Web pages for you to explore include:

http://www.bbk.ac.uk/Departments/AppliedLinguistics/VirtualLibrary.html

http://www.ed.gov/ed/index.html

http://www.edu.wsu.edu/es/esl.html

http://www.ed.uiuc.edu/edpsy-387/rongchang-li/esl/

Following is a list of WWW pages that relate to specific issues addressed in this book. Note that some WWW pages may be listed under more than one category.

Literacy Organizations Online

Adult Literacy Resource Institute (Boston)
http://www2.wgbh.org/MBCWEIS/LTC/ALRI/alri.html

Indiana Literacy & Technical Education Resources
http://www.statelib.lib.in.us//www/inrc/hp14.html

Institute for the Study of Adult Literacy (Penn State University)
http://www.psu.edu/institute/isal/

Michigan State Literacy Resource Center
gopher://edcen.ehhs.cmich.edu:/11/edcen.resource/rfrm/sirc/

National Center on Adult Literacy (NCAL)
http://litserver.literacy.upenn.edu

National Institute for Literacy (NIFL LINCS)
http://novel.nifl.gov/

Ohio Literacy Resource Center
http://archon.educ.kent.edu/

Outreach and Technical Assistance Network (OTAN)
http://www.otan.dni.us

Texas Literacy Resource Center
http://www-ehrd.tamu.edu/tirc/tlrc_exp/tlrc_exp.htm

Virginia Adult Education and Literacy Resource Center
http://www.vcu.edu/aelweb/

Literacy and ESOL Instructional Resources

AskERIC
http://ericir.syr.edu

CNN's Interactive Learning Resources for Teaching
http://www.cnnsf.com/cgi-bin/cnn/education/ed.cgi

Dave's ESL Cafe
http://www.pacificnet.net/~sperling/eslcafe.html

ERIC: Adult Literacy Information and Materials on the Internet
gopher://ericir.syr.edu:70/11/Ed/AdultLit

ERIC Clearinghouse on Science, Mathematics and Environmental Education
http://www.ericse.org

ERIC Clearinghouse on Urban Education
http://eric-web.tc.columbia.edu/

ESL Virtual Catalog
http://www.pvp.com/esl.htm

EX*CHANGE (Exchange, Xross Cultural, Hytextual Academy of Non-Native Gatherings in English)
http://deil.lang.uiuc.edu/exchange/

Fluency Through Fables
http://www.comenius.com/fable/index.html

Mega Math
http://www.c3.lanl.gov/mega-math/welcome.html

Outreach and Technical Assistance Network (OTAN)
http://www.otan.dni.us

California Distance Learning Project
http://www.otan.dni.us/cdlp/cdlp.html

Lifelong Learning Online
http://www.otan.dni.us/cdlp/lllo/home.html

Public Broadcasting Service (PBS ONLINE)
http://www.pbs.org

Purdue University's On-Line Writing Center
http://owl.english.purdue.edu/

The Virtual English Language Center
http://www.comenius.com

Technology and Education Resources

Basic Internet Guides
http://www.rpi/Internet/InerGuides.html

EdWeb
http://edweb.cnidr.org:90/

From Now On—a monthly electronic journal devoted to educational technology
http://www.pacificrim.net/-mckenzie

IBM Kiosk for Education
http://ike.engr.washington.edu/

Patrick Crispen's Internet Roadmap
http://www.brandonu.ca/~ennsnr/Resources/Roadmap/Welcome.html

Teaching with Technology
http://www.wam.umd.edu/~mlhall/teaching.html

Virtual Computer Library
http://www.utexas.edu/computer/vcl/

Funding and Grant Information Resources

FEDIX (Federal Information Information Exchange)
http://web.fie.com/

Federal Web Locator
http://www.law.vill.edu/Fed-Agency/fedwebloc.html/

The Foundation Center
http://www.fdncenter.org

HUD (Department of Housing and Urban Development)
http://www.hud.gov

New York State Education Department
http://www.nysed.gov/

Thomas Legislative Information on the Internet
http://rs9.lov.gov

TIIAP (Telecommunications and Information Infrastructure Assistance Program)
http://www.ntia.doc.gov/tiiap/

U.S. Department of Education
http://www.ed.gov

Employment, Training, and Workplace Literacy

America's Job Bank
http://www.ajb.dni.us/

Cornell School of Industrial & Labor Relations
http://www.ilr.cornell.edu/

Empowerment Zone and Enterprise Community Program (EZ/EC)
http://www.ezec.gov/

O*NET (The Occupational Information Network)
http://www.doleta.gov/programs/onet/

SCANS/2000 (Johns Hopkins University Institute for Policy Studies)
http://www.jhu.edu/~ips/scans/

School-to-Work Internet Gateway
http://www.stw.ed.gov

Training and Technical Resource Center
http://www.ttrc.doleta.gov/

Work Web Employment and Training Resource
http://www.work-web.com

National Association of Workforce Development Professionals
http://www.work-web.com/nawdp/

Family Literacy Resources

Children's Literature Web Guide
http://www.ucalgary.ca/~dkbrown/index.html

ERIC Clearinghouse on Elementary and Early Childhood Education (home of National Parent Information Network)
http://ericps.ed.uiuc.edu/

Family Involvement
http://www.ed.gov/Family/

Parents and Children Together On-Line
http://www.indiana.edu/~eric_rec/fl/pcto/menu.html

Multicultural Education Resources

Pathways to Diversity
http://us.edu/Library/QF/diversity/

CLNET Diversity Page
http://latino.sscnet.ucla.edu/diversity1.html

Multicultural Paths
http://curry.edschool.virginia.edu/go/multicultural/sites1.html

Miscellaneous Interesting Resources

CapWeb: A Guide to the U.S. Congress
http://policy.net/capweb/congress.html

Central Intelligence Agency (CIA)
http://www.ic.gov

Human Language Page
http://www.hardlink.com/~chambers/HLP/

Library of Congress
http://lcweb.loc.gov

Smithsonian
http://www.si.edu

Views of the Solar System
http://bang.lanl.gov/solarsys

Virtual Tourist II
http://www.vtourist.com/vt/

The White House
http://www.whitehouse.gov

Internet Search Engines

AltaVista
http://www.altavist.com

Excite
http://www.excite.com

InfoSeek
http://www.infoseek.com

Lycos
http://lycos.cs.cmu.edu/

WebCrawler
http://www.webcrawler.com

Yahoo
http://www.yahoo.com

Adult ESL: Politics, Pedagogy,and Participation in Classroom and Community Programs has its own site on the Erlbaum web page. The address is: http://www.erlbaum.com. The authors in the book will be able to communicate with the readers, to create real participation and discussion through this web site. We hope that as we "talk" to each other, we will be able to identify the issues with which we are each dealing, offer friendly advice, create and disseminate new ideas, and make this book a tool for participation.

I hope that many readers will join our online dialogue. This is what will make this book unique and timeless. Events in recent years have made many of us concerned about the future of our programs, our students, and our jobs. Perhaps by using this site to "talk" to each other online, ask questions, identify problems, and inform each other (of new web sites, helpful internet resources, methods for dealing with our institutions, ways to increase our students' access to the internet, and activities that have involved and maybe even inspired our students), we will begin a transformative process for teachers and practitioners to regain control over our classrooms and profession.

This chapter has been intended as a brief outline to introduce readers to the potential of the internet. For more information, I recommend two very informative source books. The first is *E-Mail for English Teaching*, written by Mark Warschauer and published by TESOL in 1995. In this book, Mark Warschauer explains in step-by-step detail how to use e-mail, the internet, and the World Wide Web; he also discusses possibilities of using the internet for distance education, and includes a list of resources on the internet. Warschauer does this in language that even the most novice internet user can understand and use immediately. This book is definitely user-friendly and highly recommended. You can order it through TESOL by calling 703-836-0774.

The second book is *Brave New Schools: Challenging Cultural Illiteracy Through Global Learning Networks*, written by Jim Cummins and Dennis Sayers and published by St. Martin's Press in 1995. In the first part of their book, Cummins and Sayers explain how the internet was used as a means of survival by a young boy in a Croatian refugee camp. The authors then theorize about the potential of global learning networks to lead to critical literacy and greater social participation. The second half of the book contains long lists of LISTSERVs, Gopher addresses, and web sites. This directory is useful, although the global network is changing and expanding so rapidly that the lists offer but a taste of possibilities for you to begin your own "surfing" of the internet and the Web.

TESOL Matters, a newspaper published six times a year by TESOL, also contains web site addresses related to ESL issues. Most news magazines and newspapers also list web site addresses.

REFERENCES

Cummins, J., & Sayers, D. (1995). *Brave new schools: Challenging cultural illiteracy through global learning networks*. New York: St. Martin's Press.

Sims, C. (1996, May 27). A web entree for Peruvians without PCs. *The New York Times*, p. A29.

Warschauer, M. (1995). *E-mail for English teaching*. Washington, DC: TESOL.

Author Index

Subject Index

D

E

F

G

H

I

J

L

Notes on Contributors

Joanne Arnaud is the executive director of the Boston Adult Literacy Fund, BALF, an organization that secures funding for the Boston adult literacy community. Arnaud was the grant recipient and fiscal administrator for the Community Training for the Adult and Family Literacy project.

Elsa Auerbach is an associate professor at the University of Massachusetts at Boston. Widely published in the field of adult literacy and critical pedagogy, Auerbach worked with community agencies to create the university–community literacy collaboration that trained literacy instructors to teach in their own communities. Auerbach is a North American whose parents were refugees from Germany. She worked in a factory before being hired first as a part-time ESL teacher at the University of Massachusetts, in Boston.

Sarah Benesch is an associate professor of English and ESL coordinator at The College of Staten Island, The City University of New York. She has edited and contributed to two collections of essays, *ESL in America: Myths and Possibilities*, published by Boynton/Cook/Heinemann, and *Ending Remediation: Linking ESL and Content in Higher Education*, published by TESOL. She has also published articles in *TESOL Quarterly*, *College ESL*, and *Journal of Second Language Writing*.

Richard Blakely received his PhD from the University of California, Santa Barbara. From 1973–1982, he taught in the Department of French Studies at Brown University, exploring and developing methods of using feature films as a means of teaching foreign language and culture. From 1983–1995, Dr. Blakely taught writing and ESL at the University of Rhode Island, eventually creating and directing a comprehensive program in English Language Studies, of which the English Language Fellows Program was an essential part. He is now director of ESL at Rhode Island School of Design.

Carol Chandler worked for 13 years with the Haitian Multi-Service Center (HMSC), a center that trained Haitian teachers for work in the community and recruited bilingual interns and work-study students as tutors and teaching assistants in their literacy programs in English and Creole.

J. Milton Clark is a member of the English Department at California State University, San Bernardino. Dr. Clark teaches composition and American literature. His current interests involve the integration of computers into the fields of composition and literature instruction and large-scale writing assessment programs.

Elaine Coburn is an instructor of ESL in the Institute for Intensive English, English Department, Union County College in Elizabeth, New Jersey. She was the assistant director of the Resource Center for Language minority Students at Kean College of New Jersey from its inception until it was defunded in 1994.

Timotha Doane teaches at City College of San Francisco and has been teaching adult ESL in various schools around the San Francisco Bay Area since 1979. Recently she has been spending her summers at Harvard Summer School at the Institute of English Language Programs. She has also worked as a facilitator in process recovery groups for women. She practices Tibetan Buddhism and writes poetry. She has been working creatively with her partner Clare Straum since they met doing political work with the African-American community in 1978. Together, they share an interest in American cultures and in interdisciplinary development of their professional fields.

Pamela Ferguson has been an adult ESL literacy instructor at Yakima Valley Community College in central Washington state since 1988 and earned tenure there in 1996. She was both coordinator of the ESL program and an instructor for 5 years. Recently, she had the opportunity to move into full-time administration, but chose to move back into full-time teaching. She has a Master's Degree in TESOL from the School for International Training in Brattleboro, Vermont.

Carol Peterson Haviland is a member of the faculty of the English Department of California State University, San Bernardino. Dr. Haviland directs the Writing Center, co-directs the campus writing-across-the-curriculum project, and teaches in the undergraduate composition and the graduate in rhetoric and composition programs. Her particular interests are in the intersections of theory, research, and pedagogy, and she is currently co-editing a book on writing centers and collaboration.

Loretta Frances Kasper received her PhD in Cognitive Psychology/Psycholinguistics from Rutgers University in 1985, and she is an associate professor of English at Kingsborough Community College of the City University of New York. Dr. Kasper has been researching the effects of discipline-based ESL instruction on student performance for the past decade. A frequent presenter at conferences, she has also published reports of her research in a number of national and international journals, most recently, *English for Specific Purposes*, and *Journal of Adolescent and Adult Literacy*. Dr. Kasper is the author of the text, *Teaching English Through the Disciplines: Isychology* and *Interdisciplinary English.*

Keming Liu is a native of Baoding, PRC. Dr. Liu is a survivor of the cultural revolution who was among the first in her country to re-enter the university system in 1978 after teaching on the elementary level in her hometown as well as enduring the harsh conditions of rural "re-education" experienced by many intellectuals of that era. She has taught on the university level both in mainland China, at the Hebei Teachers University in Shijizhuang, as well as at the City University of New York at Hunter College and at Medgar Evers College where she is currently an assistant professor of English. Dir. Liu received her EdD in applied linguistics as well as her MA in computers and education from Teachers College at Columbia University, and received her MA in TESOL at Hunter College. The co-author and editor of several books about Chinese language and customs, she has also translated works by Henry James into Chinese. She lives in Manhattan.

Kate Mangelsdorf is Associate Professor and Director of First-Year Composition at the University of Texas, El Paso, which is situated on the U.S.–Mexico border. She received her PhD from the University of Arizona, where she was Coordinator of ESL Writing. With Evelyn Posey, she has published a developmental writing textbook, *Your Choice: A Basic Writing Guide With Readings* (St. Martin's, 1997). She has also published chapters or articles in *Two Year College English: Essays for a New Century*, *Writing in Multicultural Settings*, *Richness in Writing*, *ELT Journal*, and the *Journal of Second Language Writing*. Currently, she is co-authoring a multicultural reader for developmental writing students.

Judy Manton, an ESL teacher in the New York City Adult Education Program for 20 years, has also taught in China and Peru. She has researched school-related English as form of ESP (English for Special Purposes) and the subculture of the public school and has developed related ESL lessons for parents of immigrant children. She has given TESOL presentations on empowering LEP parents through these lessons. At Fairleigh Dickinson University in Teaneck, New Jersey, she teaches "Cross-Cultural Perspectives." She has visited 45 countries and is interested in personal reasons for emigration and the adjustment and acculturation processes in immigration.

Rebecca Williams Mlynarczyk has taught reading and writing to college ESL students for the past 15 years. She is a certified Fluency First workshop consultant and has adapted the Fluency First approach for use in her classes at Kingsborough Community College of the City University of New York, where she is an assistant professor of English, and co-director of the ESL program. She is co-author with Steven Haber of *In Our Own Words: A Guide With Readings for Student Writers* (2nd ed., 1996) and the author of *Conversations of the Mind*, an ethnographic study of the uses of journal writing for second-language students (Lawrence Erlbaum Associates, 1998).

Pia Moriarty directs the Eastside Project in community-based learning at Santa Clara University and teaches as assistant professor in the Community Studies program. She has worked in multilingual ESL/literacy since the mid-1970s, specializing in California adaptations of Paulo Freire's pedagogy with adult immigrants and refugees. Her interests include participatory research, nonviolent social change, and the dynamics of culture-making.

Bonny Norton is an assistant professor, Department of Language Education, at the University of British Columbia, Canada. Her research focuses on the relationship between language learning and social identity. Recent research (as Bonny Norton Peirce) has been published in *TESOL Quarterly, Harvard Educational Review,* and *Gender Education.* She is a guest editor of the special issue of the *TESOL Quarterly* titled "Language and Identity" published in 1997.

Angela Parrino, associate professor of the MA in TESOL Program at Hunter College, the City University of New York, has teaching, staff development, and consultant experience in ESL, bilingual, and foreign language instruction on the elementary through grade school levels. She teaches second language acquisition theory, ESL methodology and materials, and supervises teacher interns in New York City public elementary and secondary schools. She collaborated with Migdalia Romero on "Planned Alteration of Languages (PAL): An Instructional Model for the Bilingual Classroom" in the *Journal of Educational Issues for Language Minority Students* and several books for children, including *The Big Chant: I Went Walking, Napping House,* and *Myrtle Marie* activity books. She created a video, "Feeling at Home With Language and You're Invited," which was aired on local television stations. Current projects include an article on the affective response to error correction in the adult second-language learner and an ESL series for middle school students with Donald R. H. Byrd.

Jessie M. Reppy is an associate professor of ESL and director of the ESL program in the English Department, Kean College, Union, New Jersey. Dr. Reppy was the director of the Resource Center for Language Minority Students at Kean College of New Jersey from its inception in 1992 until it was defunded in 1994. She is co-author of *Explorations in World Literature: Readings to Enhance Academic Skills,* published by St. Martin's Press (1994).

Leslie Robbins has been co-executive director of the Riverside Language Program since 1980. She is a graduate of Teachers College at Columbia University, where she received her MA. She also has an MA from New York University, where she did her undergraduate work as well. In addition, she is a graduate of the institute for Not-for-Profit Management of the Columbia University Graduate School of Business. She has been a speaker at numerous conferences on refugee and immigrant affairs and ESOL. She is past-president of the New York City Consortium for Adult Basic Education.

Carol Severino, associate professor of rhetoric and director of the writing lab at the University of Iowa, teaches, researches, and writes about how culture and social context affect writing and the teaching of writing. She has published in the *Journal of Second Language Writing,* the *Journal of Basic Writing, Writing Center Journal, Urban Education, Metropolitan Universities,* and *College English.* With Johnella Butler and Juan Guerra, she edited *Writing in Multicultural Settings* (Modern Language Association, 1997). She is completing a book about the history of academic opportunity programs in urban institutions, which is tentatively titled

The "Urban Mission" and the Academic Opportunity Program: Los Angeles, Chicago, and New York Stories.

Trudy Smoke is an associate professor of English at Hunter College of the City University of New York, where she teaches writing to ESL and non-ESL students as well as literature and women's studies classes. She is the Freshman English programs coordinator and writes and presents materials about ESL and developmental writing issues. Dr. Smoke is the author of *A Writer's Workbook* (3rd. ed., 1996) and *A Writer's Worlds* (2nd ed., 1995), both published by St. Martin's Press, and *Making a Difference* (1994), published by Houghton Mifflin. She is also co-editor of the *Journal of Basic Writing*.

Clare Strawn is currently working on her doctorate in Urban Studies at Portland State University. She has also been serving as a graduate mentor in PSU's "University Studies," an innovative, interdisciplinary, general education program and currently coordinates the Community Based Learning Internships program.

Stephanie Vandrick is an associate professor of ESL at the University of San Francisco, where she teaches ESL writing/reading classes as well as women's studies and literature classes. Her research interests include sociopolitical issues in ESL, multicultural and world literatures, and feminist and critical pedagogy. Her work has been published in *TESOL Quarterly, TESOL Journal, College ESL, Journal of Second Language Writing,* and *Journal of Intensive English Studies*. She is an associate director of the journal *Peace Review*.

Ana Zambrano was an ESL teacher and mentor at the Jackson–Mann Community School for 8 years. She came to the United States in 1984 from Colombia, where she had a background as an adult educator. Her sense of community activism informs her teaching and her relationship to the community. She currently works for Parents United for Childcare as a parent organizer.